2 Staff final Whistl
Best wi

CW01084857

Southwell & District at War 1939-45

Volume 2

'We'll Meet Again'

Copies available at Southwell
Library & The Cathedral Shop.

By

Roger Dobson

Edited by Michael J Kirton

Southwell and District Local History Society

2016

DEDICATION

I dedicate this book to my wife Su, our three children Bethany, Emma and Jim, and our grandchildren, Betsy, Martha, Eric, Georgina, Jolie and Julian.

ABOUT THE AUTHOR

Roger Dobson studied Modern History at Durham University and went on to a career in education, and latterly served as a Deputy Head Teacher at a Nottingham comprehensive school for fifteen years. He married in 1966 and has children and grandchildren. Roger has lived in Southwell since 1978 and after retiring he sat as a magistrate for twelve years, and was also elected onto Southwell Town Council in 2003, serving as Chairman on three occasions. As Chairman of the Tourism Partnership in 2006 he created six local heritage trails. He was a member of the team that produced *Southwell - The Town and Its People Volume 2* and in 2008 wrote *Southwell Inns and Alehouses*, published by Nottinghamshire County Council. Still a keen sportsman he is a member of Southwell Tennis Club and plays golf at Norwood Park. To celebrate his 70th birthday Roger cycled the 800 km 'Pilgrimage Route to Santiago de Compostela'.

COPYRIGHT NOTICE

© Roger Dobson and Southwell and District Local History Society, 2016.

All rights reserved. No part of this publication may be reproduced, stored or introduced into a retrieval system or transmitted in any form, by any means (electronic, mechanical, photocopy, recording or otherwise) without permission from the publishers.

Whilst every care has been taken to ensure the accuracy of the information contained in this publication, Southwell and District Local History Society cannot accept any responsibility for any error or omission.

ISBN: 978-0-9932442-3-0

Printed by:

Russell Press, Russell House, Basford, Nottingham NG6 0BT

CONTENTS

Ministry of Health Poster

ILLUSTRATIONS

FOREWORD

It is four years since the History Society decided to record the memories of local people from Southwell and district who experienced life in the Second World War. Roger Dobson took on what we thought at the time would be a relatively short-term project. However, fired by Roger's enthusiasm, a proposed book of around 200 pages has grown to two volumes totalling over 600 pages, thanks to the co-operation of many local residents - a remarkable achievement, recording an important period of our history.

The first volume was launched in May 2015 and has proved to be one of the most successful books that the Society has published. This second volume, which devotes several chapters to the experiences of local servicemen in various theatres of the war, I am sure will be equally successful. Some of the memories are harrowing and all demonstrate the undoubted bravery of those from Southwell and district who served their country so admirably. Sadly, a number did not live to tell their stories and we should remember them.

This volume is not just about those who served, but records life on the 'Home Front', which is a testament to those who had to keep the 'home fires burning' and, for the sake of their children, make life as normal as possible, in spite of wartime restrictions.

It has been an interesting and rewarding experience editing this book, with the assistance of my wife Anna, and helping Roger see the project through to the end. The Society congratulates Roger on his success in achieving this enormous task that records this bleak period in the history of Southwell and district.

Mike Kirton
Chairman
Southwell & District Local History Society
Spring 2016

Front Cover Photograph
V J Party at The George and Dragon, Church Street, Southwell

Some of the people on the photograph have been identified:
Children: Front Row Table, 4th from right, Roger Barker; 5th right, John Lukehurst;
Side Table (angled): 1st left, Linda Vast; 2nd, Jean Vast; far right by window, Peggy Vast;
Adults: starting 3rd adult from left, Vera Johnson-Cooper; Sarah Johnson-Cooper (landlady);
Bill Richardson; Jack Cobb; Lily Ross (in front of door); Nev Ross; William Johnson-Cooper (arms folded, landlord); Eric Ross.

Rear Cover Photograph

Picture taken in 1940 at the rear of The George and Dragon. The Johnson-Cooper family ran the public house and gave excellent support to the war effort. One of their enterprises was the making of dolls for 'Comforts for Servicemen'. Sarah Johnson-Cooper was the publican for 54 years and is pictured with her daughters Lily (left) and Vera (right).

(Both pictures courtesy of Vincent Johnson-Cooper)

PREFACE

We'll Meet Again, Volume 2 of Southwell and District at War has special emphasis on the memories of men who served in the Armed Forces. The role of women in the services was covered in Volume 1, *Keep Smiling Through.*

It has been a great pleasure and privilege for me to be invited into many homes to interview former servicemen and their families, and there have been some incredible stories passed on to me - stories of great courage but often followed by traumatic events - which have left me feeling quite humbled. These fascinating memories make up Chapters 1-4.

For the people back home in Southwell and the villages there was an iron determination to support their relatives serving abroad in the Armed Forces. Chapter 5 looks at the many community initiatives, such as *Saucepans for Spitfires, Wings for Victory* and *Salute the Soldier,* aimed at raising funds for the supply of new and better weaponry.

The following two chapters, 6 and 7, relate how people in Southwell and district coped with the restrictions of rationing and food shortages and the measures they took to ensure that they had sufficient supplies. In Chapters 8 and 9 people offer memories of how they entertained themselves in the war, and how local businesses were affected by being at war. Finally, Chapter 10 records people's memories of the Victory events - a succession of parties, parades and services, from May through to August 1945.

I am greatly indebted for the kind help given by a number of local organisations and would like to thank the staff at Southwell Library, especially Nicola Ellis and Gillian Starkey, and Christine Whitehouse and John Shephard at Southwell Minster Library. Grateful thanks go to John Lukehurst at Eakring Oil Museum, Tim Warner and the staff at Newark Library, and to Carol Standish, Jessica Sherrin and Karen Green at Southwell Town Council for their generous support. Thanks also must go to Catherine Hancock and the editor of the *Newark Advertiser*, also to Katherine Wood of the *Bramley,* for publishing a series of articles requesting memories.

Finding memorabilia, particularly photographs, to support the stories has been an important objective, and I am most grateful for the support given by Peter Cant and by members of Southwell Civic Society. In addition, many local residents have passed on to me memorabilia of the men in their families who served overseas. It would be remiss of me not to thank the following people from Southwell and the local villages for their valuable contributions of memorabilia and source materials: Janette Barrett, Robert Beckett, Jo Blaney, Bridget Clarke, Anne Clark, Jenny Clay, Christine Cross, Olwen Dodsworth, Malcolm Gough, David Hutchinson, Nick Linney, Deana and Ray Longden, Des Malbon, Peter Marrison, Roger Merryweather, Frank Mitchell, Ellis Morgan, Angela Nettleship, Darryl North, Ken Ogilvie, Barbara Page, Ruth Robinson, Rob Smith, Carole Spall, Celia Steven, John Stephenson, Michael Trueman, Trevor Wilds and Peter Yates.

As in Volume 1, my research was given a considerable boost by having access to the record of a series of earlier interviews with a number of local people carried out by Doreen Stevenson. She has generously permitted me to use the transcripts of these interviews. Equally, I would like to thank Paul Birks for providing me with the taped interviews with a number of residents, conducted some years ago when he was teaching at The Minster School.

I am greatly indebted to Trevor Wight for his series of excellent maps of naval and military battles, and for mapping Alan Yates' journey to 'Find Station R', also for his sketch of the Caunton POW Camp and for his valuable listing of all of the town's retail premises. Trevor has made a huge contribution to the project.

Thanks to Mike Kirton and members of Southwell and District Local History Society for their constant support and encouragement and to Mike and Anna Kirton, in particular, for spending many hours scrutinising and editing the text and preparing it for the printers. Mike has also at all times provided much valued advice in considering the selection of content.

Very special thanks to my wife Su for her patience and encouragement over the past five years and for accompanying me on many of my journeys in pursuit of background material. As well as this, she has given me excellent advice on how to improve the writing of the book.

Finally, a huge debt is owed to the many people I've interviewed and to those who have sent me their memories. I cannot thank them enough.

Roger Dobson
Southwell,
2016

Acknowledgements to Southwell and District Residents who have contributed memories and/or memorabilia and given me valuable assistance

Barrett, Janette
Barrett, Stella
Beckett, Jack
Beckett, Robert
Bentley, Jim
Bergmanis, Jill
Birks, Paul
Blaney, Jo
Branston, Pauline
Bush, Ray
Cant, Peter
Carpenter, Virginia
Chapman, Audrey
Chapman, Stanley
Clark, Anne née Barrett
Clarke, Bridget née Barrett
Clay, Jenny
Cooling, Harry
Cooling, Rosa
Craig, Tom
Cranidge, Bill
Crocker, Pauline
Cross, Christine,
Doar, Barrie
Dobson, Emma
Dodsworth, Olwen née Lister
Dodsworth, Robin
Doy, Dallas
Driscoll, Bernard

Driscoll, Dennis
Ellis, Nicola
England, Doreen née Barwise
Fairholme, Tom
Fenton, Karen
Field, Pam
Fletcher, Doug
Gascoine, Douglas
Gill, Terry
Gilman, Michael
Gough Jill née Dodsworth
Gough, Malcolm
Gregory, Andrew
Haigh, Brendan
Hall, David
Hall, Mary née Foster
Hallam, Jean née Bowes
Hallam, Joan
Hardstaff, Robert
Harrison, Margaret née Leek
Harrison, Nancy
Hayward, Antony
Hickman, Marian and Terence
Hutchinson, David
Hutchison, David
Inger, Jack,
Johnson, Brian
Johnson, Pat
Johnson-Cooper, Vincent

Jones, Karen
Kemp, Bill
Kendall, Ted
Kirby, Freda
Kitts, Olive née Sharman
Lee, Keith
Linney, Nick
Lockley, Rosemary née Richards,
Longden, Ray and Deana
Lukehurst, John
Malbon, Des
Marrison, Peter
Marshall, Eric
Marshall, Keith
Merryweather, Roger
Millard, Betty née Tyne
Mitchell, Billy
Mitchell, Edward.
Mitchell, Frank and Jean
Morgan, Ellis
Nettleship, Angela
North, Darryl
Ogilvie, Ken
Pacey, Brian
Page, Barbara
Paling, Julia
Parker, Marjorie
Patterson, Cynthia née Mitchell
Pickup, Peter
Pitchford, John
Pitchford, Ray
Postle, John
Price, Elizabeth née Caudwell
Pulford, Margaret née Fowkes
Pulford, Stephen
Quickenden, Jean née Walker
Raithby, Christine

Reeves, Bob
Riley, Elizabeth née Keetley
Riley, Geoff
Robinson, John
Robinson, Ruth née Caudwell
Savage, Dr John
Scoffield, Roy
Scorer, Peter
Shipley, Brian and Fran
Smith, Janice
Smith, Rob
Spall, Carole
Spall, Peter
Starkey, Gillian
Starkey, Sir John
Stephenson, John
Steven, Celia
Stevenson, Doreen
Stevenson, Paul
Thurlby, John
Trueman, Michael
Tuck, Addalane née Hall
Warner, Ann née Paling
Warner, Tim
Watts, John
Webb, Steve
West, Mary
Whitehouse, Christine
Whitton, Brenda née Kendall
Wight, Trevor
Wilds, Trevor
Willson, Tim
Wimble, Andy
Woolley, Cynthia née Revill
Wright, Lance
Yates, Alan
Yates, Peter

Advertisement 1944

CHAPTER 1

'... we shall fight on the seas and oceans ...'[1]

The possibility of having to endure the brutal conditions and horrific casualty rates of trench warfare, which the previous generation had suffered in the First World War, was a considerable deterrent to some men when it came to deciding which of the armed forces they might join.

By choosing to enlist in the Royal Navy they believed they were engaging in a noble cause - defending Britain's supply of food, raw materials and weapons was critical, failure to achieve this could mean starvation. There was also the opportunity to learn a wide variety of skills through the diversity of roles on board ship: seamen and signalmen; shipwrights; stokers and engineers; blacksmiths, joiners, painters and plumbers; officers' stewards and cooks. Finally, the Royal Navy offered the chance to see the world.

Des Malbon, signaller on minesweepers, Royal Naval Patrol Service

'No work has been more vital than yours; ... The Ports were kept open and Britain breathed.'[2]

Des Malbon

Des Malbon was almost seventeen years old when war broke out. He was living in Sneinton, Nottingham with his parents and younger brother, and had a job at Wm Hollins Hosiery on Castle Boulevard. He witnessed one of the early German bombing raids on the city, taking refuge in a nearby air-raid shelter.

He had been a Boy Scout and joined the Home Guard until he was old enough to go in the services at eighteen. Because he had particularly enjoyed signalling, he signed up for the Royal Navy. At this time there was a national appeal for volunteers to the minesweeping service; many merchant ships in the North Sea were being sunk by German mines.

After passing his medical, Des was selected for the Signals' branch of the Royal Navy Patrol Service (RNPS) and sent to train from Oct 1941-April 1942 at Skegness, in what had been Butlin's Holiday Camp. His courses included minesweeping, gunnery practice, general drill, seamanship and his specialism, signalling.

I found at Skegness that there was a lot to learn about things such as the Morse code and how to use hand and mast flags. The whole east coastline was a military area then, because it was feared the Germans could at any time launch an invasion. I was at the Skegness camp in February 1942 when German planes dive-bombed the camp, killing fifteen people.
Des Malbon

---

[1] Extract from Winston Churchill's, speech to the House of Commons, 4th June 1940.
[2] National Archives, Ref. PREM 3/314/5.

In early 1942 Des was sent to Lowestoft, then to Sheerness, both important bases for minesweepers operating in the North Sea. It was vital to clear the sea lanes from the Forth to the Thames to enable convoys to pass safely, bringing essential supplies of food, fuel and munitions to Britain. Over a hundred minesweepers had been sunk by German U-Boats and aircraft in the first two years of the war, and a number of ports had been put out of action. Minesweepers also escorted convoys in this channel off the east coast of England, known as 'E-Boat' alley, because German E-Boats laid magnetic mines under the cover of darkness.

As soon as war seemed certain the Admiralty had expanded minesweeping fleets by purchasing 67 trawlers recognising that, once converted, they would be ideally suited to minesweeping. Hundreds more vessels were requisitioned by the Admiralty as the war continued. There was no doubt that life on a minesweeper was very hazardous. The Germans had laid a large number of different types of mine - contact, acoustic and magnetic - and minesweeping crews needed to use a variety of techniques to counter them.[3]

The converted trawlers were reasonably easy targets for enemy aircraft dive-bombing attacks, as well as being at risk of mine explosions. There were many casualties in the service. Though the minesweepers had guns, they were limited in number and power.

Converted trawler used as a minesweeper (Private Collection)

The minesweeper I was assigned to was the *Tocsin*, but it was out at sea so I had to await its return. Temporarily, I joined the crew of the *St Tundo*, a cross channel steamer. It had been at Dunkirk, but it was now being used as a depot ship.

After a few weeks the *Tocsin* returned to port and I joined its crew. The *Tocsin* had been a trawler way back in the early 1900s and, like many trawlers, was requisitioned by the Royal Navy in 1939 and converted to become a minesweeper. It had a crew of 22 men. There was the skipper, two assistant officers, stokers as they were coal burning boats, engineers, a coxswain, telegraphist, steward and cook.

My job was Signalman, and I was known as 'Bunts', short for Bunting Tosser. As the sole signalman I was on the bridge in the open. Most of us were given a bunk below deck. We did mostly night 'sweeps' in the Harwich to Dover coastal region and aimed each night to blow up a couple of mines, though you couldn't rely on it.   **Des Malbon**

[3] *His Majesty's Minesweepers* (HMSO, 1943), pp. 32-3.

I hadn't been 'sweeping' long before our first enemy attack. We were just sitting in the dry dock at Sheerness when without warning German planes, coming in low, dive-bombed us.

The second major incident I experienced came in April or May 1942 at 2 a.m. one morning. We were lying about three miles from the east coast, sweeping as usual with two boats in front and two in the rear (aft). Then a Jerry E-boat came between us and suddenly we found we had a torpedo in our side. There was a big explosion. Sadly, about half the crew were below deck and didn't have time to get into the lifeboat. Just as I was making for the lifeboat I was ordered by the Second Officer to go back and quickly rescue the confidential logbooks, which were in a leather case.   I can remember that I only just made it into the rescue boat. When we eventually got back to port I discovered, on opening the case, there were no confidential logbooks in it but a stack of cigarettes. Fortunately, they were able to patch the *Tocsin* up. It was towed down to Surrey Docks for repair.   **Des Malbon**

Whilst the *Tocsin* was undergoing repairs, Des spent some time in London during a period of heavy bombing, as well as being given home leave. He returned to minesweeping duties on the *Tocsin* in late 1943 to early 1944, when, as part of the preparations for D-Day, it was given the task of towing invasion barges from the Thames to Portsmouth and Plymouth.

Inspection of HMS Tocsin's crew by the Duke of Gloucester at Parkestone Quay, 1943
(Des Malbon)

I will always remember that as we approached Portsmouth harbour, about dusk, I took the following signal from the shore, 'Please do not drop anchor, you are in a minefield.' It was a good job I'd taken that signal! We waited for a small boat to guide us through the minefield back to

Portsmouth harbour. I remember that once on shore, the skipper came up to me and thanked me for taking the signal.

Another brush with the enemy occurred when we were returning from a towing mission, not far off Dover. I remember it was ten o'clock one Sunday morning and I was about to take the skipper a cup of tea. Suddenly a Messerschmitt dive-bombed us. We fired back. We had a 12 lb Lewis gun in the front and an ack-ack gun in the rear. After causing our boat some damage the Messerschmitt left the scene. Our guns rarely brought a dive-bomber down. **Des Malbon**

In the late spring of 1944 Des was given a foreign draft. He received orders to join a cruiser, now a troopship, HMS *Stratheden*, which was scheduled to go via the Mediterranean and Red Sea to Bombay. The work out there would be convoying troops to Burma, to fight against the Japanese in the war in the Far East.

I counted myself a little lucky, because I had originally been drafted to a ship which was part of the D-Day invasion fleet and it was sunk.

When we got to Bombay we were transferred to a dirty old 'tramp' ship, the *London*, which was to transport us to Columbo. I remember there were cockroaches everywhere and it was far too crowded. Someone found out that the previous tramp ship bound for Columbo had been sunk by the Japanese. Sadly, it had been full of WRENS. Needless to say the waters there were shark-infested.

From Columbo we made regular trips in the HMS *Pladda*, another converted minesweeper, but bigger, with a crew of 42. Our job was to convoy troops to Burma. On one of these trips we arrived in Rangoon port with a convoy of Australian and British troops, only to be heavily attacked by Japanese dive-bombers. **Des Malbon**

Des suffered serious combat stress from the Japanese attack, and finished up in Columbo Hospital before being moved up to a hill station to convalesce, for six months. He was then sent home on a hospital ship, the *Empress of Scotland*. Des remembers seeing soldiers on board with terrible medical and mental problems. They had been captured by the Japanese in Burma and put in POW camps.

When the war ended in May 1945, it became clear that the Royal Naval Patrol Service had suffered the loss of over 250 vessels, more than any other branch of the Royal Navy. Because of the dangers and losses faced by these RNPS servicemen, they were honoured in a statement by Winston Churchill:

Message from the Prime Minister to the Officers and Men
of the Minesweeping Flotillas

Now that Nazi Germany has been defeated I wish to send you all on behalf of HMG a message of thanks and gratitude.

The work you do is hard and dangerous. You rarely get and never seek publicity; your only concern is to do your job, and you have done it nobly. You have sailed in many seas and all weathers ... This work could not be done without loss, and we mourn all who have died and over 250 ships lost on duty.

No work has been more vital than yours; no work has been better done. The Ports were kept open and Britain breathed. The Nation is once again proud of you. **Winston Churchill[4]**

---

[4] National Archives, Ref. PREM 3/314/5.

When Des arrived back at Lowestoft in July 1945 he received further treatment for combat stress, but he has never fully recovered and still receives treatment. Finally, in February 1946, he was demobilized and returned to Nottingham, and not long afterwards got a job at Boots, at their Thurgarton base, with responsibility for security. Shortly after this Des came to live with his wife at a flat in Caudwell's Mill, Southwell. Since then he has continued to live in Southwell and attended a number of Minesweepers' reunions, usually at Lowestoft or Skegness, which helped keep him in touch with some old colleagues.

After the war Des Malbon was awarded six medals; the 1939-45 Star, the Atlantic Star, the Burma Star, the Defence Medal, the General Service Medal and the Minesweeping Medal (MS/A).

Jack Beckett, shipwright on the battleship HMS *King George V*

'I was on deck checking the anchor when of all people, Winston Churchill, came on board.'   *Jack Beckett*

*Jack Beckett
(Robert Beckett)*

Jack Beckett was working for builder Bob Lee when the war broke out. In the early months he continued with his daily job and in the evenings and at weekends served in the LDV/Home Guard. In 1940 Jack volunteered to join the Royal Navy, preferring it to the Army or the RAF. He went to Nottingham for an interview.

Two weeks later I was sent to Skegness for six months' training. After only three weeks there, I was sent up to Scapa Flow, a major base for the Royal Navy fleet. I remember taking an exam to be a qualified shipwright; it helped being brought up in a blacksmith's shop as I was experienced in the use of metals as well as wood. After a very short time I joined the crew of the battleship *King George* V.

As shipwright my job was to look after the general maintenance of the battleship and specifically to undertake repairs to any wooden or metal structural damage on the ship. Other duties I had given to me was to take responsibility for the condition of the ship's anchor and for the security of the cargo.

Jack Beckett

The King George V-class battleships were the most modern British battleships used during WW2. Five ships of this class were commissioned. Their main task was to escort merchant convoys across the North Atlantic

In the early years of the war the *King George V* was heavily involved in the Battle of the Atlantic. She was required to provide distant cover for escorting convoys across the North Atlantic and the Arctic from North America and Canada to Russia. Once Hitler had invaded Russia in 1941, it was vital for us to see that supplies and food from America were delivered to Stalin. There were usually at least two destroyers attached to our battleship. As the radar on the battleship was superior to that of the destroyer, we would detect the danger first and send orders to the destroyers to deal with it.

On some occasions the *King George V* was given other tasks such as escorting an important personality across the Atlantic to America.   **Jack Beckett**

Winston Churchill on board the George V
(Private Collection)

It is possible that the escorting of an 'important personality' referred to was when the *King George V* was tasked to accompany the ship carrying Lord Halifax, the ex-Foreign Secretary and now the Ambassador to the United Nations, to Annapolis early in 1941.

There is no doubt that in Jack's mind the biggest threat in the Battle of the Atlantic was the German U-boats. The aim of Vice-Admiral Karl Dönitz was to use the German submarines to bring Britain to her knees through her dependence on overseas trade. Dönitz devised a system, known as the Rudeltaktik (the 'wolf pack'), in which U-boats would spread out in a long line across the projected course of a convoy.

The chief menace, of course, was the German submarines. These U-boats would hunt the individual merchant ships in our convoys in packs. As soon as they saw a target they would attack as a group.

We had two very close shaves. I remember seeing one torpedo pass the stern of the battleship and another go just underneath. Sometimes the submarines were difficult to locate as they used to hide underneath the ice flows. I never felt frightened but I could see some of the crew, especially some of the officers, were. They used to stay in their hammocks if there was any immediate danger.   **Jack Beckett**

However, battleships such as the *King George V* were given other significant tasks. Jack Beckett remembered that for many weeks in 1941 the main topic of conversation on board ship was that they had received orders, along with other Allied warships, to look for and ultimately sink the mighty German battleship the *Bismarck*, before it could cause more devastation.

I hadn't been that long on board the *King George V* before I heard that we had been ordered off convoy escort work and instructed to help with a British commando raid in Norwegian waters. Not long after that we received the dramatic news that we now had to concentrate on chasing the *Bismarck* before it could get back into port. What a chase that was! The battle lasted a few days and I remember the celebrations when it became clear the *Bismarck* was sinking.

Jack Beckett

At the time Jack wouldn't have known that another young Southwell man, Michael Suckling, was responsible for taking photographs from his Spitfire (pp. 105-7) of the *Bismarck* sitting in a Norwegian fiord. As a result of this, between 24 and 26 May 1941, the *King George V*, along with the *Prince of Wales*, was ordered to pursue and sink the *Bismarck*, which they did successfully, though not before the *Bismarck* had sunk the *Hood*. For two Southwell servicemen to be involved in different ways in this most historic of WW2 events is quite remarkable.

Jack didn't remember very well the details of either of these two major engagements, but it seems very likely that the support for the commando raid was in connection with Operation Claymore, the Royal Marines' raid on the Lofoten islands off the north-west coast of Norway, in March 1941. These islands were important for the production of fish oil.

Following the Allied successes in North Africa in October 1942, the *King George V* moved to the Mediterranean and to the Gibraltar naval base. This was in preparation for the Allied landings in Sicily, code-named Operation Husky. Before the landings took place in Sicily the *King George V* bombarded Trampani, and later escorted the surrendered Italian fleet to Malta and other of our naval bases. Jack remembered the attacks from the Luftwaffe as the battleship supported the invasion of Sicily, and later the mainland, providing cover for the transports carrying the landing forces to the beaches. In Jack's recollection, this proved to be a difficult enterprise. However, what stood out most in his memory was the visit on board the *King George V* of Prime Minister, Winston Churchill.

After a year or so the *King George V* was sent to the Mediterranean to support allied landings on the North African coast and then later landings onto the island of Sicily and the mainland of Italy. On several occasions I was present when the *King George V* bombarded onshore enemy defences on both the North African and Italian coast lines.

One memory that sticks out is when the Prime Minister, Winston Churchill, came on board the *King George V*. At one stage he stayed for a few days. I will never forget the first time I came across him. I was on deck checking the anchor when suddenly of all people Winston Churchill appeared and I wasn't sure whether to salute him or not because he was in casual gear. In the end I did salute him and he immediately nodded back. Each morning he would come up on the forecastle, which I had responsibility for, and exercise by walking up and down the deck. He never wore his hat and always seemed to have a cigar in a cigarette holder, though I never saw him smoking it.

Jack Beckett

Jack was not certain when Churchill came on board the *King George V*, but it is possible that it could have been in January 1943 when, along with other Allied leaders, including President Roosevelt and General de Gaulle, he attended the Casablanca Conference in French Morocco. The purpose of the conference was to plan strategy for the next phase of WW2 now that the Axis powers had been driven from North Africa. One outcome was to go ahead with an invasion of Sicily and southern Italy, which was to involve Jack as a crew member of the *King George V*.

After D-Day it was decided to transfer the *King George V* to the Pacific for future action in the war against Japan. She survived the war but was eventually scrapped in 1957. Six months before the end of the war Jack Beckett was directed to return to Britain, so his skills and experience could assist with the rebuilding of Coventry.[5]

> We were instructed to assist with Folls Hill Road, which, being centrally located, had been badly bombed. Our job was to make the street habitable again by making the roofs watertight and repairing all the broken windows. Many of the local residents had lost their homes and were still living in Nissen huts.
> **Jack Beckett**

Looking back at his war service, covering virtually all the war, Jack considered himself lucky on two counts.

> Serving on a top battleship, the *King George V,* in two major WW2 conflicts, the Battle of the Atlantic and the Allied Invasions of Sicily and Italy, was quite an experience. My other piece of luck was getting right through the war without serious injury or death. Many of my colleagues didn't.
> **Jack Beckett**

Although the outcome of the battle of the Atlantic was a strategic victory for the Allies - the German blockade ultimately failed - it was at great cost. 3,500 merchant ships and 175 warships were sunk whilst 783 U-boats were lost.

In the post-war years Jack set up his own builder's business, Beckett Builders, in Southwell. In 2007 he was one of the first local residents to receive a Civic Award for services rendered to the local community. He died in 2014 aged 100.

Philip Dodsworth, HMS Exeter

Philip Dodsworth at 17

'The crew all carried on their task as best they could, but within five minutes the thing no sailor wants to ever hear came over the loudspeakers - 'Abandon Ship!'.[6]

Philip Dodsworth, of 83 Westgate, was only fifteen years old when war broke out, but nevertheless he was very keen to join the Royal Navy as soon as possible. Fortunately, we have a detailed record of Philip Dodsworth's remarkable story, as he was interviewed in his later years by Michael Bentinck, to be included in his book *Forgotten Heroes.*

Philip did his initial training at Davenport in October 1939, and two years later, at the tender age of seventeen, he was appointed to the crew of the heavy cruiser HMS *Exeter,* which had previously played a heroic role in the destruction of the German pocket battleship *Graf Spee* in the Battle of the River Plate on 13 December 1939. Philip was very conscious of the ship's glorious past. The *Exeter* had been severely damaged in the battle, but as soon as it had been refitted,

---

[5] https://en.wkipedia.org/wiki/coventry The immediate reconstruction was headed by motor-industry magnate, William Rootes. Coventry city centre was extensively rebuilt.
[6] Michael Bentinck, *Forgotten Heroes* (Cambridge: M Bentinck 1995), p. 54.

in the spring of 1941, Philip prepared for what he expected to be a great adventure in the Pacific Ocean, where the *Exeter* was to form part of the special naval force intended to defend the Dutch East Indies (now Indonesia) from Japanese invasion. Japan had entered the war following her surprise attack on the American fleet at Pearl Harbour on 7th December 1941.

In the first few months there Philip's ship experienced a series of vicious attacks from Japanese aircraft. On the morning of 27th February 1942, the *Exeter* and her escort of smaller ships ran foul of a big force of Japanese warships, and the Battle of the Java Sea ensued. Unfortunately, the famous cruiser sustained an 8-inch shell hit to a boiler room in this fierce encounter, which necessitated her putting into the harbour at Surabaya.[7]

The next day, 28th February, the *Exeter* and her destroyer escort put out to sea again, but the Japanese were waiting.

> We all knew that the Japanese were shadowing us from the very minute we left port and not long after enemy ships were sighted ... and then from out of nowhere came a Jap aircraft. He must have radioed our position back to the Japanese ships ... for soon afterwards Japanese ships appeared.
> **Philip Dodsworth[8]**

HMS Exeter (Olwen Dodsworth)

In the Second Battle of the Java Sea the Japanese ships shelled the *Exeter* and her destroyer escorts mercilessly. Philip was stationed in the shell room of 'A' turret when a shell found its way into 'A' Boiler Room. Since 'B' Boiler Room had already suffered damage the day before, the *Exeter* lost all power. She was also hit by two torpedoes from a Japanese destroyer.[9] Michael Bentinck takes up the story.

> The crew all carried on their task as best they could, but ... the thing no sailor wants to hear came over the loudspeakers - yes - 'Abandon Ship!' Philip ... made his way along the stoker's mess deck ... up to the waist of the ship. ... he took a deep breath and jumped ... ; he noticed an oar floating nearby and he struck out for it ... it seemed ages before he got to it as the sea was quite choppy now ... he clung to the oar for dear life ... and wondered how long he could hold on; the fear of sharks came to him ... As he looked up again he could see a carley float coming towards him, ... already on board was the ship's padre, two officers and at least twenty fellow crew members. ...

7 Wikipedia, HMS *Exeter*.
8 Bentinck, p. 54.
9 Wikipedia, HMS *Exeter*.

[Then] out of the sky came enemy aircraft, homing down on them. They all gasped and thought they were going to be machine-gunned ...

It was not long before a Japanese destroyer came in sight ... rope ladders had been thrown over the side ... and Philip and the rest wondered what was in store for them. With his heart in his mouth he climbed up the rope ladder to the jeering of little yellow Japanese faces shouting out at him ... [when he] looked up he could see the flag of the rising sun fluttering in the breeze at the aft of the ship - a great feeling of fear was with him now for he still thought the Japanese would kill them.[10]

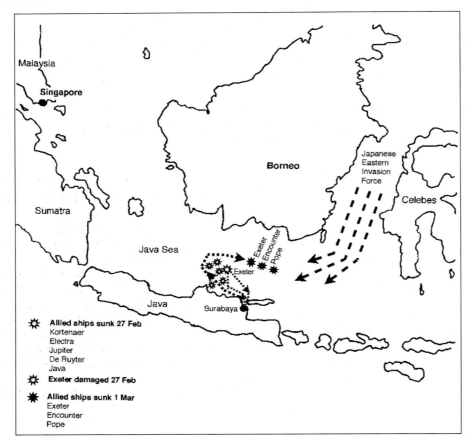

Battle of the Java Sea, 27th Feb - 1st March 1942
(Map by Trevor Wight)

After an hour the Japanese destroyer moved off, leaving many of the survivors in the water. Some of them were picked up the next day, but it isn't difficult to imagine the fate of those who were left in shark-infested waters for many hours. All the survivors were taken to a Dutch Hospital ship which had been captured by the Japanese and moored off the coast of Borneo. There Philip saw that many of the survivors were in very poor condition. Six weeks later all the survivors were told that they were embarking for Makassar, the capital of South Sulawesia province in the Dutch

---

[10] Bentinck, p. 54-5.

HOW ALLIED NAVY FOUGHT TO THE LAST GUN OFF JAVA

Japs Lose 8 Warships, Allies 12, In Great Sea Battle

TWELVE Allied warships — including the British cruiser Exeter, which helped to beat the Graf Spee—were lost in the Battle of Java.

At least eight Japanese warships were sunk or damaged.

Two British Cruisers Lost

This was revealed in an Admiralty communiqué last night, which gave these Allied losses:

BRITISH.—The cruisers Exeter and Perth; the destroyers Electra, Encounter, Stronghold and Jupiter; the sloop Yarra.

DUTCH.—The cruisers de Ruyter and Java; the destroyer Kortenaer.

U.S.A.—The heavy cruiser Houston and the destroyer Pope.

The white arrows show the threatened Jap thrusts at Australia. German radio reports parachutists have been dropped on Samau.

Newspaper Headline following the Battle of the Java Sea
(Olwen Dodsworth)

East Indies, where they would be placed in a Japanese POW camp. Philip's memories of his arrival at Makassar and the subsequent march to the POW camp are described by Michael Bentinck.

> He was pushed down the gangplank ... to be met by some very vicious-looking Japanese guards, who took great delight in hitting out at them with their pickle-sticks. All the men were craving for water and ... were all starving hungry, but there was no food or drink for them ...; the men were left standing like this for hours with the full heat of the sun beating down on them with nothing to cover their heads. Most of them had bare backs and were without shoes ... many of the Jap guards, noticing this, would stand on the men's feet to add to the pain. After a few hours of this, men were dropping like flies to the ground, then at last the order was given to quick march.
>
> ... Once out on the roadway the Jap guards soon started handing out their beatings. Men who could not keep up were those picked on; they would be hit by Japs' rifles but once a man fell to the ground ... the guards were on him like flies kicking out at him. ... If any man tried to help a fellow prisoner they received a rifle butt in the face.
>
> ... They had arrived at an old Dutch Army barracks, where they were left to stand outside the gates for another few hours ... before handing them over to the prison camp guards. ... When at last they were taken into the camp, they were in such a bad way that they knew that if the camp guards started on them as well, then many of them would just not survive.[11]

Camp conditions were appalling. POWs were crowded into small huts, which were buzzing with mosquitoes and flies. Philip showed initiative by secretly retrieving enough clothing and blankets to help him and others protect themselves against the mosquitoes. Throughout his imprisonment many POWs suffered badly from malaria, dysentery and beri beri, and it was only after many months that they were issued with mosquito nets. However, the nets were made of such thick cloth that during the rainy season, when the nights were so very hot and sticky, it was unbearable to sleep under them, so many men took the risk and slept without a net.

All they were given to eat for the first few months was rice, and when the British officers approached the Japanese commander about the need for better food and medicines for the men, they were told that what they got was more than enough. One day Philip was given meat for the

---

[11] Bentinck, pp. 59-60.

first time since he left the *Exeter* - it smelt great! He went up to the cook and said 'I really did enjoy that - was it chicken?' The cook replied, 'No, it was two cats and one dog.'[12] As to the routine at the POW camp, Philip described a typical day to Michael Bentinck:

> ... 'we were called by bugle every morning at 6.30 a.m., and ... we had breakfast, then at 7.30 a.m. we had to fall in for work. Some [POW] parties walked to work and some would be taken by lorry; ... and work carried on until noon ... then we worked on till 5. 30 p.m. But sometimes if a job had to be finished we did have to work round the clock without any breaks at all. Some of the work was much harder than other work ... if you were working on aircraft runways - many a time the rains would wash your work away.' ... Philip said that when you finally did finish work you had a four mile walk, or sometimes more, to get back to camp.[13]

Cover of Philip Dodsworth's Scrap Book (Olwen Dodsworth)

The relationship with the Japanese prison guards was not an easy one. Initially there were many beatings and some guards were especially vicious. The British POWs came to realise that if they were to survive, they had to try to build at least a working relationship with some guards. To get more food they needed to be able to trade with the natives for fruit and sugar.   These goods could be sold at 100% mark up to the Dutch prisoners in return for more food. For this 'black market' to work, some of the guards needed to be 'softened'.

He [Philip] told me how men would do anything to get more food to help them stay alive. Some of the guards could be alright to them at times, and one such guard, when on their working party, would hand him his rifle to hold whilst he went to sleep, telling him ... 'If sergeant of guard come, you wake me up.' They were only too pleased to keep an eye out for him as they could take it easy as well. Also, while the guard slept many of the men could slip away and trade with the natives. But as time went on guards like this became rare and it seemed that only the vicious guards were left, and beatings became all too common.[14]

Another problem the POWs had was that their already inadequate clothes rotted very quickly in the tropical climate, and men never had enough clothing to keep the sun off in the day or to keep warm at night. Towards the end of their imprisonment, the Japanese issued them with special white shirts and shorts; but they were only able to wear these on special occasions, such as the Japanese Emperor's birthday when the men were all expected to line up and bow towards Tokyo. As they performed this ritual, most of the POW's would spit on the ground. On this day the men received much better food and Philip wished that the Emperor had had more than one birthday.

---

[12] Bentinck, p. 61.
[13] Bentinck, pp. 64-5.
[14] Bentinck, p. 62.

In January 1945 the POWs morale was lifted by clear signs from bombing raids that the Allies were fighting back and the Japanese were unnerved. By this time many men were physically very weak, having suffered nearly three years in a Japanese POW camp, and men were dying at the rate of about four a day. When the Dutch captain approached the Japanese for medicine, again they had very little success.[15]

> One hundred and sixty Englishmen died in the first few months of 1945, with beri beri and dysentery and malnutrition being the main cause of death. When you returned from work the first question you asked was, 'Who died today?' A name would be given to you and most times you would reply, 'What a pity. He was a decent bloke.'
>
> ... You could be talking to a man who you thought looked fit, only to be told an hour later that he had dropped dead; this would come as a real shock to you and you would start to worry about yourself.
>
> **Philip Dodsworth**[16]

On 17th August 1945 we all went out working as usual, with no idea of what the day would bring. At about 11.30 a.m. the guards came over and said everyone must go back to camp. 'Suspicions were now aroused - something must be happening; maybe a forced march or even mass execution, for it was well known how heartless the Japanese could be. All the men were told to muster and put on their special white Japanese clothing.'[17]

> ... through the gates marched more Jap guards, which made everyone think, 'oh God they're going to kill us all', but the guards came and stood right in front of us and laid down their arms. The Dutch captain came out and stood on the rostrum and then in Dutch first, followed by English, he announced, 'THE WAR is OVER.' What he said after that no one heard and no one cared.
>
> **Philip Dodsworth**[18]

The Japanese guards reacted dramatically to this news. They were afraid, and suddenly better food, cigarettes, toiletries and an abundance of medical supplies became available. Philip and the other POWs were moved to a military hospital, but as far as the men were concerned 'it was too late for the Japanese to repent now; the lives they had taken, the beatings they had given, they now deserved all they got.' On the day the Allies arrived to release the POWs, the Japanese worked hard to make it look as if the prisoners had been living a life of luxury. The state of most of the men belied this, but it amused the lads to see the Japanese actually working.[19]

The British men were overjoyed to see the Australian ships come into Makasser harbour to collect them, and the realisation dawned that after all this time they were actually going home. They initially visited Perth, where they were greeted with a great welcome and fresh clothes. There followed a glorious eight days in the outback. By the time their holiday finished, most of the men were in a much better physical condition and therefore ready for the long voyage home. Stopping off at Cape Town, Philip and the other ex-POWs again received a great welcome from the South African public, and took the opportunity of buying presents for their loved ones back home. They finally docked at Portsmouth, where hundreds of relatives and the Mayor of Exeter

---

[15] Bentinck, p. 66.
[16] Bentinck, pp. 66-7.
[17] Bentinck, p. 67.
[18] Bentinck, p. 67.
[19] Bentinck, pp. 67-8.

SOUTHWELL SAILOR BACK FROM JAP CAPTIVITY

FOUR HOURS IN SEA

WHEN EXETER WAS HIT

NEARLY five years ago there set out from Southwell a young Royal Navy sailor to join his first ship. He had just finished his training at Devonport and spent a leave with his parents. He was A/B Philip Dodsworth, son of Mr. and Mrs. Dodsworth, Westgate.

Little did he dream what was in store for him, that he was to figure in one of the epic events of the war, although now he is safe back home again—having arrived in a taxicab from Nottingham at 3 a.m. on Wednesday—he would not exchange his experience for anything that could be offered him.

A Famous Ship.

Leaving home to catch the train back to Devonport in the early Spring of 1941, he looked forward to a new phase of life and perhaps to adventure and when at the Depot he was told he was to join H.M.S. Exeter he had reason to be proud, for he knew something about men o' war, particularly the glorious career of the Exeter. Had she not for one thing, just taken part in bringing the Graf Spee to her inglorious end, which itself added a fine chapter to the great story of Britain's naval might?

In due time he reached the Far East, and for a time there was nothing really eventful in life aboard unless one counts vicious attacks by enemy aircraft as of real moment.

Then, one morning in February, 1942, the Exeter and her escort of smaller ships, ran foul of a big force of enemy warships and an action ensued in which the famous cruiser sustained damage that necessitated her putting into Surabaya after the action had been broken off.

Next day the Exeter and her destroyer escort put out to sea again, but the Japs were waiting and this time there was a fight to the end. With all the Exeter's boilers damaged the crew had orders to abandon her.

Jumped Overboard

A/B Dodsworth tells how he jumped overboard and swam about for a long time before gaining one of the rafts that had been sent overboard. Meantime the Exeter moved on to its doom. Four hours passed before A/B Dodsworth was picked up by a Japanese ship, which took him to Borneo, whence he was moved to Macassar.

We know the emotion which we at home felt when the news of the end of the Exeter was received, but it was particularly distressing for those families who, like the Dodsworths, had a member among the crew. In the case of A/B Dodsworth there was a harrowing wait for the better part of two years before the news came through that he was alive and in Jap hands.

During that time and the subsequent period up to the Japanese surrender, A/B Dodsworth was under the coloured taskmaster in Macassar. When at last he was released he was taken to Australia, and it was from there that he made the journey home to England.

Thoughts of Home

Speaking of the period of captivity, he says the familiar words, "There's no place like home," never meant so much to him before as they did during the three and a half years he was in Japanese hands. "We tried not to think of home too often," he adds, "as worry soon got you down, and made you ill, and to recover from an illness was no easy matter. Since being released I have read of brutal and savage treatment in various Jap camps and consider that we in Macassar were very lucky indeed. Not that I have any praise for a Jap, far from it. We always felt that one day the Allies would win, although at times we wondered if we ourselves would win the fight to freedom again. But during all the time in captivity our spirits were very high. At Christmas time it was impossible not to think of home, but we cheered ourselves up with songs, poems and monologues."

Incidentally, A/B Dodsworth looks remarkably fit and well, and he is as keen about the Navy as ever.

Newspaper Article on Philip's return
(Olwen Dodsworth)

were waiting for the survivors of the *Exeter*. After over four and a half years home was at last round the corner.

It was early evening before Philip got away on the 12th December [1945]. He travelled through the night back to his home in Southwell, Notts, and arrived at Nottingham station at 3 a.m. He found a taxi and set off for that home he had dreamed of for the last five years. When he arrived it was all in darkness, of course, but once those inside knew who he was it was not dark or quiet for long.

... and as he [Philip] told me he was one of the lucky ones - he had come through and for him it was now 'Home Sweet Home'.[20]

On 26th December 1945 the *Newark Advertiser* covered Philip Dodsworth's remarkable story of survival against all the odds with the headline:

'Southwell Sailor Back from Japanese Captivity'.
Philip Dodsworth of HMS Exeter Safe and Well
Mr/Mrs Dodsworth of 83 Westgate have received the welcome news from their son, Philip Dodsworth of HMS *Exeter*, that he is safe and well. This was the first news since he was taken prisoner by the Japanese in 1942 when HMS *Exeter* was sunk in the Java Sea. Philip was 17 when he joined the RN and is now 21.[21]

Philip returned home to live with his parents at 83 Westgate and found a job at the Southwell Food Office, remaining there until its closure. A few years after the war he married Olwen and they took a cottage at the top of Trinity Churchyard. Philip died on the 22nd April 2006.

Ron Spall, gunner on destroyer HMS Scorpion

'I, Neptunus Rex, do solemnly declare that Ronald Spall on 7th July 1943 did ... enter the most dread region of my vast realm by Crossing the Arctic Circle. We do therefore declare him a Member of the Most Ancient Order of the Bluenose.'[22]

Ron Spall was born in Southwell and attended the National School on Nottingham Road. When the war broke out he was 16, living in Private Road, Southwell and working at The Vineries for a market gardener. He was called up on 6 May 1942, at the age of 19, and posted to Devonport for training as a ship's gunner. From May 1942 to April 1943 Ron served on two ships, HMS *Raleigh* and HMS *Drake*.

---

[20] Bentinck, pp. 72-3.
[21] *N/Adv*, 3rd October 1945.
[22] Proclamation, To all who crossed the Arctic Circle, 7th July 1943.

*Ron Spall
(Carole Spall)*

On 30 April 1943 he was transferred to the crew of the destroyer HMS *Scorpion,* which was the only weapon-class ship fitted with Limbo depth charges. It carried six 4in guns. The *Scorpion's* main task, when Ron Spall served, was to escort Arctic convoys taking goods to Russia and return as escort to merchant ships that were waiting in Russian ports. Encounters with German U-boats and other naval vessels were to be expected, as it was the express intention of the enemy to intercept the Arctic convoys and thus create food shortages in both Britain and Russia. Ron Spall speaks of these German sea and air attacks on Allied merchant ships which were being escorted.

I remember my father talking about a particular German attack on one of the merchant ships they were escorting. The ship had been destroyed and the small number of survivors were all in the icy sea struggling to cling to debris. The crew of the *Scorpion* could only stand by, look on and hope that the nearby German vessel would pick up the survivors. Sadly, father said, the German commander decided he didn't want prisoners of war, so he gave

orders to open fire on the survivors.   **Carole Spall**

*Ron Spall (middle row, second from right) with a group of new recruits
(Carole Spall)*

In between periods of action crews spent many hours being cooped up on board so, early on in his naval service, Ron learned to box. It became a way of releasing pent-up energy. He had some experience of cooking and used to get roped in on board to give the cook a break - it was mainly beef stews, dumplings and soups. Serving in the Arctic obviously left its mark on Ron Spall, as his daughter explains.

My father once described the Arctic scenery to me; he spoke of the ships being totally covered in ice and looking like ghosts sailing through frozen mists with a strange, haunting silence. Clearly one of the main issues for sailors in the Arctic was how to keep reasonably warm. He told me you had to follow the dress code and make sure every part of your body was covered and warm, or at least fairly warm. You had to try and avoid runny eyes or nose as the droplets would instantly freeze and possibly cause damage to the brain. Keeping your lips dry was hard, as licking them was the natural thing to do. Lips could freeze over causing painful blood cracks. The worst part was keeping his toes warm, so wiggling them and jumping on the spot usually helped and similarly with his fingers.

Carole Spall

HMS Scorpion (top) and the Scharnhorst
(Carole Spall)

In late 1943 the *Scorpion* became involved in one of the most important British naval actions of the war - the sinking of the legendary German battleship, the *Scharnhorst*. This took place in the Battle of the North Cape on 26th December 1943.

The *Scharnhorst* was a capital battleship, the leader of her class, and armed with a battery of nine 11in guns in three triple turrets. She operated together with the *Gneisenau* making sorties

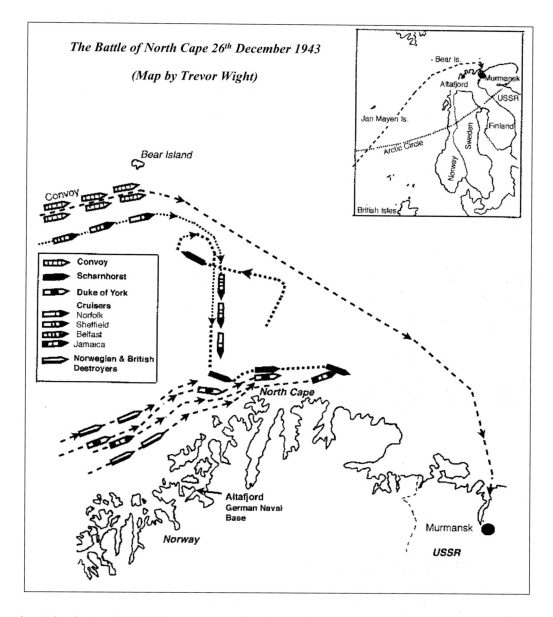

The Battle of North Cape 26th December 1943

(Map by Trevor Wight)

into the Atlantic to raid British merchant shipping and to prevent western supplies reaching the Soviet Union. The *Scharnhorst* had earlier featured strongly in the German invasion of Norway, sinking the aircraft carrier HMS *Glorious* as well as a number of her escort destroyers.

The *Scharnhorst*, escorted by five German destroyers, attempted to attack the ships of Convoy JW 55B, consisting of nineteen cargo ships accompanied by a close escort of two destroyers and three other vessels. However, the *Scharnhorst* was driven away by Admiral Burnett's three light cruisers and then cut off by Admiral Fraser's force. During the battle, the *Duke of York* hit the *Scharnhorst's* starboard boiler room with a 14in shell, slowing her briefly to ten knots. This

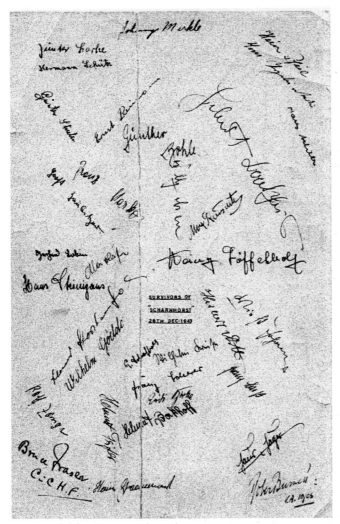

Signatures of the 36 Scharnhorst survivors
(Carole Spall)

Nottingham Guardian Article from January 1944
(Carole Spall)

NOTES BY THE WAY

Notts. Lads in Sea Fight

A VIVID account of the sinking of the Scharnhorst is contained in a letter which has reached the *Guardian* from A.B. R. Spall, who was in the action on board the destroyer H.M.S. Scorpion.

Seaman Spall, whose home is in Private-road, Southwell, mentions that on board the Scorpion are a number of Nottinghamshire lads, among them L.-S. Keeton (New Basford), L. Cook Jones (Sherwood), — Wass (Hucknall), and J. R. Vanplew (Mansfield).

It has been remarked here that this part of the country is an excellent recruiting ground for the Navy, and it would have been strange indeed if there had not been some local lads in the action which put paid to the Scharnhorst.

Hits On Scharnhorst

Seaman Spall says in his letter that the account of the engagement is sent to the *Guardian* "with the compliments of the Nottingham lads serving aboard H.M.S. Scorpion," a gesture that will be much appreciated by Nottingham people.

Details of the battle have already been published at length. Seaman Spall records the Scorpion got in three hits with torpedoes, "which must have taken them by surprise, as they started to pelt away like hell at anything."

He concludes with a passage typical of the spirit of loyalty and good discipline that dominates the Navy: "We have to thank our captain, Lt.-Cdr. W. E. Clouston, R.N., and the officers serving under him, for the daring and skill which brought us out of the battle unscathed."

Y 13, 1944.

provided the British destroyers with an opportunity to attack with torpedoes. At 18.50 hrs Ron Spall's *Scorpion* and the Norwegian *Stod* launched sixteen torpedoes at the enemy ship, causing considerable damage and driving the *Scharnhorst* into the firing range of HMS *Saumarez* and HMS *Savage*, which scored two more hits.[23] At 19.45 the *Scharnhorst* finally went down by the bows. The *Scorpion* went searching for survivors; voices could be heard calling for help from the darkness. Of the *Scharnhorst's* crew of 1,968 officers and men, only 36 survived.

> The *Scorpion* got in three hits with our torpedoes which must have taken the *Scharnhorst* by surprise, as they started to pelt away like hell at anything. … We have to thank our captain, Lt-Cdr W E Clouston RN, and the officers serving under him, for the daring and skill which brought us out of the battle unscathed.
>
> **Ron Spall**[24]

Admiral Bruce Fraser, Commander-in-Chief of the Home Fleet, had no doubt that the battle had been courageously fought by both sides.

> Gentlemen, the battle against the *Scharnhorst* has ended in victory for us. I hope that any of you who are ever called upon to lead a ship into action against an opponent many times superior in power, will command your ship as gallantly as the *Scharnhorst* was commanded today.[25]

Ron Spall was involved in the rescue of the 36 German survivors from the sea after the sinking of the *Scharnhorst*. The survivors were taken by the *Scorpion* to the *Duke of York* battleship, which was berthed in Russia. Remarkably, Ron got a copy of the signatures from all the survivors. News of the dramatic sinking of the *Scharnhorst* reached Southwell when Ron wrote home to his parents and also to a Southwell tradesman, giving a vivid account of the battle. The local tradesman immediately contacted the *Newark Advertiser*, which resulted in his incredible story being featured the following week.

In June 1944 Ron was involved in the D-Day landings, and four months later he moved back to service on the *Drake*. The following year he was in Singapore when Lord Mountbatten accepted the Japanese surrender.

After the war Ron worked for twenty-one years as an electric welder at Nicholson's in Newark. Subsequently, he spent twenty years as a garden handyman at South Muskham Prebend. He died on 23rd February 2002 at the age of 81. For his daughter Carole, Ron was always a hero.

> My father was a proud, honest, clever, caring man who stuck to his principles, strict and hard at times. He loved his family and would always stand by us but he adored my mother. Father always showed me great love; he taught me to knit and make rugs. He helped me survive and showed me how to live my life, my way. He brought many things back from the war, mentally and physically, my brave hero.
>
> **Carole Spall**

---

[23] https://en. wikipedia. org/wiki/HMS_ Scorpion.
[24] *Nottingham Guardian*, 13th January 1944.
[25] Richard Humble, *Fraser of North Cape: Life of Admiral of the Fleet Lord Fraser, 1888-1981* (London: Routledge and Kegan Paul, 1983), p. 5.

John Frederick Brooke, Officer on LCT 2337 and HMS Orwell

'Immediately after the tanks had gone ashore on SWORD beach, the enemy opened fire onto the open tank deck.'[26]

**John Brooke
(Private Collection)**

John Brooke was born in Nottingham in 1923 and joined the Royal Navy in 1941, receiving his initial training at HMS *Ganges,* Shotley.[27] From 1942-3 John served as a seaman aboard the *Orwell,* an ORIBI Class Destroyer, in GB coastal waters and in the Arctic.[28] The ship had been launched on 2nd April 1942 and by November was escorting HM cruisers taking stores and personnel to the garrison at Spitzbergen. The following year, 1943, the *Orwell* was on escort duty for several convoys to Russia.

In 1943-44 John, now an officer, was serving on LCT 2337 in GB coastal waters and preparing for the Normandy landings. He played a significant role in the D-Day landings and, in addition to recording a lengthy interview for the Imperial War Museum, he wrote a separate account of his experiences on D-Day:

My tank landing craft was LCT (CB) 2337 with Sub Lieutenant R. W. Rawlings RNVR as Commanding Officer, myself (also a Sub Lieutenant) as 1st Lieutenant (second-in-command) and ten crew. Our LCT had been refitted as a CB (Concrete Buster) so that it could carry two tanks on a raised after-deck, able to fire their guns over the bows and the other vehicles being carried on-board, at enemy targets whilst approaching the beach. Our pre D-Day exercises were with the 13/18th Hussars (Queen Mary's Own) part of the British 27th Armoured Brigade using Sherman tanks with 17-pounder, high-velocity guns, commanded by Lieutenant Knowles.

We eventually loaded the Hussars on 3 June as part of the close range support for the assault on SWORD beach. Two Sherman tanks were on the raised after-deck with a 'flail' and AVRE (Armoured Vehicle Royal Engineers) tanks forward on the lower deck. Bad weather caused D-Day to be postponed so this meant a choppy and uncomfortable experience for our army colleagues whilst lying at a buoy outside Portsmouth. At 0900 on Monday, 5 June 1944 we sailed in company with the 100th LCT (A) flotilla; still in a choppy sea and poor visibility. Heading for the Nab Tower, we joined an incredible variety of craft all meeting at a point we already knew as 'Piccadilly Circus'.

Station keeping (keeping the right distance from other vessels) became more difficult during the night as we proceeded across the English Channel, and with a full load of tanks, ammunition and army stores, the tank deck and mess decks (accommodation) were awash due to the sea conditions. The final approach to the Queen sector of SWORD beach was without incident. The Sherman tanks did not open fire on any target on the shore and the touch-down on the beach was within five minutes of the planned H-Hour with all vehicles leaving our craft safely.

However, immediately after the tanks had gone ashore, the enemy opened fire onto the open tank deck. We quickly closed the large bow door and started to turn 180 degrees to get back to sea, but as we turned we were hit by shell and mortar fire. The crew of the starboard Oerlikon gun were knocked out, and the Commanding Officer received splinter wounds to his arm and hand. Once we were clear of the beach area, we made for a hospital ship and managed

[26] www.ddnf.org.uk/memories/j_brooke
[27] http://www.iwm.org.uk/collections/item/object/80015114
[28] www.naval-history.net/xGM-Chrono-10DD-470-HMS_*Orwell*.htm

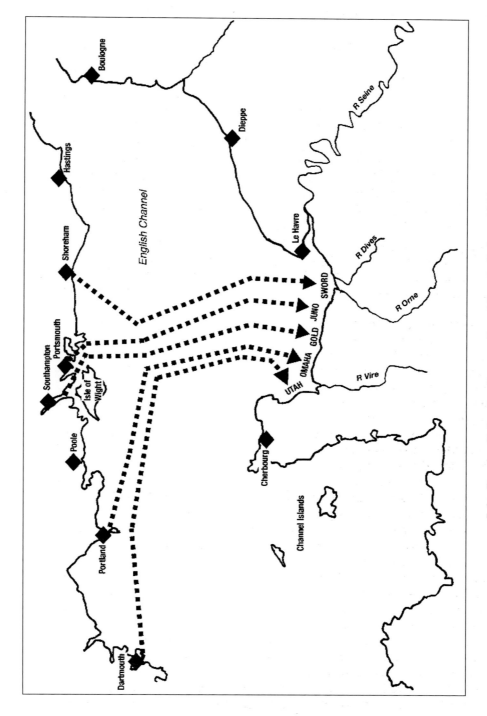

*John Brooke: D-Day landings on Sword Beach 6th June 1944
(Map by Trevor Wight)*

to transfer the mortally wounded crew of the Oerlikon gun, but Sub Lieutenant Rawlings remained on board in command.

We had problems in navigating, as the compasses were out of action. Also we had taken in tow LCT 2334 which had severe damage to the bows and was without steerage or power. This situation meant that during the night of D-Day progress was extremely slow, with our mess deck and galley damaged and persistent problems with power in our engine room; however, we did have a good supply of warm sustenance from the army's surplus stores of self-heating soup and cocoa. Early in the morning of 7 June a helpful RAF Air-Sea Rescue launch guided us onto a course to steer, enabling us to join the shipping queue back to 'Piccadilly Circus', the Nab, eventually Spithead and Portsmouth, where we arrived in the early hours of Thursday, 8 June. Sub Lieutenant Rawlings, our wounded Commanding Officer, was put ashore in Portsmouth for hospital treatment. Our craft, LCT 2337, now under my command and still towing LCT 2334, made its slow progress up the Solent to Thorneycroft's yard in Southampton for repairs. So ended my D-Day: successful, but with a loss that all the crew felt, each in his own way.

The sequel to D-Day was that Sub Lieutenant Rawlings was awarded the Distinguished Service Cross.

LCT 2337 eventually made a return trip to Normandy with US Navy DUKWs (amphibious trucks capable of carrying 25 men). These were landed successfully on OMAHA beach, but this was at the height of a great gale and after a succession of disabling mishaps in the chaos inside the Mulberry Harbour area, LCT 2337 finally had to be abandoned on 20 June without casualties.

For myself this was an end to my involvement in the European war. Many landing craft crews were either transferred to other combined operation units in the Pacific theatre or, like myself, retrained for a return to General Service duties in the Pacific.[29]

John Brooke was awarded the Arctic Star Medal for his service in the war. In the post-war period he and his family lived for many years in Farthingate Avenue and John became a regular member of Southwell and District Local History Society. He died, aged 90, on 19th October 2013.

Rear Admiral R St Vincent Sherbrooke, DSO, VC - HMS Onslow

'First, the steel splinter had to be removed from his head, a very delicate operation, then his face rebuilt over a year. He had more than 17 operations to his face, he had lost his eye and had many bone and skin grafts.[30]

Born in Oxton in 1901 Robert St Vincent Sherbrooke began his naval career at Osbourne House, then attended Dartmouth College. From an early age he was called Rupert, to distinguish him from his uncle, Col Robert Sherbrooke. He joined the Royal Navy in 1917 as a midshipman aboard HMS *Canada,* and had two years of active service in WW1. In 1935 he was promoted to commander and served on the aircraft carrier HMS *Courageous.*

He was on the destroyer HMS *Cossack* during the Second Battle of Narvik on 13th April 1940, a naval victory during the German invasion of Norway of 1940. On 9th April the Germans had launched their invasion of Norway, attacking six ports including Narvik. In the first Battle of Narvik, on 10th April, each side lost two destroyers, and three more of the German ships were badly damaged. In the aftermath of this engagement the Admiralty decided to attack the remaining German ships. On the morning of 13th April the battleship HMS *Warspite*, supported by nine

---

[29] www.ddnf.org/memories/j_brooke/
[30] www.blondmcindoe.org/rear_admiral_robert_st_vincent_sherbro

destroyers, attacked and sank the submarine U64 and an enemy destroyer. Robert Sherbrooke was at that time serving on the destroyer HMS *Cossack,* which was deployed in this action. The *Cossack* was hit, but the German ships came off worse and two destroyers were lost close to Narvik. Several more of the German ships were scuttled by their own crews. For his part in the action Robert Sherbrooke was awarded a DSO in June 1940.

On 31st December 1942 off the North Cape, Norway, in the Barents Sea, Capt. Sherbrooke, aboard HMS *Onslow*, was senior officer in command of destroyers escorting an important convoy bound for North Russia, and loaded with essential military supplies. He made contact with a vastly superior enemy force, including the cruiser *Hipper* and the pocket battleship *Lutzow*. Four times the German ships tried to attack the convoy, but were forced back each time. Eventually, the German ships had to retreat and the convoy was able to reach Russian ports without damage. Early in the action, Capt. Sherbrooke was seriously wounded in the face and temporarily blinded. Nevertheless, he continued to direct the ships under his command. His actions and the German ships' failure to neutralise the convoy, despite its superior force, were influential in persuading Hitler to scrap the Kriegsmarine in early 1943.[31]

For the heroic part that he played in the Battle of the Barents Sea, Robert Sherbrooke was awarded the Victoria Cross, Britain's highest award. Early in January 1943 the dramatic story of the naval victory and the crucial part played by Robert Sherbrooke, despite his wounds, was covered by the *Newark Advertiser*.

The then Captain Sherbrooke and his wife Rosemary at Buckingham Palace for his VC investiture

---

[31] https://en.wikipedia.org/wiki/Robert_Sherbrooke

24

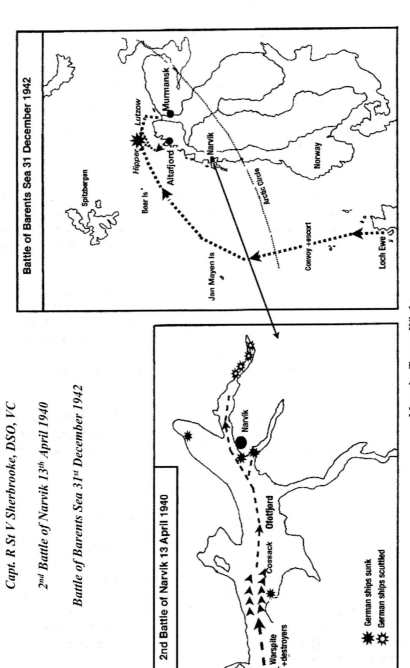

Capt. R St V Sherbrooke, DSO, VC

2nd Battle of Narvik 13th April 1940

Battle of Barents Sea 31st December 1942

Maps by Trevor Wight

Battle of Barents Sea 31 December 1942

Spitzbergen

Bear Is

Murmansk

Lutzow

Hipper

Altafjord

Narvik

Norway

Arctic Circle

Jan Mayen Is

Convoy +escort

Loch Ewe

2nd Battle of Narvik 13 April 1940

Narvik

Ofotfjord

Cossack

Warspite
+destroyers

German ships sunk
German ships scuttled

CAPT. R. St. V. SHERBROOKE
AWARDED THE V.C.

Led Destroyers' Attack

Newark joins in hearty congratulations to Capt. R. St. V. Sherbrooke DSO, of Oxton, who has been awarded the VC for his recent gallant exploits in Northern waters. ... Commanded by Captain Sherbrooke, escorting British destroyers beat off four determined attempts by a superior enemy naval force to destroy a convoy taking important war supplies to Russia.

... In a communiqué on December 31st the Admiralty announced:

'On the morning of December 31st, British destroyers, commanded by Capt. R. St. V. Sherbrooke, DSO, RN, in the *Onslow*, which were escorting the convoy, made contact with a greatly superior enemy force thought to consist of one pocket battleship, one cruiser and a number of destroyers, off the North Cape at the extreme north of Norway.

Captain Sherbrooke immediately led his destroyers into attack and closed with the enemy with great gallantry. In the semi-darkness, and with visibility further reduced by frequent snowstorms, contact was fleeting and intermittent. Fighting continued for about two hours. By resolute and skilful handling this small force of destroyers succeeded in driving off four attempts by the strong enemy forces to destroy the convoy.'

First Lord's Praise

Mr. Alexander, First Lord of the Admiralty, addressing a dinner ... in London, said: 'There never was anything finer in Royal Naval annals. There have been few periods in our naval history where destroyers had been better led or better work done. Capt. Sherbrooke led the fight on. He divided his forces. He sent a couple of destroyers against the enemy destroyers and went straight in against the pocket battleship and the 8-inch gun cruiser.'

Capt. Sherbrooke's ships were little ships, but how valuable they were to our Navy, our country and our cause![32]

Two months later, in March 1943, Capt. Sherbrooke returned home to a hero's welcome. His native village of Oxton had been bedecked with bunting, flags and messages of goodwill, and wherever he went there he was met with enthusiastic cheers. Prominence was given to this event in the local press.

OXTON'S V.C.
Capt. R. St. V. Sherbrooke Welcomed Home

Capt. Robert Sherbrooke, who was awarded the VC for his gallant exploit in bringing a Russian-bound convoy with a destroyer escort under his command, safely through, in the face of strong enemy forces, returned to his home, 'Deer Leap', yesterday.

... Captain Sherbrooke is having a week's rest before returning to hospital for further treatment for wounds received in the action which resulted in the loss of the sight in one eye.

In an interview, Capt. Sherbrooke spoke of the convoy battle. After expressing high appreciation not only of the merit of his own ship but also of the covering force which came to their assistance, he said, 'The convoy arrived intact and it is my earnest hope that this achievement may be some small consolation to the families of those who lost their lives.'[33]

---

[32] *N/Adv*, 13th January 1943.
[33] *N/Adv*, 23rd March 1943.

Robert Sherbrooke's valiant deeds were still remembered in the locality the following year, 1944.

These Events Made News in Newark and District during 1943

As the past year of 1943 opened, Newark and District took a special pride in the announcement that the VC had been awarded to Capt. R. St. V. Sherbrooke, of Oxton, for his gallant exploits with a Russian bound convoy.[34]

From July 1945 to mid-1946, Robert Sherbrooke was Commanding Officer on the cruiser HMS *Aurora*. He later achieved the rank of rear-admiral. In 1958-9 he was appointed High Sheriff of Nottinghamshire. On 13th June 1972 he died in his home village of Oxton.

Rufus Boyson Smith, steward on destroyer HMS Hecla

Rufus, born at Farnsfield in the spring of 1915, married Margaret Smith in 1937. He joined the Royal Navy as Steward D/LX 25021 and was posted to serve aboard HMS *Hecla*, a destroyer tender. This ship was attacked by the German submarine U515 when the *Hecla* was part of the convoy carrying supplies from South Africa supporting Operation Torch for the invasion of North Africa and the subsequent tank battles between Allied forces and the Africa Korps under General Erwin Rommel.

At 00.15hrs on 12th November 1942, the U-boat fired a spread of 4 torpedoes at the *Hecla*, which had apparently been misidentified as a Birmingham class cruiser, and hit her in the engine room. The other three torpedoes either missed the *Hecla* or malfunctioned. The U-boat then hit the ship with three more torpedoes at 01.28, 01.49 and 02.06, sinking the vessel west of Gibraltar. 279 of the crew of 847 lost their lives, including Steward Smith. **Trevor Wilds**

Rufus Boyson Smith was posthumously awarded the 1939-45 Star, and is commemorated on Panel 72, Column 2 of the Plymouth Naval Memorial, Devon.

Harold Brailsford

At the beginning of the war Harold Brailsford was 38, working in Dorset and married with a young daughter. His parents lived at Norwood Villas on Halam Road, Southwell. Harold was called up and decided to join the Royal Navy; he was serving on a minesweeper when tragic news came of his untimely death.

Mr and Mrs Brailsford of Norwood Villas, Halam Road have received information as to how their eldest son, Leading Cook Harold Brailsford, met his death whilst on active service with the Navy. He was engaged on a minesweeper when the ship was blown up by a mine in December. The news was sent to his wife by a shipmate. ... He was lost at sea, presumed drowned. A native of Southwell, he was 41 years old and had been in the Navy for two years. He was working in Dorset when he was called up. He leaves a widow and little girl.[35]

---

[34] *N/Adv*, 5th January 1944.
[35] *N/Adv*, 23rd February 1944.

George Warren, Royal Marines

George Harold Warren was born in Farnsfield in 1923 and lived on Main Street, between New Hill and what is now a greengrocer's shop. After the outbreak of war he joined the Royal Marines.

He served in the Royal Marines as Marine Po.X.115137. Whilst a member of Naval Party NP1686 responsible for the safety of the area around Dieppe, he was awarded the British Empire Medal (Military Division) on 15th May 1945 'for gallantry and skill in mine searching and clearing operations in the ports of Normandy and the Low Countries following the invasion of France.'

Trevor Wilds

In the autumn of 1951 George Warren married Hilda Barker and moved to Newark. He died on 9th September 2000 aged 77 years.

Robert Thorne, Royal Naval Volunteer Reserve, HMS Harvester

Only two years before the outbreak of war Robert Thorne was a nineteen-year-old student who had just completed his education, very successfully, at the Minster Grammar School. His family home was on Lower Kirklington Road. In the spring of 1941 he joined the Royal Naval Volunteer Reserve (RNVR).

Robert was quickly serving on HMS *Collingwood*. In the spring of 1942 he gained a commission as a temporary sub lieutenant. Sadly, on 11th March 1943 his ship, the destroyer HMS *Harvester*, was torpedoed and sunk and Robert, along with the other officers and 135 ratings, was reported missing in action. He was only 22 years old. My mother May Trueman, Robert's sister, said that she thought of her brother every day for the rest of her life.

Michael Trueman

Robert and Mary Thorne outside 52 Lower Kirklington Road, Southwell
(Michael Trueman)

News of Robert Thorne's sad fate was covered by the local paper.

Sub. Lieut R Thorne RNVR

His many friends will learn with regret the sad news that the only son of Mr and Mrs Thorne of Lower Kirklington Rd, R H Thorne has been lost at sea, presumed dead. He had a distinguished record at the Minster GS. In the year 1937 he was Head Boy and announced as a 'Starkey scholar', achieving the best examination results of his year. He also gained Cricket and Rugger School Colours.[36]

Charles Alan Gilbert, HMS Howe and other ships

Charles Alan Gilbert was born in Southwell on 1st February 1914. He attended the Minster Grammar School and sang in the Minster choir. After leaving school, Charles lived for a time in Easthorpe and was employed by the Southwell printers, working on accounts and letter press. In 1938 he married Joan Sharpe at Blythe Church and they went to live at Arnold, but just before the war they moved to Newark and Charles went to work at Ransome and Marles' munitions factory as a Progress Clerk.

He joined the Royal Navy in November 1942 going into the Account Division. The first ships that he served on from November 1942 - Jan 1943 were HMS *Royal Arthur,* followed by HMS *President V* from January-May 1943. He went in as a petty officer and was given responsibility for supplies, dealing with the tot of rum given out to the crew each day. Charles Alan had a longer service on HMS *Howe* from May-December 1943 and was put in charge of a gun and depth charge crew, all to do with the pipeline under the ocean. He was right in the thick of it on the *Howe* as it was on Russian convoy duty and there was a lot of action at that time in the Atlantic.

He also saw action in the Mediterranean around Malta and the landings on Sicily.

Angela Nettleship

Charles Gilbert
(Angela Nettleship)

The *Howe* was the last built of the five British *King George V* battleships for the Royal Navy.

Like her sister-ship, [HMS] *Anson,* [the] *Howe* would spend most of her career in the Arctic providing cover for Russian convoys. In 1943 [the] *Howe* took part in Operation Husky, bombarding Trapani naval base and Favignana in support of the allied invasions. Along with the *King George V,* the *Howe* escorted two surrendered Italian battleships to Alexandria.[37]

For his service on the *Howe,* Charles received the 1939-43 Star. To qualify for the Star, a seaman had to complete six months' service afloat in active operational areas. After that Charles was transferred to HMS *Victory* at Portsmouth which was used as a training establishment. Later he served on HMS *Campania* from 14th June - 31st October 1944.

---

[36] *N/Adv,* 24th March 1943.
[37] wikipedia.org/wiki/HMS_Howe

HMS *Campania* was an escort aircraft carrier … originally intended as a refrigerated cargo ship for transporting lamb and mutton from New Zealand … but was requisitioned by the British government during construction and launched as an escort carrier, entering service in early 1944.

… [The] *Campania* operated escorting convoys and doing anti-submarine work in the Atlantic and Arctic theatres.[38]

Charles Gilbert and crew aboard HMS Howe
(Angela Nettleship)

Charles got his official release in September 1946 and returned briefly to Ransome and Marles before moving to Nottingham, where he worked in the offices of Homes and Baxters in the lace trade. Around 1965 he moved back to Southwell and lived in the family home at 127 Westgate. In 1957 his daughter Angela was born. Charles died in May 2003 in Newark Hospital.

Looking Back

Reading these stories, servicemen from the Southwell area made important contributions in nearly all the key naval actions in the war - minesweeping in the English Channel and North Sea, escort protection for merchant shipping in the Arctic, targeting the most powerful battleships in the German Navy and, of course, the transportation of Allied troops and equipment to the D-Day beaches.

The loyal commitment these men made for our country must never be allowed to be forgotten.

---

[38] wikipedia.org/wiki/HMS_Campania

Returning POWs attending a dinner at Newark Town Hall to celebrate their return.
The group includes several Southwell and district servicemen.
Second row: seated 6th from left in grey suit, Major John Kirkland (next left is Lt Col. Ford)
Fourth row: 3rd left John Stephenson, 8th left Eric Rawson. Back row: 6th left Tommy Howell
(Steve Foster)

CHAPTER 2

'... we shall fight on the beaches, we shall fight on the landing grounds ...'[1]

When war broke out in September 1939, Britain had fewer than one million men in the armed services, far less than its continental neighbours. Therefore, the British government announced in October 1939 that all men aged between 18 and 41, who were not working in 'reserved occupations', could be called to join the armed forces, if required. Conscription was by age, and that same month men aged between 20 and 23 were required to register to serve in one of the armed forces. By May 1940 a large number of men from the two Southwell parishes had joined up, either by volunteering or by being conscripted. (See following page.)

Sherwood Foresters (Notts and Derby Regiment)

Before war was declared there was a considerable number of young men in Southwell and district who were territorials with the 8th Battalion Sherwood Foresters. After the declaration of war more local men volunteered to join the Sherwood Foresters; these men were quickly sent on training courses in the north of England.

In September 1939 the 2nd Battalion of the Sherwood Foresters landed in France, and took part in the early stages of the 'Phoney War' and the advance into Belgium. The 2/5th, and 9th Battalions also joined the BEF, and in 1940 these three battalions, including a number of Southwell men, defended the Dunkirk perimeter before the successful evacuation. In addition, Southwell men were part of the force that had been evacuated from Norway after the failure of that expeditionary force. Later that month Southwell Minster parishioners were given a dramatic account of what had happened.

> The escape of our BEF from Dunkirk was a stirring story of courage and steadiness. Here in the Minster on Sunday, June 9th after Evensong, we had the privilege of hearing a first-hand account from Lieutenant Dowling, who went to and fro four times on a destroyer to rescue our men. The Navy, he said, all felt it was a miracle, as there was rough weather just before, and on his last trip he ran into high seas. The calm lasted just long enough. He had been on those waters for months and never seen it calm before.
>
> The Rev. Patrick Wild was shell-shocked. Fortunately, it happened before the fall of Dunkirk, so he was brought over safely to a hospital in England. He is recovering very well.
>
> We cannot but be thankful that so many Southwell boys got back safely from Norway and France, but our hearts ache for those whose sons are missing, and for those who have no definite news.
>
> Our bells and our chimes are silenced. Instead of calling us to worship they are to tell us of danger. ... The last time such a use of our great central tower was made was in 1588 when a beacon was ready to be lighted to spread the news that the Spanish Armada was in the Channel. The Spaniards never landed. England was ready. She must be ready now[2]

---

[1] Winston Churchill, extract from his speech to the House of Commons, 4th June 1940.
[2] *Southwell Rural Deanery Magazine,* July 1940, p. 1.

List of Southwell people in the services, May 1940

This is a list of people who have left us to serve in this tragic war. They are from the two parishes of the Minster and Holy Trinity. It is hard to keep up-to-date information and the list may not be complete. … We ask God to help them in all trials and adversities. (*Southwell Rural Deanery Magazine, May 1940*)

L Abbott	H Gent	G Rodwell
John Becher	J R Gilbert	G Roberts
Richard Beaumont	George Hempsall	W Starkey
Tom Beaumont	Robert Heath	Ernest Scrimshaw
Harry Brown	C Herbert	Frederick Samuels
Frank Baxter	Rees Holden	Michael Suckling
S Baxter	Harry Hurt	James Sandover
L Bowler	George Hopkinson	Albert Smith
Basil Bowes	G Haywood	Philip Spall
Godfrey Bostock	L Horspool	John Savage
Edwin Bartlett	W Johnson	D Savage
Ernest Bell	John Kirkland	C Spencer
George Boddy	Arthur Keetley	H Saywell
Arthur Bennion	A Kendall	K Smith
R Bennett	H King	Albert Smith
C A Bell	R E Lawson	W D Shepherd
G W Brown	Arthur Lewin	G K Smith
Edward Caudwell	Herbert Lewin	W R Smith
Frederick Cooper	John Lloyd	Albert Sweet
Richard Calcraft	Eric Loughton	George Templeman
William Charity	Richard Marshall	C A Taylor
W Curzon	Charles Martin	Harry Taylor
Philip Carr	Kenneth Meaby	Charles Taylor
Charles Doubleday	John Merryweather	John Thompson
Walter Draycott	Michael Mosley	Thomas Voce
Godfrey Dowling	George Murden	Charles Voce
John Drury	B Drury	F R Warwick
Solomon Dodds	Stanley Perkins	Ernest Ware
Geoffrey Dodsworth	Fred Pearsall	Bernard Willoughby
John Elmore	R J Parkes	Ronald Willoughby
A W Foster	Cyril Parker	Revd Patrick Wild
J Featherstone	L H Postle	Nurse Ruth Mathews
Frank Felton	J Parker	Bernard Day
Joseph Fisher	Arthur Rollinson	Harold Raworth
George Gray	Eric Rollinson	Arthur Rick
Cecil Greaves	Frank Raworth	

The Norwegian Campaign and the 8th Battalion, Sherwood Foresters

By October 1939 the 8th Battalion, Sherwood Foresters, about 1,000 men, was assembled at Shildon, County Durham for training. Together with the 2/5th Royal Leicester TA Battalion, they were sent for training, with mock battles on Bellaby Moor, near Catterick. The 8th Foresters wintered at Shildon between October 1939 and April 1940. As soon as news came through that German troops had invaded Norway, the 8th Sherwood Foresters were ordered to prepare for action.[3]

The 8th Battalion of the Sherwood Foresters, including men from Southwell and district, landed in Norway as part of the ill-fated attempt to assist the Norwegian Army against the German invading force. Inadequately equipped to fight a winter battle, a situation made worse when the ship carrying its vehicles and heavy equipment was torpedoed and sunk, the 8th Battalion was forced to withdraw through mountains and deep snow, pursued by German ski troops supported by aircraft and tanks. Many of them were captured and sent off to POW camps.[4]

A group of Sherwood Foresters, south of Lillehammer, 21st April 1940.
John Stephenson 2nd left.
(John Stephenson)

The Sherwood Foresters had been given little training. There were still members of the battalion who had never had the opportunity to throw a live grenade or to fire the Bren light machine gun, the basic fire weapon of the infantry.

Yet they were deemed ready, together with a number of other territorial battalions in the same situation, to enter battle against the highly trained and equipped German army.[5]

The British contingent which landed in Norway was mainly a Territorial Army and very under equipped in weaponry and clothing considering it was still freezing temperatures in Norway. Compared with the British troops the German army was professional and well equipped. They also had air support.

John Stephenson

The Sherwood Foresters landed in Arctic conditions on the 18th April, at the port of Åndalsnes, with just the equipment and personal ammunition they carried. From Åndalsnes they turned south, with orders to link up with the Norwegian army, but this soon brought them facing the overwhelmingly superior German armoured division near Lillehammer in the Gudbrand valley, which was advancing north from Oslo. The battalion was part of the first British infantry division to engage the mighty German army in WW2.

---

[3] Richard Payne, *Frank North of the 8th Sherwood Foresters* (Nottm: Milford Printers, 1994), pp. 36-8.
[4] www.bbc.co.uk/history/ww2peopleswar/stories
[5] Cliff Housley, *First Contact: History of the 8th Battalion, Sherwood Foresters, 1939-1945* (London: Miliquest, 1997).

The Norwegian government called for the British forces at Åndalsnes to move south to support them at Lillehammer, rather than the original plan of going north as part of 'Sickleforce' to approach Trondheim from the south. After travelling south in Arctic conditions, the battalion reached the hilly area around Tretten[6], where they first came in contact with the German army.

> On the 23rd April, after fighting for five days in deep snow without food and arctic clothing, the battalion made a stand at the village of Tretten, where it bravely held the German armoured attack all day until it was eventually overrun as ammunition ran out. At 21.00 hrs on 23rd April 1940 the battalion ceased to exist as a fighting unit, having lost half of its number, killed, wounded or captured.
>
> **John Stephenson**

In this critical situation, Lt Col Ford gave the order for the battalion to break out of the position in small groups, to try to return to the main body of 148 Brigade, which was still fighting in the village of Tretten, two miles to the north.

Fortunately, several former members of the 8th Battalion have passed on their experiences of this dramatic episode. They were in different Companies, but inevitably some of the stories overlap.

Lt Col Ford (left) and John Stephenson (right) at moment of capture
(John Stephenson)

John Edward Stephenson, Eric Rawson and Tommy Howells, 8th Battalion, Sherwood Foresters

In September 1939 three Upton men, John Stephenson, Eric Rawson and Tommy Howells, enlisted at the Drill Hall in Southwell in the 8th Battalion of the Sherwood Foresters. John Stephenson lived at the Old Mill Cottage on Hockerton Lane, working as a bricklayer's labourer at Newark

---

[6] 30 British POWs were murdered at Tretten on 23th April 1940 (National Archives, WO 311/1301).

Pte John Stephenson
(John Stephenson)

before the war. In the 1920s John had been in the regular army, in the King's Own Yorkshire Light Infantry. Eric Rawson lived with his family in Church Lane, Upton and had worked at the Midland Iron Works and Henry Merryweather's Nurseries.

They began training at Newark and then were sent with the battalion to Shildon in County Durham, for further military exercises and cross-country runs. As described earlier the hastily trained three Upton men sailed for Norway following the German invasion. Their expedition, as we know, was short-lived and the fate of the three friends was soon decided.

Once Lt Col Ford had given the order for the battalion to break out of their position and attempt to reach the main body of 148 Brigade, Ptes Howells, Rawson and Stephenson were split up from each other. At approximately 18.00 hrs, the battalion HQ party, consisting of Lt Col Ford, Major Roberts, Capt. Althorpe, Pte J E Stephenson (Lt Col Ford's batman) and an unnamed soldier, were seen by a German regimental HQ party near Rindheim farmhouse, Tretten and ordered to surrender. Without ammunition, they had no option but to do so.[7]

After only a few weeks most of the Sherwood Foresters were captured and transported off to POW camps. The three Upton friends were split up; Tommy Howells and my dad were placed in Stalag XXB POW camp at Marburg, originally Polish territory now part of Greater Germany, whilst Eric Rawson was taken to Stalag 344 near Lambinowice in Poland. **John Stephenson**

CASULTIES
SUFFERED BY THE BATTALION
IN NORWAY

Company	Total	Killed	P.O.W.	Interned Sweden	Evacuated Incl. West Coast
Bn HQ & HQ	196	3	56	12	125
"A"	88	-	55	6	27
"B"	90	5	19	11	55
"C"	91	2	17	25	47
"D"	89	11	13	7	58
Tpt	71	-	11	4	56
Officers	31	4	14	4	9
Totals	**656**	**25**	**185**	**69**	**377**

Sherwood Forester Casualties in the Norwegian Expedition (John Stephenson)

[7] wikipedia.org/wiki/Sherwood_Foresters

Group of Sherwood Foresters at Stalag XXB, John Stephenson back row 3rd right
(John Stephenson)

Eric Rawson spent two and a half years in Poland at Stalag 344. It was the largest German POW camp in WW2.

Eric worked very long hours in coalmines on very meagre rations of bread and soup, varied only after Red Cross parcels started to arrive. Some German guards would be sympathetic about these parcels, whilst others would bayonet them indiscriminately and spoil the contents. From Poland, Eric and his companions were marched to Czechoslovakia, presumably because Allied troops had entered Poland. ... Many men perished on their journey. ... Once they arrived in Czechoslovakia it was a return to a harsh regime of work, first in another coalmine and later in a sugar beet factory.

It was while working here loading trains that Eric and another man escaped. They hid in forests during the day and walked at night without any real idea of where they were going, until they got a lift in a Russian truck and found themselves in Prague where they were taken over by the Red Cross. Eric saw out the rest of the war in a transit camp, working in the Officers' Mess.[8]

Tommy Howells and John Stephenson ended up being transported to Marburg in Germany via West Prussia, and assigned to different working parties.

---

[8] *Upton in the 20th Century* (Nottingham: Upton LHS, 1999), p. 46.

John Stephenson first heard of his father's capture from a friend of the family, who came to their Upton house and said that he had just been listening to 'Lord Haw Haw' on the radio, who had read out a long list of names of captured British servicemen in Norway. John's father had been mentioned. A week later his mother received the official letter notifying her of her husband's capture.

International POW Medal
(John Stephenson)

He was a POW at Stalag XXB, Marburg, until close to the end of the war. For much of the time he worked at a farm, bringing produce back to the POW camp when he could. He found the German guards perfectly civil and came across an amazing coincidence. One elderly guard, who had fought in WW1, had been taken prisoner and sent back to England where for a time he worked at Merryweather's Garden Centre, Southwell.

Dad was known to be an outstanding bugler and whilst he was at the camp the other POWs collected cigarettes so that they could afford to purchase a trumpet for dad to play. He once told me that he had played the Last Post several times when a fellow POW had either died or committed suicide at the camp.

At some time in the war I remember I was asked to go and see Major Kirkland who had been allowed to return home earlier because he had lost a leg. Both Major Kirkland and my father got 'Mentioned in Despatches'. Major Kirkland gave me two rings and said that my father wanted me to have them. They had been made in the camp by some of the POWs.

In January 1945 the German army decided to move the POWs at Stalag XXB because of the Russian advance east. The POWs, including my father, were force-marched for about 300 kilometres into western Germany [for the Death March see page 45, Frank North]. The march was an endurance test. They were made to do 20 km a day in freezing conditions. There were few places where they could sleep, little food and some POWs froze to death. After the war had ended he was released by the Americans and he returned home around May 12th.

John Stephenson

John Stephenson has good reasons to remember the day his father returned in May 1945, after being a POW for five years in Eastern Europe

He looked very thin when we saw him, not surprisingly after five years behind iron railings. Local villagers in Upton had a nice surprise for him. A banner, 'Welcome Home', faced him as he came down the main street and there was bunting everywhere. A few weeks later there was a special service at the Minster, giving thanks for the winning of the war, and my father played the 'Last Post' on his bugle.

John Stephenson

Eric Rawson was also demobilized shortly after the war finished and returned to his Upton family.

Years later Eric Rawson visited Norway as a guest of the Norwegian government, when he was able to appreciate the beauty of the country in more congenial circumstances.[9]

Tommy Howells was also released in 1945. Forty-four years later, with Eric Rawson, he travelled back to Lillehammer to take part in official ceremonies, including the unveiling of a headstone to commemorate the death of a comrade who had, until then, lain in an unmarked grave.[10]

In the immediate post-war years, John Stephenson continued to perform as a bugler. He returned to work in the building trade at Wright's of Newark and moved from Upton to live in the town. However, sadly, he suffered from nerves, probably never really getting over his experience in the war, and many times imagined there were Germans waiting to get him. He needed regular hospital treatment and died in 1961, at the relatively young age of 59.

Frank North, Sherwood Foresters

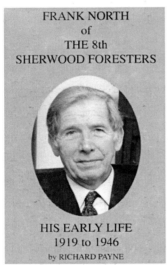

FRANK NORTH
of
THE 8th
SHERWOOD FORESTERS

HIS EARLY LIFE
1919 to 1946
by RICHARD PAYNE

Frank North
(Darryl North &
Richard Payne)

Frank North was born on 27th November 1919 and spent his early years living in Gunthorpe. After attending the Magnus Grammar School, he was fortunate to find a job in the Rating Office at Southwell Rural District Council. In the spring of 1939, as war with Germany appeared likely, Frank became aware of a recruiting campaign run by local GP Dr Roger Brooks for young men to join the Territorial Army 8th Battalion, Sherwood Foresters.

Frank, together with a number of friends - Bill Atkin of Hill Farm Cottages, Thurgarton, Ernest and John Bentley from Manor Farm, Thurgarton, Ernest Crowder, Beck Street, Wilf Hornbuckle, Beck Street, Sid Russell, who worked at Thurgarton Priory, John and George Bowley and Jack Spencer, farmer of Goverton, joined up. They all attended the first meeting of part of 'A' Company at The Pavilion Hall, Lowdham on 26th April, 1939, four months before the outbreak of the war. After the meeting they all went to enlist at 'A' Company HQ at The District Hall, Arnold. The 'A' Company Commander at that time was Captain H D'Oyley Ransom, who lived at Thurgarton Priory. In that summer 'A' Company was posted to a training camp at Trearador Bay, Anglesey. Because of Frank's experience of office work he was appointed 'A' Company clerk.[11]

As mentioned earlier, the battalion undertook training in County Durham and 'A' Company was billeted in the CIU Club. Their Company Commander was now Captain E G C Beckwith from Lowdham, a director of Players cigarettes; a junior officer was 2nd Lt James Wright of 'Hilltop', Lowdham. After their incomplete training the company, along with the rest of the battalion, set sail for Norway:

On 17th April, 1940, 'A' and 'D' Companies were sent aboard the cruiser HMS *Galatea* and set sail for Norway in a convoy of three cruisers, including HMS *Arethusa,* and three destroyers. At

---

[9] *Upton*, p. 46.
[10] *Upton*, p. 46.
[11] Payne, pp. 26-34.

A group of Sherwood Foresters, pre-embarkation for Norway
(Darryl North and Richard Payne)

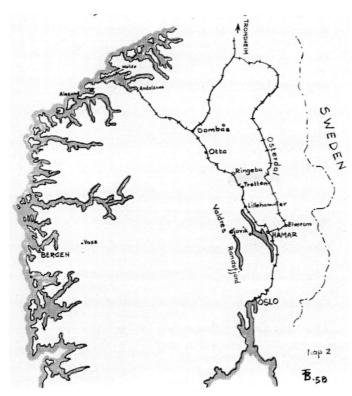

Map of Sherwood Foresters movement after landing at
Åndalsnes (Richard Payne)

night midway through the journey the men heard the explosion of a torpedo attack which sank a transporter laden with winter clothing and military vehicles.[12]

At 10.30 pm on 18th April 1940 HMS *Galatea* docked alongside the quay at the fishing port of Åndalsnes at the top of the Romsdalsfjord in Norway. This was the railhead for Oslo to the south. The 8th Foresters were greeted by the whole local population, all pleased to welcome the British force. 'A' Company was billeted at the local school; the rest of the battalion was landed at the mouth of the fiord, at Molde. There was no resistance to their landing, which was unexpected.

Next morning, 19th April 1940, 'A' Company was addressed by Captain Beckwith in the school playground. He told the 150 men that on the 9th April the Germans had taken control of most of the strategic parts of Norway, including Narvik, the Norwegian port [for] the

_____
[12] Payne, pp. 38-43.

Swedish Gällivare iron ore fields. The upshot was a British government decision to attempt the re-capture of Narvik. What the Sherwood Foresters didn't know was that the initial success by the Royal Navy at Narvik had ended; progress was prevented by deep snow and lack of equipment.[13]

'A' Company was now ordered south to meet the Germans, who were advancing north from Oslo. At 11.30 a.m. on 20th April 'A' Company was despatched by rail from Åndalsnes to Fåberg. Frank North had the job of patrolling the length of the train to see that the Bren gunners at front and rear did not fall asleep. 'A' and 'D' Companies were now assembled for battle with the German army.

On 21st April 'A' and 'D' Companies … were taken by Norwegian Army lorries to defensive positions, facing south in rocky, mountainous country among fir trees and lying snow. … On this day 2nd Lt James Wright of Lowdham was killed by enemy action. The two companies remained in this position for some days, among rushing streams by day as the snow melted, followed by hard freezing with little shelter at night. At length they were told to withdraw northwards. Frank believed that he was acting under Norwegian directions. He had no idea of his place in the situation of the British military force and its intended operations in Norway. This was just as well, for by now the evacuation of the 'Sickleforce' troops at Åndalsnes and Molde was imminent and due to be completed on about 3rd May.[14]

Sketch of the Hellerud positions
(Richard Payne)

---

[13] Payne, pp. 43-8.
[14] Payne, pp. 55-6.

For the next few days 'A' and 'D' Companies staged a fighting withdrawal north, in Arctic conditions, to allow the remnants of the Norwegian army to pass through their positions and regroup. 'A' and 'D' Companies eventually came to the village of Tretten.

They were attacked by machine gun from the air, with bullets striking the roads and ricochets from the rocks. One or two were wounded. On about 26th April they reached Tretten, followed closely by German troops in mechanised transport, and with horse-drawn artillery, advancing up the road of the valley.

'A' and 'D' Companies of British foot soldiers, each with a rifle and a few rounds of ammunition, took to the foothills to escape, and were quickly cut off by the enemy who overtook them by road. The soldiers broke up into scattered groups, and Frank was one of the 17 men, including Captain Beckwith, who rendezvoused at a large summer residence on the mountainside, which was unoccupied. There they found blankets and cut firewood and remained for two days. ... Captain Beckwith ... said that it was his intention to keep on the mountainside and try and contact our forces further north.

So for the next week the party walked through the pine woods and on mountain tracks. Captain Beckwith said they had two options. One was to go across country and get interned in Sweden, the other was to proceed north and hope to catch up with the rest of the British forces.[15]

On 4th May Frank and his companions, after a ten-day retreat in freezing conditions, reached a place on the mountain, which overlooked the settlement of Otta (20 km east of Dombås). Here Captain Beckwith said that they had to cross the valley in order to be able to get back to Åndalsnes. So they came down the mountainside and decided to go through the churchyard.

On rounding the blindside corner of the churchyard they ran straight into a platoon of German soldiers ... 'There were more of them than us', recalled Frank. Captain Beckwith suddenly had his own and at least 16 other lives in his hands; leadership was required.

Captain Beckwith: 'There's no point in resisting'.

German officer: 'Ah, Englander, for you the war is over.' So Frank, Bill Atkin, Captain Beckwith and 14 others were taken prisoner. No right-minded person could have any reproach for any of their actions, for they were a fragment of an army thrown to war by officials who did not deserve their trust.[16]

The captured soldiers were at once taken by German truck to Dombås, where they found many other prisoners. They learnt that the evacuees from Åndalsnes and Molde had got away just in time, indicating that Captain Beckwith's hope to re-join the 8th Foresters had been impossible to fulfil. Frank and the others had faced death or internment.

At Dombås the Germans provided soup ... took Frank's photograph and awarded him POW number 344. Then they were loaded into trucks for Oslo, to be embarked in a transport ship ... He then began the journey to his first camp at Poznan in Poland, during which he was separated from his officers and from the Lowdham contingent, except for Bill Atkin, not to see them again until after the war.[17]

---

[15] Payne, pp. 56-8.

[16] Payne, pp. 59-60.

[17] Payne, pp. 63-4.

They went by ship to Hamburg and then by rail to Berlin. From Berlin around 100 POWs were put in cattle trucks for a journey of 2 or 3 days to Stalag 21B, situated a few miles from Poznan at Scuben; Frank was there from May-October 1940, the first of eight POW camps in which he was interned until January 1945.

German propaganda made the most of the surrender; in Thurgarton Bill Atkin's father heard Lord Haw Haw broadcast his son's name, captured as a POW. Frank's parents, Fred and May North, were less fortunate. The first they heard was from an 8th Sherwood Forester from Woodborough, who was saying that he had seen Frank killed![18]

This story was fortunately proved incorrect when Frank's first letter arrived at the end of June. As well as putting his parents' minds at rest, he was clearly very much alive, since he concluded by asking how the local cricket team was faring.

8th May 1940

Dear Mother and all,
I expect you have been worrying a lot as you have not heard from me for over a month. ... I am sorry to say that I am a prisoner of war, having been captured by the Germans after only four days fighting. We are being treated very well indeed and the first thing they gave us when they captured us was cigarettes and cigars. ... Have you got a cricket team at Gunthorpe this season?
    Your loving and affectionate son,
    Frank [19]

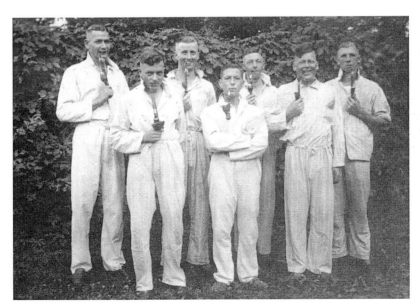

POWs in whites, smoking German Pipes

(Richard Payne)

---

[18] Payne, p. 65.

At Stalag 21B Frank and the other POWs were put to work on the demolition of buildings in Poznan, damaged by German bombs during the blitzkrieg, labouring from 8.00 a.m. to 6.00 p.m. In October 1940 he was moved to Stalag 21D.

Stalag 21D [was] an old fort, dank and dreary, mostly underground, also near Poznan, where he continued to work on demolition and loading rubble by hand into skips. By now about 2,000 British prisoners were held together at 21D, and the effects of undernourishment began to show with outbreaks of lice. This plague was stopped by the arrival of Red Cross food parcels with tins of meat, chocolate, coffee, tea and soap. These arrived at the rate of one a week, shared between four men, supplied by public subscription at home to the Red Cross and St John of Jerusalem War Organisation.

... Next of kin were able to send clothing parcels, and one arrived on Frank's 21st birthday, with clothes bought in hard times by his parents.

In the camp the POWs were given a daily ration of 1/5th or 1/4th of a loaf of rye bread, some margarine, jam and vegetable soup. On the working parties in Poznan they could meet Polish civilians, with whom they bartered the Red Cross goods for eggs, bread, sugar and oats.

Relations with the ordinary German guards were very good. These were mostly WW1 veterans, some of whom had been POWs themselves and had no grudges to bear. Discipline was organised by the RSM, senior NCO, and the other NCOs who did not have to work but acted as managers of the men in camp and outside. There were no discipline or behaviour problems at all. Particular tasks were allocated by the guards by a system of posting a selection of jobs on the noticeboard, to which the men could sign up.[20]

In May 1941 Frank, Bill Atkin and the rest of the Foresters were again moved, this time to the biggest holding camp in Poland, Stalag 8B at Lamsdorf-Lambinwice. Here, were assembled 40,000 POWs - Russians, Frenchmen, Poles, later some Australians and Canadians.

At Stalag 8B Frank was sorted out into a detachment of 18 men - nine Scots and nine English ... who were despatched by railway train to billets in a paper factory, Golgner und Mether, beside a stream in Upper Silesia. ... The job at Golgner und Mether ... was to go by lorry into Northern Czechoslovakia to load up metre lengths of wood onto lorry and trailer, for use in the paper factory. ... For this Frank was given a small pay allowance ... This logging work went on through two winters, log splitting machines operated in the frozen snow by patient men. Sundays were free. The POWs played cards and football. The guards arranged matches and took the team to play against other working parties.

... In August 1943 Frank's only short-lived stand against his captors [took place]. It happened at the paper factory when a trainload of coal arrived for the boilers. The guards called out for the POWs to work to unload the coal.

'We all got our heads together, 24 of us, and decided not to go,' said Frank. No force was used, no shouts or threats. The POWs stayed in their billet.[21]

Frank continued to send letters home with occasional photographs. In the one shown opposite, Frank's group of POWs are smoking large German pipes, a moment of levity in the relentless drudgery of life as a POW.

[19] Payne, p. 67.
[20] Payne, pp. 68-71.
[21] Payne, pp. 71-5.

Kriegsgefangenenlager

23rd November 1942

Dear Mother and Father,
Glad to know you received the photograph I sent. The pipes are not quite
as big as they look but could do with some tobacco and cigarettes. Another
thing I would like is a pair of shoes. The photos of you, Aunt Jess, Mary,
Margaret and Trev were very good. Let's have some more.
Best love and wishes,
Frank[22]

In the summer of 1943 Frank North, Bill Atkin and ten other POWs were sent to a coalmine at Katowice in Southern Poland, where they were put to work underground with pickaxes. Conditions in the barracks at the mine were decent and clean, and the food was superior to that in the main Stalag 8B camp. After a month there Frank's old cartilage injury to his right knee flared up and he was sent back to Stalag 8B, but in October returned to Katowice to work on a railway maintenance job. He remained there until late 1944. Altogether about 300-400 Allied POWs were employed in replacing the stone ballast under railway sleepers, dislodged by the continual heavy rail traffic. Whilst he was there, Frank witnessed two tragic incidents.[23]

Two Irishmen, who had escaped and been recaptured, were brought back to the camp. As the crowd of POWs rushed forward to greet these adventurers, an unpopular German guard, known by his appearance as 'Donald Duck', raised his rifle and shot into the prisoners, killing two people. Generally though, Frank thought that treatment by the guards continued to be humane.

[The second 'tragic' incident Frank witnessed] … was when Frank and the POWs looked out through a hole which they had carved in the side of the hut close to the railway junction where they worked. By night from the west onto the branch line to Auschwitz and Birkenau came trains of cattle trucks full of men, women and children, many wearing the Star of David. Often the trains had to stop at the junction. Frank spoke to his guards who told him, 'Juden, all is kaput'. It was obvious to Frank and the working party that the guards did not like this 'official policy' of the regime and so they opened the doors of the cattle trucks when stopped at the junction, to give air to the people.[24]

All was not gloom for Frank and his POW companions as in the autumn of 1944 news gradually filtered through that the Allies, both on the eastern and western fronts, were closing in on Germany.

2nd October 1944

Dear Mother and Dad,
… The news is simply great just now, isn't it? We are all expecting to be
in the mother country very soon now. … Well so long for the present, and
please remember me to everyone. By the way we had a film show last

---

[22] Payne, pp. 93.
[23] Payne, pp. 76-7.
[24] Payne, pp. 79-81.

week, and even saw good old Trent Bridge and the Old Market Place. I did feel homesick.

> *Love,*
>
> *Frank*[25]

By the end of January 1945 the Russian army had advanced deep into Poland. The members of the Katowice workforce were able to hear the roar of guns and see the flashes of explosions. The result was that, at half an hour's notice, the whole complement of the camp was ordered by the Commandant to prepare for a very long march. 'The Russians are coming', he declared.

Thus began an incredible feat of human endurance, a 1,000 kilometre march, from January to April 1945.

Frank's epic march was one of a number of forced marches undertaken by around 80,000 POWs in extreme winter conditions over about four months between January and April 1945. These notorious marches have been given various names including 'The Death March' and the 'Long March'.[26]

It began in the dead of winter, with a huge column of POWs and their frightened guards heading away from Russia to an unknown destination. The route was marked by Frank on a wartime map of Northern Europe, probably one of the few surviving records of this historic event; it spanned from Katowice into Czechoslovakia, then west into Germany, crossed the River Elbe north of Prague and turned south somewhere near Nuremburg.[27]

> As the march continued, the numbers grew to many thousands of men including Russians, Poles, English[men] and New Zealanders. Frank and his group quickly ran out of their Red Cross rations, after which there was no food except for what they could find for themselves. They survived on turnips, dug with their hands from frozen fields. … At night they lay in the open, or in farm buildings with rats in the rafters.[28]

The journey continued for three months, with some POWs dying en route and many falling ill. January and February were amongst the coldest winter months in the 20th Century in Europe, with temperatures as low as -25 degrees … Most of the POWs were ill-prepared for the evacuation, having suffered years of poor rations and wearing clothing ill-suited to the appalling winter conditions.[29]

> If they were Allied POWs, then the German SS guards put them onto horse-drawn transport. When a Russian got sick he was killed by a shot in the back of his neck. The explanation was, 'Not in the Geneva Convention'. Each morning there was a medical parade. After about 12 weeks' march, Frank's right heel became infected, 'septic'. Somehow he was put into a hospital about 12 miles outside Nuremburg; this was at the beginning of May 1945. He was there for four or five days, during which time he saw the destruction of the city take place by first American and [then] RAF bombing raids. A 'frightening sight'.[30]

---

[25] Payne, pp. 92.
[26] Wikipedia.org/wiki/The March
[27] Payne, pp. 97-8.
[28] Payne, pp. 98-9.
[29] Wikipedia.org/wiki/The March
[30] Payne, pp. 99-100.

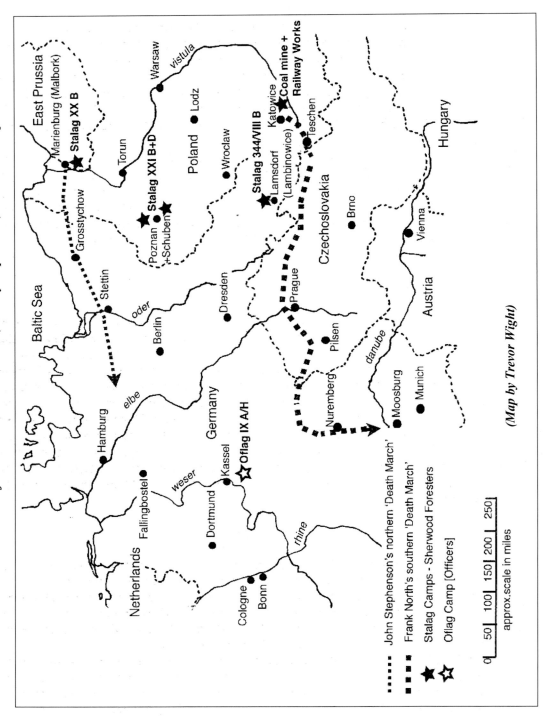

Southwell Prisoners of War: POW Death Marches (January - April 1945) and POW Camps

(Map by Trevor Wight)

On 5th May the 'liberating' Americans reached Frank's hospital; he could hear the tanks as they breached the perimeter wire. Some of the guards fled, others were rounded up. Frank probably saved the lives of some of the guards by informing the American troops that the POWs hadn't been badly treated. After a few days Frank was flown by Dakota to Bruges, sent by lorry to Ostend, by ferry to Tilbury, then to Hayward's Heath rehabilitation camp; on 11th May 1945 he arrived home by train to Lowdham to parents Fred and May North. He had survived. For a while he was posted to an infantry battalion at Amersham, eventually being 'demobbed' on 11th March 1946.[31]

In 1947 Frank married Dulcie Brown, who had taken his job at Southwell RDC after he had joined up in April 1939. Frank returned to work at Southwell RDC, even though he received a visit from Captain Beckwith of the 8th Battalion, Sherwood Foresters offering him a job at Player's cigarette factory. Frank and Dulcie, together with their children Patrick, Darryl and Rosamund lived at 'Northacre', near Hilltop Cottage, Thurgarton. The book *Frank North of the 8th Sherwood Foresters*, by Richard Payne, was published in 1994, the year Frank North died.

John Kirkland, Sherwood Foresters

John Kirkland was another Sherwood Forester. He was born in Southwell on 21st November, 1902, the son of a solicitor, he was a partner in the firm of solicitors Kirkland and Lane, Church Street, Southwell. He was appointed an officer in 'D' Company and in 1940, after training, was sent with his battalion to fight in Norway. 'D' Company was the only full Forester Company to form the rearguard force at the village of Tretten; the remainder of the battalion was situated at Rindheim, to the south of Tretten. After the Germans broke through at Rindheim, 'D' Company and half of HQ Company defended the burning village of Tretten, and the vital road bridge, where hand-to-hand fighting took place until all were overcome. He had the misfortune to receive a bullet wound in his leg, which later resulted in the need for an amputation. After a spell in Lillehammer Hospital in Norway, he was taken to an Oflag POW Camp in Germany and spent three years in enemy hands. On his repatriation in October 1943 he told the story of his captivity to the *Newark Advertiser.*

MAJOR KIRKLAND
Back At His Desk

When an *Advertiser* reporter called he found Major Kirkland back again at his office desk. In his usual cheery way, he ... told the story of his many experiences while in enemy hands.

'I was wounded in the left leg in Norway in 1940', he said, 'and when captured was taken to a hospital in Lillehammer which was under German control and where I remained from April to August of that year. The Norwegian doctors and nurses looked after me and the other wounded very well indeed and I can give them full marks for all they did for us.

From there I was moved to Oslo, where I remained only a short time with my companions, and then put on a hospital ship and taken to Swinemünde to another hospital which was attached to a Stalag camp. There was a party of 35 of us, six of whom were officers. After ten days there we were sent to Poland. In February 1941 I was moved to an Oflag (an officers' prison camp near Kassel).

---

[31] Payne, pp. 100-2.

In October that year it was rumoured we were to be repatriated and we were sent to Rouen. A hitch in the arrangements led to us being sent back to a hospital in Kassel. Afterwards we were sent to various officers' prison camps, the last being at Spangenburg.'

Swedish Reception

About the middle of August 1943 we again received news of our repatriation. Remembering our previous disappointment, however, we still entertained grave doubts until a week ago, when we actually started on the first stage of our homecoming and after a long journey by train, arrived at a Baltic port. We then crossed over to Sweden on the train ferry and received a marvellous reception from the Swedish people. The women gave us everything they could - cigarettes, tea and chocolate. We slept in a station that night and set off again on the following morning for Gothenburg where some 1,200 of us embarked on the Swedish ship, Drottningholm, which brought us safely to a northern English port.'

... The treatment I received from Germans was good. My wounds were cared for and when my leg became worse, and there was no hope of saving it, it was amputated. A few months later I was fitted with a 'peg-leg' which has been quite serviceable. It was the gift of the Red Cross.

How Time Was Spent

'In the Oflags, officers are not allowed to work. Instead they while away the time in study courses. Some of the officers I know were studying such subjects as architecture, law, agriculture and horticulture. We also had lectures by our own officers on various subjects, Languages; Spanish, German and Norwegian.

Major John Kirkland
(Newark Advertiser)

Twice a week we were allowed a 'parole' walk to the local sports platz where, under the watchful eye of German guards, some played football or hockey. In the summer one could enjoy swimming in the local baths. Occasionally, in the compound we played 'yard' cricket and hockey. We also had a considerable amount of physical training.'

... Major Kirkland said, 'You can give the Red Cross as many pats on the back as you like for their food parcels. The German ration is just a subsistence allowance. What we would have done without Red cross parcels I don't know. They kept us alive. If it had not been for them, half of us wouldn't have been able to stick it.

The method we used to employ in camp was to pool the cookable food from parcels. This was cooked in the camp kitchen by British orderlies. In charge of them was one of our officers. He was a clever caterer and produced some really good meals.'

German Fear

Questioned as to what he thought of being home again Major Kirkland replied, 'I think the average appearance of the people here is a good deal happier than in Germany. The Germans are not at all optimistic now. ...They fear a Russian invasion.'

He went on to say, 'We used to get German papers occasionally and were only allowed to listen to the German wireless news. We didn't get much news from home. We had our letters, but our chief source of information came from airmen who had been shot down.'

Major Kirkland added, 'I feel fit. I have 28 days leave and then, in all probability, shall be sent to a rehabilitation centre where I will be fitted with an artificial leg.'[32]

---

32 *N/Adv*, 27th October 1943.

Whilst in captivity John Kirkland was in correspondence with his close friend John Caudwell, who was running the family mill in Southwell.

Dear John,

... I was delighted to get your letter with its news – in fact any news is most welcome here as, although we are not really having a bad time, things get most awfully monotonous.

We really have nothing to do all day except eat and sleep and attend two parades to be counted. ... We amuse ourselves by sunbathing when the weather is fit and quite a lot of playing various games. The whole-bodied ones play cricket, hockey, deck tennis and do a certain amount of gym. We exercise by taking a gentle walk most evenings. I have learnt to play back-gammon and also play quite a bit of poker for camp money but not for very high stakes!

I was glad to hear of Edward's [Caudwell] promotion – he's getting on rapidly and will probably be a full blown Colonel by the time we get home. ... Tell them I am looking forward to a helluva party with them when I get back! Remember me to all.

Yours,

John[33]

Major Kirkland was given a hearty welcome by the people of Southwell and spent the rest of the war supporting community projects for the war effort. In October 1945, he learned that he had gained the bravery award 'Mentioned in Despatches' for gallant and distinguished action in the defence of Tretten during the Norwegian Campaign with the Sherwood Foresters. He continued to work at his solicitors' office, Kirkland and Lane, until his retirement, and died in Southwell on 27th July 1973.

Sherwood Rangers (Notts Yeomanry)

Men from Southwell and the local villages also joined the Sherwood Rangers (Notts Yeomanry), which continued as a cavalry unit, mobilising in that role in 1939 to move to Palestine. It converted to Artillery in 1940 and took part in the defence of both Tobruk and Benghazi, as well as in the battle for Crete. In 1941 the Rangers further converted to armour, initially with M3 Grant, M4 Sherman and Crusader tanks, and served in most of the major 8th Army tank battles in North Africa, including Alam El Halfa and El Alamein.

---

[33] Letter from Major John Kirkland to John Caudwell, 26th July 1941. (Ruth Robinson)

The regiment landed in France on D-Day, equipped with swimming DD Sherman and Sherman Firefly tanks, and was in the thick of the fighting in Normandy and on the advance across northern France and Belgium. Part of the regiment (the recce troop) was the first British unit to fight on German soil in 1944.[34] Two members of the Sherwood Rangers, who fought in several of these battles, were Patrick McCraith and Ron Trueman.

Patrick McCraith, Sherwood Rangers Yeomanry

Patrick James Danvers ('Pat') McCraith, a solicitor, was the son of a leading Nottingham solicitor, Sir Douglas McCraith. He was born on the 21st June 1916, and educated at Harrow School. In his early years Patrick lived in the Nottingham area, though soon after the Second World War he came to Cranfield House, Church Street, Southwell. In 1934 he joined the local Territorial Army cavalry regiment, the Sherwood Rangers Yeomanry, and in 1939 was called up.

In 1940 Patrick set off with the Sherwood Rangers, still a cavalry regiment, to Palestine, where they prepared for the war in the North African desert by riding in the orange groves and hills, on occasion drawing swords and charging rioters in Tel Aviv in order to protect Palestinian policemen. However, Patrick found the regiment's largely inactive role irksome, and was keen to take on the Axis tanks, which were threatening Egypt and the oilfields of Persia. He was much happier when they were ordered to hand in their horses and saddlery and became 6-inch coastal gunners.[35] Not long after this the Sherwood Rangers converted again to become an armoured vehicle unit. In late 1940 Patrick McCraith applied successfully to join the Long Range Desert Group (LRDG), under the direction of General Archibald Wavell. The LRDG was formed specifically to carry out deep penetration, covert reconnaissance patrols and intelligence missions behind Italian lines, although they sometimes engaged in combat operations. Because the LRDG was expert in desert navigation they were sometimes assigned to guide other units.[36]

Patrick McCraith with one of the LRDG trucks
(Daily Telegraph obituary)

Patrick McCraith raised and commanded a yeomanry patrol of the Long Range Desert Group. ... The LRDG had specialised in travelling deep into the desert in modified Chevrolet 30 cwt trucks. They navigated by the sun and stars, observing - and occasionally harassing - enemy units hundreds of miles from Allied lines. It was an elite, adventurous force ... whose contribution to winning the desert war was enormous. However, in a skirmish in April 1941 Patrick McCraith lost his truck in a minefield and was wounded. **Obituary[37]**

---

[34] Wikipedia.org/wiki/Sherwood_Rangers_Yeomanry
[35] *N/Adv,* 3rd Jan 1945.
[36] Wikipedia.org/wiki/Long_Range_Desert_Group
[37] Obituary, *Daily Telegraph,* June 1998.

Following recovery from his wound, Patrick re-joined the Sherwood Rangers in 1942 and took part in the Battle of El Alamein in October and November as Reconnaissance Officer. Towards the end of the war he gave a talk about the exploits of the Sherwood Rangers during this battle.

El Alamein - First Tank Battle

... Capt. McCraith said it was believed the Sherwood Rangers were the only armoured regiment to get through both the British and the German minefields on the first night. They suffered heavy casualties and in 12 hours all the officers of the leading squadron were either killed or wounded; and they were compelled to withdraw the next morning at dawn.

Moonlight Ordeal

The following night, with other armoured units, they were ordered again to go through the narrow gaps which had been made by the sappers. In this operation the whole of the petrol and ammunition lorries directly supporting the tanks were wiped out by dive-bombing in the moonlight. Despite very severe casualties the Sherwood Rangers got through the night and then took a prominent part in the armoured fighting through the ten days of the battle, were in the armoured break-through and the 8th Armoured Brigade was in the van in the chase up to Mersa Matruh [sic].

At Ghalal the Sherwood Rangers knocked out 22 Italian tanks. Col Kellett had his tank knocked out before Matruh, but mounted another which was the first to reach the centre of the town. Later the Sherwood Rangers were the first into the fort at Mersa Brega. The 8th Armoured Brigade led the Eighth Army as far as Sirte and were on many occasions about 50 miles ahead of the main body of the Army.[38]

Patrick was wounded once again at El Alamein and had to be evacuated. However, as keen as ever to get back to the action, he returned in time to take part in the Battles of Medenine and Tebaga Gap, in March 1943. Before the two battles he had met up again with one of his close friends in the Sherwood Rangers, Capt. Stanley Christopherson, who kept a diary of his wartime activities in the Middle East. In this entry in early 1943, just before the Battle of Medenine, Stanley mentions reconnaissance work they did together.

Sunday 22nd February 1943

This is a most enormous camp area - large enough to hold 40,000 men. All our brigade are here, the Staffs Yeomanry and the Greys practically next door. After lunch Donny Player, Pat McCraith and I went out in the Banbaur and did some navigation in the desert. The colonel and the others spent the weekend in Cairo. The colonel told me at supper that owing to the extremely anti-British activities on the part of the King of Egypt, we demanded his abdication and even surrounded his palace with tanks and with cadets with Tommy guns, but he refused to abdicate![39]

Only a few weeks after this reconnaissance, in March 1943, Patrick and Stanley took part in the Battle of Medenine. Rommel's Afrika Corps together with their Italian allies, holding the Mareth Line, planned to counter-attack at Medenine in order to delay an offensive by the advancing British 8th Army. This battle proved to be the last battle commanded by Rommel in the North African Campaign.

---

[38] *N/Adv*, 3rd January 1945.
[39] *Wartime Diaries of Stanley Christopherson 1939-45* (London: Transworld, 2014), p. 246.

At Medenine, Patrick was given command of a Reconnaissance Section of the Sherwood Rangers, with responsibility for establishing an Observation Post on vitally important ground. It was largely due to the holding of this position that the enemy attack was frustrated.

> On the evening of 24th March 1943, after the attack of 3 Royal Tank Regiment and the Sherwood Rangers Yeomanry on the Tebaga position, the regiment found itself soon after dark, almost surrounded ... by the enemy.
>
> McCraith, then a captain, realising that the ammunition was nearly exhausted, collected the required ammunition vehicles and took them across extremely difficult country to the tanks.
>
> Throughout the night, all movement was heavily engaged by machine gun and high explosive fire. As a result it was only by McCraith's determination that the column was brought up in time for the tanks to be replenished before the dawn battle.
>
> On 26th March, McCraith again led the regiment into the battle on the Tebaga-El-Madjal position. He was nearing the final objective when his armoured car was knocked out by a direct hit. But he remained in observation under heavy shell fire, giving valuable information.[40]

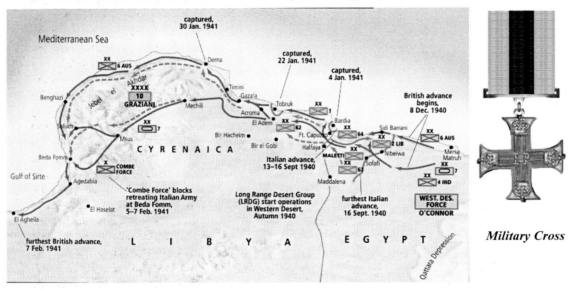

Map of the Mareth Line, 1943.
(Private Collection)

Military Cross

Following this heroic action in the battles of Medenine and Tebaga Gap in Tunisia in March 1943, Patrick McCraith was awarded an immediate MC (Military Cross), one of the very highest awards, granted only in recognition of acts of exemplary gallantry. According to the citation, he:

> ... with complete disregard to his own safety and through his coolness and courage materially altered the issue of both actions. ... This officer has twice been blown up by mines, but still continues at his job with unfailing courage and with exceptional skill which has the admiration of all who serve under him.[41]

---

[40] *Telegraph.*
[41] *Telegraph.*

After six days of severe fighting in the Tebaga Gap a hole was made in the German defences, enabling another corps to go through to El Hamma, where they supported the Maori Battalion of the New Zealand division. Although the Sherwood Rangers had suffered severe casualties they had helped to achieve a memorable breakthrough.[42]

Once German and Italian armies had surrendered in North Africa, the Sherwood Rangers returned to Europe. They were equipped with amphibious tanks and were among the first arrivals on the Normandy beaches, possibly the first yeomanry regiment and possibly the first armoured regiment from the Middle East to land at H hour on D-Day. Patrick McCraith's regiment fought its way onto Gold Beach, and advanced past Bayeux, but two days later at St Pierre, near Tilly-sur-Seulles, was caught in a burst of shell fire around the command tank.

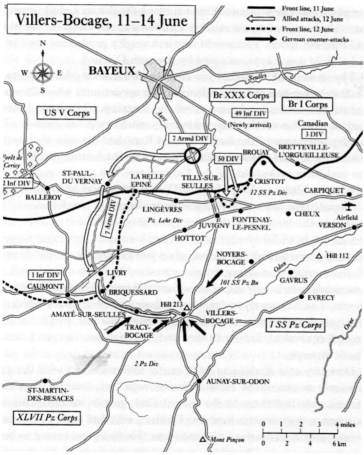

Map of Battle of Tilly Hill
Applicable also to the Ron Trueman story
(Private Collection)

The next day, 8th June, the Sherwood Rangers re-joined the 8th Armoured Brigade to advance south. Bypassing anti-tank guns, they occupied some high ground seven miles to the south-east of Bayeux known as Hill 103. It overlooked the villages of Tilly-sur-Seulles and Fontenay-le-Presnel, ... But on the next day the Sherwood Rangers and the 6th Durham Light Infantry suddenly came under attack. The Panzer Lehr Division had finally arrived at the front. ... When the advance elements of the Panzer Lehr division attacked northwards from Tilly-sur-Seulles on the morning of 8 June, the Sherwood Rangers ... received the full force. 'It was a terrible day for the regiment', wrote Christopherson in his diary. His squadron on Hill 103 lost four tanks. One of his troop leaders was killed and also his second in command, the poet Capt. Keith Douglas.

... Three days later, on 11th June, the Sherwood Rangers, again close to Hill 103, suffered another disaster. An artillery shell exploded beside the regimental headquarters' tank, named 'Robin Hood', just as an orders group was being held. The commanding officer, Michael Laycock ... was killed along with his

---

[42] *N/Adv,* 3rd January 1945.

adjutant (Capt. Jones) and signals officer. Their recce troop leader (Patrick McCraith) and the signals sergeant were also badly wounded. The Sherwood Rangers had lost two commanding officers in under a week. Christopherson, as senior squadron leader, then took over.[43]

Once again Patrick McCraith had been in the thick of the action and once again he received serious wounds. He was immediately sent to hospital in England, but this time there was no return. He was told, in no uncertain terms, that he was unfit for active service. However, determined as ever to support the war effort, in the early months of 1945, after a period of recovery, he devoted his energies to working as an instructor at Sandhurst and giving a series of lectures about the 'dashing exploits of the Sherwood Rangers' in the North African Campaign for the Ministry of Information.

> # LED THE WAY IN THE DESERT THEN INTO GERMANY
>
> ## DASHING EXPLOITS OF THE SHERWOOD RANGERS
>
> CAPTAIN P. McCraith, of the Sherwood Rangers Yeomanry is giving a series of talks for the Ministry of Information on the exploits of his regiment in the present war. The Rangers, who have always regarded Newark as their headquarters town, formed part of the brigade which led the Eighth Army, or part of it, for 1,400 of its 2,070 miles journey in North Africa. The latest honour, of course, is the S.R.Y was the first British unit to enter Germany.

(Newark Advertiser)

LED the WAR in the DESERT, then into GERMANY

Dashing Exploits of the Sherwood Rangers

Captain P McCraith of the Sherwood Rangers Yeomanry is giving a series of talks for the Ministry of Information on the exploits of his regiment in the present war. The Rangers, who have always regarded Newark as their headquarters town, formed part of the brigade which led the Eighth Army, or part of it, for 1,400 of its 2,070 miles journey in North Africa. The latest honour, of course, is the S.R.Y. was the first British unit to enter Germany.[44]

Looking back, Patrick's story is quite remarkable. Time after time he showed extraordinary courage, always leading from the front. Not surprisingly, he was wounded on several occasions but always bounced back until his D-Day+5 experience. On his return, Patrick and his family settled in Southwell, at Cranfield House on Church Street; he retained his connection with the Sherwood Rangers, becoming Commanding Officer from 1953-7 and later Honorary Colonel of the regiment. In 1967 he was appointed High Sheriff of Nottingham, then a Deputy Lieutenant of Nottinghamshire. He died on 6th January 1998.

---

[43] Antony Beevor, *D-Day, The Battle for Normandy* (London: Penguin, 2009), pp. 176-7.
[44] *N/Adv*, 3rd January 1945.

Ronald Trueman, Sherwood Rangers Yeomanry

*Ron Trueman in 1939
(Michael Trueman)*

Ron Trueman was born on 18th January, 1918 and grew up in Upton at High Farm. When the war broke out he was working in Cleethorpes as a bank clerk. In May 1939 he joined the Territorial Army as a member of the Sherwood Rangers Yeomanry, then a cavalry unit, and was sent for training to Malton in Yorkshire before moving to Brocklesby Park in Lincolnshire. The cavalry regiment was sent to Palestine in January 1940 as part of what became a four-year campaign ranging across the Middle East and North Africa, and whilst in Palestine he was promoted to Lance Corporal. In July 1940 the regiment was converted from a cavalry unit to one of coastal defence gunners. The horses were sent away and extensive gunnery training followed.[45]

Ron Trueman's battery was posted to Cyprus in October 1940, then it transferred to Crete in February 1941 to strengthen the island's north coast defences. However, shortly after, in May, the Germans conducted an airborne invasion of the island. The allied army was forced to evacuate and this was a real challenge, as Ron's diary indicates.

> **6 June 1941** I hope to God I never have to go through another evacuation ... practically the whole time there we had some heavy bombing raids, but when the blitz really started it was hell! Jerry came over one day bombing and machine-gunning and then dropped thousands of parachutists. Something I shall never forget. The evacuation ... was a great test of stamina. We had almost eighty miles to cover and I walked every yard of it, inside three days! ... The chief trouble was practically no food and one day we could not get any water at all! I think it was one of my happiest moments when I boarded one of the cruisers and the naval lads served us up with hot soup and cocoa, the first hot drink of the week.
>
> **Ron Trueman**[46]

Ron Trueman's battery regrouped in Egypt and was again converted, this time into a tank unit, as part of the 8th Army. Ron became a tank commander in B Battery. Intensive training followed and in early 1942 the regiment saw its first action as an armoured brigade in the battle of Alam el Halfa. Their second action was in October at El Alamein. This was the start of eight months of almost continuous action, pushing the German army westwards in a series of battles to a final pincer movement with the 1st Army in Tunisia. One of Ron's letters home gave an idea of the more uncomfortable aspects of campaign life in the North African desert.

> **21 October 1942** Four days ago we had a terrific sandstorm, the like of which I had never seen before. It lasted for well over thirty-six hours. ... In a matter of minutes, it was almost dark, not black darkness but a kind of dull red glow all around you. ... I slept underneath the tank and woke up next morning caked in sand and dust.
>
> **Ron Trueman**[47]

---

[45] Upton, p. 47.
[46] Upton, p. 47.
[47] Upton, pp. 47-8.

Ron Trueman's later letters home focused on hopes of returning in time to help with the harvest and he also asked after friends Eric Rawson and Arthur Cumberland, who were both serving in the armed forces abroad. The German and Italian surrender in North Africa in May 1943 was celebrated modestly.

> **22 May 1943** I suppose you were all pleased to hear the fighting had come to an end out here. … Our victory celebrations were confined to the day off for football and at night we shaped an outdoor concert and sing-song. They gave us quite a good rum ration and everybody sang with gusto. **Ron Trueman**[48]

By 1944 Ron's regiment were in training for the 'D-Day' invasion of the Normandy beaches. His 'B' Squadron landed below Arromanches and fought their way to Bayeux, St Pierre, Fontenay and Caen.

Ron and May Trueman
(Michael Trueman)

> **13 June 1944** Well here I am in the fighting line again. … We were the first troops of all on the beaches and my luck held good again … although some of the lads had a pretty rough time. … The countryside in Normandy is really beautiful, but it seems outrageous to have to fight over it and spoil so much. … thank God it never had to come to England itself. **Ron Trueman**[49]

His good luck didn't last. On 27th June 1944, two tank troops of 'B' Squadron were ambushed and destroyed by German tanks at Rauray. Ron Trueman's tank was blown up, killing his gunner and radio operator. The driver, co-driver and Ron survived. Blown out of the top of the tank with his uniform burning, Ron was rolled in corn by an infantryman to douse the fire. He returned to England that night - with one leg bruised black and a burnt arm.[50] (For a map of the battle area see previous story.)

After recovering Ron spent the remainder of the war training recruits. He was demobilized in January 1946 and returned to work at High Farm, Upton with his father, a far cry from his many war experiences abroad with the Sherwood Rangers. In 1947 he married Southwell girl May Thorne, whom he had met three years previously at a dance at the Saracen's Head, Southwell. Ron Trueman died at High Farm on 9th February 1988 at the age of 70.

---

[48] Upton, p. 49.
[49] Upton, p. 49.
[50] Upton, p. 49.

John Merryweather, Royal Artillery

John Merryweather was born on the 20th August 1908 into the well-known horticultural family. Educated at Worksop College, he developed a lifelong interest in and aptitude for sports, especially rugby and cricket, playing for Southwell Cricket Club for many years. In the inter-war years he worked for a horticultural company in Exeter, though he was destined later to join the Merryweather family firm.

In the 1930s John Merryweather became a member of the Territorial Army, attached to the Royal Artillery. Just before he was conscripted, in the summer of 1939, he had been at camp in South Wales, near Castle Martin in Pembrokeshire.

Father returned to Nottingham to be conscripted as a gunner in the Royal Artillery 284 Battery, and in the early months of the war the unit was tasked to give Air Defence to the Beechdale area of Nottingham. At some point in 1940 his battalion was given a foreign draft to North Africa and there he took part in the Eighth Army's 'Desert war' until 1944, when he returned to England. He became one of the 'Desert Rats', and kept a detailed diary for the year 1943 of his time in the Desert War.

Roger Merryweather and Celia Steven

John Merryweather 1940
(Roger Merryweather)

Army service in North Africa was no fun, as several Southwell men have testified. The desert was alien and hostile. Sand made its way into eyes, carburettors and rifle breeches; heat, averaging around 120 degrees outdoors, became unbearable inside a tank. Above all, in terms of torment, there were the flies. Flies swarmed around all day, seeking moisture in the soldiers' eyes, mouths and ears. Cuts and abrasions, constantly covered in flies and sand, developed into 'desert sores', that festered and refused to heal. If they were bandaged, the flies would penetrate between the folds and search for blood. However, the sores needed to be bandaged because if septicaemia set in it was difficult to treat.[51]

Other problems facing the 8th Army in the North African desert were boredom and inadequate rations. Between periods of military action were much longer periods of inactivity, and often the only relief from these interminable days was a weekly truck ride across the desert to the sea. Rations were extremely limited, the regular meal being corned beef and biscuits. Water was rationed, with each man only having half a gallon a day for all purposes; this inevitably led to stomach disorders, a raging thirst and filthy clothes.

John Merryweather fortunately kept a detailed diary for the whole year of 1943, whilst serving with the 8th Army in North Africa. It covered the period immediately after the Battle of El Alamein (Oct/Nov 1942), when the 8th Army were pushing the Axis armies westward, hoping eventually to take control of the whole of North Africa. The following extracts reveal this Allied forward movement, as well as the constant frustrations of fighting in the desert.[52]

---

[51] Jonathan Dimbleby, *Destiny in the Desert* (London: Profile Books, 2013), pp. 24-5.
[52] Diary of John Merryweather, 1943.

January 22nd 1943

10-00 hrs We were approaching the El Alamein battle area. There was barbed wire and a number of well-made trenches and gun emplacements, and a few derelict vehicles. Just before lunch we passed notices stating 'Allied forward minefield' on October 23rd and then 'Enemy forward minefield', October 23rd. Disabled tanks and vehicles belonging to both sides increased in numbers and there were numerous graveyards, again belonging to both sides.

13-00 We stopped for lunch and Frank Price gave me some salmon and some bully beef.

14-30 We saw our salvage boys with a simply stupendous number of tanks and vehicles of all types. We also saw enemy planes on either side of the road in fairly large numbers and various stages of destruction. ... We stopped at Fuka on the opposite side of the road from the position we had stopped in Oct. 1941.

18-30 The cooks had a good meal ready; most of the boys had bedded down, but I wanted to hear the wireless news and was pleased to hear that the fall of Tripoli was imminent.

March 1st 1943, 'St David's Day'

We had the first alarm of enemy activity but it was effectively dealt with by our Spitfires. The ground is rocky and difficult to dig but not as bad as Mischifa.

12-15 Lunch on biscuits and sardines caused some discontent but there was not much we could do about it. ... The outstanding thing to my mind was that on this military site they had three rashers of bacon per head while we only have two!

17-15 An uneventful afternoon until after dinner. Then there was the sound of an explosion out on the aerodrome followed by sundry others and we came to the conclusion that Jerry was shelling us from the other side of the hills. This went on intermittently for an hour or two. ... The guard was to be doubled with Sgt Wicks in charge and we were to stand to from 05.00 hrs until 08.00 when we should fire. ... Jerry continued to lob over the occasional shell and we conjectured how far he was distant and what his object was. Inclined to the idea he would bomb heavily during the night. In actual fact he fired odd rounds at 02.00 and 03.00 hrs and all was quiet except for this.

March 23rd 1943

16-10 Hancock illustrated on the map how our push was progressing; after a strong German counter-attack we were advancing again.

16-45 Dinner with hydrated potatoes and cabbage. After dinner I made my bed, trimmed the lamp, fixed the black-out, detailed a truck for water.

17-00 News which speaks well of our advance.

John Merryweather with colleagues in the desert 1942-3 (Celia Steven)

John Merryweather's unit, along with the rest of the 8th Army, continued through March 1943 to push the Axis powers westward and by early April the enemy had taken up positions along the Wadi Akarit in Tunisia. At this point, north of the towns of Gabès and El Hamma, there is a narrow land gap between the sea and impassable salt marshes, known as the Gabès Gap. On 6th and 7th April, the Allied armies breached the Axis defences and held a bridgehead, allowing the passage of the main Allied force to 'roll-up' the Axis defences from the flanks. John Merryweather's unit was involved in this roll-up.

April 9th 1943

Took down our tent, packed it and loaded it on to the store wagon. ... Kept the gun behind the convoy which started at 11.45 hrs. The Matadors put the gun on the truck before pulling out. I travelled with Brown's gun and we started at 12.10 hrs. We moved past the aerodrome and south-west to the outskirts of Medenine where we branched off on the road to Gabès. When we were well clear of the town we stopped for lunch. A mash was soon on; we had biscuits and herrings.

14-20 We pulled out and moved on steadily until we caught the convoy just south of Gabès. We saw several batches of prisoners on the road in trucks and a fair number in a compound, north of Gabès. The convoy now moved north nearly to the Wadi Akarit where we stopped for the night.

19-30 The cook had a meal ready. After the meal Ralph, Taffy and Thayer all went to bed but Sandbury, Weir and self stayed on until 21.45 to listen to the news. The news was that we are still advancing and the Russians holding Jerry on the Donets.

.... I slept in front of Ting Ling's Matador and wasn't particularly comfortable because in my haste I had not taken as many anti-insect precautions as usual. The night was quiet except for AA fire and flares in the distance.

A great deal of John Merryweather's diary is taken up with what food he had that day so when he came across the victor of El Alamein, General Montgomery, on the 10th April 1943, it is not surprising that he merely mentions it in passing.

April 10th 1943

04-30 I awakened the cooks and walked over to the HQ where Taffy was making a morning mash. Sanbury had got me an excellent breakfast of beans, bacon and tea.

06-15 We pulled out and soon reached the Wadi Akarit which had impressive defence works; one easily understood it was a tough nut to crack. Jerry had blown the bridge so we did a detour to pass.

08-15 We turned off the main road toward the sea where we contacted 283 Battalion. We waited until 09.15 before we moved again, preceded by 283. Progress to and then along the road was very slow; this applied to the whole journey because Jerry had blown the bridges. Much of the journey was through orange groves.

14-15 Montgomery passed us in his tank called 'Monty'. We moved slowly and after we had passed Monares, Montgomery was standing beside the road waving to troops as they went by. Next we saw a Jerry Field Gun which had faced our oncoming traffic. There were more traces of a battle in these parts.

15-15 We reached the outskirts of Fux. Our progress here was reduced to twenty or thirty yards every five minutes. The population was obviously pleased to see us. ... We dragged through the town and eventually reached the place where we were to locate all eight guns.

17-15 The guns were soon in action ... Dinner consisted of meat and veg, but we were hungry and liked it. ... I had just dozed off when five Italian POWs arrived. They were put in David's

Matador and Sgt Hardy, who was Guard Commander, collected Willams, Ashworth and Brodie to mount guard on them through the night.

Following the success of Montgomery's 8th Army in sweeping the Axis armies out of North Africa, John Merryweather's Royal Artillery unit returned to England. He was sent to the south coast, where preparations for D-Day were under way. After seeing action in the Allied landings, his unit moved on to take part in the battle for Caen, in Normandy. In the push towards Berlin, he passed through France and Belgium; while in Brussels he became close friends with a Belgian family. In the early months of 1945, John's regiment entered northern Germany, eventually being given the horrific job of liberating the infamous Belsen Concentration Camp.

Belsen had originally been planned for around 7,000 inmates, but before its liberation on 15th April 1945 the numbers had soared to around 60,000. This intense overcrowding led to a vast increase in deaths from disease, particularly typhus, as well as tuberculosis, typhoid and dysentery. Amongst the internees were large numbers of Jews, Poles, anti-Nazi Christians and homosexuals.

They also found thousands of unburied bodies and at least 53,000 inmates, many of whom were dying. 'It was hard to distinguish which was which.'

John Merryweather's regiment was part of the task group which was given the terribly distressing task of burying the dead and treating the survivors. Two weeks later, on 3rd May 1945, he wrote down his reflections in a most powerful and detailed narrative intended for his children Roger, John and Celia when they came of age.

> 1462521 W/Sgt J F Merryweather
> 284 Battery, D Troop
> 90th HAA Regt RA BLA
> 3rd May 1945

To my children when they are old enough to understand

This narrative relates to the Belsen Concentration Camp where my friends of the 113th LAA Regiment have up to now buried between 12,000 and 15,000 nameless people. The village of Belsen lies in the most entrancing country and has a most prosperous appearance. The houses are attractive, the gardens neat. The camp consists of two sections, one of which is sub-divided. One section is for the Prison Guards, the other for Slave Labour and Political Prisoners.

Let us examine the Prison Guard section, in appearance a super refined Garden City, rather better than most in England. The houses are well kept, beautifully decorated and furnished. The inhabitants who enjoyed this luxury could look out the windows into the other section of the camp and see a man working in the garden who had never washed, and whom it would be impossible to approach nearer than two yards without being affected by the smell.

Turning to the Camp proper which is occupied by Slave Labourers and Political Prisoners. The area is much the same as a military camp in England which would accommodate a regiment of artillery, or about 1,000 persons. The prisoners in the Camp varied from 60,000 to 70,000 and the death rate was such that this number would be replaced three times in one year.

In the Slave Labour section, women are on one side and men on the other, this being the only effort of decency. There is no sanitation of any kind and man or woman may squat in front of the observer so he has to step round. The person who thus excretes has no paper and will not move many feet before sitting down. You must understand that 70,000 people are doing this every day before you can visualise the general conditions in the camp. The people are accommodated in wooden huts something like the length of a cricket pitch. One enters and is assailed by a stench, in comparison with which fellmonger's waste is as lavender.

Along the sides are two-tiered bunks; in crowded times these are occupied by six persons; in less crowded times by four. A gaunt creature lifts its head and beckons; one cannot tell whether it is greeting or request. In ten seconds the creature relaxes and lays back exhausted. There is just sufficient flesh to cover the bones, and the stomach is so flat that the twists and turns of the intestines are visible through the drawn and parchment-like flesh. Many have no clothes on at all; others have been able to take clothing from dead people.

One passes down the hut and glances at one bunk where the occupants have been strong enough to tip a dead comrade over the side where he has fallen and lies literally a bag of bones, happily released. The space he occupied shows a mass of straw saturated and permeated with the excrement of many weeks. One retches convulsively, but later on understands that these are the lucky prisoners, the slave labour as distinct from the political prisoners. Here children are born and some conceived. Medical attention does not exist, a festering sore is just a festering sore. Nobody cares, possibly even the prisoners do not care. Perhaps you cannot imagine that anyone could be worse off, but the political prisoners are, though it may be beyond my descriptive powers to explain how.

Sometimes the newcomers exceed even the maw of this gigantic monster. These are taken to the lethal chamber where the operator can watch from outside what goes on inside. It is said that the doctor in charge had experimented until he had evolved a gas which took 7 to 10 minutes of agony before death intervened. He had another amusement which was to inject petrol into the veins, which resulted in death in ten minutes. Shortage of petrol put a stop to this method so creosote was used instead and resulted in death in seven minutes.

One saw the butcher who was very handy and did a good trade. His speciality was flesh which had been tattooed; he removed this and used it for fancy lampshades. One saw the strangler, who admits to strangling six women.

About one battalion at a time guarded the camp and their beat was outside the camp boundary. Only the elite SS who lived in the previously mentioned houses went into the camp. The guards? Outside they could not see inside the huts. They could see the carts which went round each morning to collect the dead, and it would be difficult to ignore a heap of dead 80 yards long and five feet high. These men could not in the natural way of things refrain from talking about what they had seen, and assuming that they were relieved with regularity news must have spread round much of the country. It must safely be assumed that the German who says he did not know about it is by at least a 200 to 1 chance a liar.

In this letter much has been omitted, not because of nicety, but just that the writer had no notes and found the conditions so incredible that the mind could not absorb it all. It should be remembered that the Belsen camp was only one of at least a dozen of such camps and by no means the largest.

John Merryweather[53]

After the burial of the many corpses the surviving prisoners were de-loused and moved to a nearby army camp. Belsen was then burnt to the ground because of the typhus epidemic and lice infestation. Massive efforts were made to help the survivors with food and medical treatment, but many were so weak that another 14,000 inmates died after liberation. Former SS staff were tried by the British Army at the Belsen court from September to November 1945, resulting in eleven of the defendants being sentenced to death and nineteen to life imprisonment.

---

[53] Letter from John Merryweather to his family, 3rd May 1945 (Roger Merryweather & Celia Steven).

John Merryweather and colleagues outside the Church of the Holy Nativity, Bethlehem 1946
(Roger Merryweather)

Following demobilization John Merryweather joined the family horticultural business in Southwell. His letter, giving a vivid description of Belsen Camp, he duly showed to his family and a copy can be found at the Imperial War Museum. Soon after the war he and his family moved from Halam Road to his parents' former house at Brinkley. John Merryweather died on the 19th February 1989.

Ray Longden, Royal Artillery

Ray Longden
(Newark Advertiser)

Born on 20th February 1923, Ray Longden, the son of Major Longden of White Cottage, Morton, was working at Farrar's Boiler Works in Newark when the war broke out. He was too young to join up so he did a spell working for McAlpine's, constructing aerodromes in Lincolnshire. On the third anniversary of the war, in September 1942, at the age of 19, he was called up, joined the Royal Signals and was posted to Ossett.

Ray didn't stay there long as he volunteered for service in the Mediterranean and was transferred to the Royal Artillery for gunnery training at Woolwich Arsenal. By November 1943, the 61st Battery of the 14th Anti-Tank Regiment was ready to do service in the Mediterranean sector of the war. Ray Longden, No. 14276026, now a gunner, was also qualified as a driver and mechanic.

We sailed from Liverpool to Greenock where we boarded the cruise liner *Franconia*, joining a big convoy which led us by Gibraltar to Alexandria in the eastern Mediterranean. From there we marched sixteen miles to Buge on the north African coast in order to reinforce the 4th British Division; by this time the war against the Axis troops had virtually finished in that part of North Africa.
Ray Longden

The Allied advance now moved to the north Mediterranean and forces had already landed, first in Sicily in September 1943 and later in southern Italy, coinciding with an armistice made with the Italians, who then re-entered the war on the Allied side. Progress through Sicily was initially good, but by the end of 1943 the Allies were faced with the strongly fortified German defensive position, the Gustav Line, stretching from west to east coast and including the obstacle of the historic hillside monastery at Monte Cassino.

The first attack on Monte Cassino had been launched as early as 12th January 1944, by Commonwealth forces, but there had been a distinct lack of progress. This was followed in mid-February by the controversial heavy bombing of the 1,400-year-old building. A further assault had been made on the stronghold in March 1944 by Commonwealth troops, but the key positions on the hill remained in German hands. Ray Longden was present at the final battle of Monte Cassino in May 1944.

Monte Cassino after Allied attacks 1942-3
(Ray Longden)

We landed at Naples in November 1943; our main objective was to give support to the Allied offensive against the German defensive position known as the Gustav Line. The main resistance to the Allied advance centred on the magnificent hilltop Benedictine abbey of Monte Cassino, which dominated the surrounding area. Until Monte Cassino was taken, the Allied advance up the leg of Italy towards Rome couldn't be continued.

Whilst the early assaults on Monte Cassino were taking place in the first three months of 1944, our regiment was based around the village of Acquafondata, seven miles or so from the monastery, and involved us digging gun emplacements for the big spring offensive that was being planned.
Ray Longden

British Troops at Monte Cassino, 1943 (Ray Longden)

By the second week in May 1944 the Allies felt that their army was strong enough to make a fourth, but this time successful, attack at Monte Cassino which would at last open up the road to Rome.

On the 11th May, actually my mother's birthday, there was the most massive artillery bombardment of the German positions on Monte Cassino. On that night our 4th British Division went in and I remember the Polish division attacked to the west of us in 'Death Valley' as it was called; the engineers of the 8th Indian Infantry succeeded in bridging the river on the other wing and the American army was also in action. There were French forces, New Zealanders and Canadian troops also involved. It was an incredibly well planned attack and it needed to be.

My biggest memory was the sheer noise and length of the barrage at the start of the battle on 11th May. You were totally deafened! Not surprisingly, when we crossed the river to advance towards the hill it was impossible to walk far before finding a shell-hole. The Allied attacks and the German counter-attacks brought very heavy losses to both sides, especially where the Polish Corps were storming the monastery ridge with very little natural cover for protection, so there was a lot of hand-to-hand fighting. The battle went on for more than five days and it was only in the later stages that the strong German resistance started to lessen. Finally, on 18 May the Polish Corps entered the ruins of the monastery on the ridge, the Germans having ordered a general withdrawal. What the victory meant was that the road to Rome lay open. **Ray Longden**

In all, the fight for Monte Cassino cost the Allies 45,000 dead and wounded. Ray's 61st Battery of the 14th Anti-Tank Regiment continued to support the British 4th Division, moving north beyond the Gustav Line in search of General Kesselring's German Army. On 4th June Rome was at last liberated.

German Propaganda
(www.naval-military-
press.com/images/T/2)

Our 61st Battery pushed north from Monte Cassino taking on the retreating Germans. However, I believe the American General, Mark Clark, made sure the American 5th Army got the praise for liberating Rome. The British 8th Army had orders to chase Kesselring's German 10th Army and I remember heavy fighting around Assisi, in the hilly Appennines; very difficult country to fight in. We then moved towards the east coast, still chasing the German army towards Rimini and Pescara and I remember, near the village of Forlimpopoli, a German shell knocked out the front of our truck.

Again, the fighting was hard but the Allies were slowly pushing the Germans back to the north of Italy to their last defensive line, the 'Gothic Line'. Eventually, after many months we were told to gather up our gear and make for the port of Taranto, down in the heel of Italy, from where we were sent to Palestine.

We weren't 'demobbed' until 1947 and I remember receiving, at Aldershot, a pin-striped suit and a raincoat before I took the train back to Nottinghamshire. **Ray Longden**

Ray returned to Monte Cassino a number of times after the war.

I wanted to go back on the occasion of the 60th anniversary in 2004, so I could pay respect to those who I fought with who had lost their lives. The Commonwealth War Cemetery, where so many Allied servicemen are buried, is situated at the foot of Monte Cassino and it was there that I met Lieutenant General David Richards, Commander of the Allied Rapid Reaction Corps, who invited my family to attend an act of Remembrance there. I laid a poppy wreath at the Cassino Memorial in the cemetery. **Ray Longden**

Ray and Deana Longden with Lt-Gen.
Richards
At Cassino British Military Cemetery
2004 (Ray Longden)

A few weeks after meeting Ray Longden at Monte Cassino, Lieutenant General Richards sent him the following letter.

From Lieutenant General D J Richards CBE DSO

> Allied Rapid Reaction Corps
> 41179 Monchengladbach
> Germany
> 20th May 2004

Dear Ray,

It was a great privilege for me to meet you in Italy last week. I much enjoyed our conversations and meeting your 'support staff'. Enclosed are some photos and a 'Gunner' magazine.

Yours ever,

David

Looking back, it cannot be overestimated what an ordeal Ray Longden had lived through by fighting in the Italian campaign. He had been involved in one of the bloodiest battles of WW2 at Monte Cassino, followed by further heavy losses as Ray's unit helped to push the German divisions out of Italy. When he returned home, he was expected to settle down to normal life - there was no counselling offered, as today.

For this valuable service he was awarded four medals, including the 'Italian Campaign Star' and the '1939-45 Star'. Following demobilisation, Ray returned to the district and married, living in Southwell for a time, and setting up a garage business in Morton with his father. On his second marriage in 1965 to Deana Smith, Ray went to live in Morton, close to his garage business.

Harry Taylor, Royal Military Police/Seaforth Highlanders

Just before the war started Harry Taylor had been working at Southwell Lace Factory as a twist hand, serving a five-year apprenticeship. He wanted to be in the military police so didn't wait to be conscripted, voluntarily joining up. The army authorities sent him to Scotland to be with the Seaforth Highlanders in the police section. Following training in Scotland, Harry was appointed sergeant in the Royal Military Police, No. 4859939. For several months prior to D-Day his company of 'Redcaps', as they were known, had been providing security on the beaches between Cowes and Ryde on the Isle of Wight. Trials had been going on for some time with tanks and vehicles that had been adapted and fitted with propellers to enable them to disembark from a landing craft

Cap Badge of the Royal Military Police

some distance offshore. The role of the RMP was to seal off all the roads leading to the beaches and to clear from the area all unauthorised persons.

Harry Taylor in training (Christine Cross)

On D-Day+6, Harry set sail for Normandy arriving on Gold beach at 8.00 p.m. in the evening of D-Day+8. His duties were to take over security and liaison between the main British Intelligence Unit and the prisoner-of-war holding cage north of Bayeux that had just been erected by the Royal Engineers. This was an extensive barbed wire compound in an orchard that had seen plenty of action, huge pieces of shrapnel were embedded in the tree trunks. Here, Harry's job was to receive and segregate prisoners and then to liaise with British Intelligence, who would conduct interrogations. The POWs were then despatched to the beach-head for transit to the UK.

At about 9 a.m. on a lovely June morning on D-Day+14 I received the first Nazi Fighter Pilot shot down behind our lines who had survived; in fact, apart from a rip in his tunic, he was in good shape. He was a magnificent specimen of a man. Athletic, good-looking, and highly decorated, including the Iron Cross hanging round his neck.

I reported to the Major in charge of Intelligence that I had just received this prisoner and also the fact that he had requested a needle and thread to repair his uniform. I was instructed to bring him for immediate interrogation, whereupon he was questioned about himself and from which airfield he had taken off before being shot down. All he would give was his name, rank and number and said that was all he was required to give. After about an hour of further interrogation I took him back to the compound and he again asked for a needle and thread to repair the damage to his tunic. He was an Officer of the German Reich and as such he could not be expected to walk about in a damaged uniform.

I reported this to the Major. He didn't make any comment at the time but said, *'I want him back in an hour's time for further interrogation.'* It was extremely important that he talked. It was now becoming necessary to put some pressure on, and the fact that he was told that he would be shot unless he came up with more than he had done made no difference. In fact, it did not matter what method was tried, he was determined to give no more.

Harry Taylor
(Christine Cross)

Back he went again to the cage. It was now late in the afternoon and we were still at square one. He again asked to be able to repair his uniform and I again informed the Major. This time he said, *'Give him what he wants and report back to me when he has completed his repairs.'* After about another hour I was able to report to the Major that the repairs had been completed. The prisoner had thanked me and I would thank the Major for him.

Reporting back what had taken place, the instructions were to bring him back for more interrogation and bring a jack-knife at the same time. I collected a knife and was on the point of leaving the cage when I heard the piercing scream of a shell. The shell thumped into a clump of trees on the compound perimeter causing no damage whatsoever. I gathered myself together and was amazed to see that the prisoner had not moved at all. He had simply stood there oblivious, or so it seemed, to any danger. I marched him back into the interrogation tent, putting the jack-knife on the table. The questioning started all over again but it made no difference, he would not divulge anything other than he already had; his name, his rank and number.

The Major turned to me and said, *'Go and get me a uniform from one of the other prisoners. I want it tatty and filthy.'* We had in the cage some Russian slave prisoners and, selecting one about the same size as the German airman, I made him strip off his trousers and tunic, which could be smelt a hundred yards away and was full of lice. I took them back to the tent where the Major informed the prisoner that he was to remove his own uniform and put on the trousers and tunic I had brought. The Major said, *'We are going to cut up your uniform as we suspect that there are things hidden in the linings.'* The Major picked up the jack-knife, the prisoner stood motionless and then started to shake and tremble. Within seconds he was completely demoralised and said to the Major, *'I will tell you what you want to know. I cannot let you cut up my uniform and I certainly can't put on the clothes the sergeant has brought in.'*

He had been completely broken by a simple threat that his beloved uniform would be destroyed and having to wear back in the cage the Russian slave labour uniform. He had resisted all kinds of pressures and threats including one that he would be shot, and yet had been broken down by what to me seemed marvellous psychology on the part of the British Intelligence Officer.

Harry Taylor[54]

Another of Harry Taylor's duties was to accompany German POWs back from Normandy to Britain, if they were identified as having valuable information to pass on. Sometimes these liaison journeys proved eventful.

Two German prisoners had volunteered very valuable information about the dispersal of Panther (tank) divisions in the Caen area. I was called to the British Intelligence tent and informed by the Major in charge that I was to get two prisoners to London (Kempton Park Racecourse) as quickly as possible.

... As soon as we were airborne I settled the two prisoners just in front of me at the rear of the aircraft. I looked round and realised that the only gun on board was the tommy gun I carried.

---

[54] Memoirs of Harry Taylor (Unpublished).

The RAF personnel had donned parachutes and I asked where was mine. The pilot said, *'You will have to take pot luck if we go into the drink. Can you swim?'* I said no I couldn't. He replied, *'It will be a good chance to learn'*, and laughed it off!

We landed at Thorney Island aerodrome near Portsmouth. A pick-up vehicle met us on the runway and we were driven to the main guardroom, arriving at the same time as a number of RAF personnel were reporting back from an evening pass out. I started to shepherd the prisoners through the main entrance covering them from the back with my tommy gun. The RAF personnel had by this time realised they were Germans and, ignoring me and my gun, immediately waded into them with fists and boots; in a flash they had them on the floor. I shouted to the RAF guards on duty to assist me in rescuing the prisoners but it was several minutes before order was restored. We got the prisoners into a cell while those responsible for the attack were detained for questioning etc. It transpired that most of the airmen were Londoners whose homes and families had, and were still suffering from V1 and V2 attacks. The mere sight of the Nazis had provoked the instant attack. ... This was the last thing we wanted to happen as both men were prepared to give vital information. **Harry Taylor**

Harry had strong feelings about many of the German prisoners he came across, which we may find uncomfortable, but were not unusual or unacceptable in the context of the time.

Many of the captured Germans were men from the elite units - the Adolf Hitler Youth Division, the SS and the Panther Corps. They made no secret of the fact that they believed they would be liberated before we could get them to the beaches. Searches of the prisoners were continually revealing photographic evidence of the most callous nature. Pictures of rows and rows of civilians hanging from crudely erected gallows were common. It was not possible to feel anything except the deepest hatred towards them.

... One day we received a batch of a hundred POWs which included some officers and senior NCOs. Many had been arrogant from the moment they had arrived. They didn't hesitate to inform me who they were and the rank they held and demanded to be treated accordingly. Through the interpreter I told them I didn't recognise rank and as far as I was concerned they were POWs.

At the point when the POWs were ready to be marched into the cage, I instructed the interpreter to turn the column round so that the lower ranks would be marched in first. A sergeant belonging to the Intelligence Corps realised what was happening, came running towards me screaming, *'You can't do that; you are humiliating the higher ranks.'* He halted the marching column. I moved towards him and in no uncertain manner told him *'to get stuffed'*. **Harry Taylor**

In spite of the hostility felt by the Military Police towards many of the German prisoners, at no time did Harry see any physical violence contemplated or used by the RMP. The only time violence occurred was when little could have been done to prevent it.

We had recently taken in a batch of Russian slave labour prisoners and had them in a separate cage. They were in a very poor condition and it was obvious they had been treated very roughly by their German masters. They were filthy and loused up, many had a body odour strong enough to make you feel sick. We had a lot of sympathy for these men and we did not regard them in the same light as the Nazis. It took some time before they realised this, that anything we could do to improve their lot we did; extra rations and a certain amount of freedom within the cage were just two ways we helped them.

It so happened that in the cage they occupied, no latrines had been dug. Normally this task would be carried out by the occupants themselves, but in this case I decided to put some of the more arrogant Germans in to do the job. Selecting half a dozen Germans, and an interpreter, they were handed spades and told what to do. As soon as the German prisoners started to dig I moved out of the cage and hardly got through the main gate when the Russians attacked the Germans and were giving them a right going-over. With the help of some of the guards we managed to extricate them and get them out of the cage for their own safety. The Russians now had to dig their own latrines after all, because there was no way we could risk that happening again! It appeared that the Russians knew of the Germans and were getting their own back.

Harry Taylor

Harry Taylor (left) in France post D-Day
(Christine Cross)

Towards the end of the war Harry developed diphtheria and ended up in a field hospital. In the bed next to him was a German prisoner, also suffering from diphtheria, and to Harry's amazement a close friendship developed between them. After this interesting encounter Harry was given a convalescence break and sent to Paris.

One morning my CO sent for me saying, *'I've got good news for you. We are waiting to move to Antwerp as soon as the port is taken, but in the meantime we have to send a token force to fly the flag in Paris, which has just been liberated by the Americans. You are to be part of that force.'* The next day my new address was the Hotel Metropolitan in the Rue Cambon right in the centre of Paris, complete with the full treatment, waited on for meals

The Americans had liberated Paris, but without doubt it was the British the Parisians wanted to see and we happened to be the only ones there at that time. Bottles of wine and champagne were handed to us and disposed of as though there was no tomorrow. To celebrate the liberation, a huge Charity Concert was put on at the Opera House; this was to pay tribute to all the Allied Forces and we were to represent the British Forces. The reception we received was truly fantastic and the respect shown to the Union Jack and the playing of the National Anthem was out of this world.

At the end of December, we had another outstanding experience. Winston Churchill and General de Gaulle met at a banquet at the British Embassy, and we provided some of the security necessary. The precautions we had to take had to be seen to be believed. Sometime previously Mussolini had been released from captivity by German parachutists from a remote hotel in the Italian mountains and the authorities were taking no chances that German intelligence knew what was going on in Paris. Happily, it all passed off without incident.

Harry Taylor

In March 1945, close to the end of the war, Harry Taylor was moved from Paris to Antwerp on security duty at the docks.

> The outstanding memory for me in these last weeks of the war came at dawn on a lovely spring morning. As we were finishing our last patrol of the dock area, we observed hundreds of civilians, men, women and children, gathering on a large area of waste ground in the vicinity of the docks. We discovered that a Belgian collaborator was to be publicly executed so we decided to watch the proceedings. The crowd occupied three sides of the area which was roped off. The condemned man was brought out of a building nearby and very unceremoniously lashed to a stake. At the same time a crude wooden coffin was placed a few yards away to his right but fully in his view. The collaborator was then blindfolded and a disc placed over his heart.
>
> The execution squad of six Belgian gendarmes took up a firing position some twenty paces away. We were standing immediately behind when the officer in charge of the firing party gave the order to fire. It was all over in a split second. The victim slumped on the stake and the crowd turned away and started to disperse. We stood our ground until the body had been untied and put in the coffin. One person who spoke very good English came up to me and said could he have a word. He said, *'Do you know you have broken the rules, you should have turned and walked away along with everyone else as soon as the execution had taken place?'* I replied that I hadn't realised that was the case, but surely the person who had broken the rules that counted had just been executed.
>
> **Harry Taylor**

On his return Harry Taylor went back to his work at Southwell Lace Factory. On its closure in the mid-1950s he bought 101 Westgate, where he lived and set up a grocery and green-grocery business. In the 1980s his family moved to Derby and he died in 1992.

Geoff Mosedale, Royal Engineers

Geoff Mosedale was born in Southwell on the 14th April 1923, living for many years at 17 Queen Street. After attending the Minster Grammar School, part of the time as a choir boy, he worked before the Second World War in the family business, G Mosedale and Sons, bakers, on King Street.

> My father started in the Territorial Army, finally enlisting for active service in May 1942, when he joined the Royal Engineers as a private in the Northamptonshire Regiment, selected to be a driver or mechanic.
>
> Dad was initially based in the United Kingdom before doing active service in north-west Europe. Early on in this service he was taken very ill with meningitis and was admitted to hospital for several months.
>
> He rejoined his regiment in early 1943 and continued to do active service in north-west Europe until he was posted to the Middle East in October 1945, when he was promoted to Lance Corporal, returning to the UK in April 1946, being finally discharged in June 1946. **Jenny Clay**

On his return Geoff resumed work at the family bakery business, and in 1947 he married Kathleen Saunders from Oxton, who had been a state registered nurse in the war. He died in 1996 having lived in Southwell for the whole of his life.

Edward Caudwell, Royal Army Service Corps

In 1939 Edward Caudwell, along with his brother John, was managing Caudwell's Flour Mill on Station Road. At some point in 1940-1 he was called up, joining the Royal Army Service Corps (RASC) as a Welfare Officer, eventually being promoted to Major. He was sent to Iceland, which was regarded by the British government as strategically important being so close to the North Atlantic trade routes. In view of Germany's interest in neutral Iceland, British forces had invaded on 10th May 1940, occupying the island with two armed brigades. It was now possible to stop shipments to Germany, as part of the British naval blockade. From his Icelandic base, Edward was in regular touch with his family back in Southwell.

**Edward Caudwell
(Liz Price)**

10 BSD (Base Stores Depot)
RASC, Iceland, 'c' Force

20.7.41

Dear John,

... All the world now know that we have American troops here in Iceland, so I don't suppose the censor will mind that information being given away – they certainly are a very pleasant crowd of fellows.

... I don't think you can expect me home for some long time yet – and to tell you the truth I don't mind stopping in Iceland, there are lots of worse places going at the moment and I never was fond of sand and flies.

... Hope you are all well,

Best wishes,

Edward[55]

Edward was still stationed in Iceland at Christmas 1941 and had met Helga, his future wife, who worked for an Icelandic shipping line. At Christmas he sent presents to the Caudwell family including a doll in Icelandic dress to his niece Ruth Mary (Robinson) and some salmon, a real luxury item at that time.[56]

---

[55] Letter from Edward Caudwell to his brother John, 20th July 1941 (Ruth Robinson).
[56] Letter from Edward Caudwell to his brother John, 9th December 1941 (Ruth Robinson).

By 1942 the defence of Iceland had been transferred from Britain to the United States. Consequently Edward's army regiment was sent to North Africa to support the war fought against the Axis powers in the desert, and was later posted to Italy, where it took part in the 8th Army's campaign to push the Germans out of the peninsular. Edward continued his correspondence with his family, making clear his dislike of the North African desert.

> Major E. Caudwell
> 45. BSD
> RASC
> BNAF
> June 13 1943.
>
> Dear John,
> ... How often I think of 'Brandreth' and the cool looking trees alongside Spring Terrace. What would I give for half a day without flies – they are everywhere? I hear from the wireless that the Conservative member got in at Newark by a small margin of 3,000 – it sounds a big drop from Titchfield's figures – I suppose the new member is Colonel Sheppard.
> ... I am enclosing a postcard for Ruth Mary – Constantinople, it is one of the places I have passed through in my travels. This is Sunday evening, how I should enjoy a pint of 'White Lion' ale, all so refreshing! One cannot get beer out here.
> Kind wishes to Joan,
> Edward[57]

After the war Edward returned home, visiting Scapa Flow, where he married Helga on the ship on which she was then based. He resumed working at Caudwell's Mill whilst also running a farm at Morton, where he lived. Edward died in 1979.

Derek Warwick, Sherwood Rangers

In 1939 Derek Warwick, son of Col and Mrs Philip Warwick of Normanton Prebend, Southwell had recently finished his education at Oxford University and was commissioned in the Sherwood Rangers Yeomanry. In January 1940 Captain Warwick went overseas with the regiment to Palestine and later to North Africa. The following year, 1941, he spent five months in Tobruk at the time of the long siege.

However, it was during the Battle of El Alamein (October-November 1942) that the Sherwood Rangers Yeomanry, part of Montgomery's 8th Army, fought with distinction. Derek Warwick was involved in the 'regimental attack which found a hole in the enemy's defences and which possibly turned the scales in our favour on the Tel el Aqqaqir Ridge.'[58]

---

[57] Letter from Edward Caudwell to his brother John, 13th June 1943 (Ruth Robinson).
[58] *N/Adv,* 30th December 1942.

On the night of 3rd November Derek was wounded but soon after learnt that he had been awarded the Military Cross, granted in recognition of acts of exemplary gallantry. News of this heroic action was reported the following month.

Middle East Heroes

DSO for Lt-Col Kellett
Capts. Warwick and Brooks - Military Cross

Lt-Col EO Kellett, MP, Commanding Officer of the Sherwood Rangers Yeomanry has been awarded the DSO for gallantry in the Desert fighting. Two officers of the same regiment, Captain F R Warwick, son of Col and Mrs Philip Warwick of Southwell, and Captain G O Brooks, the Medical Officer, both receive the Military Cross.

… In Tobruk
Captain F R Warwick was wounded on the night of November 3rd-4th. He was hit in the forehead just above the right eye, and the latest information … is that he was going on extremely well, and he has made an excellent recovery. He may even possibly be out of hospital.

Captain G O Brooks was MO to the Regiment … and both he and Captain Warwick went overseas with the Regiment in January 1940. … Colonel Kellett, Captain Warwick and Captain Brooks were all in Tobruk for five months in 1941. They are now part of the Royal Armoured Corps.[59]

Honour for Lieut Derek Warwick
The award of the Military Cross was given to Lieut Derek Warwick, the only son of Mr and Mrs Warwick of Normanton Prebend. He was awarded the MC for gallantry and distinguished service in the Middle East. This has been reported previously in the *Advertiser*.[60]

George William Fletcher, gunner, Royal Artillery

Bill Fletcher came from Oughtibridge in the Sheffield area. Early in the war he was stationed at Maythorne camp; his Release Book indicates that he was a gunner in ACC, 65 Medical Regiment, Royal Artillery (Field).

My father, Bill Fletcher, came from the Sheffield area, and when the war broke out he joined the Army Catering Corps because of his cooking capabilities, although later he transferred to the Royal Engineers. At one point he was sent for training to the Maythorne Army camp at Southwell. One night he went down to The Crown and met my future mother, Vera Stafford, who lived at the top of Burgage Lane in a cottage, where Burgage Court is now. Soon after this my father's regiment was sent to France but he still kept in touch with Mum. On his return at the end of the war he made a visit to Southwell deliberately to renew his friendship with Mum. Being a little nervous of Mum's response, he sent a soldier friend to Burgage Lane with the message that 'Bill Fletcher is waiting for Vera in The Saracen's Head.'

Karen Jones

---

[59] *N/Adv,* 30th December 1942.
[60] *N/Adv,* 13th January 1943.

At the end of the war Bill Fletcher was awarded three medals; the 1939-45 Star, the Defence Medal (Campaign Medal) and the 1939-45 War Medal. On the 10th August 1946, shortly after being demobilized, he married Vera Stafford at Southwell Minster and they lived initially on Burgage Lane before moving to Landseer Road. They had three girls, Karen, Beverley and Lindsey. Bill died on 9th September 1982, aged 64.

Bill Fletcher (right) in Germany, 1945

(Karen Jones)

Ted Kendall, driver, Royal Army Service Corps

In 1939 Ted Kendall was seventeen years old, living with his parents and sister Brenda (later Whitton) in one of the Sunnyside Cottages, Westhorpe. Before he could join the Army he volunteered to join the ARP and do some fire-watching. In 1941 he was called up and asked to go to Mansfield Army Hospital for a medical. Having passed, he was then sent to Derby. Ted's father, Albert Kendall, a veteran of the First World War, had also been called up and joined the Royal Army Service Corps. Ted was attached to the 26th MLBU, driving army vehicles, especially lorries, and was for a time billeted in Wisbech.

> Early in 1942 I was sent to Liverpool and told that I would be joining the 26th MLBU (The Mobile Laundry and Bath Unit) who were going to North Africa. We sailed on the SS *Ormonde* of the Orient Line and I remember we were in the bowels of G deck. We docked at Algiers and for some time we moved back and forth between Tunis and Algiers. My job was to give vehicle support to the army in the North African campaign. We didn't see much action on the ground but there was plenty going on in the skies.
> **Ted Kendall**

After the Allied military success in North Africa in 1943, Ted Kendall's unit took part in the invasion of Italy, landing in Sicily at Syracuse, crossing the Straits of Messina in small crafts, eventually arriving at Anzio.

> Our unit's job was again to support the army by transporting supplies to their bases. We made our way up the leg of Italy, via Naples, Rome and Florence, passing Monte Cassino, where there was a huge battle. I remember transporting supplies to the Infantry Training Camp in the Naples area. At one point we stopped the army lorry, got out, sat down and watched Mt Vesuvius erupting!
> On our journeys we came across many Italian and German prisoners of war and received a friendly reception from the local Italian population wherever we went. Driving army lorries in the hot climate was tough and we enjoyed the breaks, often with a glass of red Italian wine.
> **Ted Kendall**

Towards the end of the war Ted Kendall's unit got more leave and he remembers visiting Trieste and having a photograph taken there, which he still possesses. Throughout the war Ted kept in contact with his family back home in Southwell, especially with his sister Brenda and her husband, Frank Whitton.

> *Dear Brenda,*
>
> *Many thanks for the photo of Derek. He is getting a bonny boy. I am glad to hear you're in the best of health as these few lines leave me the same. The weather is good, plenty of sun and I am very brown now.*
>
> *Give my best regards to Frank. I expect he is busy working at the factory. I hear from mother that father is on leave but is not very well. I hope you see him before he goes back. I seem to be getting plenty of mail just now. I hope it keeps up. Well, Brenda, I will close now, sending you all my love.*
>
> *From your loving brother,*
>
> *Ted* [61]

Christmas Card from Ted Kendall to his sister Brenda, 1944 (Brenda Whitton)

When VJ Day came along he was at Udine, working with the 1st Battalion of the King's Own Royal Regiment. He stayed in Italy with the army until 1946, when he was 'demobbed'. As soon as Ted returned home, he got engaged and went to live in Netherfield, Nottingham.

---

[61] Postcard from Ted Kendall to his sister, Brenda, Christmas 1944.

Cyril Flowers, South Staffordshire Regiment

Before the war Cyril had been working at Carey's Lace Factory on The Burgage as a qualified twist hand. He was called up in April 1940 and joined the South Staffordshire Regiment.

> He went by train to Sutton Coalfield and by bus to a new camp, Erdington, near Birmingham. Here he was trained for 12 weeks before going to Scotland as part of the South Staffordshire Regiment, although he was later transferred to the Yorks and Lancs 9th Battalion. In 1941 he returned from Ireland to get married, but four days later he was back in the army.
>
> He sailed on the *Stirling Castle* to Durban and then on the *Nova Scotia* to India, finally serving as one of the Chindits behind enemy lines in Burma. Their aim was to stop the Japanese getting food and supplies, thereby enabling the 14th Army to advance. They blew up railway lines and booby-trapped bridges, but were forced to stop the latter when the Japanese started to use local villagers as human shields. Food was dropped by Dakota aircraft with a fighter escort. The American food was K rations. Each drop supplied three meals a day for five days, and consisted of tinned meat, fruit bars, chocolate, cheese, coffee powder and a tablet that was the equivalent of vegetables. Water was obtained from rivers and dykes. Apart from this, Cyril never spoke to Doll or anyone else about his experiences. … 'We had no counselling; only our pals.'
>
> In December 1945, Cyril returned home on the *Andes* that made a record-making trip; Australia to India to Southampton. He was then ordered to Woodhall Spa from where he made his way to Southwell station. With no telephone at No 22 it was uncertain when he would arrive. Throughout his time in Burma he had not been allowed to write home, but the Army sent notification each month that he was well. Doll's letters and home-made cakes arrived regularly for him. The great excitement of his arrival was marred by his appearance; he was now 9st 6lb, having lost 2 stone. He had brought home a spare kit bag full of tinned fruit and sugar that he had been able to buy on the boat. Doll had also kept tinned food for the welcome-home party. After the celebrations Cyril was at Lincoln HQ for five months and then went to York for demobilisation.[62]

In 1945 Cyril returned to Carey's Lace Factory to take up the job he had been promised, but after the war the demand for lace fell dramatically. In 1956 Carey's closed and Cyril was the last man to be paid off.

Robert Page, signalman, 8th Army

Born in 1906 Robert William Page was working as a clerk at the Westminster Bank, Southwell and living with his wife at 11 Newark Road when the war broke out. He was 33 and settled into country life. Two years later, in 1941, he was sent to Huddersfield to train as a signalman.

> From Huddersfield father was sent to North Africa on the *Queen Mary* via the Cape. He joined the 8th Army under Montgomery and arrived just after El Alamein. He boasted that Rommel never advanced after he arrived on the scene. He enjoyed working in Cairo, loved the climate and had plenty of time to read, explore and go to the cinema, one of his passions. Later with the 25th Brigade he moved across North Africa; he called his unit, 'the rear, rear, brigade'. He never talked of the fighting or the devastation he must have seen.

---

[62] Stevenson, Doreen, *Twentieth Century Lives of Southwell* (Southwell: Stevenson, 2001), pp. 65-66.

Throughout his war service my father wrote copious letters home - I still have them - but there is little about any action around him. Out of boredom he began writing two novels based on his early life in Nottingham and he shared with my mother every detail of his stories, they are far more prominent than the world about him. His first novel was *'We Give Today'* and had as its heroine, Dorothy, who father based on a young girl he had got to know when he attended Army training in Huddersfield. The second novel he wrote was *'To Err is Human'* and had as its main character a young girl called Marjorie. He had never done any writing before he went into the services.

Barbara Page

In 1943 he crossed with the 8th Army into Italy and, awaiting his turn to cross from Sicily, he watched two vessels before him torpedoed and sunk. Robert moved up the Italian peninsula with his brigade and when peace was declared in May 1945 he had reached Venice.

With a friend he hired a gondola and, incredibly for anyone who knew this gentle man, thinking the gondolier was charging too much, threw the poor man into the canal. **Barbara Page**

Letter home from Egypt sent 1943 (Barbara Page)

Though Robert had come home on leave in the spring of 1945, he wasn't finally demobilized until the beginning of 1946, when he walked home to Southwell from Newark in the middle of the night and as dawn broke reached Galley Hill and saw the Minster before him. It was a glorious homecoming (see page 289).

After the war Robert resumed his job at the Westminster Bank until his retirement at the age of 60. He continued to write and finished another four books in the post-war years, though they were never published. The family continued to live on Newark Road. Robert died in 1978 at the age of 71.

Philip Spall, Royal Leicestershire Regiment

Philip was born on 2nd April 1919 and was the brother of Ron Spall whose story appears in Chapter 1. He was educated at The National School in Southwell before taking a job before WW2 at Ransome and Marles' factory in Newark.

He was called up in 1939 to join the Royal Leicestershire Regiment and after training they were sent to Northern France as part of the BEF. His unit was the 2/5th of the RLR and his service number was 4860245. During the retreat from Dunkirk in May 1940 his regiment found themselves in a defensive position against a canal. On either side of the British positions the line was held by French soldiers. He always told of how in the night the French soldiers, on either side, disappeared and in the morning they found themselves surrounded by the Germans and they were captured.

His date of capture was 27th May 1940 and his place of capture was Carvin, France. Following his capture he was sent to Stalag XX-A and then Stalag XX-B. Towards the end of the war he recalled watching the Allied 'planes bombing nearby German cities such as Marienberg in Southern Germany. During the winter of 1944/5 the German authorities decided to move the POWs westward and away from the advancing Russians. This was a very cold and bitter winter and on this forced march, the 'Death March', he witnessed many of his fellow POWs die through disease and malnutrition. This made a very lasting impression on him and made him appreciative of food we have today. He hated food wastage, having known what real hunger is.

As the war ended in May 1945 he recalled one morning that the POWs woke up to find the German guards had disappeared. Not knowing what to do they headed west and eventually were met by the advancing American army, who liberated them. He was flown back to the UK and ended up in a holiday camp, Pontins, near Blackpool for recuperation. **Peter Spall**

Philip met his wife to be on VJ night at the Winter Gardens in Blackpool. They were married in 1946 and moved to Southwell to live. Philip resumed his job at Ransome and Marles, before moving to Blackpool in 1959, where he worked as a bus driver until retirement in 1984. He enjoyed a happy retirement until his death on 1st January 2000 and is buried in Holy Trinity graveyard in Southwell.

POW Certificate
(Peter Spall)

Edgar Bowring, Royal Artillery

Edgar Bowring joined the Royal Artillery regiment in WW2, serving in Iceland from 1940-2 and later in North West Europe from 1944-6.[63] Whilst fighting in Germany towards the end of the war, Edgar won the prestigious Military Cross (MC) for showing 'outstanding courage and devotion to duty'.

Southwell Officer Wins MC

Major E R H Bowring

It is announced that the Military Cross has been awarded to Major Edgar Rennie Harvey Bowring, Royal Regiment of Artillery, of Southwell for service in NW Europe.

The citation states: 'Throughout Major Bowring has shown outstanding courage and devotion to duty. Under the heaviest fire he remains as calm and collected as on parade. On at least two occasions his half-track hood has been riddled with mortar splinters when he was in it and on one of these occasions a wireless set inside the truck was smashed by a splinter. He remained completely unmoved and gave those around him the impression that he was rather enjoying the battle.

The morale value of his example was incalculable. By his calmness and skill under the most adverse conditions he has undoubtedly made material contributions to the success of many actions. For example at Wustwezel in October a platoon of 11 Royal Scots Fusiliers was attacked by a JAGD Panther Tank, 2 self-propelled guns and about 40 infantry. Major Bowring, by the skilful handling of his fire, cut off the enemy infantry from their armour 400 yards from our position. The armour got into the village but dared not come out from behind the houses. Meanwhile an attack by our infantry on our left went in. The German infantry, who had been pinned by our fire, dropped their arms and fled and were all accounted for. Twenty-seven rifles, three spandaus and a revolver were left in the ditch in which they had taken cover. The Panther tank was destroyed later by our armour. Major Bowring, by cutting the enemy infantry off from their armour, undoubtedly created the opportunity of destroying the enemy, and it was taken.

Major Bowring, by his complete indifference to enemy fire, by his calmness and cheerfulness has been an inspiration to all who have come into contact with him'.[64]

Joffre Boonham, Leicestershire Regiment

Joffre Tallis Boonham was born on 17th November 1918, in the Southwell district. He served with the Leicestershire Regiment during World War II, from 1939 to 1946, and was promoted to Sgt Major.

After three years on East Coast defences, he was posted to India and spent the rest of the war in the Far East. He was awarded the Burma Star for his services with General Orde Wingate's 'Chindits', operating behind enemy lines in North Burma. He was released onto the Army Reserve in 1946.
Trevor Wilds

---

[63] Eastbourne College War Service Record 1939-46.
[64] *N/Adv,* 18th July 1945.

In March 1946, he married Edith Swinburn at Durham. He was the sub-postmaster at Farnsfield until his retirement in 1986, and a leading light in the Royal British Legion, officiating each Remembrance Sunday as Parade Marshall, resplendent in his bowler hat and pace stick.

P Roach, Royal Tank Regiment

In 1939 P Roach, living in Winkburn when he received his call-up papers, joined the 1st Royal Tank Regiment (RTR). He served in Europe, and in the autumn of 1944 was involved in the liberation of S'Hertogenbosch, a city in southern Netherlands, when he came face to face with the enemy in a house 800 yards behind the German lines, while carrying out a patrol with his platoon officer during the fighting. He told his interesting story to the *Advertiser* soon after the war had ended.

WINKBURN SERGEANT
Got a Hun and a Hairdressing Kit

'The enemy were in some houses a little way down the road or at least they were a few days earlier, because we came under their fire and we wanted to know [if] they were still there,' he said. 'So we set off on a walking patrol, the platoon officer and me. Everything went alright until we got separated entering the village, but I decided to go on alone.'

'I got about 800 yards behind the Bosche lines and found myself near a cowshed adjoining a house. I went through the cowshed and peered out into the yard, where I saw a pair of Jerry jack boots standing outside the back of the house. I tried 'em on but they did not fit, so I left them there and went into the house to see if anybody was about. The first room I went into was the main one and it was obviously occupied by Bosche, the usual dirt, machine guns, some 'ammo' and a bazooka or two lying about. But I also spotted a hairdressing kit which wasn't bad so I "swiped it".'

Door Opened

'While I was about it, I thought I might as well finish my look round, and went into the other room, which was on the opposite side of the corridor, but it was empty, so I decided to get out. Just then the second door in the room I had examined first opened and I flattened myself pretty quick against the corridor wall. I knew I should see whoever it was first, because the door opened inwards.'

'I stood waiting and slipped the safety catch of my Sten and in a couple of seconds, through the door, comes a Jerry sergeant major walking in his stockinged feet, obviously the owner of the pair of boots outside. I think he must have been half asleep. Anyway, as he got through the door, he saw me and his jaw dropped about a mile. We seemed to stand looking at each other for hours but I suppose it was only a couple of seconds, and then he took a backward jump through the doorway.'

'If I could, I would have liked to have taken him prisoner, but I don't know any German, and didn't even know how to say "Hands up", so I just stepped in the room and "let drive". I don't know whether I killed him but he stopped about ten rounds before the gun jammed. Then I hopped it pretty sharp, expecting any minute for some of the others to appear. No crouching on the way back, I just went. But no shots came, and I made it OK. Anyway, it's a nice hairdressing kit.'[65]

---

[65] *N/Adv*, 24th January 1945.

Frank Felton, gunner

Frank Felton lived at 70 Easthorpe. He was called up and trained as a gunner in the army. When serving in the North African Campaign he was captured and sent to Italy to a POW camp. Towards the end of the war, Frank was involved in a very daring, successful POW camp escape.

Gunner F Felton's escape from Italian POW camp

Among men repatriated from Switzerland who passed through Nottingham yesterday week was Gunner F Felton. All the men were taken prisoners at Tobruk or Knightsbridge [Libya] and later escaped from Italian POW camps at the time of the Italian surrender.

When they escaped from the Italian camp they lived for about seven days on grapes and water and scraps of food they could obtain from civilians. They had to hide during the day and make their way by night across the fields becuse the roads were being used by the Germans. Gunner Felton said that on one night 80 POWs had pushed the Italian guards aside and surged out into the open and fanned out in small groups to make their way to the Swiss border.

The most difficult time was spent in getting over the mountains and they were two days in a shepherd's hut. When they reached the Swiss border they saw soldiers with helmets like those of the Germans and, mistaking them, put their hands up but were relieved to find they were in Swiss territory.[66]

The 'escapees' passed through Nottingham on their way to a dispersal camp before going home. Some of the men were met by relatives, and Gunner Felton had a happy reunion with members of his family and his fiancée.

Harry Coghill, Sherwood Foresters

In 1939 Harry Coghill, eldest son of Canon and Mrs Coghill, lived at Orchard Cottage, Southwell. When he was called up, he joined the Sherwood Foresters and in 1940 went over to France and Belgium where he was caught up in the battle for France. He was taken prisoner at Dunkirk and spent the rest of the war in a POW camp.

First-hand information has been received about Major Coghill, eldest son of Mrs Coghill, Orchard Cottage, Southwell and of the late Canon Coghill. Members of the family were recently in conversation with two British ex-prisoners from Major Coghill's regiment who have recently been re-patriated from the same camp where Major Coghill has been interned in Germany for several years. Both these men had been batmen to Major Coghill. They say he is well and in good spirits. The family's friends will be glad to hear this re-assuring news and will look forward to what we hope is now the not far distant day when all British prisoners will be home again.[67]

In April 1945 the advancing allied armies liberated the German POW camps in northern Europe and Harry Coghill was able to return home, where he received an excellent welcome, especially from the people of Westhorpe.[68]

---

[66] *N/Adv,* 1st Nov 1944.

[67] *N/Adv,* 6th September 1944.

[68] *N/Adv,* 11th April 1945.

Godfrey Samuel Bostock, Sherwood Foresters

Born in 1920, Godfrey Bostock was living at 108 Westgate, Southwell when war broke out. In 1940 he joined the Sherwood Foresters regiment, went over to France and was involved in the evacuation of Dunkirk. He was then sent with the Sherwood Foresters to the Far East, but in April 1943 news came to his mother that he he had been captured by the Japanese.

Captured by the Japanese

News has just been received by Mrs Bostock of 108 Westgate that her only son, Pte Bostock of 1/5th Sherwood Foresters is a prisoner-of-war in Japanese hands. He had been reported missing since the fall of Singapore. He is 23 years old and took part in the evacuation at Dunkirk.[69]

Eventually, news came through that Godfrey Bostock had been released and was in Rangoon, waiting to return.

Pte Bostock Freed from Japanese

Southwell people will be glad to hear good news of Southwell boys who have been prisoners in the Far East. Mrs Bostock of 108 Westgate, Southwell has received a cable from her son, Pte G S Bostock, 1/5th Sherwood Foresters, saying he is safe and well in British hands at Rangoon and hopes to be home soon.[70]

Godfrey Bostock died in Southwell in 2007 at the age of 88.

Colin Johnson, Royal Army Service Corps
Clifford Johnson, 1st Army

In 1939 Colin Johnson, son of Mr and Mrs F Johnson, was working in the Nottinghamshire coalfield and living in Fiskerton. He joined the Royal Army Service Corps (RASC) and was stationed with the 8th Army in North Africa. Around the same time, Colin's brother Clifford joined the 1st Army and also served in North Africa, taking part in Operation Torch from 1942. Both armies were involved in successfully freeing North Africa of Axis troops after the Battle of El Alamein.

On one occasion Colin Johnson, my father, was driving a water tanker in the desert close to El Alamein; after an exhausting drive through the desert their unit pitched tent just after nightfall. Next morning they woke to find themselves in the middle of a minefield.

Once the Axis powers had been pushed out of North Africa, Colin's unit, still attached to the 8th Army, landed in Italy continuing the fight against the enemy. When Colin's unit reached Rome they were given some time off after the rigours of the Italian campaign. Then a most extraordinary event happened. One night Colin and some army friends found a bar in the middle of Rome when who should walk in but his brother Clifford, who had been fighting with the 1st Army in Italy.

Brian Johnson

The *Newark Advertiser* picked up this incredible coincidence.

---

[69] *N/Adv*, 21st April 1943.
[70] *N/Adv*, 26th September 1945.

Colin and Clifford Johnson, the sons of Mr and Mrs F Johnson from Fiskerton, met in Italy. Of the two brothers, Colin was in the 8th Army in Egypt, Clifford was in the 1st Army in N Africa.[71]

Colin and Clifford Johnson at their meeting in Rome, 1945.
On the back is written:
'Rome 1945. All the best Mum, Dad, Mag and Brian.'

(Brian Johnson)

After the war, Colin and Clifford Johnson returned to live at 'Kendor', Station Lane, Fiskerton, where they bought a couple of ex-army lorries. They set up a business making and delivering concrete blocks.

Allan Arthur Beckett, King's Own Yorkshire Light Infantry

In 1939 Arthur Beckett was 16 and working at Caudwell's Mill, living with his parents Fred and May Beckett in Church Street. Too young to enlist at the outset of the war, he became a member of the local Home Guard, before joining the King's Own Yorkshire Light Infantry regiment. Arthur's battalion saw action in the Allied invasion of Sicily, and later the invasion of Italy, including the Battle of Anzio. He was only on active service for twelve months before he died in the fighting.

Mr and Mrs Beckett of 59 Church Street received the sad official news that their son, Private Arthur Beckett, had died of wounds on the 29th November 1943 while serving with the Central Mediterranean forces. He would have been 21 in June. He worked at Caudwell's Mill and was a member of the Home Guard. He had been in the army for 12 months and saw active service in Sicily.[72]

Arthur Beckett's grave lies in the Sangro River War Graves Commission Cemetery in Italy.

---

[71] *N/Adv*, 17th May 1945.
[72] *N/Adv*, 5th January 1944.

Walter Hart, Royal Corps of Signals

In 1939 Walter Hart was working at Farrar's Boiler Works, Newark. His parents ran the post office at Fiskerton. Walter was called up and joined the Royal Corps of Signals. Early in the war he was sent to France, coming through the Dunkirk evacuation. Later he was posted to Malaya and, on the fall of Singapore, became a Japanese POW.[73] Better news arrived in September 1945, that Walter was soon to return home to Fiskerton.

> **Signalman W Hart returns from the Far East**
>
> Mr W J Hart from Fiskerton received a cable on Wednesday from his son, Signalman Walter Hart, stating that he had arrived in India from No 1 Camp, Thailand. He was captured at the fall of Singapore and only three cards had been received from him by his parents in 3½ years. Before enlisting in the Royal Signals in 1936, Signalman Hart was employed at Farrar's Boilerworks.[74]

George Raymond Hipwell, OCTU, Sherwood Rangers

In 1939 George Raymond Hipwell lived at Hall Close, Farnsfield. He had been educated at the Minster School, Southwell and Nottingham College of Art. He was a playing member of Nottingham Tigers RFC and worked as an assistant in the County Architect's Office at Shire Hall, Nottingham. In 1939 he married Irene Jean Fraser.

> He served as an Officer Cadet in 141st OCTU, prior to being commissioned as a 2nd Lieutenant on 18 January 1941. He had previously served with the Sherwood Rangers Yeomanry and was commissioned into the Royal Engineers. In February 1943 he was taken prisoner at the fall of Singapore but survived the war.
>
> **Trevor Wilds**

On his return, George decided to continue his army career and was promoted to Captain in April 1947, eventually retiring from the Army as a Major in 1959. He later moved to Aberdour in Scotland to live with his son and died there on 18th May 2004.

Horatio Hucknall, Leicestershire Regiment

In 1939 Horatio Hucknall, born in Farnsfield, worked for the local butcher, J Hatcher. He was called up in 1939, aged 20, and enlisted as Private 4860137 in "A" Company, 1st Battalion, Leicestershire Regiment, serving in India, Malaysia and Singapore.

> He was taken prisoner at the fall of Singapore on 15th February 1942 and put to work on the notorious Burma-Siam Railway. He died as a prisoner of war on Wednesday 18th August 1943, aged 25, at the POW camp at Nam Chon Yai (229 kms north of the start of the railway), from acute enteritis. He was originally buried in Grave No 30 at the camp cemetery but was later interred in Grave 6 C 24 in the Kanchanaburi War Cemetery in Thailand, the last resting place of many who perished working on that railway.
>
> **Trevor Wilds**

Posthumously, Horatio was awarded the 1939-45 Star, the Pacific Star and the Indian Imperial Medal.

---

[73] *N/Adv*, 26th May 1943.
[74] *N/Adv*, 19th September 1945.

Angus MacAskill, Sherwood Foresters

In the summer of 1937 Angus MacAskill married Joyce Atherley, the daughter of the local baker at Farnsfield. He was a gardener at Calverton Colliery before joining the Territorial Army and then the Sherwood Foresters, serving as Lance Sergeant 4977349 in the 1st/5th Battalion. He fought at Dunkirk, India and then Singapore.

He was posted with the Battalion to Singapore in February 1942 and they had only been there for a fortnight when the order to surrender to the Japanese was given at 3 p.m. on 15th February. The captured prisoners were then marched to Changi, on the eastern tip of the island. After six months on Singapore Island, the troops were moved in batches to Ban Pong, near Bangkok in Siam (Thailand) to work as forced labour on the infamous Burma-Siam railway.

On 4th September 1944, Angus was put aboard the Japanese POW ship *Kachidoki Maru*, one of the so called 'hellships' with 900 other POWs to be taken to Japan. Alistair Urquhart, a POW who was also aboard, described the atrocious conditions in his excellent book 'The Forgotten Highlander'.

These Japanese ships carried no markings so there was no way of knowing what their cargo was. At 22.40hrs on Tuesday 12 September 1944 the ship was torpedoed by the American submarine USS *Pampanito* north east of Hainan Island off China, and sank with the loss of 244 POWs, of whom Angus was one. He is commemorated on Column 70 on the Kranji War Memorial in Singapore. USS *Pampanito* is now a tourist attraction at Fisherman's Wharf, San Francisco.

Trevor Wilds

There is a commemorative plaque in memory of Angus in St John's Church, Inverness. He was posthumously awarded the 1939-45 Star and the Pacific Star. Of the 900 Sherwood Foresters of the 1st/5th Battalion who were sent to the Far East, 50 died in action before the capitulation of Singapore. A further 300 died of sickness, malnutrition and ill-treatment as prisoners of war.

Arthur and Neville Rollinson

Early in the war two Southwell brothers were called up around the same time, Arthur Rollinson joined the Sherwood Foresters and Neville the Seaforth Highlanders. In 1944 the two brothers had an unplanned meeting, which was covered by the local paper.

Southwell's Rollinson Brothers Met in Middle East

News has been received by Mr and Mrs Rollinson of Westgate, Southwell that their two sons, L Cpl A Rollinson, late of the Sherwood Foresters, and Pte N H Rollinson of the Seaforth Highlanders, have met in the Middle East after Arthur, who is lying in a military hospital suffering from injuries received after being thrown from a horse, was greatly surprised to see his brother walk into the ward. He had no knowledge that he was in the neighbourhood. This was a very happy reunion. Arthur has been abroad for four years and two months, having been all through the Desert Campaign. Neville has served in several theatres of war and was enjoying a rest from active service when he met his brother.[75]

---

[75] *N/Adv*, 25th October 1944.

Charles Dexter, Sherwood Foresters

Born in 1903, Charles Dexter married Alice M Richards at Farnsfield in the autumn of 1937. Early in the war he joined the Sherwood Foresters and served as Corporal 4796209 in the 2nd Battalion, which accompanied the original British Expeditionary Force and was the first battalion of the Regiment to enter a theatre of operations in World War II. In northern France, they were separated from the Germans by the neutral states of Belgium and Holland and they were not called upon to fight at this stage. This all changed on 10th May 1940, when German troops advanced dramatically into these two countries, thus ending the so-called "Phoney War", which led to fierce fighting, covering the retreat of the BEF to Dunkirk.

On the morning of 28th May 1940 the 2nd Battalion was instructed to move forward to fill a gap in the Brigade line along the Wambreck stream, near Ypres, between the 2nd Wiltshire Regiment and the 143rd Brigade. For various reasons, the Battalion was unable to locate the gap it was supposed to fill but did locate the 2nd Wiltshires, albeit in a different position from that which they had been given. They then took up a position to the right of the Wiltshires. On the evening of 28th, around 9 p.m., the Battalion began withdrawing by motor transport through Poperinghe to Hoogstrade, where they were to come into reserve to troops holding the line of the River Yser. Although the War Diary is incomplete for this period, it is known that there were many casualties at this time, one being Corporal Dexter, who died aged 36. **Trevor Wilds**

In June 1940 Charles Dexter's wife received the sad news. She was left a young widow with six children. Charles is buried in Oosttaverne Wood Cemetery, Heuvelland, Belgium, some 6 kms south of Ypres. Posthumously, he was awarded the 1939-45 Star.

Kenneth and Harold Smith, East Yorkshires and Royal Warwicks

The Smith family from Maythorne had four sons serving in the army in WW2. Two of them, Kenneth Smith in the East Yorkshire regiment, and Harold in the Royal Warwicks, met up unexpectedly whilst on active service in India.

Smith Brothers Meet in India

One of those rare events in this war of two brothers unexpectedly meeting on 'active' service. Mr and Mrs A Smith, Maythorne, received a letter telling them the story. Both sons are stationed in India. One, Pte Kenneth Smith being in the East Yorkshire Regt and Pte Harold Smith in the Royal Warwicks. It appears that one of them went into a shop in the locality where he is stationed and was astonished to meet his brother coming out of the same shop. Although located within a few miles of each other neither was aware of the fact. Pte Kenneth Smith served in France, coming out of Dunkirk evacuation. The Smiths have two other sons serving in the army. One is a POW in Germany.[76]

---

[76] *N/Adv*, 8th March 1944.

Cyril Davis, Hampshire Regiment

Cyril Davis was born in Farnsfield in 1920 and attended the local Wesleyan School. When Cyril was called up he served as Private 6411191 in the 1st/4th Battalion, Hampshire Regiment.

The Hampshires formed part of 128th Infantry Brigade of 46th Infantry Division, which left Britain on 6th January 1943 for North Africa as part of 'Operation Torch'. On 27th February the 2nd/4th Battalion, with 1st/4th in support, was attacked at Hunts Gap. Extensive minefields and heavy dive-bombing kept the German tanks at bay, but the enemy had success in overrunning some positions, before they withdrew on 2nd March. During March the Brigade was engaged on defensive patrolling, under heavy shelling. 1st/4th Battalion lost 100 casualties during March, of which Private Davis was one. By the end of April, the rifle companies of 1st/4th Battalion only had 3 officers and 80 men left between them.   **Trevor Wilds**

Cyril Davis died on Monday 15th March 1943, and is buried in the Oued Zarga War Cemetery in Tunisia.

Looking Back

From the stories provided here most of the major theatres of war are covered, from Norway and the Dunkirk beaches in 1940 to North Africa and Italy in 1942-3, and finally to Western Europe and South East Asia in 1945.

For young men from the rural district of Southwell, most of whom had travelled little in their lives, it must have been an eye-opening experience suddenly finding themselves in the middle of the Norwegian winter, driving across the Libyan desert or arriving in tropical Singapore to protect the famous naval base against Japanese aggression.

Whilst they must have had many uneventful days, the young men mentioned here clearly experienced plenty of action, with some stirring moments contrasting with others showing the unpleasant side of war. Fortunately, many local young men were able to return home, in some cases after very lengthy and challenging POW experiences. Others, sadly, never came home.

Leaving the army after a period on operational service and after injury can be a very daunting experience. Nowadays, there are in existence many organisations which offer 'post traumatic stress disorder' support to soldiers and their families, when in need. This can offer a lifeline of support in mental and physical health and in educational assistance. For the returning soldier in 1945 this support was, compared with what exists today, very limited.

Whatever their fate, people in the Southwell area, then and now, respect them for their valued contribution to a memorable and much needed victory.

..*Shoot straight, Lady*

You've got a fighting job on hand, too. These are significant days and anyone — man, woman, or child — who is less than fighting fit is a pull back on the total war effort.

FOOD is your munition of war. The Government sees that you get the right stuff and it's vital that you should know how to use it to full advantage . . .

There's cheese : it makes muscle and bone.

There are potatoes : they give energy and warmth.

Carrots, that give vitality and help you to see in the dark.

Green vegetables, with their valuable salts and vitamins, which are so very important for clear complexions and sound teeth.

Did you know that 5 quarts of summer milk — milk at its richest and when it is most plentiful — go to the making of 1 lb. cheese?

Or that swedes, the juice of which you used to give to babies because of its valuable Vitamin C, are now to be had at most greengrocers cheap enough and in big enough quantities for you to serve as a second or third vegetable to the entire family?

All good live stuff. And you need them all : *every day.* Serve everything appetisingly as you so well can do. Then you can be proud of your vital, active part in the drive to Victory.

(Bombers & Mash)

CHAPTER 3

Special Operations Executive

'The Ministry of Ungentlemanly Warfare'[1]

Find Station 'R'[2]

The Special Operations Executive (SOE) was officially formed by the Minister of Economic Warfare, Hugh Dalton, to conduct espionage, sabotage and reconnaissance in occupied Europe (and later in SE Asia) and to aid local resistance movements.

Few people were aware of SOE's existence and because of this it was sometimes referred to as 'Churchill's Secret Army' or the 'Ministry of Ungentlemanly Warfare'. As the SOE operated in Europe and South-East Asia it was important for recruits to be fluent in a number of languages, allowing local communication with resistance groups and guerrilla armies.

For their operation in South-East Asia, the SOE set up a branch known as 'Force 136'. Its purpose was to promote and organise internal resistance groups in the British imperial areas of Malaya and Burma, threatened by the territorial ambitions of Japan.

Alan Yates

Alan Yates on enlistment
(Peter Yates)

Alan Yates came to Southwell in 1936 when he was appointed to teach Languages at the Minster Grammar School on Church Street, and to assist in the Boarding House. When war broke out, Alan immediately volunteered to join the Army, but was not accepted as at that time teaching was regarded as a 'reserved occupation'.

A few days after war had been declared, I heard an appeal on the radio for anyone who had a good background in Western European languages to apply to join the Armed Forces. So I decided to volunteer. I was 25 years old, fit, male and had no dependents. Like many men I felt I wanted to have a go at this sod Hitler.

I was quickly contacted and asked to travel down for an interview at Aldershot. There, I was interviewed in French by an elderly gentleman. The interviewer said they were looking for three attributes – the ability to speak languages well, the ability to ride a motor bike in daylight or in darkness, road and off-road, and thirdly, the ability to shoot a .38 revolver accurately and quickly. My immediate thought after the interview was that this job sounded a lot more exciting than teaching languages to reluctant pupils in Southwell.

Alan Yates

[1] Wikipedia.org/wiki/Special_Operations_Executive.
[2] Alan Yates, *Find Station R* (Southwell: Unpublished, 1999).

Alan continued teaching in Southwell until after the Dunkirk evacuation in June 1940. Shortly afterwards he received a letter from Army Recruitment stating, 'Owing to the changed position in Northern France, be prepared to be called up.' This happened very soon afterwards and he was asked to go down to Trowbridge.

Alan was given a post in the Royal Signals and assigned to the Special Operations Executive (SOE). Making use of his linguistic skills, his job was to intercept German or French Enigma messages which were in Morse code. He had to record the messages and make notes of any suspicious statements. It was often frustrating because reception could be bad and he could never ask for a repeat. The speed was about twenty words a minute. **Peter Yates**

Some months later he was recommended for commission training, at the time that Japan had broken through in the Far East and was threatening various parts of the British Empire. Alan was told that he would be working in the SOE and be based in India. On the troopship going out he and his fellow recruits had to start learning Urdu. He was commissioned into a Sikh Regiment as Second Lieutenant, and told to report to a Major Watt once he arrived in India.

Special pass on joining Force 136 (Peter Yates)

Having arrived in India, I was involved in one of the daftest interviews I have ever experienced. My interviewer wouldn't tell me about ME 9 because of the Official Secrets Act. On the other hand, I had been told not to reveal anything about the work of the Royal Signals. We boxed clever for twenty minutes until he finally opened up that I would be involved in supporting 'long distance communications'. So I was now transferred to ME 9, which later changed its name to FORCE 136 (Far East Section of the SOE). **Alan Yates**

Alan's base was in a seedy part of Calcutta. The main function of the SOE in the Far East was to work on sabotage exercises; some of this work was in administration. At the time of Alan's arrival British imperial territory in India, Burma and Malaya was faced not only by Japanese aggression but also by the hostile colonial administration of French Indochina, modern-day Vietnam, Laos and Cambodia, which was in the hands of the Vichy French government, a puppet state of Nazi Germany. In his early days in India Alan was expected to use his excellent French to intercept messages sent to and from the French colonial government out there.

Alan's language skills were invaluable during covert operations in what was then French Indo-China. I believe on one occasion he impersonated a French military policeman in an operation against the French forces there.

He once told me that he took the message, over the radio, unencoded - the single word, 'Mauvais' - that was the night when the entire allied communications operation in French Indo-China collapsed - the Japanese had infiltrated the lot. Signals should never have been sent in open language but this one was. That was the last message they got out. **Michael Yates**

Alan Yates in India
(Peter Yates)

At other times it was much more dangerous work, involving operations in the field, especially in Burma.   One such operation was 'Find Station R', and in 1999 Alan Yates wrote a most fascinating account of this mission.

Station 'R' was in fact a clandestine radio station in Burma, belonging to Force 136.   Though it was not situated behind enemy lines, Japanese activity in the area was creating problems for Cpl Jones, the SOE operative, who had established himself and his team in a remote mountain village called Mualnuam.   Mualnuam was perched in the Chin Hills of North Burma, at a height of about 7,000 feet above sea level.

Jones had with him two civilian operators, Mr Joseph and Mr van Ket. Mr Joseph was of Anglo-Burmese extraction and Mr van Ket of Dutch-Malay.   Station 'R' was operating in an isolated spot, some distance from the nearest British forces and accessible only via difficult mountain tracks. During the retreat from Burma, Jones had done a first rate job in keeping his station on air in spite of the severe difficulties inevitably associated with any large scale withdrawal under enemy pressure.   The Japanese forces had already swept through South-East Asia and were knocking ominously on the door of the Indian sub-continent. Alan Yates explains why the SOE operation was urgently needed.

For a time all went well ... but, eventually, unexpected difficulties began to occur. The cause of these difficulties was a progressive failure of power supplies. ... Station 'R' possessed a petrol jenny ... As often happens with things mechanical, wear and tear, aggravated by the many vicissitudes through which Station 'R' had passed, began to take their toll. ... Gradually, very gradually, we began to lose contact. The incoming signals grew weaker, more intermittent, and finally there was complete silence. ... Our transmissions therefore ceased and the final link was broken. Until such times as necessary replacements could be got through to Station 'R', the station and its personnel were on their own.[3]   **Alan Yates**

Two unexpected events quickly changed the situation, the first of which was the surprise arrival in Calcutta of Mr Joseph bringing several pieces of bad news about Station 'R'. He passed on that morale there was understandably very low, and that the operators felt they had been abandoned by Calcutta; the Japanese were very active in the area and there was no certainty that Station 'R' would still be in British hands by the time he got back.

Field Work in India - Alan Yates is the passenger
(Peter Yates)

---
[3] Yates, pp. 4-5.

The second event that came out of the blue was that Alan Yates was summoned to Group HQ and informed that he would be in charge of the relief party, which would be sent to Station 'R' without delay. The relief party had four main objectives; the first and second tasks were to make contact with Station 'R' and then to take fresh supplies of vital stores and other equipment. The third task was to hand over details of the projected new stations, and the fourth was to take in an operator to relieve Jones. The NCO chosen as Jones' replacement was a Cpl Muir.

Now that the relief plan had been decided Mr Joseph was instructed to retrace his steps and alert Jones to what was happening. It was at this point that Alan began to think of likely problems in store.

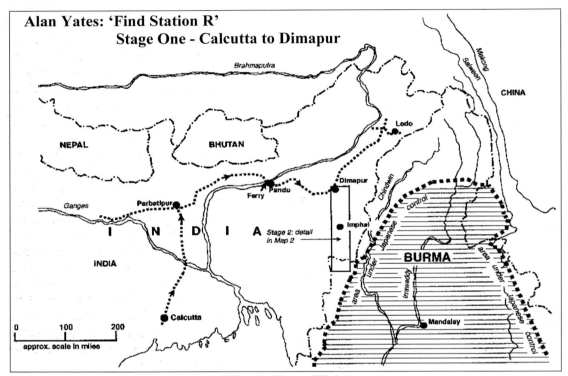

(Map by Trevor Wight)

These were, however, minor matters when compared with the problem of language. The elementary scraps of Urdu which I possessed would see me through India and well on the way beyond ... [but] my total ignorance of any Burmese dialect would surely create difficulties ... However, from the moment I met Ling my cares vanished. So who, you may wonder, was Ling?

Ling was a native of Haka, a village in the Chin hills. For a considerable time it had been occupied by Japanese forces ... but Ling had left his home and joined the British forces in Burma. The plan was that Ling should accompany Muir and myself, together with a team of mules and their drivers as far as Mualnuam. Ling would be in uniform and would act as our interpreter until we reached Station 'R'.

At first meeting Ling I mistook him for a Gurkha ... He was wearing a uniform similar to that of a Gurkha infantryman and the illusion was completed by the murderous kukri hanging from his belt ... squarely behind his back.[4]   **Alan Yates**

---

[4] Yates, pp. 8-9.

A second concern for the relief party was the difficulty of the terrain, and the somewhat 'menacing' traditions of the hill tribes whose territory they would have to pass through.

> ... villages were dotted about those mountains and were linked together by primitive, narrow tracks. A few hours' march separated each village from its neighbour. ... Many of the houses possessed high pointed gables on which were displayed row upon row of skulls ... Until quite recent times, head hunting had been widely practised in these regions, as also in the Naga Hills through which we were also to pass, and occasionally there had been disturbing rumours of even darker practices.[5]
>
> **Alan Yates**

Alan Yates in Colonial Dress
(Peter Yates)

The relief party was now able to get started. Later that day an army lorry collected Ling, Muir and Alan Yates, together with a miscellany of stores, and deposited them at Sealdah station, where they boarded a train taking them to the western bank of the Brahmaputra River. In the absence of a bridge, a ferry conveyed them to the eastern bank and they resumed the railway journey as far as Dimapur. There they were collected by a large military convoy, which took them through the Naga Hills, fortunately without any interference from Japanese planes, which occasionally strafed vehicles proceeding in either direction. This part of the journey ended with a winding descent towards Imphal, the main town of Manipur State and the HQ of IV Corps.

Finding transport from Imphal was hindered by the major withdrawal of British and Indian forces as most of the available vehicles were needed for this operation. In addition to this problem, the Japanese air force arrived and delivered a series of attacks on Imphal. The relief party seized the first opportunity which came along - a small Indian Army truck unit - and 'escaped' to 'Milestone 109'.

> Milestone 109 was a major staging area. Situated on more or less level ground in a valley watered by a river, it contained a wide variety of personnel, stores and transport. ... In addition to wheeled transport, there was a well-stocked mule line, which, although we did not then know it, was able to play an essential role in our mission.

---

[5] Yates, p. 3.

Apart from the urgency of our mission itself there were two other reasons for wanting to move quickly. We were aware of the proposed plan for British withdrawal and the prospect of heading off into the hills in search of Station 'R' and, on return to the British forces, of finding that the area had been taken over by the Japanese, was hardly comforting. The second worry was that the onset of the monsoon rains was imminent. A further consideration was that if we were to suffer further serious delay, Japanese activity in the area of Mualnuam or Siang Pikot might well force Jones and his companions to move their station before we could reach them, in which case we would be faced with a needle-in-a-haystack type of search.

... An unexpected informant [on a road gang] assured Ling that he knew a mountain track leading directly from Milestone 109 to Mualnuam. The track was quite impossible for wheeled transport but was perfectly suitable for mules.

The officer in charge of mule transport was a Major Vernon-Harcourt. Although he gave me a sympathetic hearing, he gave nothing else. Politely, but very firmly, he pointed out that mules were in heavy demand and that every one of his animals was already earmarked for other duties for several days ahead. There was no, repeat NO, possibility of authorising us to use mules.[6]

Alan Yates

Help for the relief party came when Alan sought out the local Signals Officer, Capt. Alan Smith. He discovered that a unit had been allocated nineteen mules, which were no longer required. Alan immediately returned to Major Vernon-Harcourt, who reluctantly agreed to let the party have nine mules and three Indian mule-drivers. Very early the following morning they set off before any further snags arose.

Ling and I led the way, followed by three strings of mules, each trio being led by its own driver, and Muir brought up the rear since he had a rifle and fifty rounds, as did the mule drivers; this seemed a wise arrangement.

The undulating nature of the track was further emphasised by the fact that, whilst the main ridges of hills ran roughly north and south, our own course lay diagonally across the general line. Many of the hillsides were scored by gullies of varying depth and width, some with mountain streams tumbling and foaming down them, others practically dry. Whenever such a gully cut across our route, we had to wind our way down to it and cross the stream bed by a primitive sort of bridge.[7]

Alan Yates

They reached the village of Khaw Bem and were soon the centre of a friendly crowd of people, some wearing virtually nothing, others were very well clothed, including beads and bones. After leaving Khaw Bem they arrived at a further village, Tui Tang. Facing them were two upright stone pillars about shoulder high, one set on either side of the track. Attached to each pillar was a wooden pole. These poles were decorated with scraps of coloured rag-like material and on each pole was transfixed a number of animal skulls. Their fears were immediately aroused. Was human headhunting still practised?

Whether these grisly installations were intended to warn off unwelcome strangers, to scare away evil spirits or merely to mark territorial boundaries I have no idea ... I think that we were all somewhat relieved by the absence of human skulls for the Chins, like the Nagas, had very recently been notorious headhunters.[8]

Alan Yates

[6] Yates, pp. 18-20.
[7] Yates, p. 24.
[8] Yates, p. 26.

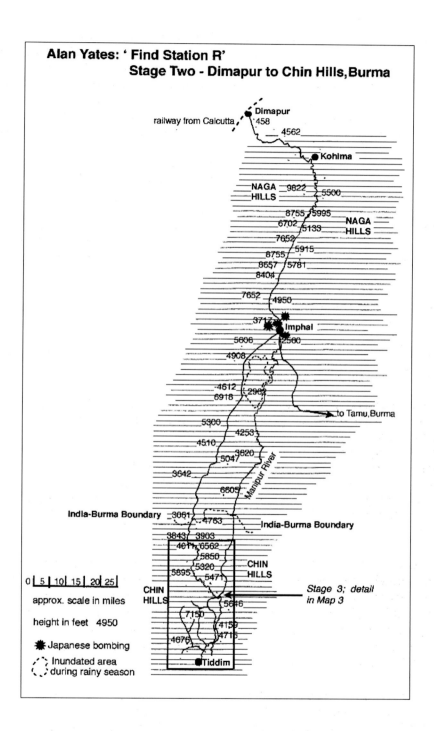

(Map by Trevor Wight)

The party passed through several more villages, most of which had the gable ends of huts liberally decorated with skulls of animals, before camp was struck. They were keen to remain long enough in the villages to establish friendly relations since they might need local support on the way back. Usually the headman of the village provided a tribesman guide to take them to the limit of their territory, but they would never venture beyond that limit. On this first day progress had been rather disappointing, due mainly to the arduous nature of the track; on the other hand, they had been lucky to 'escape' from Imphal with the mules, and even luckier to meet Ling's friend at Milestone 109, with his valuable information.

Day 2 started with an exhausting footslog up hill and down dale, beneath an unforgiving sun and punctuated by anxious moments each time the mules were called upon to cross the tree trunk 'bridges' over the numerous mountain streams.

> It was at one such bridge that we suffered our first and only loss of stores. One of the mules - the tail-ender of the middle trio - missed his footing and fell into the almost dry stream bed below. The drop was only a matter of a few feet ... and we were able to haul him out and get him onto the track again. The animal itself was undamaged but unfortunately it was carrying two containers of concentrated sulphuric acid, one on either side. An examination of its load revealed that one of the containers was cracked and that very corrosive acid was beginning to seep out. ... There was only one thing to be done - to remove and dump the damaged container. ... Had it broken in the process, the consequences both to beast and to burden could well have been horrific.[9]
> **Alan Yates**

On their way through Panzang and Tungzang, where again they saw huts decorated with skulls, some possibly human, they acquired a few additions to their provisions, partly by barter, partly by purchase. After a heavy tropical storm they struck camp for the night. In the evening they reflected that they had been lucky that the container of acid only cracked, when it could have been broken.

When the third day dawned, they were aware that they were now within striking distance of Mualnuam but a real challenge awaited them. Their route lay along the crest of a long mountain ridge and the state of the track was worrying following a minor landslide. Where the track had once been there was now a drift of loose scree and, to make things worse, both the inner and outer slopes were very severe. Whilst a man could turn and twist in such a location, it was difficult for a loaded mule to do so.

> An outcrop of rock projected into the path. There was sufficient space for a man to pass without falling over the outer edge, but for a mule, especially a loaded mule, such a passage seemed out of the question. ... The situation seemed quite hopeless.[10]
> **Alan Yates**

In this critical situation Alan requested the NCO in charge of the mules not to risk more than one mule at a time. The NCO led the first mule as far as the rock, where Muir and Alan were waiting to help get it safely around. The plan was to repeat this process with the other mules, but it didn't quite work out.

---

[9] Yates, p. 28.
[10] Yates, p. 33.

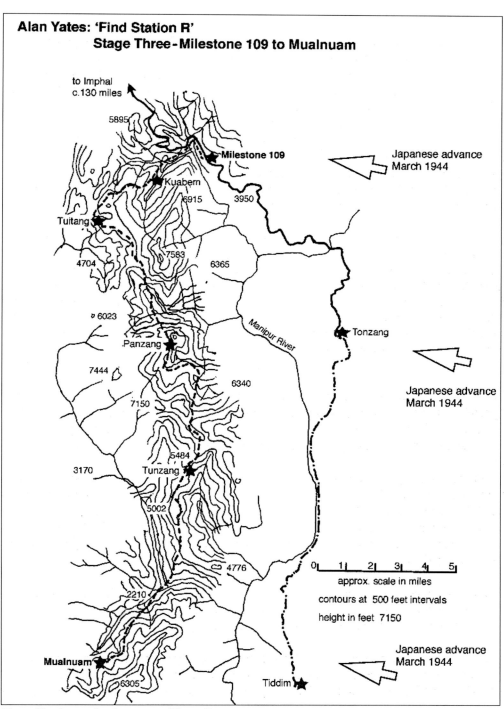

Alan Yates: 'Find Station R'
Stage Three - Milestone 109 to Mualnuam

to Imphal
c.130 miles

5895

Milestone 109

Japanese advance
March 1944

Kuabem

6915   3950

Tuitang

4704

7583

6365

6023

Manipur River

Panzang

Tonzang

7444

6340

7150

Japanese advance
March 1944

5484

Tunzang

3170

5002

4776

0 1 2 3 4 5
approx. scale in miles

contours at 500 feet intervals

height in feet 7150

2210

Mualnuam

6305   Tiddim

Japanese advance
March 1944

Note: Kuabem, also known as Khaw Bem

(Map by Trevor Wight)

On next looking round the bend to see how he was getting on with the first animal, I froze with horror. Instead of bringing up a single animal, he had released everyone from its companions and now all nine were making their way up the track entirely unaccompanied! ... As if to add to our worries, one or two of the mules would pause briefly to help itself to a bit of edible plant and would move on only when butted from the rear by the next in line.[11]   **Alan Yates**

Muir and Alan now expected the worst - at least one mule, if not more, falling from the track - but they had both underestimated the qualities of an army mule. One by one the animals passed round the rock without so much as a pause though the distance between the upper edge of the rock and the lower part of the loads could not have been more than an inch or two.

From there progress to Mualnuam was resumed, the now familiar pattern of long winding climbs alternating with similarly long winding descents. After wading across the River Psao, Mualnuam was now close by, perched high on a hill. Was it still in British control? They were soon to find out. A group of three figures came out to meet the relief party. One of the trio was a tribesman, the second proved to be Jones and the third was Mr Joseph. Jones was clearly happy to know that his relief had at last arrived.

Station 'R' had been established in one of the native houses. Like its neighbours it was well built of wood and consisted essentially of one big, general-purpose room. In one corner stood the long defunct generator, the prime source of the problem. The mules were unloaded and the stores brought into the hut before Jones took Muir on a conducted tour of the station.

When they returned Jones surprised Alan with an unusual invitation. A member of the village community had recently died and the early part of the funeral ceremony was taking place. The headman had told him that two of their party could witness the Chin funeral ceremony if they wished. Since to decline such an invitation would have seemed rude, Jones and Alan made their way to the hut where the funeral rites were being observed. A rectangular slab of hard pressed earth occupied the centre of the floor, and in the middle of the slab a small fire of smouldering logs provided a steady stream of smoke. The corpse was positioned near the edge of the slab.

The corpse had been secured sitting cross-legged in a rather Buddha-like position, its sightless eyes staring fixedly on the dully glowing embers ... The redness of the light given off by the smouldering logs and the fact that such light fell obliquely onto the dead face from a sharp angle below, created a macabre effect ... The corpse ... was being slowly dehydrated by the heat of the fire ... causing a shrinkage of the body tissues ... the resulting contraction of a sinew or a muscle would produce a slight movement ... The combined effect of the changing play of dim light on the face and the unnatural movements of the limbs was something I shall long remember.[12]

Alan Yates

Returning to their hut, they re-joined Muir, Ling, van Ket and Mr Joseph. Stories were exchanged and a celebration meal prepared. The atmosphere was positively festive; it had been a good day. On the return journey Alan Yates and his relief group expected to make much better time since the major obstacles had been dealt with. They decided to reduce their rations to a minimum so that the extra food could be left at Station 'R'. They wound their way down the track and took one last look back at Mualnuam, aware that they were unlikely to return again. There were still some hours of daylight left when they arrived at Panzang, but Alan decided to call it a day as he was concerned about the state of Jones' feet.

---

[11] Yates, p. 34.
[12] Yates, p. 38.

While we were still preparing our meal, we had our first surprise in the shape of an odd-looking figure who arrived, unannounced. The unexpected visitor was a young man dressed not in native fashion like the rest of the villagers, but wearing a turban and a sort of knee-length off-white coat partially embroidered with coloured threads. Round his waist he wore a broad, red belt in the style of a cummerbund, and gave the general impression of being an imitation of an Indian mess waiter. But a far bigger surprise followed his arrival, for he addressed me in English ... For some reason I was most uneasy about his presence and felt instinctively that he must be treated with caution.[13]

Alan Yates

The stranger explained that he was 'son of headman' and had learnt to speak English while serving as an NCO in the local levy [conscription of men for war]. He proposed to Alan that he would be his 'bearer' during their stay in his village and seemed keen to show the villagers that he knew the ways of the British, including speaking to them in their own language. By now a sizeable crowd had arrived on the scene, but a few words from 'son of headman' and the crowd moved out quietly. Alan's party settled down to what they thought would be a good night's sleep. How wrong they were.

How long we had been asleep it is impossible to say but well after dark I was awakened by a wild confusion of sounds. Human voices, some chanting, some yelling, some hysterically laughing, mingled with the clash of metal against metal and the rhythmic thudding of some form of percussion device; even more worrying was the sporadic discharge of firearms. For a short time I lay still, listening to the din and trying, without success, to decide exactly what was happening. The noise seemed to be coming not from within the village itself, but from a short distance beyond its limits.[14]

Alan Yates

With some alarm the party looked out into the darkness and saw, on the hillside above the village, the light from burning torches. The tribesmen seemed to be in a state of considerable agitation. A long procession formed and began to wind its way towards the village.

It is one thing to have been assured, as we had been, that headhunting was by now a thing of the past; it is quite another to find oneself completely outnumbered and sleeping in a village such as this, still well out of contact with any British forces or other possible sources of help ... I think that both Jones and I were again uneasily conscious of the many skulls that decorated the gable ends of the houses.[15]

Alan Yates

Jones had his rifle and the usual fifty rounds, Alan had his pistol and twelve rounds, and the three mule drivers were also armed. They could do nothing but wait. When the crowd arrived there followed renewed shouting and loud banging on the wooden poles, but to their great relief no attempt was made to force the gate.

Next a bonfire was lit, and this was the occasion for a further outburst of yelling, chanting, clashing of metal and the firing of numerous shots. They had no means of knowing what it was all about, so they didn't go back to bed until they were reasonably certain the tribesmen had no intention of harming them. The next morning 'son of headman' re-appeared.

---

[13] Yates, p. 43.
[14] Yates, p. 44.
[15] Yates, p. 45.

I assured him that we had slept very well - we thought that there had been some degree of noise through the night but that, being tired from our earlier march, such disturbance, if any, had not caused any problem - especially as we knew that we were among friends! He appeared well pleased by this reply and added: 'You see, much noise, big wedding'.[16]   **Alan Yates**

Alan Yates with an SOE colleague in India/Burma
(Peter Yates)

A few hours later a friendly departure followed and, apart from a few problems selecting the right tracks and finding a suitable camp for the night, Milestone 109 was reached without too much difficulty. By the next night the relief party had re-joined their own forces. Their first duty was to report back to Major Vernon-Harcourt and return his mules and drivers. Major Vernon-Harcourt announced with a certain satisfaction that Alan had to report back immediately to HQ IV Corps, where he felt there would be a ticking off in store for taking nine mules when they were needed elsewhere. However, Alan felt he had no cause for concern as the task of finding Station 'R', relieving Jones, installing Muir in his place, and getting the station on the air again had now been accomplished.

Looking back many years later, Alan Yates recounted his principal memory of the mission.

I am unlikely to ever forget Jones, Muir, Ling, Mr van Ket and Mr Joseph; all were involved in this eventful journey which, beginning in the outskirts of Calcutta, led through North-Eastern India, across the Brahmaputra River and from there via Assam, to a remote village in the Chin Hills of Northern Burma ... at a moment when the forces of Imperial Japan were knocking ominously on the door of the Indian sub-continent.[17]   **Alan Yates**

He also wrote of what happened to his colleagues in the period immediately after the return from Station 'R'.

---

[16] Yates, p. 46.
[17] Yates, p. 1.

Jones was immediately promoted to the rank of Sergeant but equally instantly he burst into song! Day in day out he hummed, 'I'm dreaming of a White Xmas' until we were all driven out of our minds. ... Ling successfully made his way back into his native Haka and spent a very useful period there without being discovered by the enemy. ... [As for Muir] not long after he had taken control of the station, the Japanese overran the whole area. Not only did he save himself and his two assistants, but he saved a major part of his equipment, including all the top secret material ... His efforts earned him a well-deserved 'Mention in Despatches'.[18]   **Alan Yates**

Not long after Alan's mission to Burma, in the spring of 1944, Japanese armies attempted to destroy Allied forces at Imphal and invade India. After an epic struggle the British 14th Army, under Lieut-General Slim, drove the Japanese back inflicting heavy losses. Together with the Battle of Kohima, the Battle of Imphal was the turning point of the Burma Campaign. Alan Yates, by now promoted to Captain, was still in India when the war in Europe, and later in the Far East, ended. He remembered being told of the German surrender by the Argyll and Sutherland Highlanders. This was the day before the news filtered through to England.

Everyone was over the moon in Calcutta about the war finishing. I remember seeing a Brigadier enthusiastically pulling a rickshaw and gesturing to the old Indian lady to go and sit in the seat!
                    Alan Yates

On his return home Alan resumed his teaching post at the Minster Grammar School and remained there until the 1970s, when it became a comprehensive school. He lived on the Ropewalk with his wife Betty and three sons, Michael, John and Peter. Peter encouraged him to write down at least some of his wartime experiences, which he did in 1999. Alan died on 25th February 2013, aged 98.

---

[18] Yates, p. 50.

(Home Front)

CHAPTER 4

'... we shall fight with ... growing strength in the air ...'[1]

The enormous importance of air power in modern warfare was recognised in 1936-9, when the German Luftwaffe played such a prominent role in the Spanish Civil War. To be able to compete with the Luftwaffe, the RAF had to start producing aircraft on an ever increasing scale, along with essential equipment and armament.

In addition, there was a need to form new squadrons and recruit both air and ground crews to fly and maintain the aircraft coming off the production line.

The image of the RAF was probably deceptively glamorous compared with the more established armed forces. However, life for the 'Brylcreem boys' was often unimaginably stressful and tragically short.

One of the many dramatic stories of WW2 is the sinking of the great German battleship *Bismarck* on 27th May 1941. A key person in this remarkable story was Michael Suckling from Southwell.

Michael Suckling, photographic reconnaissance in Coastal Command

Michael Suckling with a model of the Bismarck
(Southwell History Society)

'... the picture that sank a mighty battleship ...'[2]

SPOTTED THE BISMARCK
Flying Officer M Suckling of Southwell
Behind the sinking of the German battleship, *Bismarck*, lies the story of the vigilance of a young Southwell airman, Flying Officer Michael Suckling, while on reconnaissance patrol.[3]

Michael was the son of Frank and Marjorie Suckling of 'The Gables', Southwell and the great-grandson of horticulturist Henry Merryweather. He attended Southwell Minster Grammar School and then, thanks to the British Legion, transferred to Ellesmere College, where his father had been. After two years working at Merryweather's nurseries he joined the RAF in the spring of 1939 and was commissioned as a Pilot Officer, seeing service over Dunkirk during the evacuation in June 1940.

Michael was then appointed to Coastal Command's Photographic Reconnaissance Unit and sent to the north of Scotland, to the PRU outstation at Wick, located at a wild and lonely place on the top of

[1] Extract from Winston Churchill's speech to the House of Commons, 4th June 1940.
[2] Taylor Downing, *Spies in the Sky* (London: Little Brown, 2011), p. 135.
[3] *N/Adv*, 13th January 1943.

Michael Suckling with his Mother and Nana at The Gables, Southwell
(Peter Yates)

the Caithness cliffs not far from John O'Groats. The base housed a handful of pilots and a small team of First Phase interpreters. The selection of pilots for photographic reconnaissance work was rigorous as the job was regarded as being extremely hazardous. To be selected for this role Michael Suckling must have been an exceptional pilot, and his familiarity with flying Spitfires would have been a great asset.

The purpose of photographic reconnaissance was to record German naval activity. Keeping the sea lanes open was of critical importance for Britain's survival.

> It takes a special sort of individual to be able to fly for hours at a time, unarmed, over enemy territory simply to take a set of photographs, perhaps of a single factory or ship, and then to get home again. ... In 1940 Air Chief Marshal Bowhill, the head of Coastal Command, laid down three qualifications for new pilots joining the Photographic Reconnaissance Unit. First, they must have considerable experience; second, a real ability to navigate; and third, they must have ... an 'above average combination of conscientiousness, daring, self-reliance and initiative.[4]

After his move to Photo Reconnaissance, Michael went on a training programme at RAF Wick to learn the new skills required. The course lasted 2-4 weeks, during which time pilots also converted from twin-engine aircraft to single-engine ones, such as the Spitfire which Michael flew. One problem for Michael and all PRU pilots was that when faced with enemy fighters their natural instinct was to engage the 'bandit' at once. This was not an option as the guns and armour plating had been removed from the aircraft to enable the pilot to fly faster and to attain greater height. 'You don't need guns when you're flying the fastest planes in the sky.'[5] Another problem PRU pilots faced on long sorties or missions was the risk of running out of aviation fuel. A Spitfire

[4] Downing, pp. 130-4.
[5] Downing, p. 133.

used about a gallon of fuel every minute, so some pilots returned with only a few gallons left in their tanks. That was cutting it very fine.

   A Spitfire flown by a PRU pilot was likely to be heavy with fuel at the start of its flight, and the pilot needed the longest possible run to get airborne. Then he would climb to maybe 25,000-30,000 ft. At this height it is bitterly cold and cockpits were unheated; there was always the possibility that gauges or measures would freeze up. Most aircrew didn't like to wear electrically heated suits but dressed for the intense cold. At great height a pilot's main problem, apart from preventing his hands from freezing, was stopping his Perspex canopy misting up.[6] Two further difficulties for PRU pilots were finding the precise location and then carrying out the photography. The Spitfire was single-seated - it was all dependent on the pilot. In later years the Mosquito fighter-bomber was developed for photo-reconnaissance, with a navigator on board - a major step forward.

Michael Suckling (fourth left) and pilot colleagues (Celia Steven)

The reconnaissance pilot had just in front of him, in the pouch on his knee, a map. After several hours flying across enemy territory, he needed pinpoint navigation skills to know his precise location. … But a higher wind than anticipated up in the altitudes … could throw out all his calculations.

   … Once over the target … the pilot would begin his aerial photography. Aiming the cameras was not easy and required experience. They were mounted behind the cockpit, so the pilot had to bank the aircraft steeply, straightening out only when the target was disappearing under the nose, and turn the cameras on as it passed below the aircraft. … Each camera (usually 2 or 3) could take up to 500 separate exposures.[7]

Despite these challenging circumstances, most PRU pilots were happy just to be flying Spitfires - quite simply it was most pilots' favourite aircraft. They felt it fitted them like a glove and the

---

[6] Downing, pp. 1-2.
[7] Downing, pp. 139-40.

aircraft almost became part of them by reacting to their every move. However, the Coastal Command flights were a long, lonely business.

Michael Suckling arrived at RAF Wick Coastal Command at a critical time. During the winter of 1940-1 it was feared by the British government that the biggest battleships and battle cruisers in the German Navy would leave their docks, enter the Atlantic and have a field day hunting the convoys and unescorted merchantmen en route to British ports. This fear became real when two of Germany's largest battle cruisers, the *Scharnhorst* and the *Gneisenau*, left their docks at Kiel at the end of December 1940. Fortunately, the photo reconnaissance pilots spotted the battle cruisers and a later air raid caused major damage to the *Gneisenau*.[8]

Coastal Command's major target, however, was the *Bismarck*, the most powerful battleship in Germany's navy, with eight 15" heavy guns. Despite its size it was faster than any battleship in the Royal Navy. For weeks RAF pilots were sent on photo reconnaissance missions to find the *Bismarck* and to report immediately its location.

> On 19th May 1941, Germany's newest battleship, [the] *Bismarck*, slipped its moorings in the port of Gydia in the Baltic and accompanied by its escort, the heavy cruiser *Prinz Eugen*, sailed across the Baltic … towards the coast of Norway en route to the Atlantic Ocean. … On crossing the Baltic, two large ships were spotted by a Swedish warship and the Swedes alerted the Admiralty in London. At this point it was not known which ships had been spotted - only that they were large.[9]

In view of this report, the Air Ministry realised that if the German ships had reached Norwegian waters they would be in range of the photo reconnaissance flights out of Wick. On 21st May 1941 the senior officer instructed Michael, or 'Babe' Suckling as he was nicknamed, to photograph enemy ships including, hopefully, the *Bismarck*. Her mission was to create havoc with the Atlantic convoys, thus threatening the supply lines to Britain; she had to be stopped at all costs.

Thus, at just after 11 a.m. on 21st May, Michael Suckling took off in his Spitfire to photograph the enemy ships in the Norwegian fiords in the Bergen area, on what proved to be one of the famous PR sorties of the war. Michael's Spitfire hit Norway just below Bergen and he followed the coast at high altitude, banking left every few minutes to look down on the grey fiords below. Whilst on his reconnaissance, Michael located a large battleship he felt sure was the *Bismarck*, in Grimstadfjord south of Bergen.

> On one of his many banks to the left he suddenly saw something that made him nearly leap out of his seat. He threw the Spitfire into a steep vertical dive to get a better look. Far below he could see in the fiord the specks of … six ships. One was large, probably a cruiser, and it was surrounded by destroyers. Suckling levelled off, turned his camera on and flew across the fiord, carrying on to Bergen … He was just turning for home when he spotted another group of ships in the fiord below. Here was yet another large ship and three more merchantmen. At 1.15 p.m. Suckling turned on his cameras again, flew the length of the fiord and then turned west. He had got what he came for![10]

---

[8] The *Gneisenau* was seriously damaged in an air raid on 26th February 1940 whilst still in dry dock. It was beyond repair.

[9] Downing, p. 143.

[10] Downing, p. 144.

To complete his task, Michael Suckling needed to return safely to headquarters with his special collection of photographs, so he flew straight back to Wick and landed at about 2.30 p.m. As he climbed out of the cockpit, he called out excitedly to the aircrew, 'I've seen them! Two of them! I think they're cruisers, though one could be a battleship.'[11] It took an hour for the photographs to be processed. When Michael returned to base, the Chief Interpretation Officer, David Linton, could barely believe what he saw. In his mind there was no question that Michael Suckling's photographs showed the location of the *Bismarck*.

The first ship that Suckling had photographed was the heavy cruiser *Prinz Eugen* and in the second fiord was none other than the most powerful ship in the German navy, the *Bismarck*, but Linton was able to confirm that there were no booms around the ship to protect it from torpedoes. It looked like the ships were about to sail.[12]

However, Coastal Command headquarters were not prepared to take the word of a mere Pilot Officer, and Air Chief Marshal Bowhill demanded to see the photographs himself. No aircraft were available to fly the photographs south, so Michael Suckling jumped into his Spitfire, despite just returning from his long sortie, refuelled and offered to deliver the photographs himself. The exciting story of Michael Suckling's dash to London was covered by the *Newark Advertiser*.

Spotted the Bismarck
Flying Officer Michael Suckling of Southwell

Michael Suckling's famous photograph of the Bismarck (Spies in the Sky)

The exploits of this daring officer are told in 'Coastal Command' ... which is now on sale ...

Delivered the Pictures
No communication aeroplane was available to fly south, so Suckling jumped into a Spitfire and took the pictures himself. Night forced him to land on the outskirts of Nottingham (actually Newark) and not far from his home town, but he refused to be beaten. In the town a friend of his owned a garage. Suckling 'phoned him, had a car filled with petrol and, with the garage proprietor at the wheel, drove south through the black-out at more than 50 mph. At 1 a.m. the precious pictures were on Sir Frederick Bowhill's desk.

Flying Officer Suckling, who was 21 when he took the momentous photographs, which meant the end of the *Bismarck*, and who was reported missing on 21st July 1941, was 'Mentioned in Despatches' for his 'fine piece of work'.[13]

The photographs revealed the great news that Michael Suckling had indeed photographed the *Prinz Eugen* and the mighty *Bismarck*. Then began one of the most famous chases in naval history. Warships were immediately

---

[11] Downing, p. 145.
[12] Downing, p. 146.
[13] *N/Adv,* 13th January 1943.

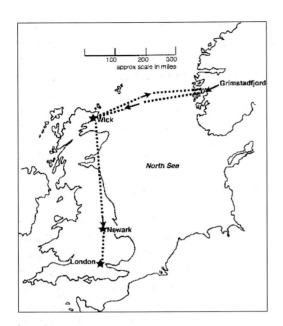 

Michael Suckling's flight to Norway and route to London with pictures of the Bismarck
(Maps by Trevor Wight)

despatched to intercept the *Bismarck*. The order was sent out by the Admiralty, 'Sink the *Bismarck*.' After losing HMS *Hood* early in the naval engagement, six days later the battleships HMS *Rodney* and HMS *King George V* closed in for the kill. The *Bismarck* was badly damaged and its rudder was so severely disabled that it could do no more than sail around in a circle; the *Bismarck* finally went down with the loss of nearly two thousand crew.

For his work in finding the *Bismarck*, Michael Suckling 'became a hero within the RAF. Along with this acclaim, the work of the photo reconnaissance and interpretation teams suddenly became famous.' Two months later Michael was flying another mission, this time from St Eval in Cornwall. On 21st June 1941 he was sent to take pictures of two other German battleships, the *Scharnhorst* and the *Gneisenau* in the French port of La Rochelle. He did not return. It is understood that Michael needed to go in at low level, as was often required, to supplement the less risky high level shots. At low level an unarmed Spitfire was relatively easy prey for the flak defences. 'No one ever knew what happened to him. Such was the life and death of a pilot in photo reconnaissance.'[14]

Air Ministry records show that on 23rd July, two days after Michael Suckling's failure to return from his mission, a letter, signed by Charles Evans, was sent to Mrs Suckling informing her of his regret that Michael was reported missing, but at the same time suggesting that it wasn't impossible that Michael might now be a POW, in which case he would contact his mother first rather than the Air Ministry. If this occurred, Mrs Suckling was requested to pass this information to the Air Ministry.[15] A further letter was sent by the Air Ministry to Mrs Suckling on 29th

---

[14] Downing, p. 147.
[15] Air Ministry Records, 23rd July 1941. Charles Evans was the principal assistant secretary, personnel. (Paul Stevenson)

By the KING'S Order the name of
Flying Officer M. J. Suckling,
Royal Air Force,
was published in the London Gazette on
11 June, 1942,
as mentioned in a Despatch for distinguished service.
I am charged to record
His Majesty's high appreciation.

Archibald Sinclair

Secretary of State for Air

Mentioned in Despatches Certificate awarded to
Michael Suckling
(Celia Steven)

November 1941 revealing that 'in view of the lapse of time, it is felt that there can now be of little hope of his [Michael] being alive, but action to presume that he has lost his life will not be taken until at least six months from the date on which he was reported missing'.[16] Mrs Suckling replied to this in a letter dated 3rd December in which she reluctantly agreed with the conclusions reached by the Air Ministry. 'There is very faint hope that more will ever be known of his fate.'[17]

In tribute to Michael Suckling his Commanding Officer said that his work was outstanding, both for his keenness and sheer bravery, while his Intelligence Officer described him as an 'Ace' among them. Unsurprisingly, Michael Suckling was posthumously awarded a 'Mentioned in Despatches' certificate. This award was published in the London Gazette on 11th June 1942. It wasn't until the following year, 1943, that people in Southwell and district were made aware of Michael Suckling's historic mission in locating the mighty German battleship *Bismarck*.

Ian Stanley Cash Linney, bomber pilot in 107 Squadron

'The Mosquito was the best aircraft you could possibly fly.' Ian Linney

Born in Farnsfield in 1922 and educated at Oundle School, Ian Linney later lived for a time in Ravenshead before coming in postwar years to reside on Burgage Lane, Southwell. Ian had always had a passionate interest in aircraft, so it was no surprise when he signed up to join the RAF in December 1940. His early days were spent in training on various airfields from Stratford-on-Avon, to Aberystwyth in Wales and Montrose in Scotland. At some point in 1942 he became a Flying Instructor at RAF Sibson near Peterborough in Cambridgeshire. This airfield was first used in 1940 for training naval pilots; from January to June 1941 the Oxfords of No. 14 Service Flying Training School RAF were based there. Ian Linney's

Ian Linney (left) at Epinoy, France in 1944
(Nick Linney)

[16] Air Ministry Records, 29th November 1941.
[17] Letter - Mrs Suckling to Air Ministry, 3rd December 1941.
(Paul Stevenson)

preference, however, was to become an operational pilot, so he asked to see his local Commander and requested a change of role. Around this time, as was the custom amongst aircrew, Ian found he had acquired a nickname, 'Bull' Linney, chosen because he was blessed with a wide neck.

Ian's request to be given an operational role was granted and he was selected for 107 Squadron, which by October 1944 had moved to Lasham in Hampshire. From early 1944 107 Squadron replaced its Boston bombers with Mosquito FB.VIs. The Mosquito FB.VI, which Ian Linney came to worship, boasted the same armaments as the fighter version, but had the additional capability of being able to carry two 500 lb bombs in the rear half of the bomb bay - the forward half was taken up with cannon breeches.

Mosquito Aircraft together with Pilot's Notes
(Nick Linney)

As far back as September 1939, Sidney Cotton had predicted the demand for a two-seater photo reconnaissance aircraft with a range of at least 1,500 miles. The De Havilland Mosquito was the answer to this prayer. Geoffrey de Havilland had years of experience for designing and building high speed aircraft and many of these had fuselages made of wood. ... With metals in very short supply in wartime Britain, the De Havilland team set about building a fast bomber that could outfly enemy fighters, with a shell built out of birch plywood filled with lightweight balsa wood. Designed with two engines for a crew of two, a pilot and navigator-bomber, it was a brilliant piece of engineering. ... With the power of a bomber and the speed and agility of a fighter, the Mosquito was a winner. In its trials in early 1941 it established itself as the world's fastest operational aircraft. It would remain so until the era of jet-powered fighters.[18]

Wing racks were fitted on the Mosquito FB.VI to carry two 50-gallon drop tanks or a further two 500 lb bombs. It had a two-man crew, could undertake a round trip of 1,000 miles, carrying 4,000 rounds of .303 ammunition, 1,000 rounds of cannon shell and 2,000 lbs of bombs, and still be able to cruise at between 255 and 325 mph.[19]

---

[18] Downing, p. 148.
[19] Martin Bowman, *Mosquito Bomber/Fighter-Bomber Units 1942-45* (Oxford: Osprey, 2010), p. 54.

THE SQUADRON CREST

107 Squadron's Crest
(http://www.raf.mod.uk/history/
107squadron.cfmt)

In early 1944 the Mosquito FB.VI units were kept busy destroying V1 flying-bomb launch sites in the Pas de Calais. Following the successful D-Day landings, 107 Squadron's Mosquito FB.VIs' role was patrolling across and behind enemy lines, attacking troop movements and anything in the way of enemy activity on the ground. In September 1944 the 'Mossies' played a supporting role in the airborne landings at Arnhem.

Ian Linney's third pilot's logbook reveals that he became an intruder and photo reconnaissance pilot. He first became involved in nightly intruder missions from Lasham on 1st October 1944. These missions were offensive operations, by day or night, with the primary object of destroying enemy aircraft in the vicinity of their bases. Other targets were enemy held railway stations, engines, railway junctions, bridges and viaducts, yards, buildings, points and sidings - anything to stop enemy reinforcements being brought up.

Operating mainly along the Rhine from the Ruhr to the Dutch border, 107 Squadron's operations were designed to cut off the enemy forces west of the Rhine from the supplies and reinforcements east of the river. The operations were so successful that the German forces in western Holland were virtually without supplies from Germany and it took as long as four days to cover 300 miles by rail.[20]

A typical operation was on 1st October 1944 when twelve squadron crews claimed successful attacks on 27 trains and several strings of barges without loss to themselves. Later in October, during a period of bad weather which restricted operations, eight aircraft joined in the final softening-up of the enemy defences on Walcheren Island prior to the Canadian Army's final assault. In that month Ian Linney's pilot's logbook (no. 3) shows that he was involved in a number of these strikes.[21]

Oct 1st 1944 Mosquito Z, F/Sgt Bilborough navigator. Patrol - Cleves - Wesel - Dorsten - Munster - Osnabruck. Attacked two trains with cannon. No strikes seen.

Oct 5th 1944 Mosquito Z, F/Sgt Bilborough navigator. Patrol - Deventer - Almelo - Hengelo - Rheine - Osnabruck. Attacked train, bomb overshot, cannon, strikes seen on troops.

Oct 9th 1944 Mosquito Z, F/Sgt Bilborough navigator. Patrol - Walcheren Island. Nothing seen. Landed Thorney Is.

On 19th November 107 Squadron moved from Lasham to the Continent and, despite the worsening weather conditions, from 21st November ten aircraft operated against the enemy from its new base at Cambrai/Epinoy in Northern France. While based near Cambrai 107 Squadron adopted a 'song' composed by Fl. Lt Jim Lee. An extract from the song captures perfectly the Squadron's mood during this period of the war.

---

[20] B S Northway, *A History of 107 Squadron* (107 Squadron: unpublished, c1963), p. 61.
[21] 107 Squadron, pp. 60-1.

107 Squadron Song

When late at night they send us out
To give the Hun another clout
Through sleet, fog, flak and fighter flare
Nous y serons, nous y serons
We shall be there.

When peace breaks out and fighting's done
No more we'll blast the bloody Hun
When booze flows freely everywhere
Nous y serons, nous y serons
We shall be there.

When Hawkers stand in Civvy Street,
With tattered sleeve and ragged seat
And 'Buy One!' is their plaintive prayer,
Nous y serons, nous y serons
We shall be there.[22]

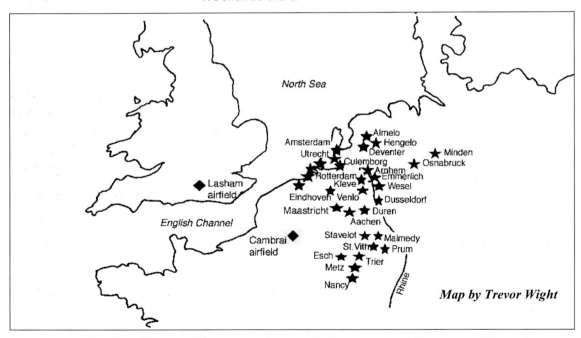

The Rhine Barrier: Targets attacked by 107 Squadron, Sept 1944 - Jan 1945

During November 107 Squadron continued its attacks, ranging beyond the Rhine to the Dutch coast. Key cities such as Dusseldorf, the German capital of the state of North Rhine/Westphalia, important for its industry and oil facilities, were targeted.

[22] 107 Squadron, pp. 66-7.

The bombing campaign at this time also aimed at preventing supplies and reinforcements being brought in from Germany as Ian Linney's logbook for November 1944 showed that Zutphen, an important regional centre, and Deventer and Hengelo, key towns on the railway route east, were specially targeted. The November logbook (no. 3) entry also indicated that when the Germans were forced to use barges because the railways couldn't cope, the barges were attacked as well:

Nov 1st 1944 Mosquito Z, F/Sgt Bilborough. Patrol - Walcheren. Gun position attacked, cannon MG. Diverted to ford.

Nov 5th 1944 Mosquito Z, F/Sgt Bilborough. Patrol - Zutphen - Dusseldorf - Roermond - Arnhem. 2 trains attacked, bomb and cannon. Flak. No strikes seen.

Nov 29th 1944 Mosquito Z, F/Sgt Bilborough. Patrol - Zutphen - Hengelo - Almelo - Deventer. Barges bombed (4). No results, cannon strikes on two barges.

On 16th December the German General von Runstedt launched his surprise counter-attack in the Ardennes, eventually known as the 'Battle of the Bulge'. This offensive was the enemy's final bold effort to stave off defeat. Good progress was made by the German army at first, largely because poor weather conditions prevented proper use of allied air forces. 107 Squadron could only operate eleven aircraft on 17th/18th December and only seven the next night. Ian Linney's logbook entry reveals the lack of progress.

Dec 17th 1944 Mosquito Z, F/Sgt Bilborough navigator. Patrol - Lemmer - Leeuwarden - Groningen - Delfzijl - saw nothing.

However, on the nights of 22nd and 23rd December, fifteen sorties were made as the weather in the target area was excellent. The ground was snow-covered and with clear visibility and a half moon, roads and railways could be seen quite clearly. All aircraft in the sorties achieved some hits. The following night seventeen sorties were flown against General von Runstedt's army, again with considerable success, and on Christmas Eve 107 Squadron learned of the award of eight DFCs to its members. On that night 34 sorties were flown with great success and it fell to 107 Squadron to supply the main effort from the 2nd Tactical Air Force, since all airfields in Northern Europe, with the exception of Cambrai and Driffield, were fogbound that Christmas Eve night.[23]

Dec 23rd 1944 Mosquito Z, F/Sgt Bilborough navigator. Patrol - Pronsfeld area. Railway bridge attack; hit line. Transport attacked, one left burning.

Dec 24th 1944 Mosquito Z, F/Sgt Bilborough navigator. Patrol - Stadkyll - Mechernich - Grasdorf. Attacked transport with cannon RM/G. Hits.

Ian Linney was never likely to forget his involvement in the Battle of the Bulge. On his second sortie on Christmas Eve 1944 he had an amazing escape.

At this critical time in the Battle of the Bulge, Mosquito pilots were instructed to do two or, if possible, three bombing sorties on the advancing German tanks. The Mosquitos received a heavy 'pasting' from the German armour and father needed all his piloting skills to get away from the

---

[23] 107 Squadron, pp. 62-3.

Ian Linney with
F/Sgt W Bilborough Dec 1944
(Nick Linney)

flak. When he eventually returned to base the ground crew immediately noticed that an incendiary bullet had lodged between the Mosquito's two petrol tanks. Fortunately for my father the bullet had failed to explode but it made his aircraft unserviceable. Father was not able to use the plane for his third sortie that night which denied him, he always believed, the DFM award. **Nick Linney**

Ian Linney's pilot's logbook (no. 3) tells the story:

Dec 24th 1944 Mosquito Z, F/Sgt Bilborough navigator. Patrol - Doren Rheinbach - Wittlich - Vianden. Attacked two trucks with cannon 2 flames. Hit between petrol tanks.

Although the weather was again unfit for operations on Boxing Day 1944, nineteen sorties were flown on 27th December. Flares were dropped and all crews were able to find targets, which included over 100 hundred railway trucks.

Dec 27th 1944 Mosquito Z, F/Sgt Bilborough navigator. Patrol - Prum - Rodach - Bollingen. Roads attacked. Bombs, cannon M/G.

The weather didn't permit operations again until New Year's Eve, when sixteen crews of 107 Squadron set the pattern for the following year by bombing, cannoning and machine-gunning von Runstedt's transports and barracks. On New Year's Day twelve aircraft again attacked German transport in the salient with moderate success, in spite of the Luftwaffe's great effort to achieve superiority.

Dec 31st 1944 Mosquito Z, F/Sgt Bilborough navigator. Patrol - Daun - Mayen - Euskirchen - Zulpich Line - Coblenz - Lengerich. 3-500 - Bombed on railway, 1 hit.

Jan 1st 1945 Mosquito Z, F/Sgt Bilborough navigator. Patrol - Vianden - Wallerstein - Arsfeld - Vianden. Bombed railway east of Limerle. 1 hit.

By 16th January von Runstedt's attempted breakthrough was virtually halted. 'Operation Blackcock' was now put into action - to clear German troops from the Roer Triangle on the borders of Belgium and Germany so that they would be forced back over the Rivers Roer[24] and Wurm, further into Germany. On the night of 16th January 107 Squadron resumed its task of softening up fortified villages west of the Rhine, prior to the thrust of the 21st Army Group. On that night eleven sorties were flown in a strike on the villages of Wegburg and Klinkum. On 17th a further sixteen sorties were made against Wegburg and Heinsburg. Finally, on the night of 19th January thirty sorties were flown against troops in the villages of Birgelen and Erkelenz, which were heavily bombed and cannoned at the cost of four aircraft damaged, but no casualties to the squadron.[25]

---

[24] The German spelling is Rur, and the Dutch/French is Roer.
[25] 107 Squadron, p. 66.

AEROPORT DU TOUQUET
TOURISME ***
S Escale
Tél. 403 RESTAURANT-BAR R. C. Boulogne 40 B 26

Bar bill at Le Touquet, 1944
(Nick Linney)

Jan 16th 1945 Mosquito Z, F/Sgt Bilborough navigator. Strike - Wegburg attacked with 2-500 INC cannon. Fires seen.

Jan 17th 1945 Mosquito Z, F/Sgt Bilborough navigator. Strike - Heinsberg, 2-500 INC dropped. Flare over Wegburg, low cloud.

Jan 19th 1945 Mosquito Z, F/Sgt Bilborough navigator. Strike - Birgelen, 2-500 INC dropped, cannon. Fires burning.

Jan 19th 1945 Mosquito Z, F/Sgt Bilborough navigator. Strike - Birgelen, 2-500 INC dropped cannon, large fires burning.

During the remainder of January and February 1945, 107 Squadron continued its attacks on enemy transport on both sides of the Rhine with considerable success; in this period the Allied Armies were advancing slowly but inexorably towards the Rhine.

Jan 27th 1945 Mosquito Z, F/Sgt Bilborough navigator. Patrol - Erkelenz- Neuss - 270 Koln 10. 2- 500 GP on DP. Missed.

Jan 28th 1945 Mosquito Z, F/Sgt Bilborough navigator. Patrol – Paddeborn - Unna - Brilon - Winerberg. Train attacked with bombs Overshot. Cannon ,M/G, brakes u/s.

Jan 29th 1945 Mosquito Z, F/Sgt Bilborough navigator. Patrol - Paderborn - Unna - Winerberg. 2-500 GP on Muttlar by Gee Train attacked near Monreal. I blew up, others HE.

Ian Linney's Mosquito Z continued its intruder missions into February 1945, concentrating on bombings in the Bad Oeynhausen and Hamm districts, especially on the railway south east of Siegen. On 3rd February Ian Linney received a real fright on a mission to the Hanover-Brunswick district.

> The crew took a wrong turn and they found themselves in a field of barrage balloons, which was terribly difficult to extricate the plane from. If the Mosquito had got tangled with the long cables of the balloons, then it could have caused maximum damage to the plane. **Nick Linney**

Ian Linney's matter-of-fact entry in his logbook gives no indication of how frightening this must have been for the pilot and navigator.

Feb 3rd 1945 Mosquito Z, F/Sgt Bilborough. Patrol - Greene- Hanover - Brunswick - Magdeburg. Dropped flare in balloons, came out over Cologne, dropped bomb. GKW.

By the middle of February 1945, Ian Linney had completed his tour of 30 sorties for 107 Squadron. Still based at Cambrai /Epinoy, he spent the last weeks of the war on flying missions from his base, usually to England and back, but no more bombing missions were assigned. Ian's activity on VE Day plus one was recorded by Canadian pilot, Jonny Conlin.

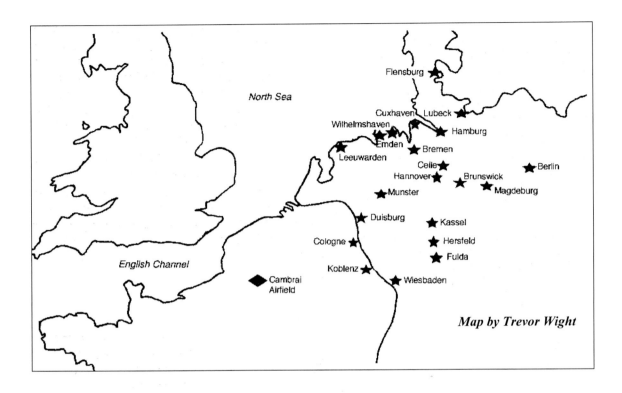

The Final Collapse: Targets attacked by 107 Squadron, Jan 1945 to end of the war.

Getting over to England for repatriation to Canada was far from easy. ... For four days in a row we went out to meet the aircraft [for England] and found it full. Ultimately we prevailed on the CO to let us borrow the squadron 'Oxford' so that we could be flown to England ... But we couldn't get any of them (instructors) to take the time to fly us over until 'Bull' Linney agreed to do so, although he had never flown or been in an Oxford.

... Next day six of us piled into the aircraft with loads of kit ... [in spite of] standing orders stating four people and no kit. By the time we had got into the aircraft the entire ground crew had assembled to see us crash. It took us an hour to reach 1,000 feet ... when we were crossing the Channel, Smith [co-pilot] took control while Linney read his note-book 'to learn how to land'. ... We got down at Blackbush without incident although we very nearly ran out of aerodrome. ... I haven't flown since save as a passenger. **Jonny Conlin, Canadian pilot, 107 Squadron**[26]

On his return home from war service Ian felt bereft.

Father once said to me, 'I'd been flying the best aircraft you could possibly fly, the Mosquito FB.VI for the last eighteen months and now it was all over. It was the most desolate day of my life.'

Nick Linney

---

[26] 107 Squadron, pp. 69-70.

Following Ian's distinguished service, as an RAF pilot during WW2, he took over W and J Linney's printing company in Mansfield. In 1946 the business employed 18 people and had annual sales of just £20,000. Today it employs nearly 700 people and has a turnover approaching £370 million.[27] Clearly, much of this success was due to Ian's drive and vision. In 1997 he was awarded an OBE for his services to the community in Nottinghamshire, and was appointed a Deputy Lieutenant the following year. In April 2013 Ian Linney died, aged 91.

Reunited in later years Ian Linney and W Bilborough with a painting of a Mosquito
(Nick Linney)

Frank 'Bish' Barrett, Sqn Ldr, gunner in 26, 407 and 279 Squadrons

'From one sportsman to another, I salute you.'

Hermann Goering[28]

Born on 28th June 1908 Frank Barrett was the son of well-known local photographer Howard Barrett, of Station Road, Southwell. Before WW2 Frank attended the Minster Grammar School as a chorister (1919-25) and became Head Boy. From an early age he developed a deep love of the countryside and country sports, above all riding, probably influenced by his work as a freelance journalist for *The Tatler* before the war. He also wrote for the *Newark Advertiser*; in fact Frank was the original 'Rex', writer of the regular Southwell Topics column. When war broke out in September 1939 Frank Barrett immediately decided to enlist.

Frank Barrett's story is most remarkable for both the variety and the length of his wartime service experience. When he was in 26 Squadron, based south of London, he was involved in the Battle of Britain in the role of Army Co-operation 1940-1. Then, in June 1941, he joined the

---

[27] *Nottingham Post*, 26th April 2013.
[28] Believed to be a verbal message passed on to Frank Barrett regarding a sporting photograph taken by his father Howard Barrett.

Frank Barrett (Anne Clark)

'Demon' 407 Squadron, part of RAF Coastal Command, and participated in low level attacks on German shipping in the North Sea. Later in 1941 he moved to 279 Squadron, based in Norfolk and formed to provide an Air-Sea Rescue capability in the North Sea. In the later war years his role changed again to that of a Gunnery Instructor and Armament Officer in the north of Scotland, concluding with Frank, now Squadron Leader, in March 1945 leading a team to take over the running of the Luftwaffe Air Ministry, as part of the Allied Control Commission.

At the outbreak of the war he was determined to enlist rather than have no choice where he was placed. His preference was to join the RAF; he didn't fancy the military due to the terrible conditions faced in WW1. At Tollerton Airfield he paid for flying lessons, intending to be a Fighter pilot. He got his pilot's licence and entered the RAF as a Commissioned Officer in early 1940. Unfortunately, he was deemed too old at 32 to be a fighter pilot, but at Cranwell they discovered my father was a crack shot and that sealed his fate. On 19th April 1940 he passed his Gunner Exams with distinction. **Anne Clark**

Frank Barrett's detailed memoirs of these momentous years inform us that on 9th March 1940, following his Cranwell training, No. 77924 Acting Pilot Officer on probation, F Barrett - the lowest of the low - reported for No. 6 Air Gunner Officers' Training Course at RAF Manby, near Louth in Lincolnshire. Manby was the Centre for Armament Training in the RAF and became the home of the RAF's No. 1 Armament School, since it was only a few miles from the east coast and had good ground and air firing ranges at Theddlethorpe and Donna Nook.

The rear gunner was often known as 'Tail-end Charlie'; his primary role was to be a lookout, defending his aircraft from every fighter attack from the rear of the plane and to warn the pilot when to take evasive manoeuvres. This meant being crammed into a confined space, a see-through turret, enveloped by the pitch-black sky and constantly revolving to scan the eerie darkness for a shadow that could be an attacking night fighter. Loss of concentration was not an option as relaxing this constant vigilance for even a moment could result in death for everyone on board.[29]

CERTIFICATE OF COMPETENCY.

Photograph   of Holder.

Signature of Holder... *Frank Barrett*

This Pilot's Certificate of Competency for private flying machines No. 20045 dated 24th July, 1939 has been issued to F. Barrett

for the following types of flying machines :

All types of landplanes.

Given at London this 24th day of July, 19 39.

Director of Home Civil Aviation.

Certificate of Competency (Anne Clark)

The forty or so men I joined in training at RAF Manby had come from all parts of the world, many at their own expense, including two gold and diamond prospectors, an Australian insurance salesman, a master builder, one

---

[29] Website: https://themedthemod.com/tag/life expectancy-of-a-rear-gunner

of the best syncopated dance pianists I ever heard, a tea planter, a professional gymnast and the shooting editor of *The Field*.

The great skill of instructor Wing Commander 'Bonzo' Franks led to the successful training, in about six weeks of successive courses, of fairly competent air-gunners to fly with all the operational bombing squadrons. ... The non-commissioned staff too matched up to this high standard, but alas the equipment of aircraft and weapons were obsolete and in short supply.

... The aircraft we flew in were 'Demons', two-seaters of little better quality than 1914-18 types. Totally out of date but I suppose adequate for the job. The procedure for air firing training was thus: the aircraft took off to a carefully limited area by the coast where it towed a drogue - that is a fabric stocking of roughly the same length as a small aircraft. The second 'Demon' , with the trainee and his guns, flew on a parallel course at the same height and about 150-200 yards apart. The firing would consist of 200 rounds from a Lewis gun. When the towing aircraft landed, the drogue was examined and the number of hits recorded as a percentage of the rounds fired.

... With the day's work done, mess life was often enlivened by the dance music brilliantly played by 'Charlie', the syncopated pianist. He had at one time been with Billy Cotton, but his somewhat erratic behaviour did not suit that great bandleader for long.

... The final examination results became available at the end of the course and I saw mine was at 92%, very high, and my flying logbook had the entry for air gunnery 'above average'. ... The postings were then made, mine being to Army Co-operation Command, Old Sarum, near Salisbury, for a further short course of training.

Frank Barrett

Lysander Training Aircraft
(Private Collection)

The aircraft Frank was using in training was the high-winged single-engined Westland Lysander. The 'Lizzies' were capable of flying at very low speeds, land on virtually any grass field and generally regarded as fun to fly. They also had great qualities of strength and manoeuvrability and needed only a short landing and take-off area. However, Frank quickly came to the conclusion that the methods used at Army Co-operation Command were somewhat dated.

Our course was mainly one of airborne 'spotting' exercises ... flying up and down railways or to specified depots to report back what had been seen, or sometimes photographed. ... It was abundantly clear that the whole conception of Army Co-operation was still in the 1914 era. On the Continent the fast thrusts and advances of a highly organised and equipped German army were covered by a vast Luftwaffe. The very idea of artillery spotting or any forward reconnaissance by Lysanders was a condemnation of the Army Commanders' responsibility for pre-war planning. ... After the Dunkirk retreat it was obvious that the concept of Army Co-operation as taught at Old Sarum was dead, pilots were posted away to squadrons whose needs were immediate.

Frank Barrett

Following these two courses, Frank Barrett was ready to join an operational squadron. In June 1940 he joined No. 26 Squadron at RAF Lympne where the officers' mess was in a famous country house belonging to the wealthy Sassoon family. However, by 14th June the squadron was despatched to RAF West Malling, near Maidstone. Almost immediately a roster went up in the mess for trips over to Dunkirk, where events were dramatically unfolding.

The main role for 26 squadron at that time was Army Co-operation - assisting the ack-ack batteries in south London; providing the army with photographic reconnaissance and using the Lysander aircraft, which could fly low, for dropping messages to ground troops.

By June 1940 enemy activities in the London area increased daily. One day we stood with a bunch of young, eager aircrew grounded with no suitable aircraft to take part in the fighting. We stood in the grounds of 'The Hermitage' (our mess, previously a lovely country house) as Stukas dive-bombed our airfield only a mile away. Our curses turned to ecstatic cheers as a Hurricane squadron followed them down and had a wonderful opportunity to pick most of them off as they pulled out of their bombing dives. It was a tremendous boost to our morale to see the Stukas one after the other shot down while still too low for any of the aircrew to parachute to safety.

Frank Barrett

Frank Barrett did not only experience the Battle of Britain in the air in his Lysander:

One glorious Saturday afternoon we were grounded and I went off to play cricket against a village team some miles away ... The air raid warning siren had gone off as soon as the game started and high up above the broken cumulus clouds the machine guns stuttered and there was a haze of enemy bombers. The game went on.
... The village batsman hit the ball high in my direction; just as the ball was reaching its highest point my eyes travelled straight past it on to a German Heinkel bomber with a Spitfire on its tail. My eyes fell on the scene just as the German aircrew baled out with their parachutes billowing open. But like a flash my eyes picked up the ball again. I caught it; as the batsman walked away he looked at me, looked at the fallen parachutes, shook his head ... and smiled. The game went on undisturbed.

Frank Barrett

By September 1940 the Battle of Britain was at its height and the threat of invasion was growing. The fleets of invasion barges could be seen clearly across the Channel from a few thousand feet above the aerodrome. As a result 26 Squadron aircrew officers were given a new, special role, should an invasion be attempted.

Our new role ... was to spray poison gas on the enemy on the beaches and landing craft. Technically it was a simple matter to fit and carry a large gas container on the rigid undercarriage of the Lysander. ... Obviously no harmful substance could be used in our training runs with the containers and some readily visible volatile pinkish substitute filled the practice gas tank. It was coloured violet. What the practice spray was I never found out but it had a smell rather like aniseed.
... The role we were trained for with poison gas was, of course, 'Top Secret', in fact, 'Super Secret' and luckily the explanation that the tank was a smoke-screen container was accepted without question. The smell was more difficult to explain away.

Frank Barrett

Another new task assigned to 26 Squadron at the height of the Battle of Britain was to give extra support to anti-aircraft batteries, in light of the daylight attacks of the Luftwaffe.

The idea was simple. A Lysander was to take off and go to certain positions and heights over London prior to an anticipated attack. The aircraft batteries took their estimates of our height and speed from their range-finders and the pilot of the Lysander radioed his actual height and speed to the batteries for adjustment to be made. In the meantime the air-gunner kept a very sharp look-out for enemy intruders.

Frank Barrett

Inevitably, some of these sorties above London assisting the anti-aircraft batteries brought contact with enemy invaders.

On this occasion the sortie was north of RAF Gatwick over the Staines area and what is now Heathrow. There was a good deal of air activity, a lot of chatter being picked up by our intercom. We were at about 17,000 ft and a lot of beautiful cumulus clouds formed as the morning wore on. Then everything happened at once. A lone JU 88 bomber broke cloud not far from us and I swung my guns towards it. The anti-aircraft batteries opened fire and black puffs burst all round us - after all we had just given them our exact speed and height. We did 'get the hell out of it', but just as Dingle (pilot) put 'Lizzie' into a steep dive there was a crack and some of the fabric of the fuselage tore away in a sheet and the Perspex of the pilot's cockpit splintered. Whether we had been hit by a splinter from the anti-aircraft fire or by enemy action I could not guess ... a few spots of blood blew back on me as we pulled out of the dive clear of the balloons and set sail for home.

Frank Barrett

Frank's pilot, Dingle, had in fact been injured, but he was able to get the Lysander back to base without any major mishap. This incident indicates how hazardous the role of 26 Squadron was helping the anti-aircraft batteries around London. Aircrew needed breaks from the daily conflict during the Battle of Britain. On one rare occasion when this was possible Frank Barrett, along with some aircrew friends, decided to go into London for the evening and have a night out.

On the train into London we said we would have an evening at The Café de Paris. However, as we walked off the station at Victoria, Aubrey thought things over and said we should go elsewhere and have a wonderful celebration with a friend.

The following morning at breakfast we learned that The Café de Paris had received a direct hit, 'Snake Hips' and his Band had received the full force and those patrons of that famous watering hole that had not been killed were injured.

Frank Barrett

Frank's daughter Anne remembers two other occasions in later years when luck played a big part in Frank's survival:

On the first occasion he was given a 24-hour pass and so decided to ride his motorbike back to Southwell. On returning to his airfield in the evening, he came off his bike and damaged a tyre making him have to walk to his local garage. When he got back to the airfield his crew had already taken off with another Gunner in his place. The plane never returned; they were shot down.

The second close shave was somewhat similar. He was on twenty-four hour leave when a telegram arrived at his mother's house asking him to return immediately for another sortie. My father was out when the telegram came and so he again missed his crew taking off. This time they were shot down by a Messerschmitt 109 over Germany and became POWs. As a result of this father became known as the lucky person to have as your gunner, though I strongly believe he was an exceptional shot and that was his secret.

Anne Clark

Towards the end of the Battle of Britain, Frank Barrett was involved in another skirmish over the skies of London.

> The air was alive with a big battle raging above us when a Messerschmitt 109 came towards us with a Hurricane emptying his guns into it and then climbing away. The 109 was already smoking furiously as it lost height and crashed onto the concrete apron close to the Headquarters buildings. It had lost most of its petrol because the fire was fierce but not explosive, and the pilot, inevitably badly shot up, had tried to get out but had died with his legs over the outside of the cockpit and his body drooping inside. The fire crept on and the boots and lower legs dropped on to the ground. At this point an officer arriving late on the scene saw the boots and said, 'Those boots, I must have them as a souvenir.' I touched him on the arm and told him, 'Don't - there are feet still in them.' He took a closer look and retreated looking very sick.
> **Frank Barrett**

In late April 1941 Frank Barrett was instructed to leave 26 Squadron and move to No. 16 Squadron at Weston Zeyland, Somerset, still with Army Co-operation flying Lysanders. Frank had been with 26 Squadron nearly a year, during which time he had flown with fifty-three different pilots. He was only at 16 Squadron a few weeks, but one event stood out in his memory. This was when the squadron held its annual shooting contest firing revolvers and all officers were ordered to compete.

> Shortly before the contest I was told that the Wing Commander had won all pistol competitions from the year dot and he expected this would always be the case. We were equipped with Smith and Wesson .38 revolvers and I had a fair amount of experience with them. My score easily won the competition, but it was received with glowering looks from those present. 'My God, the old man's bad enough at the best of times. What will he be like now?' One or two officers were critical of my temerity and one or two delighted. Fortunately, I had no reaction from the CO, who I thought might at least have congratulated me.
> **Frank Barrett**

Shoulder Badge
(407 Squadron)

Frank Barrett was pleased to hear of his next posting. In June 1941 he joined No. 407 'Demon' Squadron composed mainly of aircrew from the Royal Canadian Air Force (RCAF), one of seven RCAF units to serve with RAF Coastal Command. It was given the title Demon squadron after a visiting journalist wrote a glowing account of the pilots' dangerous low-level attacks on German shipping along the Dutch and Belgian coasts. The name Demon stuck. Frank took an instant liking to the Canadian youngsters, who, whilst very inexperienced, were keen and seemed anxious to know where all the Englishmen with monocles were! After flying, the Canadian airmen would be rolling dice to *'Baby needs new shoes'*. Not a care in the world, yet.

407 Squadron base was at RAF North Coates, close to Grimsby in north-east Lincolnshire, and their main role was to attack enemy ships, which either singly or in convoy were going along the Friesian Islands' coastline from the Channel ports to Bremen and Hamburg. RAF Coastal Command also protected allied shipping from aerial attacks by the Luftwaffe. Frank's daughter Anne remembers her father having fond memories of these days.

> Some of the time when father was flying sorties for Coastal Command he was based in the north of Scotland and on the Shetland Islands. The role of the RAF bombers there was to fly out of the sun and dive-bomb enemy shipping, which was intent on sinking Allied merchant boats in the

North Atlantic. All bombers were told to look out for the *Bismarck* but father did not come across it.

Anne Clark

The squadron's aircraft were Lockheed Hudsons, a proven civilian aircraft adapted for military service with a bomb-rack and doors and a power-operated rear turret with four Browning guns. The Hudsons were twin-engine and to Frank were a welcome change from the dear old Lysander. Two particular sorties stood out for Frank.

On the 7th September I did my first operational sortie with 407 squadron ... It was a roving sortie, hopefully to find a convoy off the Friesian Islands. We flew south from Borkum without seeing anything and the pilot, F/Lt John Hill, then decided to try Terschelling Harbour. In the good visibility we could see a ship or two on the first run, and running in low we got a stick of bombs across a coastal vessel at the wharf. We landed back after a sortie of 4 hours, feeling pleased with this successful initiative. However, a day later we were justifiably peeved to be told by the CO that Queen Wilhelmina was not pleased to have her Dutch ships destroyed. Since the Nazis controlled the whole Channel coast and had confiscated all shipping that seemed an inappropriate attitude.

Frank Barrett

Sept 7 20.00 hrs F/Lt Hill, pilot, Bombing Recco - Bombed shipping in Borkum-Terschelling, Terschelling Harbour 4 hrs.[30]

In the winter of 1941-2 407 Squadron were to claim 150,000 tons of enemy shipping, sunk or damaged. However, the dangerous nature of the low-level attacks and the bad weather the aircrews experienced often created difficulties.[31]

Early in October I started to fly regularly with Sq Ldr Paul Lynam, my flight commander, and on 10th we took off on a daylight 'Rover'. That is a sortie to find a convoy in a certain area off the Friesian Islands. ... The weather was bad with low cloud and poor visibility. Three aircraft took off in a 'Vic' formation with the CO leading, but the weather was so bad that the Hudsons on our port and starboard were quite close in.

'Bomb doors open', ordered the CO, as we flew in - not onto a convoy but smack on to the heavily defended island of Borkum. The bombs of each aircraft straddled gun posts, from which flew at us a curtain of bullets. I had seen the other two aircraft pulling safely away after bombs were gone, but only one reformatted with us as we turned for home. The third aircraft landed some ten minutes after us and we were relieved to see the rear-gunner leave his turret unharmed. The Perspex panels of the turret had eleven bullet holes in them, and since they surrounded the turret seat it was a miracle that he, too, wasn't riddled.

The next day I was given a 24hr leave and I flew to Balderton. I started walking over to the old A1 when a truck driver offered me a lift, and as I was settling down in the seat it was announced on his radio that the RAF that morning had successfully attacked the heavily defended island of Borkum. The truck driver nodded, saying, 'That's right, give 'em Hell.' I nodded too, 'I was on that raid', to the truck driver's delight.

Frank Barrett

October 10 0715 hrs S/Ldr Lynham, pilot 'Rover' - Daylight, Terschelling, Borkum 3.15 hrs.[32]

---

[30] Frank Barrett's logbook.

[31] Patrick Otter, *Lincolnshire Airfields in the Second World War* (Newbury: Countryside Books, 1996), pp. 185-86.

[32] Frank Barrett's logbook.

The *Daily Sketch* sent a staff photographer and reporter to RAF North Coates to write an article about this successful Canadian squadron, and on Monday 17th November 1941 the newspaper carried a full page of photographs ... with the headline 'These men sink the NAZI ships'. It would have gone down nicely in Canada. No names could be mentioned for security reasons. (See next page.)

After about six months in 407 Squadron, Frank was posted to Bircham Newton in north Norfolk in November 1941. Bircham Newton was where the new Hudson No. 279 Squadron was being formed. He was keen to go as Sq. Ldr Lynam had insisted he wouldn't move to lead the new squadron unless his whole aircrew went with him. For Frank, this was a compliment to the aircrew.

Squadron 279's role was to provide long-range air-sea rescue over the North Sea - this task was very different from Frank's previous experience. An efficient Air-Sea Rescue system was urgently needed, because too many badly damaged planes were being ditched a long way out in the North Sea with very little hope of the aircrews being picked up from their escape dinghies. Whilst the new 279 Squadron did make a difference, it was not possible to retrieve all the dinghies.

Frank Barrett at RAF Bircham Newton 1941-2
(Anne Clark)

On the night of 13th March, 1942, a Wellington badly damaged over enemy targets, was at last forced to ditch a long way out in the North Sea. The pilot ... had kept in touch with his base where he had been tracked accurately. His position and time of contact were immediately passed to No 16 Group HQ and to Bircham with a request for help.

My logbook shows that it was 00.00 hrs on 13th March, 1942, when W/C Lynam took off in Hudson OSV with his usual crew ... including myself in the rear turret. The flying conditions were appalling. Cloud was very low with a freezing mist below. Approaching the fix area I saw a Verey cartridge Green/Green explode only a few hundred yards away. 'There it is', I called ... our position radioed back to Bircham. This was an exceptional piece of flying and navigation by pilot and navigator in atrocious conditions and steadily getting worse. ... The CO kept on circling vainly hoping for a break in the weather to get that sight of the dinghy that would give the ditched aircrew's spirits a lift. ... Eventually, W/C Lynam called to me, 'We must go home now - I'm afraid I'm beginning to fly dangerously. There had been no moon, just freezing mist and no visibility at all. We landed back at Bircham having been airborne for five hours. For several days after this the weather remained dreadful, and no further contact was made with this dinghy. We heard no more of them but I hope they drifted to some shore if only to remain POWs for the remainder of the war. We - the searchers - felt only frustration and dismay. **Frank Barrett**

Daily Sketch article, 17ᵗʰ November 1941 (Anne Clark)

March 13th 00.00 W/C Lynam - ASR for Wellington 3 E - Contact twice by Verey Lights from sea - Fixes obtained - Low cloud, bad visibility, no moon. 5hrs. 10.[33]

However, in many cases 279 Squadron was able to carry out a successful rescue.

We were to do the last trip together - the usual four of us - on the 23rd June, when we shared the patrol over a dinghy full of relieved aircrew, when Spitfires and a Walrus completed the rescue. **Frank Barrett**

June 23rd 08.45 W/C Lynam - ASR - Relieved Wellington crew dinghy. Walrus and Spit completed rescue. 3.05 Hrs[34]

By July 1942 Frank Barrett was 34 years old and had served as a Senior Gunnery Officer in four different operational squadrons for the last two years. It is likely that at this point the RAF administration considered that he now needed to play a less demanding role. Frank's daughter shares this view.

The job of Rear Gunner did take its toll on my father. For many hours a gunner would be squeezed into a tiny turret, flying in cramped, freezing and solitary conditions. The sorties were carried out without oxygen and they did have a lasting effect on father's ears and hearing. The life expectancy of a rear gunner would be desperately short - around five operations, I believe was the average. One sortie they went on resulted in the landing gear being shot off by flak and he said that returning to base was a very hairy thing. They had to do a belly flop to land and the plane could easily have gone up in flames.   Father always said the worst experience was looking across to the empty seats at breakfast after a sortie. He lost so many good friends that he never wanted to talk much about his wartime life in the RAF; he didn't find retelling stories easy. **Anne Clark**

Thus in July 1942, Frank Barrett's operational squadron service ended and that saddened him. However, he was still highly regarded by the service and was posted as a Gunnery Instructor to No. 16 Group Armament Practice Camp at Thorney Island and other RAF stations. Frank's role was to provide air-firing training of aircrew from all squadrons within 16 Group. Not surprisingly, Frank's heroic work at Coastal Command as a Rear Gunner was given due recognition on 1st January 1943. The *Newark Advertiser* covered the award to Frank of 'Mentioned in Despatches'.

Honour for Flight Lieutenant Barrett

Flight Lieutenant Barrett, the son of Mr and Mrs Barrett of Station Road, Southwell, has been 'Mentioned in Despatches' for his service in Coastal Command. Mr Barrett was born in Southwell and educated at Southwell Minster Grammar School and was granted a commission in RAFVR early in 1940. He was the original 'Rex' of Southwell Topics.[35]

In October 1943 Frank was appointed Armament Officer and posted to Sumburgh in the Shetland Islands. The following year came further recognition of his value to the RAF when in July he was promoted to Squadron Leader and posted to RAF Brackla, as Squadron Commander to the Air Crew Allocation Centre in north-east Scotland.

---

[33] Frank Barrett's logbook.
[34] Frank Barrett's logbook.
[35] *N/Adv*, 13th January 1943.

Frank Barrett, 'Mentioned in Despatches' (Anne Clark)

Frank Barrett's final wartime role came in early 1945 when, with the end of the war in sight, senior experienced servicemen were needed to go to Germany as members of the Control Commission. Its function was to take control over all aspects of enemy territory, the Air Division being responsible for the running of the Luftwaffe Ministry itself.

A squadron leader was needed to lead the Aircrew branch at the British Air Forces of Occupation headquarters at Bückeburg, in the province of North Rhine/Westphalia. The decision was made that the Occupation headquarters should be in the ancient palace of the Princes of Schaumburg-Lippe, with close links to the German imperial family. The palace was noted for its outstanding architecture, its prized wine cellar and its fine arts. The task was one of disarmament, to take over the vast stock and stores of all types of weapons and equipment in the hands of the Luftwaffe at the end of the war. The German palace had a fine library, with a great selection of books, magazines and prints and when Frank visited it one day he came across an amazing coincidence. The *Newark Advertiser* took up the story.

Squadron Leader Barrett visits former Palace of Kaiser

Writing from Germany, where he is stationed with the RAF, Squadron-Leader Frank Barrett, third son of Mrs Howard Barrett, Station Rd, Southwell relates an interesting incident.

A former Palace of the ex-Kaiser is being used as the Officers' Mess. Upon his arrival

Frank Barrett was based at the ex-Kaiser's palace in 1945, working for the Allied Occupation Force (Anne Clark)

Squadron-Leader Barrett went into the library where he saw a familiar photograph, a picture of 'Foxhounds' taken by his father, the late Howard Barrett, photographer.[36]

Frank Barrett's daughter was given more information about this amazing coincidence and was able to add another interesting angle to the story, involving the notorious Nazi Luftwaffe chief, Hermann Goering. As Frank and his staff were given the responsibility of running the Luftwaffe Ministry, it is very likely

---

[36] *N/Adv*, 26th September 1945.

that there would have had to be some personal contact with the ex-Minister of the Luftwaffe, Goering, now a prisoner of war.

> Apparently Hermann Goering had seen this photograph of the 'Foxhounds' by Howard Barrett in the library of the palace and was aware my father was the photographer's son. He sent my father a message, 'From one sportsman to another; I salute you.' My father always wished this message had been written, not verbally relayed, as it might have brought him a fortune! **Anne Clark**

'Foxhunting at Rufford' by Howard Barrett
hanging in the ex-Kaiser's library
(Anne Clark)

After the war ended, Frank received a number of medals for his long and distinguished war service including the 1939-45 Star medal, the Atlantic Star medal and the Defence Medal 1939-45. In addition, he had won a 'Mentioned in Despatches' certificate in 1943 for his work in Coastal Command.

Frank stayed in the RAF and became Commanding Officer at Bicester RAF Station for four years, retiring from the RAF in 1958. He then went into farming, something he had always wanted to do. Frank died on 3rd February 1998 at the age of 89.

Norman Robert Norfolk, fighter pilot in 72 Squadron

Norman Norfolk was born in Nottingham on 21st November 1912, and educated at the Minster Grammar School as a boarder. He joined the RAF on 29th June 1936 as a direct-entry trainee pilot, serial number 44929, and in October 1939, a month after the war started, Norman was serving with 72 fighter squadron at Leconfield.

In June 1940 72 squadron moved south to assist in the evacuation of Dunkirk and by September was based at RAF Tangmere in West Sussex, famous for its role in the Battle of Britain. Among the WW2 aces who served at Tangmere were Douglas Bader and the then inexperienced Johnnie Johnson. Norman was listed as one of the Battle of Britain 'Few'. The fighter planes used by the pilots at Tangmere were Gloster Gladiators, Hurricanes and Spitfires. Norman was commissioned on 17th September 1940.

RAF Tangmere was one of the main targets for the Luftwaffe in the Battle of Britain and Norman was serving there at the time of a destructive Luftwaffe raid.

> The worst raid on the station [RAF Tangmere] came on 16th August 1940 when hundreds of Stuka dive-bombers and fighters crossed the English coast and attacked Tangmere. There was extensive damage to buildings and aircraft on the ground and 14 ground staff and six civilians were killed, but the station was kept in service and brought back into full operation.[37]

---

[37] en.wikipedia.org/wiki/RAF_Tangmere

RAF Tangmere

Badge of RAF Tangmere (En.wikipedia.org/wiki/ RAF_Tangmere)

The life of a fighter pilot was exhilarating, but also exhausting, dangerous and stressful. At the height of the Battle of Britain, in August and September 1940, pilots were expected to undertake several sorties a day, intercepting often up to a hundred enemy bombers and fighters. In addition to the sheer physical fatigue, the mental strain built up day by day as pilots faced the possibility of their aircraft being shot down or catching fire during encounters with the enemy. Even returning to base was often risky because of poor visibility. Once at base it was often to discover that several of their colleagues had been killed or reported missing. We are fortunate to have a number of Norman Norfolk's Combat Reports, recorded by him at the height of the Battle of Britain. On 1st September 1940, 72 squadron, flying Spitfires, were ordered to intercept up to 160 enemy bombers and fighters over the south coast.

COMBAT   REPORT 43[38]

Date	1/9/1940	**Flight, Squadron**	'B', 72 Sq
Number enemy aircraft	100+	**Type enemy aircraft**	ME 109
Time of attack	13.30	**Place of attack**	5m E Dungenness
Height of Enemy	12,000 ft	**Enemy casualties**	1 ME damaged
Our casualties	Nil		

General Report

Flying 'Blue' 2 with 72 Squadron over Hastings when an enemy formation was intercepted of about 60 bombers and 100 ME 109s. We attempted to attack the bombers but were attacked by the ME 109s. A dog fight ensued in which I was able to get a deflection shot on an enemy aircraft. My fire was a little ahead of enemy aircraft at first, but he flew into my view and I was able to tracer into his cockpit as he was so close (50 yds). He did a complete roll and dived apparently out of control. I was able to follow him down.

Signed *NR Norfolk, Sgt, 'Blue', 'B', 72 Sq*

Norman returned from this sortie on 1st September 1940 with a severely damaged tail unit, but the very next day his section was ordered to intercept another wave of over 100 Luftwaffe bombers and fighters. This resulted in his being shot down by a Messerschmitt (ME) 109 whilst in combat in his Spitfire K9938 over Herne Bay. His aircraft crashed and burnt out at Garrington Farm, near Bekesbourne emergency landing ground. Norman survived this ordeal by the skin of his teeth.

---

[38] National Archives Records for Battle of Britain Pilots, AIR-50-30-19_1Norfolkcombatlogvol1.pdf (Ken Ogilvie)

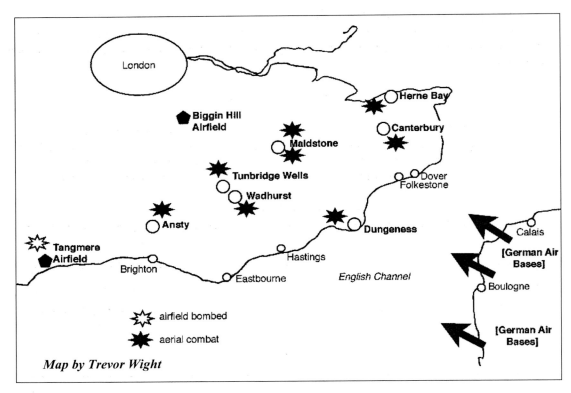

Norman Norfolk: Battle of Britain, actions involving enemy aircraft

COMBAT REPORT 45

Date	2/9/1940	**Flight, Squadron**	'B', 72, Spitfire
Number enemy aircraft	100+	**Type Enemy aircraft**	Dornier 17, ME 110
Time of attack	12.45	**Place of attack**	Canterbury
Height of enemy	20,000 ft	**Enemy casualties**	1 ME110
Our casualties	1 Spitfire	**Range fire opened**	300 yds

General Report

I was flying 'Blue' 2 with 72 Squadron over Canterbury at 20,000 ft when enemy aircraft were intercepted. Then I delivered an attack on ME 110. I opened fire at 300 yds and closed to 50 yds. Enemy aircraft was smoking badly when I broke away. No more was seen of him as my aircraft had been hit by the enemy fire and the engine put out of action. I glided down and landed with undercarriage up at Canterbury airport (airport blocked). My aircraft burst into flames and was completely destroyed.

Signed, NR Norfolk, 72 Sq

At this stage in the Battle of Britain, Norman's section of 72 Squadron was required for duty on most days. His Combat Reports show that on 7th and 11th September he destroyed two, one each day, Dornier 17s. On 15th September, the day now regarded as 'Battle of Britain' day, Norman recorded a hit:

COMBAT REPORT 46

Date	15/9/1940	**Flight, Squadron**	'B', 72 Sq
Number enemy aircraft	28 bombers, fighters	**Type enemy aircraft**	HE 111, ME 109s
Time of attack	14.35	**Place of attack**	Maidstone
Height of enemy	15,000 ft	**Enemy casualties**	1 probably

General Report

I was leading 'Yellow' section when 72 Squadron was ordered to intercept enemy aircraft proceeding towards London from the Kent coast. The squadron intercepted 28 HE 111 with fighters. We attacked the bombers from the rear quarter position. My section each took a bomber. I fired almost all my rounds into a Heinkel 111 but I did not see it go down, although pieces flew off it.

Signed, NR Norfolk, Sgt, 72 Sq

Formation of Dornier 17s (https://en.wikipedia.org/wiki/Dornier_Do_17)

Norman's Combat Reports show that 72 Squadron was still acting as a key part of the RAF defence force from October 1940 until the end of that momentous year.[39] At some point in 1941 the squadron was moved to North Africa, to support the Tunisian campaign, before being supplied with the updated Spitfire Mk 1X in 1942. It then assisted the British 8th Army as they advanced through Italy and France up until the German surrender. In March 1943, whilst on leave, Norman was asked to act as a role model, when he was invited to give a talk at The Ideal Cinema about setting up an Air Training Corps at Southwell.[40]

---

[39] Combat Reports of Pilot Officer N R Norfolk. (Ken Ogilvie)
[40] *N/Adv,* 17th March 1943.

Norman's worth as a pilot had been quickly recognised as early as December 1940, when he was awarded the Distinguished Flying Cross (DFC), being credited with the destruction of at least four enemy aircraft.[41] Two years later further recognition of his gallantry was covered in the local paper.

Pilot N R Norfolk's Success

Among the RAF pilots to distinguish themselves is an Old Southwellian who was a particularly fine rugger player and cricketer. He is Pilot Sgt N R Norfolk who is one of three brothers who were educated at the Minster GS. He participated in a recent attack on a German raider which resulted in the Heinkel crashing. Local sportsmen will be pleased to learn that the 'dash' which contributed to so many Rugby victories is being continued in the greater sphere of activity.[42]

Norman survived the war and was released from the RAF as a Flight Lieutenant in 1945. His survival is remarkable as a high percentage of Battle of Britain fighter pilots were either shot down or went 'missing'. He must have been a very daring, brave and skilful pilot with leadership qualities; this was recognised when he was asked to lead a fighter wing and further taken into account when he was awarded the DFC. Norman was awarded the OBE for his service as a fighter pilot and his contribution to Air Traffic Control, he was officially identified as one of the 'Few'. Norman Norfolk died on 13th March 2005 at the age of 92.

Reginald James Cook, bomber pilot in 15 and 608 Squadron

Reginald Cook (en.wikipedia.org/ wiki/RAF_Tangmere)

Born in 1918, Reginald Cook was educated at the Minster Grammar School, Southwell and later at Bemrose School, Derby. He lived on King Street, Southwell, where his father was the local chemist, before moving to Melbourne in Derbyshire.

He enlisted in the RAF in March 1939, six months before the outbreak of war, and was commissioned in 1942, having completed his training as an operational pilot. Reginald was assigned to 15 Squadron, based at RAF Abingdon, at that time flying Battles, Stirlings, Blenheims, Wellingtons and, possibly later, Lancasters. From 15 Squadron's Operational Record Book, it seems that the main bombing targets in 1942 were German cities and European ports under their control, such as Brest in western France, where German capital ships were berthed.

Badge of XV Squadron

(https://en.wikipedia.org/ wiki/No._15_Squadron_ RAF)

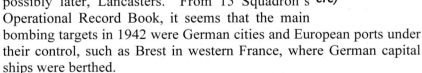

Bomber Command despatched 508 sorties, compared with 424 last week, and lost only three aircraft. A total of 514 tons of HE bombs and 24,000 incendiaries were dropped. Unsuitable weather prevented operations on two nights. The principal effort was directed against the *Gneisenau*, *Scharnhorst* and *Prinz Eugen*, which were attacked on each of the remaining nights of the week.[43]

---

[41] *N/Adv*, 25th December 1940.
[42] *N/Adv*, 27th March 1942.
[43] Air Situation Report for 5-12 Jan 1942 as reported to British War Cabinet, TNA CAB66/20/46.

Not long after these sorties on Brest, in early 1942, Reginald Cook was awarded the Distinguished Flying Medal (DFM).

Reginald Cook has received the Distinguished Flying Award for his bravery in repeated daylight bombing of a German warship at Brest.[44]

At some point later in the war, Reginald transferred to 608 (North Riding) Squadron, a Reconnaissance squadron in the early war years, which reformed in August 1944 at RAF Downham Market, Norfolk as a Mosquito 'Pathfinder' squadron, carrying out night attacks on Germany. 608 Squadron's 'Operations Record Book' shows that Reginald Cook was on bombing assignments to Berlin and other German cities right to the end of the war. His last bombing mission appears to be on 8th April 1945, but he didn't feature in the final bombing raid of the war on 2nd May, when 608 squadron dropped a 4,000 lb bomb on the naval port of Kiel.[45]

OPERATIONS RECORD BOOK
Secret
608 Squadron

Place	Date	Time	Summary of Event
608 Sq	8/4/45	22.49 hrs	KB 236 (A) F/L Cook, F/O Millership

Owing to weather conditions at base, these aircraft were all diverted to Gransden Lodge and interrogated there.[46]

Close to the end of the war there were further flying awards for Reginald - the DFC in March 1945[47] and the DSO in September 1945. The Distinguished Service Order (DSO) was one of the highest awards a serviceman could receive, many were awarded to squadron commanders for a long period of leadership, but in exceptional cases junior officers received it.

Fl. Lieut Cook Awarded DSO

The King has approved the following award of the DSO in recognition of gallantry and devotion to duty in the execution of air operations to Flight Lieutenant Reginald James Cook, DFC, DFM.

He enlisted in March 1939 and was commissioned in April 1942. He was awarded the DFM in Feb. 1942, and the DFC in March 1945 and is entitled to the Star. Flight Lieutenant Cook has proved himself to be a most skilful and courageous operational pilot.

He has recently completed a third tour of operational duty. His sorties have all been completed over enemy territory in Germany and occupied Europe and heavy aircraft defences have frequently been encountered. This officer took an effective part in the final prolonged bomber offensive against Berlin. Flight Lieutenant Cook has operated continuously from the early days of the war until the present time. His many successes have made him a valuable asset to his squadron.[48]

---

[44] *N/Adv,* 25th February 1942.
[45] wikipedia.org/wiki/No._608_Squadron_RAF
[46] 608 Squadron Operations Record Book.
[47] *N/Adv,* 28th March 1945.
[48] *N/Adv,* 26th September 1945.

After his success in the RAF, Reginald decided to move into commercial aviation, working as a pilot for British South American Airways, flying an Avro Lancastrian Mk 111. Sadly, his new career didn't last long, as this dramatic report shows:

This Day in Aviation - 2nd August 1947

2 August 1947: At 1.46 p.m., British South American Airways Flight C559 departed Buenos Aires, Argentina en route Santiago, Chile. The airliner was an Avro Lancastrian Mk 111, reg. G-AGWH, named RMA *Stardust*. The flight was under the command of Reginald J Cook, DSO, DFC, DFM ... On this flight, in addition to the five-person airline crew, there were just six passengers.

... The airliner never arrived. A five-day search was unsuccessful. ... The fate of *Stardust* remained a mystery until 1998, when two mountain climbers on Mt Tupungato ... found a wrecked Rolls-Royce aircraft engine in the ice of a glacier at the 15,000 ft level. A search of the glacier in 2000 located additional wreckage and it was confirmed that this was the missing Lancastrian. Investigators determined that the airliner had flown into the glacier at high speed and the crash caused an avalanche, which buried the wreckage.

In 2002 the remains of eight persons were recovered from the glacier, five of which were identified through DNA.[49]

Reginald Cook's life was eventful but sadly short. As a bomber pilot he had come through the war years, which many didn't, but after only two years in commercial aviation he failed to survive a tragic air accident.

The Avro Lancastrian Mk.III, G-AGWH,
R.M.A. Stardust
(This Day in Aviation)

Bill Graham, bomber pilot in 304 Squadron

William Monteith Graham was born on 4th July 1911 at Ipoh in the Malay States, where his father was a rubber plantation manager in the Cameron Highlands. Between the wars the Graham family came over to live in England, and Bill was educated at his father's old school, then called Haileybury and ISC (Imperial Service College), near Hertford. After leaving school Bill enrolled in the RAF on 6th January 1933, No. 34005 and began flying training. Soon after he saw action in a low-scale war in a part of the old North West Frontier, fought by the Raj against dissident tribesmen. Bill received a number of promotions before war broke out in 1939. He had been Pilot Officer in 1934, then Flying Officer in 1935 rising to Flight Lieutenant in 1937. After the outbreak of war Bill was posted first to RAF Bramcote and then to RAF Syerston.

From 1940 up to his death at the age of 29, Bill was RAF Liaison Officer to a new Polish Bomber squadron 304(P) Sqn. On 1st November 1940 he was appointed Acting Wing Commander. He was with it [304 (P) Sqn] as it started flying training at RAF Bramcote (near Nottingham) in 1940, on Handley Page Hampdens and as it then graduated onto the Wellington MK1.

---

[49] www.thisdayinaviation.com/2-august-1947

It was Bill's responsibility to ensure the squadron was fit to fight according to the RAF training and operational procedures, bearing in mind that some of both air and ground crew had seen action during the Nazi invasion of Poland in 1939 and all the Poles in the squadron had tales to tell of escaping either to France, where they continued to fight the German forces, before escaping to Britain, or making their way directly to the UK through Rumania and thence eventually Portugal.

Two comments of Bill's have been passed down to me. The first was that he considered it an honour to work with the Poles; he thought they were a very fine group of people; the second was that they made better Fighter than Bomber aircrew because of their utter determination to see as many Germans die at their hands as possible - not an easy task from 30,000 feet at night.

Ken Ogilvie

In December 1940 304 squadron moved to its new operational base, RAF Syerston. By the time the King and Queen visited the squadron in January 1940, Bill was living with his wife Jean in Bleasby.

My mother had married my father in September and they moved to a cottage, then called Roseneath Cottage, Main St, Bleasby ... the cottage still stands ... renamed Forge Cottage. In April, my mother now expecting me, was sent down to Colchester where she would be closer to good maternity facilities. [It was also felt by Bill Graham's family that occupants of Bleasby were vulnerable to enemy raids on Syerston].

Alastair Graham (son)

Flying training was continuing all the time and the Syerston RAF station logbook recalls events such as practising defence against enemy paratroopers and another time against enemy aircraft.

On the night of 8/9th May 1941, No 1 Group mounted one of its first raids of the war: a 77 aircraft raid on 3 targets in North Germany, one of which was on some shipyards in the Bremen area where it was said invasion barges were under construction.

I learnt many years later from the British station adjutant at Syerston at the time ... that 304 squadron was not considered quite ready to supply more than a handful of aircraft to this task but what was wanted were volunteers to Pathfind. This technique was still in its infancy in Britain. It required first class navigation first to find a target, which of course would be subject to blackout, and then to approach it very steadily and at low altitude to ensure that marker munitions landed on it with precision. Apart from difficulties of locating the target at night with possible partial cloud cover, the optimum approach to target altitude brought the pathfinder aircraft well under the Flak ceiling. A crew did indeed volunteer at Syerston. Including Bill Graham, they were all 'Brits' involved with flying training and probably there was a feeling that to the Poles under their tutelage albeit for not much longer, leading by example was the only option.

Bill Graham's plane was shot down and crashed some way from the Bremen target area. ... Initially the dead were buried close to the crash site and after the war their remains were moved to the Commonwealth War Graves site in the Forest of Cleves near Cologne. **Ken Ogilvie**

Bill's son Alastair remembers going out to Cologne with his mother Jean in the years after the war in order to meet his maternal grandfather, who was posted there in the civil service. It can't have been an easy time for either of them being so close to where Bill's plane had crashed and to the place he was buried.

Petrus Helgard Hillebrand, warrant officer in 34 Squadron

Petrus Helgard Hillebrand was born in 1916 and married Millicent Lilian Minnie Strutt from Oxton. After joining the RAF he served with 34 Squadron and became a Warrant Officer.

> 34 Squadron was based at Tengah (Singapore), flying Bristol Blenheim 1 fighter bombers. They suffered the fate of every Allied squadron in the areas attacked by the Japanese in early 1942 - heavy casualties followed by a forced retreat.
>
> On 9th/10th January 1942, Blenhiem IV V5597 (Pilot Sgt James Ellis Smith RNZAF) took off with five other aircraft to attack Sungei Patani airfield, Malaya. Only two of the aircraft reached the target in the poor prevailing weather. All returned except V5597, which was thought to have been brought down at about 03.30 on encountering severe turbulence in a tropical storm. All three crew were lost, including W.O. Hillebrand, who was 26 years old. **Trevor Wilds**

A family headstone in Farnsfield churchyard reads 'Warrant Officer Petrus Helgard Hillebrand, Royal Air Force, missing on active service Singapore 10.1.42.' He is commemorated in Column 413 of the Singapore Memorial in Kranji War Cemetery. He was awarded, posthumously, the 1939-45 Star and the 1939-45 War Medal.

Bert Ulyatt 1908-96, RAF driver

Before WW2 Bert Ulyatt lived in a cottage on Nottingham Road with his daughters, Barbara and Doris, and then in later years moved to Lower Kirklington Road. In 1940 he joined the RAF.

> I went to Padgate near Manchester on a free train. After square-bashing I was stationed in Lincolnshire where I was a driver of service vehicles. Then I was sent overseas on the liner *Queen Elizabeth* to Simonstown in South Africa. There were about 5,000 of us aboard. Near Cape Town we were in a tented camp
>
> We were then sent to North Africa to help the fight against Rommel. I saw Winston Churchill when he came out. We also saw plenty of Germans and Italians, some of whom had absconded. They'd had enough of it. Life was difficult until we reached Benghazi. We were a mobile aircraft depot repairing them on the job but, at Benghazi, I was put on ambulance work for three years. I was never in the firing line. They came from the front to us and we took them to the hospital. I was frightened. I didn't think that I could do it but I got used to it.
>
> The first time was New Year's Day and the first man I got hold of was dead. When war moved on to Italy, I stayed and gained great satisfaction by visiting the sick and writing letters home for them. The food was better than in the desert where it was stewed apricot and sacking [sic] and the usual corned beef. We also had square dog biscuits. All you could do was suck the corners, but the Red Cross sent lots of things and we'd always got water on the ambulance. Water was rationed, but if you'd got one mug of water and twenty chaps, everyone would have a sip. It was wonderful comradeship. When we were settled, ENSA came to entertain us and some men converted a little place into a chapel on the aerodrome. **Bert Ulyatt**[50]

In 1945 Bert was demobilized, given a 50s suit, and returned home

---

[50] Stevenson, p. 34.

Back at our cottage I couldn't believe it. I was half mad. I couldn't believe there were flowers in the garden; couldn't believe there was paper on the walls and carpets on the floor. I walked about our fields for hours. I couldn't believe I had survived. **Bert Ulyatt**[51]

Bert Ulyatt died in 1996 at the age of 88.

Leslie Wellbourne Jackson-Wynch, navigator in 76 Squadron

Leslie was born on 16 November 1910 at Farnsfield and was educated at the Church School. In June 1942 he married Helen Cecilia Lawe, and close to two years later in March 1944 he was appointed as a Pilot Officer on probation in 76 Squadron, Royal Air Force Volunteer Reserve.

[In1944] 76 Squadron was a bomber squadron based at RAF Holme-upon-Spalding Moor in Yorkshire, flying Halifax bombers. It appears that Leslie was trained as a navigator. In September 1944, he was awarded the Distinguished Flying Cross 'for high skill, fortitude and devotion to duty'. In that same month he was promoted to Flying Officer. **Trevor Wilds**

After the war Leslie stayed in the RAF and in March 1946 was promoted to Flight Lieutenant. By 1950 he was serving in Singapore; seven years later he retired from the Royal Air Force and went to live at Rose Cottage, South Scarle. Leslie died in August 1993, aged 82 years.

Charles Howard Barrett

Charles Barrett was born on 16th October 1906, the son of Howard and Emma Barrett. He went to Miss Wales's Infants School, the National School and then the Minster GS, where he was a chorister from 1918-22. After school he helped his father in the photographic studio, before joining Carey's Lace factory. He was a pattern corrector and designer. He married Stella Savage in 1928 and they lived on Lower Kirklington Road, moving to Easthorpe in 1932, bringing up five daughters there.

At the start of the war before he was called up he was a member of the ARP in sub-section 3 of the Southwell district. He joined the RAF reserves on 3rd July 1941 and served with 1658 Heavy Conversion Unit, RAF Riccall and also with 199 Bomber Command as a fitter on various aircraft, including Spitfires, Hurricanes and later Lancasters and Halifaxes. He was based at various times as a member of the ground crew at a number of air force stations including Scampton, Mildenhall and Hemswell, where he served in a Polish squadron.

I remember him saying that when the aircraft that he had been working on went out on a mission, the ground crew would wait and listen for their plane to return, as they could recognise the sound of the plane that they had worked on.

He was 'demobbed' on 8th November 1945 from the Personnel Despatch Centre at Cardington. Father was then sent to the Auxiliary Fire Service for six months' service at Long Eaton. **Bridget Clarke and Janette Barrett**

---

[51] Stevenson, p. 34.

Christmas Menu at
RAF Ricall, 1944

Charles Barrett at work on an aircraft engine,
RAF Ricall
(Both pictures Janette Barrett & Bridget Clarke)

Charles Barrett eventually returned to live in the family home in Easthorpe, Southwell and to work in the lace industry in Nottingham until his retirement. He died on the 24th September 1990.

John Robert Gilbert

John Robert Gilbert was born in Southwell on 4th April 1920, the son of Robert James Gilbert and Edith Watson. John joined the RAF in 1935 and did his basic training at Cranwell. He served in the RAF as an administrator in various units of Bomber Command in the United Kingdom. In September 1942 John got leave to get married to Eileen Jasper in Birmingham.

Two years later, in 1944, he was posted to India, serving on Lord Mountbatten's staff in Bombay, New Delhi and the Hindu Kush, coming home after independence had been granted in 1948.

In the post-war years he served in Ceylon, returned to work at RAF Manby as Personal Assistant to 'Bomber' Harris and was later promoted to Warrant Officer. He also became Chief Instructor to the boy entrants. In the 1960s John Gilbert completed a tour at RAF Episkopi, Cyprus, and then returned to the UK taking a last posting at RAF Linholme, nr Doncaster, before leaving the RAF in 1967. He retired to live in Birmingham with his family and eight years later, in 1975, died leaving a wife and two daughters.
Pauline Crocker and Angela Nettleship

Looking Back

RAF recruiting adverts in 1939 were quick to claim that by joining bomber and fighter squadrons young men would have the opportunity of finding excitement and adventure. What these adverts didn't mention, not surprisingly, was that intensive training was required for anyone wanting to be a pilot, navigator or gunner and that once on action stations many dangers faced these young men.

It takes a special kind of bravery to fly for hours across hostile territory, often with poor visibility, threatened by anti-aircraft artillery from the ground and Messerschmitt 109s in the air. Despite the tragically high casualty rate in both bomber and fighter squadrons, young men volunteered in their hundreds to play their part in this noble cause. Without their contribution the war could not have been won.'

<table>
<tr><td>(Home Front)</td><td>(Bombers & Mash)</td></tr>
</table>

BRITAIN'S SECRET WEAPON
For the "HOME FRONT"

is doing good work in 9 million homes, all day and every day.

A good wireless set is the best tonic for depression, bringing entertainment and news to your own fireside. And . . .

a good wireless set is

The New "90" MURPHY at £11

Call and hear one at

HUNT & CO. (NEWARK) LTD.

26, Stodman Street Newark :: Tel. 286

(Newark Advertiser)

HENRI

★ See HENRI of Appleton Gate for Re-conditioned Cycles, and limited number of New Cycles.

All Accessories

(Newark Advertiser)

CHAPTER 5

'Saucepans into Spitfires'

'Women of Britain, give us your aluminium and we want it now ... We will turn your pots and pans into Spitfires and Hurricanes.'[1]

By 1939 Germany had been preparing for a European war for over six years; Britain, on the other hand, had only seriously started concentrating on increasing its armaments since the 1938 Munich crisis. The need for a great boost in the production of aircraft, tanks and ships became even more urgent when, in June 1940, the German army overran the Low Countries and France, resulting in the British army's evacuation at Dunkirk. Britain faced the prospect of an immediate attack by air, probably followed by a seaborne invasion. To help pay for this vastly increased output, the British government called for financial help from each local community. It reasoned that this would also make people feel as if they were actually doing something for the war effort.

To provide a framework for the initiative, the government organised a number of designated weeks during the course of the war when people were encouraged to help raise funds for a specific type of weapon. During these weeks, there were promotional campaigns when local authorities, such as Southwell Rural District Council, held special events to persuade communities to invest in National Savings Certificates. This was a means for people to save small sums of money on a weekly basis, offering a low level of return, with the safety of a government guarantee. As a result the government could invest in new weapon production.

'Saucepans for Spitfires' and 'Save for a Spitfire' Campaigns July 1940

Supermarine Spitfire.

Designer: R J Mitchell

Produced: 1938 - 1948

No. built: 20351

(Wikipedia)

---

[1] Lord Beaverbrook, July 1940, Susan Briggs, *The Home Front 1939-45* (Weidenfeld: London, 1975), p. 185.

In 1940, when Britain was at great risk of invasion, an increase in aircraft production was essential. Lord Beaverbrook, the Minister for Aircraft Production, quite rightly took the credit for achieving this.

The 'Spitfire' was the key. These were the planes which captured the public's imagination, even though the majority of sorties in the 'Battle of Britain' were carried out by Hurricanes. A Spitfire was better at altitude, it was faster than the Hurricane and more agile. With its slim fuselage and graceful elliptical wings, it was beautiful. For those on the ground it was always the distant sight of the instantly recognisable Spitfire, with its delicate lines, its swoops and wheeling turns, engaging ME 109s through the clouds, that thrilled. The Spitfire seemed a symbol of defiance and of hope.

Lord Beaverbrook launched his 'Saucepans for Spitfires' campaign in July 1940, enabling housewives to feel that they were playing an active part in the battle against Hitler. On 10th July 1940 the head of the Women's Voluntary Service (WVS), Lady Reading, broadcast an appeal:

> The Minister of Aircraft Production is asking the women of Great Britain for everything made of aluminium, everything that can be given to be made into aeroplanes. ... I am asking for the things that you are using every day, anything and everything new and old, sound and broken, everything that's made of aluminium. ... We can all have that tiny thrill of thinking that, perhaps, it was my saucepan that made part of that Spitfire.[2]

Will You Help to Provide a 'Spitfire' Fighter Plane ?

Of course, You Will ! - Then you have your chance !

Generous Donations are invited towards the Cost of a Spitfire - £6,000

People in Newark and District Works, Factories, Offices, Shops, Clubs, etc. as well as private individuals who value the opportunity of subscribing to a fund in a Free Country to help to Keep it Free are asked to assist.

Subscriptions sent to the Midland Bank, Newark, will be acknowledged in the Press.

MR. H. M. L. HUTCHINSON
Hon Treasurer, Midland Bank.

MR. J. HICKMAN
Hon. Secretary.

(Newark Advertiser)

The response to Lady Reading's appeal was instant and overwhelming. Almost before she had finished speaking, saucepans, kettles, dishes, colanders, zinc baths, and toys were being handed in to WVS centres. In total, the WVS reckoned that their collection added up to nearly a thousand tons of aluminium by the time the appeal finished in mid-September.

---

[2] Norman Longmate, *How We Lived* (London: Arrow, 1973), p. 281.

There was real community interest in the campaign to collect any scrap metal and pass it on so it could be converted into aircraft production. In the Ideal Cinema foyer, there was a 'Pay for a Spitfire' appeal and I can remember going with my Mum to Holy Trinity School, carrying old saucepans and other scrap metal from Sunnyside. The teachers kept a stack of scrap metal collected locally.

Brian Pacey

Under another of Beaverbrook's schemes people could help pay for a Spitfire. The basis of his appeal was that it would cost £5,000 to build a Spitfire, though the true cost was closer to £12,000. Presumably, the underestimate was to make the appeal within reach. He then cleverly went on to itemise a Spitfire's constituent parts, so that every component was 'priced': £2,000 would buy a wing, £5 a compass, a guinea a thermometer, 15s the blast tube of a machine gun, and, for mere pocket money, for a rivet 6d could be contributed. It was a brilliant stroke of public relations, as people felt that putting their shilling in the collection box connected them to heroic events.

The 'Spitfire Fund' was taken up in almost every town and city in the British Isles. Those places that 'bought' a Spitfire could have it named after their town, in letters four inches high in yellow paint on the fuselage. Individuals and businesses also raised large sums of money. Garfield Weston, MP for Macclesfield, presented £100,000 to the Spitfire Fund. The Nizam of Hyderabad donated so much that 152 (Hyderabad) Squadron was named in his honour. As far as businesses were concerned, Fighter Command got the aircraft while the business got excellent publicity. No-one lost out. In all, £13 million was raised.[3]

Southwell residents recall the 'Save for a Spitfire' campaign in the summer of 1940. During the campaign Squadron Leader Fidler of the RAF arranged for a Spitfire to be on display in Newark Market Place. Southwell had an exhibition of original posters and artwork by Aircraftman Thomas and Aircraftman Lorimer.

 A "SPITFIRE" IN MARKET PLACE

R.A.F. DISPLAY TO-MORROW

(Newark Advertiser)

Throughout the year there always seemed to be concerts at the Saracen's Head and the Ideal Cinema to raise funds for the war effort, like the 'Save for a Spitfire' campaign. Often Joan Thomas's Dance School would perform.

Janette Barrett[4]

Mother always found money for the Spitfire Fund, but my father didn't earn enough for regular payments to the National Savings scheme.

Keith Marshall

---

[3] Juliet Gardiner, *Wartime Britain* (London: Headline Publishing, 2004), p. 309.

[4] Interview with Paul Birks.

The *Newark Advertiser* gave a list of Southwell residents who generously supported the 'Spitfire Fund'.

Southwell Contributions[5]

Previously acknowledged	**£177**	**7**	**0**			
Mrs John Caudwell	1	0	0	Mrs Emily Bird	2 10 0
Mrs C G Caudwell	5	0	0	Mr Herbert Ellis	1 0 0
Mr/Mrs F Schumach	1	0	0	Mrs Herbert Ellis	1 0 0
Miss Dorothy Leivers		10	0	Miss S Roberts	5 0
Miss Joan Garland		5	0	Mrs E E King	1 0 0
Mrs May	2	0	0	Mr/Mrs W Mountney	5 0 0
Mr George Burrows	1	0	0	H Merryweather, Sons	10 0 0
Mr R L Lee		10	0	G F Mosedale, Sons	2 2 0
Miss Barbara Starkey		10	0	Mr/Mrs Blair	2 10 0
In mem. E H Olulow	1	0	0	Mr H Rickett	2 2 0
Mr Leonard Steel	1	0	0	Sale of tickets	13 17 9
Mr Joseph Keetley		10	0	Mrs Cundy	10 0
Mrs Reginald Wright		10	0	Mrs Suckling	1 0 0
Mrs Nielson		10	6	Mr Roach	10 0
Mr G B Hempsall		5	0	Mr/Mrs Bates	10 0
Mr E J Ridgeway		5	0	Miss Goodwin	10 0
Mr/Mrs E A Walton	3	3	0	Mr J Caudwell	2 2 0
Mr George Cholerton	1	0	0	Mrs Marshall	10 0
Dr J F D Willoughby	2	10	0	Mrs Conybeare	1 0 0
Mrs Kennedy	2	10	0	Mrs Davage	1 1 0
Miss Barbara Warwick		10	0	Mr. J A Elliott	1 10 0
Mr/Mrs J J Jones	1	0	0	Miss Eva Gibson	1 0 0
Rev J S Wright	2	0	0	Mr John Gibson	1 0 0
Mrs J S Wright	2	0	0	Mr Henry Hore	5 0 0
Miss M B J Wright	1	0	0	Mrs Henry Hore	2 2 0
Miss E Ford	2	0	0	Mrs A G Merryweather	2 2 0
Mr/Mrs Whysall	1	0	0	Mrs H E Steel & Miss Porter	3 3 0

---

[5] *N/Adv*, 16th October 1940.

'National Warship Week' January 1942

The signal is SAVE for YOUR WARSHIP WEEK

There's a 'bite' about the Navy's attack. They're doing their job famously. Here's your chance to lend them a hand. CLEAR DECKS FOR ACTION and make your Warship Week a shattering broadside against the enemy. The Signal is SAVE! Invest for all you're worth in War Savings.

Go to a Post Office or your Bank or Stockbroker and invest your money in 3% Savings Bonds 1955-65, 2½% National War Bonds 1949-51, 3% Defence Bonds, or Savings Certificates : or deposit your savings in the Post Office or Trustee Savings Banks, Buy Savings Stamps at 6d. and 2/6d. each from a Post Office, Trustee Savings Bank, or your Savings Group.

INVEST ALL YOU CAN IN
3% Savings Bonds
2½% National War Bonds
3% Defence Bonds
Savings Certificates
Post Office Savings Bank
Trustee Savings Bank

(Newark Advertiser)

In 1940 the government had come to the conclusion that it was absolutely necessary to raise substantial sums of money for more weapons. Towns and districts were encouraged to set up their local 'National Savings Group', persuading people to buy savings stamps on a regular basis. Southwell RDC were quick to take up this initiative; a local group was formed and centred on the Food Office in King Street. Miss Galloway and Miss Starkey were put in charge of the sale of savings stamps, and by June Miss Galloway expressed her delight in the number of residents who had joined the Savings Movement.[6]

To raise the profile of this National Savings Movement, 'Savings Weeks' were held proclaiming the patriotic duty of raising target amounts through individual savings in government bonds and national savings certificates. Southwell and District held their first Savings Week from 24th to 31st January 1942 - 'National Warship Week'.

Early in the war the Royal Navy had not only lost many large ships, but was facing pressure to provide escorts for precious convoys in the Atlantic. Ships sunk by enemy action had to be replaced. Each region was provided with a savings target to achieve, based on the region's population, with each level of savings having a class of warship assigned to it. Towns and villages would focus on paying for smaller ships such as cruisers, destroyers and submarines.

In Southwell Rural District a target of £425,000 was set. If this target was achieved, the community would be permitted to 'adopt' a submarine, HMS *Tempest* and its crew. Events were planned for each day of the week. The National Warship Week was inaugurated at a meeting in the Assembly Rooms when the proceedings were opened by the Marchioness of Titchfield, and by the rousing delivery of a speech by Rear Admiral J B Pulliblank DSO, OBE.

The Navy is ready to do it. They don't want any sympathy. What they do want is more ships and more ships. You could double the Navy and we should not have too much. It is very difficult to realise how much they are in need of ships and men, and the men take some time to train. For these ships we need the money.[7]

---

[6] *N/Adv,* 17th April 1940 and 12th June 1940.
[7] *N/Adv,* 4th February 1942.

The Rear Admiral gave impetus to an entire week of special events. The Saturday opening was followed by a Church Parade on the Sunday. The organisations involved assembled on Burgage Green and paraded to a service at the Minster, to which the congregations of all the churches in the town were invited. On the Monday there was a public meeting at the Ideal Cinema, with two short documentary films, followed by the popular Hollywood film *Gunga Din*. A dance was organised on the Tuesday at the Assembly Rooms, and the Wednesday was given over to a Schools' Day with a concert by all the Southwell Elementary Schools. Thursday was dedicated a Civil Defence Day, with a further concert. Finally, on Friday, 'Ladies Day', a Whist Drive was held at Holy Trinity Church in the evening.

During the whole week, the ground floor of the Assembly Rooms was opened all day for the sale of National Savings stamps and certificates, while stocks and bonds could be purchased on any day through the banks.[8]

By 11th February £280,000 had been collected during the Southwell and District 'Warship Week', though it was reported that there was more to come. About £45,000 was raised in Southwell alone. Although this fell short of the ambitious target, the Committee was very happy with the result, which amounted to more than £7 per head of the population of the district. The local schools had contributed £600, raised from the purchase of stamps and certificates and the concert at the Assembly Rooms.

The normal practice after a successful 'War Savings Week' was for the local community to be presented with a special plaque, in recognition of their outstanding contribution to the war effort. The local community would then hand over a plaque to the Royal Navy to mark the adoption of the warship [i.e. an exchange of plaques]. This occurred in April 1944, when Vice-Admiral MacKinnon handed the 'Warship' plaque to Ald. C G Caudwell JP, Chairman of the Southwell RDC Savings Committee.

HMS Storm (Private Collection)

The Vice-Admiral said that although many things in the navy had changed, there were some things [that] never changed and they were traditions - traditions that had been handed down to them by their forefathers ... One of those traditions that was impressed very firmly on him when he went to sea was that nothing was impossible until you had a jolly good try.

Mr Straw, on behalf of the Southwell RDC, handed to Vice-Admiral MacKinnon a plaque in commemoration of the adoption of HMS *Storm* and for presentation to the ship's company in the hope that it would remind them of the good feeling that existed between Southwell and the ship.[9]

[8] *N/Adv,* 11th February 1942.
[9] *N/Adv,* 5th April 1944.

At the end of the war it was finally revealed to local residents the full extent of HMS *Storm's* success, operating as it did in Japanese-held waters in the Far East, specifically hitting the enemy's supply routes off Southern Burma.

SOUTHWELL'S HMS STORM

Sank Nine Enemy Ships In One Day

... The name of Commander Young's submarine may now be revealed. It is, most appropriately, HMS *Storm* the ship adopted by Southwell Rural District. The Lieut-Commander's record has been summed up by the commanding officer of the Far Eastern Flotilla with which the *Storm* operated as follows: 'In a series of patrols in shallow and often restricted waters, the *Storm's* intrepid commanding officer, with the full support of his well-trained team of officers and men, has made history for the British submarine service.

A Bold Leader

(HMS Storm Badge)

... Lieut-Commander Young has carried out his patrol with almost unbelievable audacity, combined with cool judgement and profound sagacity, and has shown what results can be obtained ... by bold and determined leadership.

Most of the *Storm's* successes have been achieved by gun action. She has sunk 20 of the enemy's coastal supply vessels - 19 of them by gunfire, one by torpedo - and has damaged or probably sunk many others. In addition, she has accounted for one destroyer and four patrol or escort vessels.

Lieut-Commander Young ... said on his return to his country: 'Our commission would have been more profitable if targets had been more plentiful. Most of them were coast-crawling supply vessels, small in size but valuable to the enemy because they were laden with ammunition and materials for carrying on the war against our troops in Burma. On one of our last patrols we managed to put down 11 of these craft, nine in one day.'[10]

'Wings For Victory' Week June 1943

1943 saw 'Wings for Victory Week', June 19th-26th. This time the target was lower, £25,000 for Southwell and £250,000 for Southwell Rural District. The objective was to purchase a twin-engine Lancaster bomber and a fighter. It was agreed beforehand that the officer commanding a nearby RAF Station would assist with a display of planes over the town during the week's campaigning. An RAF dance band was available for social gatherings. As in the previous year, the town planned a programme of events on each day of the week. These opened on Saturday evening, when the speaker was Group Captain R V M Odbert, followed by a Ministry of Information film.

---

[10] *N/Adv*, 30th May 1945. - HMS *Storm* Badge: *https://en.wikipedia.org/w/index.php?Curid=12053153*

'Wings For Victory Week'
'CRUSHING NAZIS IN THEIR LAIRS'

... Group Captain Odbert said that 'Wings for Victory' weeks aimed to provide the RAF with the overwhelming air power they needed to obtain final victory. They would all recall that during the first phase of the war they were on the defensive. The slogan was then, more fighters - more Spitfires.

We are now on the offensive. Our appeal today is plainly for more fighters and bombers so that we can continue to bring the war home to the heart of the ruthless Nazis who created it.[11]

(Newark Advertiser)

On Sunday afternoon there was a church parade to the Minster and a service. The parade, including RAF and WAAF from the district, met on Burgage Green and proceeded to the Minster, accompanied by the North Midland Regional band and the local Home Guard band. The lessons were read by Wing Commander J H Searby and Fl. Lieut A C Bradbury. An address was given by Revd C E Wright, and Wing Commander Baxter took the salute near the Memorial Cross.[12]

On Monday there was a dance display by pupils of Miss Joan Thomas' in the Assembly Rooms. Tuesday evening was given over to a display by the National Fire Service, followed by a demonstration by the Home Guard on the Recreation Ground and music by the RAF band. Wednesday and Thursday brought a Schools' Display in the Assembly Rooms and a Whist Drive, organised by the WI, in the Holy Trinity Schoolroom.

One of the features of the week's events was the concert at the Assembly Rooms on Wednesday evening when a joint programme by the children at the Southwell elementary schools was compèred by Mr R Matthews.

Schools' Concert – 'Wings for Victory Week'

The concert opened with an action-song, *"Soldier, soldier, won't you marry me?"* by the Methodist School children. This was followed by a fairy play, *"The King's Cobbler"*, and two rhymes, *"Hide little Mousie"* and *"Where are you going to my pretty Maid?"*, by the small pupils of Holy Trinity School. Then came the play, *"The Rabbit who wanted red wings"*, by the Methodist Infants, followed by the Methodist school choir.

During the interval an appeal for public support during "Wings for Victory Week" was made by Mrs Swingler. After the interval came an entertaining act by a troupe of Nigger Minstrels from the National School followed by a scene from *"Alice through the looking glass"* by senior girls of the National School. £31 was raised.[13]

---

[11] *N/Adv*, 23rd June 1943.
[12] *N/Adv*, 19th May 1943.
[13] *N/Adv*, 30th June 1943.

The RAF band reappeared at Friday's dance in the Assembly Rooms, which was organised by the Youth Council, and the week concluded with a Sports Gala at the Recreation Ground, including a PT display, sideshows and sports races.

Saturday's 'Wings for Victory' Sports Meeting

'Wings Week' was brought to a triumphant close on Saturday evening when a children's sports meeting rounded off the week of festivities.

The children of the Methodist School gave a Physical Training Display which was followed by an exhibition of folk dancing from the girls of the National School. The Girl Guides' Camp was another feature. Later a programme of sports took place. The evening concluded with addresses by Ald. C G Caudwell and the Chairman of the Parish Council, Mr Matthews, both of whom thanked the public for their magnificent response which had enabled Southwell to reach a figure very much in excess of the target.[14]

The success of our "Warship" and "War Weapons" Weeks showed the Navy and the Army our determination to save for their vital ships and weapons.

Now it's the turn of the R.A.F. We must back them too, to the limit. Let's break all savings records during "Wings for Victory" Week. Show them that we too, by reaching our objective and going bang *over* the target, can win wings—"Victory Wings" for our district.

PUT EVERYTHING INTO IT—

3% Savings Bonds 1960-70

2½% National War Bonds 1951-3

3% Defence Bonds

Savings Certificates

Savings Stamps

Post Office Savings Bank

Trustee Savings Bank

The week was an outstanding success. The target had been £250,000, and this was 'smashed' by £120,252, the grand total being £370,252. Among the contributions made during the week were £10,000 each by the Westminster, National Provincial, Lloyds, Barclays and Midland Banks; £25,000 by the Mansfield, Sutton and District Co-operative Society; £23,009 by the Nottingham and District Miners Pension Scheme, £32,500 from Bolsover Colliery Co. and £10,000 from Hall and Earl Ltd. This meant that the average contribution was £10 per head of the population. Since a good weekly wage was then about £3, it can be seen how extremely successful the series of fundraising events were.[15]

In recognition of Southwell Rural District's fine achievement, a 'Wings for Victory' plaque should have been presented by Squadron-Leader P A MacKenzie, but in his absence the duty was performed by Captain W F Macdonald, Commissioner for Nottingham Savings, on 5th April 1944 at the Southwell Rural District offices. Certificates of Honour were also given to the various committees and Alderman Caudwell presented three logbooks to the Squadron.

(Newark Advertiser)

---

[14] *N/Adv,* 30th June 1943.
[15] *N/Adv*, 5th July 1943.

'Salute the Soldier Week' June 1944

1944 brought 'Salute the Soldier Week', beginning on 28th June. Southwell's target was set at £30,000, whilst the Rural District's was £250,000. The money was needed to buy more tanks and other army materiel. A glade in Sherwood Forest was the picturesque setting for the opening of Southwell Rural District Council's campaign. American troops took part in the procession from the local school to the Forest Cricket ground.

The procession was headed by the band of the Rifle Brigade and the American troops, followed by members of the Home Guard, Army Cadet Force, Air Training Corps, Girls' Training Corps, British Legion, Parish Council, Special Constabulary, National Fire Service, Wardens' Service, Land Army, Thoresby Ambulance Brigade, Girls' Brigade and Boys' Brigade.[16]

Southwell's local campaign was inaugurated in the grounds of Dunham House by two ex-POWs, Colonel C N Roney-Dougall MC and Major J Kirkland.

Timely Tribute

Colonel Roney-Dougall, declaring the campaign open, mentioned how he and his friend, Major J Kirkland, had been POWs in Germany for what seemed to be a century and a half.

The 'Salute Week' gave them the opportunity to pay a timely tribute to their fighting soldiers. The more material object was to provide the best soldiers in the world with the best weapons in the world (applause).

The speaker referred to Dunkirk, Hong Kong, Singapore and Burma - a whole series of events in which the best soldiers in the world met defeat, because they were too few in numbers and were too poorly equipped.

Then came the come-back - the campaign in Africa and Italy and now in France which was to end in the liberation of Europe. That come-back had been made possible very largely because of the savings of the people at home.[17]

The Salt of the Earth

They came from the North lands,
They came from the South lands,
They came from the mountains,
They came from the fens,
They drilled hard with rifle,
They drilled with their bayonets,
They practised with mortars,
They practised with Stens.

Now they're fighting our battles,
And in spirit we're with them.
They're fighting our battles,
And proving their worth.
They won't *all* get medals
They won't *all* get mention,
But they're *all* British soldiers,
The salt of the earth.

SALUTE THE SOLDIER

Let us salute him, the man who fights our battles for us. Let us Salute the Soldier by going without just a little more, by giving up just a little more, and by saving even more.

(Newark Advertiser)

Local school children played an active and enthusiastic part in all the week's fundraising events. Nearly £90 was raised by two displays given by Miss Joan Thomas' Dancing Class at the Assembly Rooms. A concert was arranged by the Head Teachers and Capt. G T Francis, with local school children providing the first part of the programme. The entertainment opened with a varied performance of songs, admirably rendered by the Methodist school scholars who were trained and conducted by Mr J Dixon. The Methodist Infants followed with a pleasant little play *'Gifts for Mother Hubbard'*, which featured a number of nursery rhyme characters. There were other more military presentations.

---

[16] *N/Adv,* 21st June 1944.
[17] *N/Adv,* 21st June 1944.

In 'Salute the Soldier Week', there were plenty of army men and vehicles in town and we all went down to the Recreation Ground where a big field gun was fired, using live ammunition, in the direction of the Old Golf Course which had recently been ploughed up. **Keith Marshall**

Embarkation leave

Sheila carries daddy's gas-mask,
Peter carries daddy's gun.
Mother's chattering on and laughing
As if parting were just fun.

She's put apples in his pocket,
He's got photos in his book,
When he isn't busy fighting,
He'll have time to have a look.

Dad is going to fight for England,
For a world where men are free,
Better times for all but — mostly
He'll be fighting for these three.

SALUTE THE SOLDIER

The soldier is giving up all he holds most dear. What can we do to show our gratitude? We can salute the soldier by saving. SALUTE THE SOLDIER

Issued by the National Savings Committee

(Newark Advertiser)

As in 1943, the week's campaign was a huge success. Southwell Rural District's target of £250,000 was beaten by the huge amount of £124,556. Southwell itself reached the splendid total of £44,988, against a target of £30,000. The recent D-Day operation must have helped to spur on the campaign.[18]

The 'Salute the Soldier Week' showed a fine result, all the better because the success was due chiefly to many small investments, rather than big firms giving large sums. The two services in the Minster were intended to lift our effort onto a higher level than mere commercialism, and connect the week with self-dedication and a call to personal service. The first Sunday saw our Nave filled with a great congregation, and we can never forget the inspiration of the Rifle Brigade military band ... they played two pieces which brought out the loveliness of such music as heard in such a building as our Minster is.[19]

One of the local people most responsible for the town's impressive performance during the National Savings Weeks was William Leek. His death came as a shock at this particular time.

Mr William Leek's death - A Genial Southwell Resident

Southwell has lost a respected resident by the death of Mr William Leek which occurred at his home on The Ropewalk last Wednesday. ... Mr Leek was 68. He left his position at Messrs Warwick and Richardson Ltd, Newark to become the Assistant Overseer for Southwell, an office he occupied until 1927, and up to the time of his death he was Rating and Valuation Officer for Southwell Rural District Council, an office he had held since 1927. ... He also held the office of Clerk to the Southwell Parish Council since April 1918.

... The National Savings movement found in Mr Leek an enthusiastic worker and keen organiser. In addition to being Hon. Secretary of the Dunham House Savings Group, he was Hon. Secretary of the National War Savings for the Southwell Rural District and was responsible for the organisation of the various Savings Weeks Campaigns.

... Mr William Leek was a true lover of sport. He was Hon. Secretary of the Southwell Cricket Club for twenty years ... and he was a former Captain of the Club and an old member of Notts. County Cricket Club. In 1902-3 he was Chairman of St Mary's Football Club and was for many

---

[18] *N/Adv*, 28th June 1944.
[19] *Rural Deanery Magazine,* August 1944.

years on the Committee of the Southwell Horticultural Society. He was a member of the Southwell Lodge of Freemasons. He leaves a widow, two sons and one daughter to whom much sympathy has been extended. There was a large attendance at the funeral on Saturday when a service was held in the Minster.[20]

Salvage Collection Campaign

A 'Salvage Drive' was one way in which the entire Southwell community was encouraged to join in the war effort.

(Home Front 1939-45)

Collection of Salvage

Southwell RDC is actively involved in salvage work and appeals for the following materials, giving instructions for the collecting of the various types of material.

1. Waste Paper and Cardboard

Save all newspapers, magazines and books and bundle together. Save wrapping papers, cardboard and cartons, large or small, compress and bundle them together. Hand the bundles to the refuse collector.

2. Metals

Keep iron, steel, copper, brass and aluminium separate and place near the side of the ashbin on the next bin day. (Aug. 2)

3. Tins

Tins, drums, galvanised baths and buckets should be placed as usual on the pavement edge for collection. Please do not mix with glass and pot, these may go in the ashbin each week.[21]

Southwell RDC decided to have two main centres for the collection of all salvage. The Minster and Holy Trinity Churches were quick to offer their services; the two people designated to organise the collection centres were Mrs Coghill at Holy Trinity Vicarage, and Mrs Conybeare at The Residence, Church Street.

Local residents were asked to take scrap metals and waste paper there as regularly as possible. It wasn't just individual households that were urged to support the Salvage Drive. Throughout the war the schools, the Boy Scouts and the Girls' Friendly Society organised collections of waste paper, including newspapers, magazines, periodicals, books and cards.

I belonged to the Girls' Friendly Society which was one of the church organisations. We were asked to collect newspaper and scrap metal, including saucepans for the war effort.

Jean Quickenden

---

[20] *N/Adv*, 1st July 1944.
[21] *N/Adv*, 17th July 1940.

155

(Imperial War Museum)

I remember being asked to take aluminium and other metals into school to be collected for the war effort.

Harry Cooling

A Salvage Committee ran a house-to-house collection, with the help of the children from the school and the Pioneer Club.

Lowdham Local Village History[22]

However, the idea of the Salvage Drive was not without controversy. Southwell RDC decided in the summer of 1941 that scrap metal collection needed to be increased to enhance Southwell's contribution to the war effort and that the only way this could be achieved was by removing iron railings from around the town. The main areas affected were around Southwell Minster, the entrance to the Minster Broad Walk and along the main streets, especially Westgate and Church Street. The Council was careful to promote this move in a positive way, by suggesting that the removal of railings would open up town vistas and add an air of spaciousness. However, not all residents saw it this way.

To the Editor of the Advertiser
Re. Removal of Southwell railings

In last week's 'Southwell Topics' you stated that the removal of the railings improved the town. I don't know where this comes in as damage has been done to the stone walls. The iron posts and chains removed from the Minster entrance were a safeguard to cattle eating the Yew trees, a deadly poison.
   What has resulted at Rufford Park, Norwood Park and at Averham Rectory? And the person who selected the railings to be taken down missed several railings in Easthorpe. Elsewhere, flowers and shrubs were burnt by the gas used in the work.   **J F D, Southwell.[23]**

The removal of the railings made a strong impression even on the young people in the town.

The railings in front of most of the big Prebendal houses were taken away. Those in front of Vicar's Court, at the Minster end, were also taken as were those in front of the Old Grammar School on Church Street. Any metal that could have the faintest use for the war effort was taken.

Steve Pulford[24]

I remember the railings in front of the buildings on Westgate and the Prebendal houses on Church Street being taken down to provide metal for aircraft and warship construction. When I later purchased Normanton Prebend there was only wooden fencing. I replaced this with metal railings.

Douglas Gascoine

I can remember the launch of the Salvage Campaign when they took away our railings in Easthorpe.

Janette Barrett[25]

I remember being in Easthorpe one day and seeing men get out of a lorry and take the railings down, alongside the terrace between The Hearty Goodfellow and where the shop is now.

Peter Cant

---

[22] *The 20th Century in Lowdham* (Lowdham LHS, 1999), p. 112.
[23] *N/Adv,* 2nd July 1941.
[24] Birks.
[25] Birks.

Where railings were taken down, ugly stumps were left. In some cases, now modern replacement railings have been installed. The removal tended to be on the main streets, especially Westgate, Queen Street and Church Street.   **Robert Beckett**

In May 1942 a special two-week Salvage Drive took place. Southwell householders were required to do their utmost by searching for all potentially suitable materials. Southwell RDC especially stressed the need for waste rubber.

(Imperial War Museum)

Waste rubber of all kinds, including old tyres, hot water bottles, Wellington boots, in fact everything rubber is urgently required for the war effort. Please put the rubber waste on the roadside by 9 a.m., commencing 8th May.[26]

---

[26] *N/Adv,* 6th May 1942.

A few weeks later, in June 1942, Southwell RDC put out a further plea for salvage.

Southwell and Salvage

To The Editor of the Advertiser

Sir, - The present world conflict is not only on the battlefield, it is a war of production and raw materials. The country has responded magnificently to the call for salvage - indeed 12, 000 homes are vital sources of raw materials.

A further important step to obtain raw materials is the Ministry of Supply 'Salvage of Waste Materials (No 3) Order' which makes it an offence to destroy or throw away any rag, rope or string or put rags, rope or string in a refuse bin. ...

A considerable extra tonnage of rags will thus become available for salvage - they are urgently needed to provide the raw materials for the production of numerous forms of equipment for the fighting Forces.

I feel sure that everyone - housewives particularly - will respond to this order in the spirit in which it has been made - the spirit to win the war; but I would like to ... appeal to them to release for salvage all the worn out woollen, cotton and linen rags, pieces of carpet, sacking, rope and string that they can spare, not forgetting those old suits, frocks, underclothing, rags and upholstery which can no longer serve their owners any useful purpose, but can now render a valuable service to the nation.

Rags should be kept as clean as possible, separate from other salvage, ready for the collector. It is a good idea to keep a rag bag in which every bit of rag, rope and string can be kept for salvage.

Yours obediently,

ALEX STRAW, Chairman of the Southwell RDC[27]

The Salvage Campaign continued into the later years of the war, with a fortnight in May 1944 dedicated to a 'Book Collection', where targets were once again set. The Southwell Rural District target was 72,000 books, and the town expected to contribute 6,000 books. Housewives and owners of business premises were called upon to turn out every book or paper they did not really need. Local people were asked to give the books to a Salvage Steward or to a school child, or they could be taken to the local schools. The books were then organised by competent sorters into those for the Forces, those for restocking raid-damaged libraries and those for re-pulping to provide vital munitions.

As part of the Salvage Campaign I can remember at school being asked to collect and hand in books and magazines. To encourage children to collect there were a series of rewards given. If you collected ten books/magazines, you were rewarded with a corporal's stripes, twenty books a sergeant's stripes. If you collected 100 you could become a Field Marshal, like Montgomery. Our family knew the local printer, Mr Padgett, so one day I took my father's wheelbarrow and asked Mr Padgett if I could take away any cast-offs he might have, I knew he liked to get rid of slightly blemished booklets. I got a barrowful and as a result I became a Field Marshal! At school I proudly showed off my rank and in return got a bit of stick for it. I felt the only thing I didn't have was the car.

Keith Marshall

---

27 *N/Adv*, 29th July 1942.

Other Community Projects

Comforts for Servicemen

Various local groups provided comforts for servicemen in the armed forces. The central organisation was the 'Southwell Hospital Supplies and Comforts for the Troops', and in November 1941, after one year's work, £270 had been collected and 2,175 knitted hospital garments had been made. Two depots were used by the organisation: The Great Hall at Bishop's Manor and the Church Street residence of Mrs Warwick. Subsidiary working parties were held at Holy Trinity Vicarage, Brackenhurst and Eakring Rectory and help was also forthcoming from Upton, Halam and Edingley. Various schools, members of the WI and the Methodist Church also contributed. The British Legion assisted, supplying lists of servicemen and dispatching the parcels.

(Newark Advertiser)

At the end of the first year (Nov 1941) the garments had been distributed as follows:

To the Comforts for the Troops County Fund - 1627 knitted garments
To the Upton Searchlight Company - 16 knitted garments
To Colonel Starkey's Regiment - 78 knitted garments
To Newark WVS for the Navy - 7 knitted garments
For the Southwell Easter Parcels - 110 pairs of socks
To Individual Soldiers, Sailors and Airmen - 40 pairs of socks
To the Finnish Troops' Comforts' Fund - 116 Hospital garments
To the British Red Cross Society, per WVS - 472 Hospital garments
Socks and mittens are now being made for the Christmas parcels for local men serving with the forces.[28]

---

[28] Harold Robinson, *Rural Deanery Magazine,* November 1941.

Southwell WI held demonstrations on the making of soft slippers for wounded servicemen and thrift slippers from the felt hats that many people wore at that time. Both Southwell and Lowdham WI organised working parties to knit comforts for the troops, and a whist drive was held every Saturday evening to raise money for the Comforts' Fund. The WVS collected donations and packed and dispatched hundreds of parcels. Private individuals also did their bit.

Congratulations to Mrs Johnson-Cooper

Mrs Johnson-Cooper and her family of the George and Dragon, Southwell, are to be congratulated on their sustained effort to organise a fund for Soldiers' Comforts.

Their scheme, run from the public house, originated about two years ago when Mrs Johnson-Cooper and her family decided to run a Comforts' scheme on their own to include not only Southwell lads, but also men in the Armed Forces who had been billeted in the town. The idea had the hearty support of the customers of the house.

At Christmas 1942, when the effort had just been launched, each man received a postal order of 3s each. Last Christmas, 1943, the 257 men on the list received 4s each. This included 4s for the POW Relatives' Association to be dispatched through their organisation.

Mrs Johnson-Cooper has received over 200 letters and air graphs and Christmas greetings from grateful boys in all parts of this country and abroad.[29]

Geoff Dodsworth served with the Sherwood Foresters and remembers receiving parcels from the Johnson-Cooper family at the George and Dragon.

Sarah Johnson-Cooper arranged for parcels to be sent off to soldiers serving abroad. I was a beneficiary of those parcels when I was in France with the Sherwood Foresters. I used to get a parcel consisting of 20 cigarettes, usually Players, a handkerchief, some food and a balaclava. The Johnson-Coopers, as landlords, had photographs of all the Southwell men and women who were abroad with the armed services pinned up on the walls of the public house.

Sarah at this time laid on free 'Tripe Suppers' in the Tea Room. Throughout the war local women used The George for knitting socks for soldiers. In August 1945 a lavish celebration took place at the inn when there was a 'Victory over Japan' street party held there.

Geoff Dodsworth

I remember when my father was in the army he would receive food parcels from the mother of Neville Ross, who ran the George and Dragon. Neville Ross was the clerk to the magistrates.

Douglas Gascoine

My mother, who could knit a pair of khaki gloves in an evening, found time to belong to a group that produced comforts for the troops. Everybody seemed to be doing something for the war effort.

John Watts

Girl Guides, Brownies, Girls' Friendly Society (GFS) and King's Messengers were all heavily involved in knitting clothing and blankets for servicemen. The Girl Guides and the GFS group usually met at the Residence in Vicar's Court. The kitchen there had been fitted out and decorated for use as a Youth Centre by the Minster. Mr Ellis, the greengrocer next to Bull Yard, also made a room available, the 'Ellis Room', for youth groups.

---

[29] *N/Adv*, 23rd February 1944.

Girl Guides Marching outside Holy Trinity Church (Malcolm Gough)

I belonged to three local girls' groups, the Girl Guides, GFS and King's Messengers. All three encouraged girls to contribute to the town's war effort. As I was interested in knitting, along with many other people, I would pick up wool from Mrs Warwick at Normanton Prebend and then later take back what I had knitted for our soldiers abroad, whether it be a scarf, balaclava or mittens.

Margaret Pulford

We used to knit scarves, socks and mittens for the soldiers, and Colonel Warwick's wife at Normanton Prebend would supervise the project. Quite by chance Enid sent some knitted garments to Edward Caudwell, who was in the forces in Iceland. Edward had previously lived here and he replied, thanking Enid.

Janette Barrett[30]

I was in the Girl Guides and one task we were set was to help the war effort. We were shown how to knit squares for blankets and then asked to sew collars.

Betty Millard

At the outbreak of war, I belonged to the Girls' Friendly Society which met in the old Trebeck Hall and was run by Mary Becher. I also joined and later helped with the Minster Youth Club which met at the Residence. We had plenty of fun and I remember taking part in a concert at the Minster to raise funds for the war effort.

Jean Hallam[31]

As Girl Guides we were all expected to knit scarves, which were taken to Mrs Warwick at Normanton Prebend. The scarves were then distributed to soldiers. Our leader was Miss Margaret Peet, and the meetings were either in the WI Hall, Trebeck Hall or in the Ellis Room off Bull Yard.

Jean Quickenden

---

[30] Birks.
[31] Doreen Stevenson Interviews (Unpublished).

The Air Training Corps

Many boys joined the Boy Scouts and spent a lot of time supporting the war effort, regularly collecting scrap metals and waste paper. For older boys, later in the war, there was the opportunity of joining the local squadron of the Air Training Corps.

Local squadron of the Air Training Corps formed

Under the chairmanship of Mr J H Stark, Regional Traffic Commissioner, Bleasby Hall, a squadron of the Air Training Corps has been formed for Southwell and District. Premises have been obtained for headquarters and it is hoped that the eligible boys of Southwell and neighbourhood will quickly enrol so that training may be begun.

A public meeting will be held at the Ideal Cinema on Sunday, 21st March at 3 p.m. when the movement will be fully explained. ... Fl. Lt Norfolk, DFC, an old Southwellian, will address the meeting. Everyone interested is cordially invited, especially boys and their parents. Enrolment forms may be obtained from the Council offices. A display of model aircraft made by the ATC cadets can be seen in the windows of Messrs Dowse, King Street.[32]

There was a flourishing Minster Grammar School Scout Troop. I lived a bit too far from town to join this, but many in my form did, and vied with each other in earning all sorts of proficiency badges. The aim was to achieve an armful and they were displayed on the sleeve. Quite a few boys joined the Air Training Corps, one of whom was Peter Wendels, my friend and desk-mate for three years. A keen aero-modeller, he was inducted into basic gliding in the ATC.

John Watts

Detachments of the squadron visited local Bomber Command aerodromes, learned about work in the RAF and helped the regulars there. A number of cadets were later at Syerston, assisting in preparation for the D-Day offensive. In addition, annual camps were held - the first one at Elsham Wolds, Lincolnshire.

I joined the Air Training Corps and used to visit RAF stations at Newton and Syerston and the American 9th Air force bases at Bottesford and Langar; a few flights in Wellingtons, Lancasters or Dakotas made it all worthwhile. The Americans always gave us a good time with ice cream and tinned fruit and rides in their jeeps. On leaving school I joined Rolls Royce as an engineering apprentice and worked on the first jet engines; later in 1946 I joined the RAF.

Jim Bentley, Thurgarton[33]

A detached flight of the Air Training Corps of Lowdham Squadron was formed at Bleasby with my husband as C. O. At least eight boys (16 years and upwards) joined and with boys from surrounding villages about 20 paraded on Sunday mornings using the road as a parade ground. Lectures were held on Thursday evenings. Subsequently my husband with the Bleasby flight formed No. 2054 Squadron at Southwell.[34]

---

[32] *N/Adv,* 17th March 1944.
[33] Thurgarton Village website.
[34] Wright, Beatrice, *Bleasby in Wartime* (Beatrice Mary Wright, 1994), p. 13.

Like other friends we were keen to do anything to help the war effort and when we were old enough some of us joined the ATC. Our local group was run by the Head of Lowdham Village School and some of our training sessions took place at Syerston Airfield.

Jack Inger, Minster GS, Woodborough

Funding was needed to provide the Air Training Corps with equipment and costs for training and transport.

Air Training Corps

A whist drive was held in the Women's Institute on Thursday in aid of the Welfare Funds of the Southwell Squadron of the ATC. P-O N Walker, Adjutant of the Squadron, acted as MC and presented the prizes to the following: Ladies 1. Miss E Robinson 2. Mrs N White 3. Mrs Tong Consolation: Mrs Rhodes: Gents: 1. Mrs Smith 2. Miss K Robinson 3. Mrs Marsden [*sic*]; Consolation: Mrs Shepperson. A net sum of £4 3s was realised. P-O Walker thanked the organisers.[35]

A report on the progress of the Air Training Corps was given in August 1944.

Southwell Air Training Corps Gala

'Sword of Honour' Presented to Sgt J K Jones

Southwell's Gala Day in aid of the Air Training Corps Benevolent Fund was opened by the Regional Commissioner, Mr J Stirk, at Lowe's Wong on Saturday. A 'Sword of Honour' was presented to Sgt J K Jones, a former Cadet, now in the RAF.

… Many attractions were provided for the large number of visitors. These included sports and games, pony rides, displays by the Guild of Magicians, and a performance in the Residence grounds of the *'Merry Wives of Windsor'* by the Nottingham Shakespeare Society. The tea stall was an attraction and music was played by Ransome and Marles' Band.

At the opening ceremony those present on the platform were Ald. C G Caudwell, Mr J Stirk, J T Clark, N Metcalf, T H Field, Sqdn-Ldr A J E Behm, Flying Officer R L Wright (Commanding Officer), Flying Officer N Walker (Adjt) and Flying Officer Burton

Formation of the Southwell ATC

… Mr Stirk intimated that the Government gave a grant and in addition there was a Welfare Committee whose duty it was to collect funds … to raise money for the betterment of the boys in training - to provide transport, sports and equipment - by whist drives, dances and public subscriptions.

Busy Cadets

Flying-Officer Wright … spoke of how the Cadets were trained, saying that people did not realise the amount of work the Cadets were doing. Briefly, their training covered engineering, navigation, drill, physical training, mathematics, signalling, armaments, map-reading, hygiene and swimming. … The lads responded very well and they benefited very much from that pre-Service training. In a little over 13 or 14 months they had some 75 Cadets through their hands. … It was largely taken per head of the population.

'Sword of Honour'

The speaker then intimated how the first of the Corps to obtain the 'Sword of Honour' for Proficiency was Sgt Brothwell who had gone into the Forces. At the conclusion of the opening ceremony Sqdn-Ldr Behm presented Sgt Jones with the 'Sword' amidst much applause.[36]

---

[35] *N/Adv,* 9th August 1944.
[36] *N/Adv,* 30th August 1944.

Women's Institute and the Fruit Preserving Centre

Southwell Women's Institute were quick off the mark in setting up a Fruit and Jam Preserving Centre at their WI Hall, in response to national recommendations. Damsons and plums could now be purchased on ration book points from Southwell shops. A report of this early progress was made in the local newspaper.

Among a host of other areas of responsibility, the WI also took on the preservation of fruit that would otherwise have gone to waste.

(Women's Institute website)

Preserving Centre at the WI Hall
The canning, bottling and jam-making at the Centre, organised by the Southwell Women's Institute, in conjunction with the Ministries of Food and Agriculture, is now in full swing. Although the centre has only been operating during Thursday and Friday of the first two weeks, a large quantity of fruit - all surplus garden produce - has been preserved, the total being about 500 cans, 150 bottles of fruit and a large quantity of jam. The coming weekend will be given over to the canning of tomatoes and pears. It is hoped that this valuable work of saving the nation's surplus fruit and vegetable crops will be continued until the end of the plum and damson season.[37]

The Women's Institute also used their monthly meetings to raise awareness on a variety of topics, all connected with support for the war effort; talks on subjects such as 'How to plan your allotment or garden', 'Self-Help in Air Raids', or demonstrations for example on 'Making soft slippers for the wounded'.

These wartime meetings followed a familiar pattern. Each opened with the singing of 'Jerusalem', followed by the specific talk/demonstration and concluded with a whist drive and tea and biscuits. The money from the whist drive was always given to a deserving cause; beneficiaries included the Red Cross, Salute the Soldier, Aid to Russia, Women of France, Comforts for Troops, and the European Civilian Relief Fund.

It is impossible to overestimate the contribution of the Southwell WI. The members were active in so many areas of civilian life helping people to cope with the difficulties of managing in wartime.

---

[37] *N/Adv*, 28th August 1940.

Dig For Victory

'Dig for Victory' was one of the most famous campaigns of the Home Front. The merry grins of 'Potato Pete' and 'Dr Carrot' became an increasingly familiar sight. Although vegetables were not rationed, they were scarce in the shops. Local residents were encouraged to support this national campaign, not only by growing vegetables in their back gardens, but also by digging up their lawns and flower beds.

(Newark Advertiser)

Dig! Dig! Dig! And your muscles will grow big
Keep on pushing the spade
Don't mind the worms, just ignore their squirms
And when your back aches, laugh for glee
Just keep on digging, till we give our foes a wigging
Dig! Dig! Dig! For Victory.

Dig for Victory[38]

Every possible scrap of land was used for agriculture. Southwell Golf course, off Park Lane, was ploughed up, as was some of the land in the Recreation Park, where the children's play area is today. Harvey's Field had cattle grazing in it. One of the local 'Dig for Victory' projects close to The Ropewalk had surprising results.

One of the major results of the campaign was the increase in the number of allotments in the town, as well as the change of use of people's lawns and back gardens.

Folk were encouraged to 'Dig for Victory'. It was expected that we should not only grow vegetables on our back land but dig up our lawns as well. We had six White Leghorns and six Light Sussex until a fox came to play games with them and they had to be replaced with Rhode Island Reds.' **Beatrice Mary Wright, Bleasby[39]**

Clearly, as well as proving to be a highly successful campaign, 'Dig for Victory' also encouraged people to eat a healthy diet and take plenty of exercise, a good model for our present times.

---

[38] Raynes Minns, *Bombers and Mash* (London: Virago, 2012), p. 101.
[39] Wright, p. 8.

Role of the Southwell Churches

Southwell churches were in the forefront of all the major community campaigns. Leading figures behind this ecclesiastical effort were Provost Conybeare and his wife, Bishops Mosley and Barry and their wives, all from the Minster; Canon Ernest Coghill and his wife from Holy Trinity Church and Revd John Almond from Southwell Methodist Church.

When army regiments arrived in the town, the servicemen were clearly in need of places for recreation when off duty (see Volume 1, Ch. 4, pp. 113-14). An appeal was made through the local newspaper for people to offer servicemen facilities for relaxation. There was an immediate response from all the churches. The servicemen were offered space at the Methodist Sunday Schoolroom, the Workmen's Rest and the garden at the Residence. Churches also took the lead in offering accommodation to evacuees. The Bishop of Southwell, Provost Conybeare, and the Archdeacon of Newark took in several (see Volume 1, Ch. 2, pp. 29-32). After the Dunkirk evacuation people's spirits suffered a severe jolt. Morale had to be raised. Once again the churches stepped in and a joint leaflet was circulated to all houses, backed up by a report in the local paper.

Bishop Mosley
(Dean and Chapter)

MORALE - *How to Play Your Part*

... At this critical hour all of us want to know how we can help our nation. Events have clearly shown that the underlying strength of a nation is the morale of her citizens. Here are five practical ways in which each of us can play a part.

Forget yourself by helping your neighbour

In days of tension this casts out your own fears and worries. Help them to work out all the instructions about air raids, evacuation, rationing and waste.

Keep the moral standards of the nation high

Don't weaken the home front by trying to wrangle something for yourself on the quiet. Make a break with all the personal indulgence, selfishness and private wars which undermine national morale and unity. Everyone has his part to play in the spiritual and moral re-armament of the nation.

Be a rumour stopper
Those who love their country sacrifice the luxury of being the one to pass on the 'news'. Any patriot shoots a false rumour dead on sight. ... Faith, confidence and cheerfulness are as contagious as fear, depression and grumbling.

The secret of steadiness and inner strength is to listen to God and to do what he says. ... His voice can be heard wherever you are; in the home, in the factory, in the air-raid shelter, in the first aid post.

Forearm yourself by listening to God first thing every morning. ... In time of listening, God takes away fear and fortifies against uncertainty and hardship. He gives foresight and cool judgement. He offers limitless reserves of energy and initiative. He comforts the bereaved.

A British General who has fought through two wars said this, 'Telephone wires may be cut, wireless stations be destroyed but no bombardment can stop messages from God coming through if we are willing to receive them. To listen to God and obey him is the highest form of national service for everybody, everywhere.'

W J Conybeare Provost Southwell Minster, **Ernest A Coghill** Vicar Southwell Holy Trinity, **John W Almond** Minister Southwell Methodist.[40]

In the early years of the war until his retirement in May 1941, Bishop Mosley took the view that in difficult times when families had lost fathers and sons to the war effort, local communities should give them as much support as possible. He recognised the importance of giving people a chance to escape from their worries for a while and was even prepared to speak out against some of his fellow clergy who supported the ban on the opening of theatres on Sundays.

It seems to me only fair that having allowed cinemas to open on Sundays, the Home Secretary should remove the ban on the opening of theatres. I find it difficult to share the unqualified disapproval that has been expressed by some of my brethren.

... Leaving music aside, I regard the drama as much the most desirable and satisfying of entertainments and while cinemas are open, to give the theatre a similar right is to remove all obvious injustice. ... To oppose the opening of theatres and other places of amusement on the ground that this will draw people away from public worship, is a wrong and mischievous argument.[41]

On his retirement in the summer of 1941, Bishop Mosley admitted he was reluctant to leave his position. 'The time is coming, however, and I am sure it is right, to hand over this lovely diocese, the best in England.'[42]

The new Bishop of Southwell, Dr F R Barry, was enthroned on 1st November 1941. He energetically threw himself into supporting the local war effort by encouraging a number of wartime initiatives such as the 'Comforts for Soldiers' scheme and the 'Warship Week'. Dr Barry's wife took a leading role in the Girls' Friendly Society and the local Girl Guides. Bishop Barry attracted much publicity, perhaps inadvertently, when, in January 1942, he was taken to court by the police and ARP for having lights visible at Bishop's Manor during the blackout. He vigorously

[40] *N/Adv*, 28th August 1940.
[41] *N/Adv*, 5th March 1941.
[42] *N/Adv*, 28th May 1941.

defended his actions, but was nevertheless fined £12 (see Vol. 1, Ch. 3. pp. 75-82). In June 1944 Bishop Barry was responsible for organising a very significant wartime event - the 'Diocesan Diamond Jubilee Celebrations'.

Diocesan 'Diamond Jubilee' Commemoration

In the historic Southwell Minster, on Friday, a large assembly of clergy and laity attended the diamond jubilee celebration and thanksgiving services. The Archbishop of York, Dr Cyril Garbett, preached at the morning and evening services. In the afternoon there were nearly a thousand guests at a reception by the Bishop Dr F Russell Barry, at the Bishop's Manor. Sixty years ago the Minster became a Cathedral on the formation of the Southwell Diocese.

Youthful Diocese

The Archbishop of York, in his sermon, expressed his great happiness at being able to join in the 60th anniversary of the founding of the diocese. The 700-year old Minster had been associated for centuries with the See at York...

... Fully 800 people filled the nave for the afternoon service and among those present were the Duke and Duchess of Portland, the Lord Mayor and Lady Mayoress of Nottingham.[43]

Bishop Barry realised that once the war was over there was a great need to take stock and rebuild the life of our own country, spiritually as well as physically. In January 1945 he sent a pastoral letter to all churches in the diocese, offering a ten-year plan.

If the church is to fulfil its mission, if it is to meet the outstanding needs and opportunities of the post-war period, it requires increased financial supply. It must be able to send out living agents, adequate in number and equipment into the parishes and new estates. It must train good men well for the Ministry. It must provide churches in new areas. It must recondition its school buildings to the standards of the Education Act and provide for the training of Christian teachers, youth leaders, social and moral welfare workers. Not least it must deal with the stipends of the clergy and offer its servants a fair living wage. This involves a large sum of money. The Diocesan Conference has resolved to ask for £150,000 for these purposes. We want to raise that during the present year.[44]

The bishop made a more controversial contribution to the public debate in late August 1945, just after the two atomic bombs had been dropped on Japan resulting in enormous loss of life. He publicly called for the immediate destruction of the factories which produced the atom bomb.

The Bishop of Southwell and the Atom Bomb

In the course of a letter to *The Times* last Wednesday, the Bishop of Southwell wrote, 'The Great Powers have now a unique chance of moral leadership. Let them appeal to the cause of humanity. Let them now demolish the factories from which the atom bomb was produced and destroy all records of the formula. History would not forget the gesture.

I am fully aware of the counter-arguments and the balance of ethical judgement here is delicate. But, perhaps, it is only some striking act of deliberate voluntary renunciation which can convince the world of our sincerity or help to break out of that vicious circle in which it is so tragically imprisoned.

---

[43] *N/Adv*, 14th June 1944.
[44] *N/Adv*, 31st January 1945.

Let me make it clear that the Great Powers have, in my judgement, a moral obligation to remain heavily armed for many years. This is no plea for a sub-Christian pacifism nor for any premature disarmament. I am only concerned with this particular weapon. The suggestion is, needless to say, conditional on the full agreement and consent of Russia who is now, presumably, in on the secret.'[45]

Bishop Barry's views led to an outburst of letters sent to the Editor of the *Newark Advertiser*. The bishop was strongly supported by the Vicar of Balderton, who declared he was 'horrified and sickened' about the use of the atomic bomb. However, many people sent letters opposing the two church leaders, on the grounds that the use of the two atomic bombs shortened the war and saved many allied servicemen's lives, possibly including members of their families.

The Provost, the Very Revd W J Conybeare, demonstrated an excellent example of how to build community spirit in times of adversity. He had been appointed before the end of WW1, and in the years of the Depression in the 1930s his active work in support of the unemployed and poorer sections of the community had endeared him to the local population. Whilst he was Provost,

W Conybeare, Provost of Southwell Minster. An impression in watercolour by W Bryan. 1937

Provost Conybeare

he was responsible for many improvements at the Minster. He had central heating, electric light, and a new organ installed. The grounds were levelled and beautified, and many gifts made to the Minster.[46] In August 1944 Provost Conybeare retired. A major event at the Minster marked his retirement, and a farewell gift from the laity of Southwell diocese was made to him by the Duke and Duchess of Portland.

Earlier in the war, in 1941, a member of the clergy who had done a good deal to minister to troops billeted in the town was Canon Ernest Coghill of Holy Trinity Church, who always had a high sense of duty. For just over 50 years he had treated his Westhorpe parishioners with love and affection and it was clear from the tributes at his funeral in February 1941 that these feelings were reciprocal. One example of his tireless work, continued into wartime, was his opening up of The Workman's Rest in Westhorpe to servicemen billeted in the Southwell area. There they could find 'a refuge for relaxation and entertainment in the form of billiards, whist drives, dominoes, bagatelle, newspapers and refreshments'. As Marjorie Hustwayte and Penelope Young state in their book *Holy Trinity, Southwell 1846-1996,* 'Any vicar succeeding Canon Coghill must have found him a daunting act to follow.'[47]

Southwell Methodist Church was equally unstinting in supporting the war effort. The Revd J W Almond rallied chapel members to help the troops stationed under canvas nearby on Lowe's Wong and in accommodation at Maythorne, Kirklington Hall and Southwell Racecourse. In

[45] *N/Adv,* 22nd August 1945.
[46] *N/Adv,* 30th May 1944.
[47] Marjorie Hustwayte and Penny Young, *Holy Trinity Church 1846-1996* (Southwell: Self Published), p. 27.

February 1940 the Sunday school room was officially registered as a Social Centre and Canteen, organised by Miss Marjorie Dowse. It catered every evening for men and women of HM Forces. To keep spirits up, a number of new organisations were set up by the Methodists. The minister's wife instigated the Women's Bright Hour; the Headmaster of the Methodist Day School, Mr Dixon, started a Boys' Brigade, and Mrs K N Hoare was asked to form a Guide company for some of the girls connected with the chapel.

Minster Choir in Wartime (Malcolm Gough)

Looking Back

It is quite astonishing to read about the amounts collected in Southwell and the villages during the special 'Weapon Weeks'. How could such a modest population raise so much money? No doubt people wanted to feel they were playing an active part in the war effort. The business community were happy to be seen doing their bit, contributing money for a Spitfire for example, which undoubtedly enhanced their standing in the community. The local churches took a significant lead in showing the true meaning of Christianity, by giving practical support in a time of need. This admirably positive attitude is well summed up by Steve Pulford.

> The local people were determined, not depressed. As soon as it was seen that we were suffering casualties, when the Sherwood Foresters returned from the Norwegian Campaign and from Dunkirk, then people were determined that the job should be finished properly. There were some well-known casualties, all displayed on the plaque in the Minster School, including the Headmaster's son, the Bishop's son and boys who had been in my form, like Eric Scraton and John Cox. So people were anxious, but most of all they were determined to do everything necessary to finish the job off. This could be seen in the way everyone volunteered to raise funds by holding events like whist drives and concerts. These public activities both raised money and kept people cheerful.
> **Steve Pulford**[48]

---

[48] Stevenson.

CHAPTER 6

'Doctor Carrot Guards Your Health'

'Call me often enough and you'll keep well.'[1]

As soon as war was declared Ministry of Food posters encouraged everyone to grow their own fruit and vegetables, because, at that time, 70% of all food consumed in Britain was imported. There existed a real risk that the German U-boat campaign around our shores would cut off crucial food imports. At the same time a ploughing initiative was started to provide additional land.

Food Rationing introduced

The increase in home production could not fully compensate for the loss of imports, resulting in rationing. A national identity card scheme was introduced in September 1939 and registration forms were delivered to each household; ration books were only issued to those on the register. Buff-coloured ration books were issued to most people, with green books for children under 6 years old and pregnant women, who were given extra milk and orange juice. In Southwell people collected their ration books from the Food Office, originally in King Street, then at Kelham House, Westgate.

Wartime Food Office in King Street

Mr John Ellis, the Clerk to Southwell RDC, has been made Food Executive Officer, a corresponding post he held in the last war. His experience will be invaluable. The shop in King Street formerly occupied by Messrs Mills has been taken over as Food and Fuel Office and Mr J H Barber has been appointed chief assistant to Mr Ellis …

40,000 Ration Cards

Preparations are also being made with regard to the issue of ration cards. There will be about forty thousand of these, but if there is any further drift of evacuees back to their homes, complications may arise when the time for issue comes.[2]

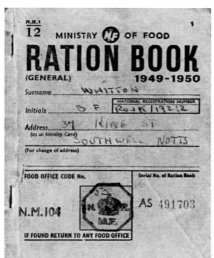

Ration Book (Brenda Whitton)

In January 1940 rationing began in earnest. Bacon and ham were limited to four ounces per person per week, butter the same amount, and sugar limited to twelve ounces. Each family had to register with a specific grocer and butcher; rationed goods could only be purchased through that retailer. The normal procedure was for the customer to go into the grocer's or butcher's shop and hand over the ration book to the proprietor, who clipped out the appropriate coupon. The retailer's stock was replaced based on the number of customers registered with him.

---

[1] Dr Carrot tells mothers, Ministry of Food leaflet 1941.

[2] *N/Adv,* 4th October 1939.

We had to register at a local grocer's. The Cooperative shop was just at the top of Burgage Green, not far from Dornoch Avenue and so we registered there. Many people registered at J H Kirkby's on Church Street. You could register at any shop you preferred, but you had to get everything from one book from that shop. If another member of your family had a ration book, then they could register at another shop. So in that way you could split your family. There was also a points system to get things like tins of fruit.

Julia Paling[3]

In the weeks and months that followed further items were added to the rationing list: cheese, preserves, tea, margarine, cooking fat and a wider range of meats. Because the rationing system could only be applied to items for which supply could be guaranteed, many food items where supply tended to be erratic were never included, and it was for these items that people queued. To make distribution fairer, two new systems were introduced: an allocation one and a points one.

"We 'ave to take what fish we can get these days, Madam."

(Home Front 1939-45)

The allocation system was organised by the local Food Office, which tried to ensure that goods in short supply were distributed to all shops. Eggs were one such item and were delivered to retailers on the basis of one egg per registered person per week. Milk, too, was allocated and in March 1943 the allowance stood at three pints a week. Imported fruit was also restricted; retailers were instructed to sell oranges for children only in the first five days they had any in stock, thereafter they could offer them to any customer.

The points system, first introduced in December 1941, applied to a variety of tinned goods. Each person was allocated a number of points - for most of the war 20 points could be used for tinned food every four weeks. Each chosen item was then given a points value: a luxury item such as red salmon was 32 points, while it was two points for a tin of baked beans or pilchards. As with rationing, the points' system was extended over time; rice and dried fruit were added in January 1942, cereals and condensed milk in April 1942, and biscuits in August 1942.

In addition, from January 1940 food prices were pegged by government subsidies; by changing these subsidies the government could attempt to control eating habits. For example in 1941, because of growing shipping losses, the price of bread was allowed to rise, whilst the subsidy on potatoes was increased to lower their price, encouraging consumption. To stop profiteering, maximum prices were also fixed for many products.

How did local people cope with the small rations?

In rural areas most families seemed to cope well with food shortages, and Southwell was fairly typical. The majority of houses had a garden, which, as part of the 'Dig for Victory' campaign, could be dug up to grow vegetables in place of a lawn and flower borders, indeed many people were already quite self-sufficient. It was common to keep a few chickens, and the cultivation of allotments around the town supplied additional produce. There was usually a barter system when people had a glut of a particular crop. The children missed having sweets, and it was difficult to

---

[3] Birks.

bake cakes and puddings on the meagre sugar and fat rations. It was certainly a healthier diet, and recipes using 'alternative' ingredients produced quite palatable results.

Both adults and children were encouraged to gather wild fruits and berries, to be sold to the local Southwell WI Fruit Preservation Centre for jam-making. Rose-hips were a particularly rich source of Vitamin C and made into rose-hip syrup, usually given to children or stirred into milk puddings. Mothers were helped to see what was available to give their children a nutritious diet by recipe leaflets provided by the Ministry of Food, and often endorsed by celebrities such as Gert and Daisy Waters. They were regular visitors to the Saracen's Head when appearing on the Nottingham stage.

The housewives were the real heroes. I remember the big queues they had to go through in order to collect their rations or food not rationed. It must have been a real struggle finding enough food, especially with many husbands away on active service duty. One example of 'making do', near us, was women cutting up sugar beet and then boiling it at home in order to compensate for the shortage of sugar. **Tom Fairholme**

Gert and Daisy - regular visitors to the Saracen's Head (Home Front)

My mum came from a farming family and I remember one day going on the train with her to a Kegworth farm where a pig was due to be slaughtered. We took two suitcases with us in order to bring back the pieces of ham and bacon. On the way back from the farm we prayed that the taxi-man wouldn't see. It helped that the taxi-man was a friend and I remember him advising us, 'Whatever you do, don't look guilty if we're stopped by the police.' **Margaret Pulford**

You depended on local orchards for your fruit. I think I was nine years old before I saw a banana. Occasionally we got an orange each and a grapefruit perhaps twice a year. Like many people we grew vegetables and some fruit for ourselves. You were entitled to an egg ration, but we gave up our egg rations so we could buy meal for our hens. This gave us more eggs than the ration. **John Postle**[4]

We kept hens and that meant we could have an egg a week. I remember we used to go down Challands Lane and take blackbirds' eggs and fry them. Sometimes my brothers and sisters and I would eat the roots of a small white flower. The roots were very edible and were called 'pig nuts'. There was another plant we ate that had leaves which tasted of vinegar. Something else we would do if we were hungry was to go into one of our fields and lick a block of salt which had been left for the cows to lick. **Olive Kitts**

Fortunately, our family had ways they could supplement their food rations. I remember my grandparents, the Caudwells, had two Jersey cows, pigs and hens here at Easthorpe Lodge. The bacon was cured and hung up, the eggs put in waterglass. I can also remember large bowls in the dairy filled with milk and the butter churn, which I think I took a turn on. I can remember the sound of it churning into butter. We also had plenty of fruit in the orchard. **Ruth Robinson**

---

[4] Birks.

It wasn't really a problem for our family. My mother worked at the Food Office where ration books were taken and I got the impression this helped us. Also, we had a large garden at the back where my father grew all kinds of vegetables and we had three Bramley Apple trees and one plum tree. My mother always seemed to be making apple and plum pies. My father also built a pig sty in the garden and so we rarely seemed short of meat, especially as he had a gun and he and his friend Joe Arnold up at Stubbins Farm would go shooting pheasants and pigeons. Joe Arnold saw that we never went short of eggs.

Keith Lee

Another way of supplementing the food supply was by taking an allotment. There were more allotments in the town then - at Cundy Hill, Westhorpe, close to the junction of Nottingham Road and Westgate, Landseer Road, where Honing Drive is now and, as today, allotments off Fiskerton Road. This meant more vegetables and fruit could be grown.

(Home Front)

A lot of people had allotments to provide more food for their families. There were allotments higher up Landseer Road and also where Honing Drive is today.

Douglas Gascoine

We registered at the Cooperative Stores on Westgate, but on occasions we shopped at Kirkby's if they had something special that we wanted. Rationing wasn't a problem for us because we were a large family and had plenty of coupons, and dad grew vegetables and fruit in his allotment as well as using our garden. I can remember mother giving Mr Hall, the milkman, some of our cheese ration. Also, mother was a good cook, so we never seemed to go without.

If we needed eggs we could always get them from a nearby Westhorpe farm, and as an alternative to sugar we just used condensed milk.

Rosa Cooling

The shortage of food was never a problem for either my father's or uncle's family. Uncle Cecil was a gardener and he also had milk from his goats; my father, Gerald Marrison, had an allotment next to his wheelwright's depot in the park. He grew vegetables and potatoes; he had a greenhouse for his tomatoes and he had hens as well. I can never remember either family being short of anything.

Peter Marrison

Going out to a café for a meal, if you could afford it, was another way round the rationing problem. Meals at cafés and restaurants were not rationed, although menus were very limited and items frequently off the menu.

In Southwell there were two cafés in the Old Market Place. One, where the Chinese Restaurant is now, and one next to where Beckett's shop is. But eating out would be very expensive for most people.

Dallas Doy[5]

---

[5] Birks.

Special Wartime Dishes

Mothers clearly had to improvise to make meals out of what they were able to get hold of. Offal and sausages were not rationed, although only a small quantity of offal was ever available, and the percentage of meat in a wartime sausage was another of life's mysteries. However, these were a welcome supplement to eke out the rations. For many, the dish known as 'Woolton's Pie' is likely to be the abiding memory of wartime food. Lord Woolton was the Minister of Food and this vegetable pie was named after him. It was an inexpensive dish, made without meat but with a selection of nutritious and fibrous root vegetables. The crust could be a standard pastry or potato. The Ministry of Food and the local WI frequently issued recipe books suggesting substitutes for sugar and fat.

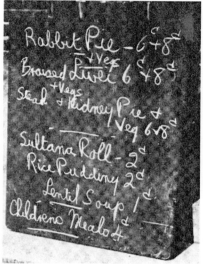

(Home Front)

Recipe – Woolton Pie

Ingredients – potato (or parsnips), cauliflower, swede, carrots, turnips, oats, spring onions, cheese. Cooking advice – top the dish with potato or pastry and grated cheese.[6]

Mother would regularly give us offal and I would really enjoy it, but not now. I remember the butcher, Harry Harvey, saying to her, 'You've had the animal's brains this week, it's the Bishop's turn next week!'
Nancy Harrison

I can remember mother taking me to queue for a sheep's head. Mum would then boil it and we'd use the tongue in a sandwich. The sheep's brains would be fried and put on toast - quite a delicacy! Soup would be made from the remains.
Harry Cooling

My mother used to make a delicious dish - 'Woolton's Pie' - made of spam I think.   **Freda Kirby**

The appearance of SPAM, in exports to the UK from America after the signing of the Lend-Lease agreement in March 1941, was an overnight success as an alternative to fresh meat. This was a brand of canned, pre-cooked meat product and was a mixture of chopped pork shoulder, ham, salt, water and potato starch. It became the basic ingredient of SPAM Yorkshire Breakfast, SPAM Spanish Omelette, SPAM Hash and SPAM Fritters, adding much needed flavour to their otherwise bland ingredients.[7]

Mother said we had to be prepared to eat things we wouldn't normally eat. So we used to eat Spam fritters and occasionally she would buy horse meat for the dog and make potted meat with it. I can also remember a man from Thurgarton, who worked with my father, and he would let us have some streaky bacon. Mother would refer to the bacon as 'fat tiger'. **Jean Quickenden**

---

[6] www.cookit.e2bn.org/historycookbook/1157-woolton-pie.html
[7] www.skylighters.org/encyclopedia/spam.html

As we had a very small sweet ration, my grandmother used to make home-made chocolates from sweetened milk and cocoa powder.

Cynthia Woolley

Housewives were especially creative when it came to making various soups.

We lived off 'nature's bounty'. Nettles were very nutritious. My mother used to make nettle soup. She'd also make plum and damson jam.

Nancy Harrison

Recipes from the Kitchen Front
Nettle Soup

- half a carrier bag of nettle tops
- large onion, large potato, dried garlic clove
- 1 ¾ pints chicken stock
- 4 tbls double cream
- salt, pepper, chives and 2 oz butter.[8]

Whilst many people in and around Southwell were able to supplement their meagre egg ration by having their own hens, others had to make do with 'dried eggs'. Dried egg powder came from America and became available in 1942. A tin of it contained the equivalent of a dozen eggs and was extra to your egg ration. Among other uses, dried eggs could be re-constituted to make scrambled eggs or included in a cake mixture.

Rules for Using Dried Egg

Store in a cool, dry place. To turn a dried egg into a fresh one, mix one level tablespoon of the powder with two tablespoons of water. This mixture equals one fresh egg. Now treat the egg as you would a fresh one. Don't make up more egg than necessary for the dish you are making. Beat as usual before adding other ingredients.[9]

"How would you like your egg this month, dear?"

(Home Front)

We didn't get many eggs. We had to use dried eggs for baking and some people would pickle their eggs and use them that way. The dried egg was made of yellow powder and looked like mustard.

Rosemary Lockley

---

[8] www.cookit.e2bn.org/historycookbook/837-nettlesoup.html
[9] wikipedia.org/wiki/powdered_eggs.html

We had a farm nearby and could get milk and cream from there. Mum collected the cream and poured it into a jam jar, shook it up to make butter. We kept chickens so we had plenty of eggs and we also had pigs at the bottom of the garden. Apart from growing our own vegetables, we preserved everything that we could. We used to pickle eggs and put waterglass in it, so we always had eggs. We had a stock of preserving jars to put fruit in. We'd bottle tomatoes, put sliced beans in salt and keep carrots in sand at the wash-house. **Janette Barrett**[10]

Private arrangements

Another way people coped was by making private deals, sometimes involving the exchange of coupons. There were also deals made with local farmers especially. For farmers, rabbits, poultry and eggs were always in plentiful supply.

I remember my father used to play in the Southwell brass band, which disbanded when the war started. He had a cornet which a particular farmer wanted. The deal my father made was a cornet in exchange for half a side of a pig! In the war little money seemed to change hands as things went back to a barter system. **John Postle**[11]

My father, Joseph Keetley, worked as a saddler and this involved him doing repairs on several local farmers' binding canvas. These farmers were keen to show their appreciation, so mother would take baby Sheila in the big pram up to Twidale's Farm near Kirklington. Whilst there she would carefully fill the pram 'well' with eggs, which she would then put in isinglass in a large tin bath to preserve. We were never short of eggs. **Elizabeth Riley**

My father farmed at Maplebeck and he could always find rabbits for people. He had a regular deal with a Mr Smith who would give him cartridges in exchange. Cartridges were so incredibly valuable for farmers for shooting rabbits and game. **Brian Johnson**[12]

As my father was Underground Manager of Bilsthorpe Colliery, he was able to access as much coal as he wanted. We could barter for everything with coal. Father had a 'special arrangement' with a farmer in the district. In return for the coal that my father took him in bags hidden in the boot of the car, the farmer gave us extra meat and vegetables. On one occasion my father's car was stopped by the local police, who were looking for suspicious black market activity; fortunately, they didn't find the coal. **Pam Field**

With the Mitchell family being so large we had a lot of sweet coupons, which we didn't need because sweets cost so much. I remember we 'swapped' the sweet coupons with friends for margarine, butter and sugar coupons. **Cynthia Patterson**

The Marshall family numbered thirteen! It might be thought we would have struggled with getting enough food. But I don't think we did. I think we were helped by my father visiting most of the farmers in the neighbourhood, delivering Kirkby's groceries. He got to know the farmers and I'm sure he was offered extra food and clothing cast-offs as well. We always seemed to have enough

---

[10] Birks.
[11] Birks.
[12] Rachel Gardner, *Maplebeck - Continuity and Change* (Mansfield: Notts Living History Archive, 2002), p. 45.

meat despite our big family size and father often brought rabbits home with him. I can also remember that each week we seemed to have a tin of salmon. **Eric Marshall**

Living on a farm at Rolleston brought big advantages. We made our own butter and we could keep a pig and have it all to ourselves. I think our only problem was getting hold of sugar and tea. But many people would solve this by having private arrangements with family and friends. We had friends from Caunton who would bring tea in return for eggs. **Frank Mitchell**

My mother was never short of eggs because she would keep poultry in our garden. She had chickens, rabbits and geese also as a sideline to make some income. I can remember she would sell her produce each week to Newark Egg Packers. 'Ginger' Flint, from Southwell, would come to the house in his van every morning on his way to Newark and collect the produce. My mother also used to deal with Clarrie Hall, the local carrier. If she wanted him to stop and collect poultry from her, she would always tie a newspaper to the gatepost to let him know. **Mary Hall**

Bilsthorpe residents were regularly given tinned meat, nylons and chocolates by American and Canadian servicemen from RAF stations and army camps all over the Sherwood Forest district. I can remember mother inviting three servicemen from RAF Ossington to supper on a number of occasions. They would always bring some food with them as gifts. **Pam Field**

As a dairy farmer Dad used to have certain 'arrangements' with some people; he would get me to deliver extra milk usually in return for something. On one occasion I was delivering some milk to the Grants at the Westhorpe Vicarage when I was stopped by two old ladies and asked what I was doing. I immediately 'fibbed' that I was going to see Mrs Grant at The Vicarage who was helping me with my homework. Another deal we had was with two ladies who were excellent cooks. My dad would supply them with cream and in return they made us chocolate eclairs. **Michael Gilman**

The Black Market and Poaching

Where items were rationed or difficult to obtain they could be bought and sold at inflated prices on the black market. The items most sought after, by both individuals and businesses, included petrol, red meat, silk and sugar. It was possible to obtain them by private deals with a trader or by 'under the counter' arrangements with local shopkeepers. The authorities seemed to be generally more relaxed about black market activities than on enforcing the blackout regulations, possibly because some of them were not above the occasional 'benefit' themselves.

We were certainly aware of a black market. When the opportunity came we would jump at the chance of buying tins of fruit, tins of tomato juice and especially tins of salmon. Sometimes we'd be offered rabbits and hares and we would ignore the probability that they might have been poached. **Janette Barrett**[13]

---

[13] Birks.

At the beginning of the war I was living on a farm up Crink Lane. I don't think that we were ever short of food in this area. There was sufficient stuff on the black market, and then you had the local farmers killing pigs on the side and then carting them around for people who were prepared to pay.

Steve Pulford[14]

I think my father, the Upton baker, used to do some bargaining on the black market. I can remember him at night regularly taking wheat, which he had got from the local farmers, to Caudwell's Mill. Presumably he got paid for this deal. I used to be worried that he would be caught.

Mary Hall

During the war Bob Reeves worked on his grandfather's farm and then later moved to help his Uncle Fred at Breck's Farm, Maplebeck.

(Black Market Website)

Because of the shortage of meat some farmers and butchers were aware of the attractions of the 'black market'. But if found out, the police and the local magistrates' court would come down heavily on anyone caught dealing. I remember my Uncle Fred coming back to the farm one day, white as a sheet. He'd been taking a side of bacon to a customer. He'd put the bacon on the back seat of the car and left it uncovered. As he was driving to his customer, he suddenly saw a policeman standing by his police car, flagging him down. 'By Fred, how pleased I am to see you', said the policeman, 'I've had a puncture. I'd be grateful if you could take me back to the police station.' On the way back to the police station, Uncle Fred tactically kept talking so that the constable wouldn't have the opportunity to look round at the back seat.

There was a lot of black market activity. It was well known that some farmers would send meat for their Nottingham 'customers' in a cattle lorry because local police were less likely to stop and search these vehicles. It wasn't just farmers involved in black market activities. I can remember soldiers selling petrol on the side and one soldier sold my father a jungle knife.

Bob Reeves[15]

There was a similar story of black market activity in other villages often involving the dubious slaughter of pigs.

For Percy Whitworth at the Beehive at Maplebeck, the soldiers at the Maplebeck battery and the Polish airmen based at Ossington meant extra custom. The Polish airmen were great suppliers of nylons and other restricted goods. They were also very keen to buy ham from the local farmers and were willing to pay £1 per lb, which was a tremendous price at the time when wages were only about £2 per week, and even less for some. Such was the extent of the black market trade that it occasionally aroused the suspicion of the Rural Agricultural Committee, whose job it was to see that food production was maximised. Doug Rose remembered a ministry official calling at the farm whilst his parents were at market. Desperately trying to explain why they had no eggs to sell he remembers saying, 'Oh the hens, they've stopped laying.'[16]

[14] Birks.
[15] Stevenson.
[16] Gardner, p. 44.

My dad, Henry Sharman, farming at Edingley was in on a particular 'arrangement'. He provided the pump which was needed to clear up quickly the site of the slaughter - a cellar I think. Obviously, those involved needed to remove any trace of evidence of their misdeed. Anyhow, someone must have snitched on dad and the others because shortly afterwards a policeman called on him at Littledale Cottage, but obviously dad knew nothing about the report.

Robin Sharman

Whilst I was working at the Thorney Abbey family farm I was aware of strong rumours of black market meat at Epperstone. You could get meat at twice the normal cost, provided you kept your mouth closed. **Bob Hardstaff**[17]

Another way of supplementing the meagre rations was by poaching. This had always been a way of providing meat for the less well off in rural areas - a free source, but slightly risky.

There were many Westhorpe families involved in 'poaching' in the nearby countryside. Halifax's Farm, near The Holme, was a favourite target for many Westhorpians. Shooting rabbits was a popular illegal activity up there. We can remember seeing one particular farmer regularly shooting rabbits whilst he was 'combining'. **Brian Pacey, David Hall, Tony Hayward**

Poaching was rife among country people. The Kemps always had guns. We were well fed; we were never short of food. **Bill Kemp**

My father, as the local police constable, would quite often have to visit local farms because there had been reports of poaching and pinching stock, especially chickens. Sometimes he would take me with him in the Ford Prefect. **Roy Scoffield**

Catching rabbits and selling them was clearly a popular and lucrative activity. David Hutchinson, living on Westwood Farm, Normanton, and Bill Cranidge at Rolleston both did well out of it.

We were not short of food. We could go at any time down to the Dumble and shoot rabbits. I used to make some money by selling rabbits at school for about 3s 6d; that was my pocket money.

David Hutchinson[18]

If you lived in the countryside rationing of food didn't really hit you. Father was a good shot and, more importantly, he had a shotgun. If you had a £3 licence, as opposed to a 10s licence, you could shoot game. I can remember my mother saying many times, 'Oh, Charles, I don't know what we're going to eat tonight.' Father would then get his gun and go out and shoot a rabbit or pheasant. He had been given permission by the big local landowner, Mr Pentecroft, to shoot on his land near the Trent below Rolleston - he was keen to keep vandals away. Crows were also a problem as they would often take pheasant eggs, so father would put poison into egg shells to kill them. **Bill Cranidge**

---

[17] Stevenson.
[18] Stevenson.

Pig Clubs

(Bombers and Mash)

One way of obtaining meat to supplement the meagre ration was by rearing pigs; in fact, rearing pigs was a lifeline for those on a low income. Each family or producer was allowed to kill two pigs a year, but before they were slaughtered they had to be registered with the Ministry and permission granted. Once a pig was killed, the owner was supposed to return the bacon and ham ration book to the local Food Office. Because of this system it was tempting not to inform the authorities that you had a pig, then you could not only rear and kill more than two pigs a year, but you could sell some of the meat and also keep your ration book. Not surprisingly, many local families kept pigs, usually in sties or outhouses at the bottom of their gardens, and fed them on kitchen scraps. The fat was taken off the carcass, the intestines made sausages, nothing was wasted, and even the bladder could provide the local boys with a football. Children often had mixed feelings about keeping pigs. For some, the pig became a pet and for them the day when the slaughterer was called in was a day of heartbreak. Other children saw the event as entertainment and hid nearby to witness the gory details.

I remember one 'kill a pig' day when Charlie Watts came to do the slaughtering. Just before Charlie came, my dad walked 'Jenny' round the garden as usual to give her exercise. She would normally do what he told her, but when she saw Charlie bring out his slaughter table she bolted back to her sty. It must have been the smell from Charlie's table which made her suspicious.

Ray Bush

Pig Clubs were formed all over Southwell district. Local people joined the club in order to get extra meat; in return the members collected scraps which fattened the pig. Tom Fairholme and Robert Beckett's family remember Pig Clubs at the Shoulder of Mutton and at the Reindeer. There was also a very popular Pig Club at Halam. Sometimes there were private arrangements made, rather than any official club being formed.

I remember my mother had an 'arrangement' with 'Pigswill' Suter who would provide mother with a bin so she could supply him with scraps for him to collect. In return 'Pigswill' would give her some of the pig when it was killed. **Keith Marshall**

There is no doubt whatsoever that the rules were bent. I always found it laughable that no animal seemed to have more than one baby. In practice, what happened was that if there was more than one baby, the others were put carefully to one side and eventually slaughtered. The 'slaughterer' would take so much and then the rest of the meat would be split up. So those people who kept pigs were always able to have an amount of meat which they didn't have to account for. **John Postle[19]**

---

[19] Birks.

There was pig meat to be had. Across the road from us at Upton, Mr Bentley always had a pig. I can still hear it squealing when it was due to be killed. We always got some of the meat. Some of the Upton ladies made pork pies from the meat and they would take them to my father for him to bake. When the ladies collected the pies they would always leave him one for our family. As kids we were told that Walter Reeves, Bob Reeves's uncle, would come and stab the pig with a carving knife in the throat.

Mary Hall

The Halam Village Pig Club

Chairman: N. Storer
Treasurer: J. Shaw
Secretary: E. Walker

— RULES —

1. The name of this Club shall be "The Halam Village Pig Club" hereinafter referred to as the Club.

2. The objects of the Club shall be:—

(a) To encouragement of pig-keeping by cottagers, householders, allotment holders, and other small pig-keepers as a means of saving waste and providing meat for members and others so far as the law permits.

(b) The provision of facilities to help members in acquiring or disposal of pigs or in obtaining requirements for pig-keeping.

(c) The arrangement of insurance.

3. All members shall pay an entrance fee of five shillings on joining the Club, and thereafter a monthly fee of one shilling (1/-). The committee may in their discretion expel a member for any reason whatsoever. Any person who is expelled from membership accepted). The amount of compensation shall be at the discretion of the committee.

8. The members shall elect from amongst their number the following officers:—A Chairman, Secretary, Treasurer, and Committee.

9. The committee shall, as soon as practicable after the end of the financial year, convene the annual general meeting.

10. The committee shall submit to the annual general meeting:—(a) The audited accounts of the Club for the period covered by the accounts; (b) Such other matters as should, in the opinion of the committee be considered at the meeting.

11. The committee shall (a) Establish a fund and cause to be paid into that fund all moneys received on behalf of the Club, and cause to be paid out of the fund all moneys required for the Club's activities; (b) Cause proper accounts to be kept and an income and expenditure account to be made out in respect of the period ending the 31st day of March each year.

12. If upon the winding up or dissolution of the Club there remains, after the settlement of all its debts and liabilities, any property whatsoever, the same shall be distributed among members of the Club, or otherwise disposed of, provided that whatsoever is decided shall be the unanimous vote of the members present and entitled to vote at a meeting of which not less than fourteen days notice must be given.

Partners Press, 22, Barnbygate, Newark.

(History of Halam Village)

Many people in the Rolleston area would rear more pigs than they were legally permitted, so that they could barter meat for sugar or other produce. I remember a police sergeant opposite us being party to this 'private deal', warning people to 'keep their mouths shut'. **Bill Cranidge**

There was a Pig Club in Bilsthorpe, set up by a group of miners, and my father was a member. The pigs were kept in a field opposite our house. What a size they grew to. One pig weighed 20 stone before it was slaughtered. There was so much food from it that I remember we had the meat hanging from our bedroom walls. **Pam Field**

During the war a Pig Club was established at Halam. The entry fee was five shillings and the monthly subscription was one shilling. The Chairman was N Storer, Treasurer J Shaw and Secretary E Walker.[20]

---

[20] John Jackson, *A Living History of Halam* (Farnsfield: Unwin Print, 2001), p. 62.

Rearing pigs secretly, or not registering the correct numbers of pigs to be reared, could lead to court action if the owner was found out, as reported here in the *Newark Advertiser*.

PIG KILLED TO SAVE ITS LIFE
An Illegal Deal at Southwell

The story of a 'screw pig' that was boiled down was told at the Southwell Police Court on Friday, when Samuel Boonham, of the New Inn, Farnsfield and James Hatcher, butcher, of Main Street, Farnsfield were fined for breach of the regulations.

Mr R P Marchant prosecuted on behalf of the Ministry of Food and Mr P A Foster defended. Mr Marchant said the charge against Boonham was selling a pig without a licence, and Hatcher was charged with buying the pig. There was also a charge against both defendants for slaughtering the pig in contravention of the regulations. Mr Barber, Southwell Food Executive, said that on September 17th, Boonham had applied for a licence to kill four pigs and was granted sanction to slaughter one under certain conditions

Inspector's Questions

Mr G Seaton, an inspector of food from East Retford, said that on September 27th he visited Boonham's premises at Farnsfield and asked to see the pig which he had received permission to slaughter. Boonham hesitated, saying 'Is it necessary?' On making an investigation witness saw two pigs and reminded Boonham that he had told the Southwell office that he had four pigs.

'I asked where the other two were', said the Inspector, 'and [the] defendant replied he had sold them to his son in May. Witness went to see Hatcher, who lives next door, and that defendant observed, 'I know what you have come for: it is about that pig. I gave him 5s for it.'[21]

Southwell and District 'Produce Association'

The idea of a 'Village Produce Association' was thought up by the Ministry of Agriculture in 1941 so that villages, or small towns, could become self-supporting. It was made attractive to local residents by the Ministry enabling recognised organisations to buy seeds, plants, animal feed and fertilisers at considerably cheaper rates. Other benefits of a Produce Association were that expensive tools and advice could be shared, new allotments could be created and surplus produce could be sold at a market stall once a week.[22]

It seems that several villages in the district decided to go ahead with setting up a local Produce Association in the spring of 1942. In the Southwell branch, Ald. C G Caudwell was elected Chairman, Mr A L Davies (National School headmaster) Vice Chairman, Mr J D Dixon (Methodist School headmaster) secretary and Mr A E Walton (bank manager) treasurer. By 1944 the membership of the Southwell Produce Association had risen to 115.

Produce Association

The newly-formed Southwell and District Produce Association will hold a show in connection with Southwell Gala Day on August Monday. In addition to a show of vegetables and flowers there will be a Ladies section as well as two classes for dogs. Entry forms can be obtained from Mr Cumberland, butcher, King St or from the secretary, Mr J D Dixon, Methodist School. Entries close on 29th July. A display of bottled and canned fruit is being staged by the WI. Proceeds for the Southwell Red Cross Ambulance Fund.[23]

---

[21] *N/Adv*, 13th November 1940.
[22] http://somerton.co.uk
[23] *N/Adv*, 28th July 1942.

Reading the regular reports in the *Newark Advertiser*, it appears that competition amongst the members to grow the finest produce and flowers was quite intense, so it wasn't surprising when the idea of an Annual Show was introduced. The judges wouldn't have had an easy ride.

Produce Association

The show and gala was held on August Bank Holiday Monday, when over 1,000 attended. The President, Ald. C G Caudwell, introduced Lady Starkey to open the show, and she was presented with a bouquet of roses. Mr Davies, the Chairman, thanked the judges, the committee and all who had supported the effort including Mrs G M Jackson who loaned the grounds at St Mary's House.

The pig was given as a prize by the Pig Club. Miss Thomas' Troupe was very efficient and proved an added attraction with a display of dancing. Several tug-of-war teams competed including the ladies and the Army Cadets. Refreshments were served by ladies from the WI.

There was an excellent entry of fruit, flowers and vegetables. Messrs Pearson showed a fine display of gladioli, etc., which was afterwards sold for the benefit of the Fund.

The Rabbit Show together with cavies and bantams had a large entry, this was efficiently conducted by Mr C B Marrison MBRC, who recently won the Victory Cup for the best rabbit. The music was relayed by Mr Carey and his son, home on leave. ... Dancing terminated the evening's pleasure in the grounds.[24]

Southwell Poultry and Domestic Rabbit Clubs

As well as the Produce Associations, the Ministry of Agriculture also suggested that local groups should create clubs for the rearing of poultry and rabbits. Southwell residents were quick to set up both. Local secretaries were Mr P Ballard and Mr Spencer of 132 Westgate, and, as with the Produce Association, fierce competition was the order of the day.

Poultry Club

An Egg Show was held on Saturday by the Southwell Poultry Club at the Dairy Shop, King St by permission of Mr Storer. This resulted in a large number of eggs being sent to the Red Cross Military Hospital, Norwood Hall. The exhibits were judged by the Assistant Area Organiser, Mr Sidney (Nottingham). The prizes were awarded to: Brown Eggs - 1. Mrs Umber, 2. Mrs Suter. White Eggs - 1. Mr A Hall, 2. Mrs Cropper, 3. Mr T Parker. Dried Eggs - 1. Mr Shorthose, 2. Miss Fletcher, 3. Mrs Porter. Duck Eggs (green) - 1. Mr G W Rogers, 2. Mr T Parker. Duck Eggs (white) - 1. Mr G W Rogers, 2. Mrs Cundy.

The committee thank those who sent gifts of eggs for the hospital, especially the YHA Burgage House.[25]

The Ministry of Agriculture encouraged people to buy domestic rabbits and breed them for food. Rabbits breed all through the year, and not only were they a great source of alternative meat, but rabbit skins were sold for making boots and coats. The meat of the domestic rabbit is white and virtually indistinguishable from chicken. By joining the local Rabbit Club, people qualified for a bran ration to feed their rabbits, which enabled them to grow more quickly and fatten.

---

[24] *N/Adv*, 8th August 1945.
[25] *N/Adv*, 2nd May 1945.

Southwell Domestic Rabbit Club

The Southwell Domestic Rabbit Club held the Annual Show on Saturday in the Gymnasium, Private Road, by permission of Mr R Matthews. There were over 100 entries. Mr C Mawson was awarded the Certificate of Merit signed by HRH the Duke of Gloucester, his exhibit being an Old English Rabbit. This gained three firsts. The proceeds together with the many subscriptions will be given to the Red Cross (Agriculture) Fund, Rabbit Section.[26]

Other problems caused by rationing - catering for weddings and sporting events

Rationing could cause problems when a big social event was planned, such as a wedding. Although at the beginning of the war a few engaged couples decided to postpone getting married until the war ended, many felt that they wanted to be united before the call-up, evacuation, or bombing separated them. There was, too, a practical reason for speeding up the progress of courtship. The new wife had a status which the long-standing fiancée lacked - the Forces paid a marriage allowance and, if the worst should happen, a widow's pension. However, most women were no doubt moved by more romantic considerations.

The church ceremony may have provided a reminder of war in the shape of boarded up windows, and there might not be many photographs for the wedding album as photographic materials were scarce, but it was at the reception that the real difficulties began. In July 1940 the long-hallowed tradition of the wedding cake was struck a heavy blow by a ban on making or selling iced cakes. Obviously, this was caused by the shortage of the main ingredients - sugar, butter, dried fruit and almonds.

"Are you ready to cut the cake, Madam?"

(Home Front)

Yet, photographs of wartime weddings show the cake to be every bit as impressive as in peacetime - a towering, decorated, three-tiered creation. The explanation is simple: one could borrow from many bakers a splendid cardboard cover, looking like the most expensive, traditional iced cake. Usually the cake was made of whatever the family could collect from relatives and friends, often saved over several months. The rest of the food for the reception probably came as a result of a joint effort - friends queuing at all the grocery shops in the town for what was available.[27] The Southwell Food Office issued permits for the extra food allowed for such occasions under the regulations. The limit of numbers - usually forty - was not necessarily

[26] *N/Adv,* 10th March 1943.
[27] Longmate. pp. 159-60.

annoying as it provided an excuse for not inviting unwelcome relations and saved the pocket of the bride's father.

At sporting fixtures, when it came to putting on the traditional catering for visiting teams, rationing caused a few headaches.

> Rationing definitely did have an effect on the people of the town. I came across the problem when trying to arrange catering for rugby teams after the match. If you wanted to entertain the visiting team, you had to go to the Food Office in Westgate and apply for permission to get X loaves, X lbs of butter and X tins of jam.
> **Steve Pulford**[28]

Clothes' rationing and its impact on local residents

'I know all the women will look smart, but we men may look shabby. If we do, we must not be ashamed. In war the term "battle-stained" is an honourable one'.[29]

(Newark Advertiser)

Clothes' rationing had come into effect on June 1st 1941. Supplies of wool and cotton had fallen to 20% of pre-war levels, so, just as with food rationing, the purchase of clothes required coupons as well as money. At first everyone received 66 coupons a year, though the allocation was reduced to 43 coupons in 1943.

Every item of clothing was given a points value, varying according to how much labour and material was needed to produce it. For an overcoat a woman had to surrender 14 points, for a dress 11, for a pair of panties 3, and for a pair of stockings 2. For children's clothes the points values were lower, to allow for their rapid growth. Clothing coupons could be used anywhere, and though officially it was illegal to offer loose coupons this was one regulation that was regularly broken. Most shopkeepers were happy to accept loose coupons since they did not want to turn away trade.[30]

To encourage women to take a self-help approach to the problem of clothes' rationing, the Board of Trade produced numerous 'Make-Do-and-Mend' leaflets, to prolong the life of garments by giving tips on basic darning and patching. 'Mrs Sew and Sew', a fashionably thin puppet figure with a cotton reel body and clothes-peg legs, explained in women's magazines 'How to patch a shirt', 'What Mother can do to save buying new' and how to 'Keep them tidy underneath'. Fashion journalists showed in short films how to turn 'an old coat, that is on the long side ... into a useful two-piece dress and jacket'. In addition, there were 'Make-Do-and-Mend' evening classes in Southwell, supporting the slogan 'Mend and make do to save buying new', and similar catchy little slogans.[31]

---

[28] Birks.
[29] Oliver Lyttleton, President of the Board of Trade, 1st June 1941.
[30] Juliet Gardiner, pp. 567-8.
[31] Longmate, p. 254.

The Utility Mark, 'Civilian Clothing 1941' appeared on all utility items.

(*Beating the Invader - Beeston & Chilwell in WW2)*

One scheme that was successfully introduced by the Board of Trade, to help provide adequate supplies of good quality clothes, was the 'Utility Clothing Scheme'. This offered a restricted range of garments of simple but sound design, low price and guaranteed quality, made to detailed specifications. The specifications were very strict: the number of buttons on a jacket was prescribed, as was the depth of hems, the length of the skirt, the number of pleats, tucks, pockets and belts; there must be no superfluous trimmings of velvet, fur fabric, or decoration such as embroidery or lace. Trouser turn-ups were banned for men, no double-breasted suits were permitted, and the number of pockets was restricted to three for coats and jackets and two for waistcoats. The term 'Utility' became a source of jokes. 'Heard about the utility woman?' 'She's single-breasted.'[32]

So what impact did clothing rationing have on everyday life? Did people find ways of getting round the problem of shortages in the same vein as they had with food rationing?

I don't think clothing rationing had the same impact as food rationing. I can never remember being out of clothes. Boys at the Minster Grammar School still managed to come in blazers and flannels.
Steve Pulford[33]

We seldom had new clothes anyway, even before the war. It was quite normal for clothes to be passed down or on to a nearby relative or friend's family. There was no question then of 'I don't want that!' For most people fashion was not important then; they simply couldn't afford many new clothes. I remember a lot of children going to school in clogs as you didn't need clothing coupons for clogs. A lot of women made their own clothing.
John Postle[34]

I think fathers suffered most from clothes' rationing because their coupons were used for the children in the family.
Joan Hallam[35]

Clothing rationing wasn't too much of a problem. I can remember having a dress made from other people's clothes. It was lucky that we were four girls so we could wear the same dresses.
Janette Barrett[36]

Whilst clothing rationing didn't appear to present the same problems as food rationing, much depended on the ingenuity and practical skills of the housewife and women of the family. Many mothers knitted gloves and scarves for their children or had someone else knit them, as the alternative was finding coupons. Also, knitted garments were undone and the wool was reknitted. Two other ways round the problem were finding 'hand-me-downs', especially outer garments,

[32] Longmate, p. 255.
[33] Birks.
[34] Birks.
[35] Stevenson.
[36] Birks.

and buying and selling second-hand clothes among friends. Old coats and dresses were cut into strips and made into rag rugs. Nothing was wasted.

In each locality 'Clothes Exchanges' were set up and run by the WVS. Here, mothers could take outgrown, but not outworn, clothing and exchange it for items sized to fit their children. Thus cash and coupon expenditure was minimised and wear of garments maximised. Shoes were frequently included in these exchanges and parachute silk suddenly became a popular, if not strictly legal, alternative material for baby clothes and underwear.

(Bombers and Mash)

Mother was a good manager. Once a year she cleared out our clothes and sent those clothes we didn't need to 'our poor relations'. My cousins at Grimethorpe Colliery had all my outworn clothes. I didn't think how lucky I was. That was life and how it was usually lived.   **Malcolm Gough**[37]

Parachute silk suddenly seemed to be available on market stalls. It was rather nice silk and if you had the ability to make delicate underwear it could be most attractive. I think even wedding dresses were made of it.   **Margaret Marrows**[38]

If you were lucky enough to acquire a parachute, this would be carefully unpicked and made into a nightgown, petticoat or panties.   **Nancy Harrison**

We didn't really suffer from the clothing shortages as my grandmother was a seamstress who had made clothes for some of the well-off families in their big houses in the Dukeries. She was brilliant at taking bits from old coats to make dresses and things. Any bits she didn't use she would make rugs out of.   **Cynthia Woolley**

Clothing coupons didn't go very far. Underskirts were often made from parachute material and I remember making a pair of PE pants from blackout material for use at school.[39]

---

[37] Stevenson.

[38] Farnsfield LHS, *Memories of Farnsfield* (Nottingham: Farnsfield LHS, 2000), p.13.

[39] Notts. Federation of WI, *Nottinghamshire Within Living Memory* (Newbury: Countryside Books, 1995), p. 185.

Mother was good at 'Make-Do-and-Mend'. She made rag rugs for the hearth by using old sack bags from the bakery as a base, like canvas. She would also make tea towels from old flour bags, but only after they had been soaked for days to get rid of the smell of the flour.

Mary Hall

School uniform was bought from Randall's in Newark but mother made our blouses. She was very clever at making things. I did OK because of mum's ability. I remember putting round buttons onto paper clips to use as earrings. I still have a bangle that was plastic with flowers on it, but I painted it and wore it often. **Jean Hallam**[40]

(Home Front)

Petrol rationing and its impact

'Is Your Journey Really Necessary?'[41]

Petrol rationing was introduced in September 1939. The number of coupons issued was dependent on the horsepower of the vehicle, with the most popular eight horsepower engines being allocated five gallons a month. It was estimated that this would give private motorists enough petrol for 1,800 miles a year. Essential car users, such as doctors, could apply for enough coupons to drive an extra 7,200 miles, whilst semi-essential car users, such as commercial travellers, could be allocated coupons for up to an extra 3,000 miles. However, in 1942, with submarine warfare at its height in the Battle of the Atlantic, these allowances changed. In the spring months, the basic petrol ration halved, and in July it was abolished altogether for private cars.[42]

Since very few people owned a car, petrol rationing was not a major problem. Everyone was used to walking or cycling, if they owned a bicycle. Buses were infrequent and routes restricted because of petrol shortages, so public transport was difficult, although Southwell had a railway connection, known as the 'Paddy'. Even with more generous allowances, farmers often struggled to find enough fuel for their farm machinery and there was even a move back to horse-drawn transport.

(Home Front)

---

[40] Stevenson.
[41] WW2 poster.
[42] Longmate, pp. 307-8.

Most people didn't own a car. However, petrol rationing was a problem when people needed to get a bus to Nottingham or Newark. There were fewer buses in the war and those to Newark gave preference to munitions workers at the Ransome and Marles' factory. Travelling a distance was difficult. Our parents lived in Hull and near the coast in Norfolk. Both places were very difficult to get access to. **Dallas Doy[43]**

Petrol rationing affected us because two of us were at Newark High School and we needed transport from Southwell. As there were few cars or buses, we often used the local 'Paddy' to Newark, but coming home wasn't so easy. Sometimes we would have to hitch a lift. Once I remember with friends getting a ride on the back of a tar wagon. **Janette Barrett[44]**

During the war my grandfather, who happened to be a highly successful racehorse trainer, enjoyed his regular visits to the Saracen's Head. With petrol extremely scarce he would come from Kirklington on horseback. On arrival at the Saracen's he would give his horse to Fred Dooley, the 'Bootman', who was both barman and yardman. After several drinks at the inn he would collect his horse and make for his Kirklington home. However, there were a number of occasions when only the horse would return, so his family became used to making midnight tours of the ditches and hedge bottoms between Southwell and Kirklington.

Anne Reeves

(Home Front)

It was virtually impossible to get around much unless you could get black market petrol. As we lived on a farm it was important for us to go to Newark Market twice a week. **Steve Pulford[45]**

My mother shopped at Kirkby's once a week and travelled by pony and trap from Westwood Farm, Normanton. We had a car but it was put away during the war. Our petrol, obtained by coupons, was used for the starting of tractors. Like a lot of people, we used bicycles and of course walked much more than people do today.
David Hutchinson[46]

We seemed to go back to the horse and cart because people couldn't get petrol. I remember Rainbows, the local delivery

---

[43] Birks.
[44] Birks.
[45] Birks.
[46] Stevenson.

service, using a horse and cart. There weren't many buses so people working at Newark travelled by the 'Paddy'. I can remember one day as it was going round the bend near Rolleston the train disappeared in a snowdrift. The snow went down the chimney and put the fire out. As the engine couldn't get going the people on board had to walk home. **John Postle**[47]

Our car could only be used for something special as petrol was in short supply. Uncle Fred at Maplebeck though had a pony and trap which we used when we went to dances in Southwell at the Ideal Cinema. **Bob Reeves**[48]

Many more people cycled to work in those days as few owned cars. Wartime restrictions made cycling even more popular as the roads were quieter than usual, but it was not without problems. It was quite normal for Southwell residents to cycle to work to Newark and Nottingham, but getting home in the winter months in the blackout wasn't easy. Although some minimal lighting on bikes was permitted, the battery shortage affected cyclists badly and often they only had the reflector on the rear mudguard. Collisions with motorists and stray animals were quite common, and there was the added danger of coming off the bike when suddenly confronted by a huge pothole.

My grandmother, who lived on Dornoch Avenue, had a Polish RAF Air Traffic Controller billeted with her, a lovely person. She used to cycle to either RAF Syerston or Newton every day and return at the dead of night in the blackout with virtually no lighting to help her.

Cynthia Woolley

As most builders' businesses closed down in the war, my brother Ken went to work at Ransome and Marles. He would cycle to Newark as would many of the local people who worked at either R and M or Worthington and Simpson munitions factory. This was good business for my brother Arthur Beckett's Cycling and Electrical business. Arthur was an agent for Raleigh and Hercules cycles. **Jack Beckett**

Because of the wartime transport difficulties, I would cycle a lot, like most people. I always remember not long after the war had ended I went down to London to take my exams so I could qualify as an estate agent. For some reason I left my cycle by the side of the Saracen's Head arch and when I returned from London, a week later, the bike was still where I'd left it! It just shows how honest people were in those days. **Douglas Gascoine**

In 1940 George Harvey from Church Street was sent to help in the sugar beet campaign. George would cycle to Newark to begin the night work of cleaning out the silos. 1940-1 was a bitterly cold winter but directed work was very important. 'And do you know what happened next? I was sent to Ransome and Marles, in a hot factory enclosed at night. I would cycle to Newark in the summer months and use the 'Paddy' in the winter.' **George Harvey to Doreen Stevenson**[49]

---

[47] Birks.
[48] Stevenson.
[49] Stevenson.

Looking Back

Like those living in other rural areas, the residents of Southwell and the surrounding villages appear generally to have managed quite well for food, despite wartime rationing. Unlike the urban areas, where people were used to relying very much on 'bought' food, they made good use of their gardens and allotments, as well as the natural resources, which could be freely found in the surrounding countryside. As well as an abundance of fruit and vegetables, meat was not in short supply for those who joined Pig Clubs, kept poultry or rabbits. There was plenty of game to be had, if not always legally.

It seems the law was frequently bent, or even broken, in making sure there was food on the table, although it was generally accepted that this was not criminal in the usual sense. Indeed, the local police and Southwell Magistrates' bench showed a relaxed attitude to all but the most blatant irregularities. Today, the wartime diet is recognised as having been healthy, particularly as it contained very little sugar or fat.

Clothes' rationing was to some a problem, although many women already had some knitting and dress-making skills. The less well off were also used to recycling clothes, handing down outgrown garments or unpicking and remaking those that were worn. Possibly those who found it hardest were the better off, who were used to having a more extensive wardrobe and employed staff to look after their clothes. Most people were used to a frugal way of life, unlike our wasteful attitude nowadays, so did not have a sense of hardship at going without what they never had.

The impact of petrol rationing was mainly felt by those who worked outside the town, particularly in Newark, Nottingham or Mansfield, although some of the Newark munitions factories provided special buses. The 'Paddy' was a reliable method of transport, as were the horses which were brought back into service by farmers and some businesses. However, most people either walked or cycled. With very little traffic on the roads, this was a much safer and more pleasant way of getting about than it is today - except during the blackout.

On the land horse power was still customary in some areas.

(Wartime Farm)

CHAPTER 7

'Lend a hand on the land'

'Plough now by day and night. Grow for the nation feeding stuffs for your farms, keep our ships and money free for buying vital arms '[1]

Farming had been in the doldrums in the years before WW2 as more and more of Britain's food was imported. As a result of this, an average of 10,000 agricultural labourers a year were leaving the land to work elsewhere, and many arable farms were being given over to pasture and livestock.

When war broke out in September 1939, the Ministry of Agriculture decided to conduct the 'Battle for Food' on four main fronts. First, because we imported two thirds of our food and much of this could be threatened by the U-boat campaign, a ploughing offensive was launched to provide enough land to grow the necessary food. Second, the process of mechanisation needed accelerating. Third, with so many farm labourers called up, the labour shortages had to be addressed. Finally, an overarching administrative framework was required for the effective running of the campaign. The urgency of these demands created real problems for local farmers who, in many cases, possessed very little machinery and were having difficulty finding labourers.[2]

> Everything needed on the farm was scarce. You couldn't get machinery. Much of it came from abroad, like bits for the tractor. Implements were difficult to find. **Bob Hardstaff**[3]

Wartime Poster (Home Front)

> My father rented Lodge Farm of 84 acres from Mrs Tuplin of Westhorpe. Early in the war we had no water, gas or electricity. We got water from a well. We didn't get a tractor until later in the war and so we relied on two shire horses. When finally we did get a tractor I learnt to drive it. The farm was mainly arable, growing wheat, oats (for the milk cows) and sugar beet. Yet we did have 10-12 cows and when I got back from school I was usually left two of them to milk; the idea was to give me experience of working with animals. **Geoff Riley**

> I went to Brockilow Farm, Laxton where my Mum's family was. There was a labour shortage. I also helped my Uncle Fred on his mixed farm at Breck Farm, Maplebeck. It was a time of very gradual change on farms. Early in the war horses pulled the machinery. **Bob Reeves**[4]

[1] WW2 poster.
[2] P Ginn, R Goodman, A Langlands, *Wartime Farm* (Mitchell Beazley: Lion Television), p. 18.
[3] Stevenson.
[4] Stevenson.

Ploughing Campaign

On the outbreak of war the Ministry of Agriculture, under the Emergency Powers Act, set up County War Agricultural Executive Committees throughout the country. These were made up of farmers chosen jointly by the Ministry of Agriculture's expert advisory officers and the National Farmers' Union. The country was split up into districts, each with its own committee. These 'War Ags', as they came to be known, visited the farms and arranged with the farmers which fields had to be ploughed. They then issued official ploughing orders, which had the force of law.

(Wartime Farm)

Agricultural committees could order farms deemed to be too small, and therefore inefficient for purpose, to be tacked on to a neighbouring farm to make a more viable unit and, in the most extreme cases, the War Ag could recommend to the Ministry that a farm be requisitioned and placed directly under its control, or that of a tenant farmer of their choosing. Farmers were told what crops to sow, depending on national need.

In such a situation there was potential for a huge amount of resentment on the part of the farming community.[5] Many farmers did not take kindly to either advice or direction, though none seem to have refused the government grants and subsidies that accompanied the orders. The assumption that arable land was more important than grazing land, because crops were more efficient as foodstuffs, was not accepted by all. Many farmers felt that they lacked the equipment needed for efficient working of arable land, and the argument that animals should be slaughtered to save land used to feed them was not universally accepted either. Some pastoral land was hard to cultivate and farmers needed grass for their dairy herds. Even if the pastoral land could be cultivated, some levelling out was often needed.

Most fields around Thurgarton were undulating with humps and hollows; they had to be levelled out and so to do this Fowlers of Leeds designed a large Gyrotiller; it was a vicious looking monster on tracks like a tank with large contra-rotating tines, which not only levelled the ground but took out hedges in one fell swoop and uprooted large trees. It ran on diesel and was certainly a mean machine the like of which we hadn't seen before. **Jim Bentley**[6]

---

[5] Ginn, Goodman, Langlands, p. 24.
[6] Thurgarton Village website.

Despite misgivings from certain quarters, the local War Ag didn't take long to show its teeth.

FARMERS DID NOT COMPLY WITH PLOUGHING ORDER
At Bleasby and Hockerton

Failure to comply with the directions of the Nottinghamshire War Agricultural Committee resulted in two farmers being fined at the Southwell Police Court. The defendants were William Hemington from Bleasby and Clarence Pykett, Gables Farm, Hockerton. There were two counts against the latter. Both pleaded guilty. Mr A Graves prosecuted on behalf of the Ministry of Agriculture and Fisheries and Mr W Scott, of Nottingham, defended.

Mr Graves said the offence to which Hemington had pleaded guilty was his failure to carry out certain works of cultivation (ploughing up most of his grassland) as directed by the Notts. War Ag Executive Committee on October 10th 1940. The first order was made in August 1940. The defendant objected to the Order

No Longer Self-Contained

The defendant wrote: 'I must strongly object to plough[ing] up further grass on my land.' He added that 41 acres already had been ploughed and now the Order was for 53 acres. His farm was practically self-contained and if further land was ploughed, the farm would no longer be self-contained. It was a dairy farm, and further ploughing would mean increasing corn at the expense of milk.

Mr Graves, prosecuting, said, 'I ask you to take a serious view of the case. The defendant has refused to carry out the instructions of the Committee merely because he wants to keep his grassland. In these times it is essential that the needs of the community should come before the personal needs of the farmer. I hope the penalty you will inflict will be such as will be a warning to farmers in the neighbourhood that you will not tolerate a refusal to carry out these instructions.'

Mr Pykett 'Gables' Farm, Hockerton

Mr Pykett's farm comprised 200 acres and if he complied with the instructions he would have something like 120 arable and 79 grass. His stock consisted of six heifers and one bull, 20 yearlings, eight calves and 100 sheep. It was considered that the grass left was sufficient for the farm.

Mr Graves thought the bench would be satisfied that there was an actual refusal to carry out the Orders. When the defendant, Mr Pykett, was interviewed in August 1941, he told the Committee he was quite tired of their interference, and was abusive to the officer.

'In this case there was a wilful refusal to carry out the Orders', said Mr Graves. 'The whole farm was sold in 1930 as arable land so he must have turned it into grassland.'

Leather Jackets

Mr Scott, defending lawyer, said that the land in question was infested with leather jackets and wire worms, and the defendant told the Committee that to attempt to crop it would be a waste of money.

The Bench fined the defendant £15 of which £10 was in regard to the unploughed field 167. He was also ordered to pay three guineas costs. The magistrates were Sir W N Hicking (Chair), Sir William Broad, Mr A Straw and Ald. C G Caudwell.[7]

John Watts, living at Springs Farm, Edingley and David Hutchinson at Westwood Farm, Normanton both recall how interventionist the new War Ags were and how they put pressure on their fathers.

---

[7] *N/Adv,* 26th November 1941.

The number of regulations was massively increased by the War Ag and we were quickly told that we had too much pasture, so we had to plough up about 40 more acres. Some months later my father received a 'Notice to Quit' because the War Ag was unhappy about him not getting his winter corn grown early enough. Father appealed against this and a hearing was held in Nottingham. He was allowed to carry on farming, but the category of the farm was reduced by the War Ag from Category 'B' to 'C'.

Nevertheless, the War Ag did their best and, as most of the committee were farmers themselves, they meant well. They did some valuable work renting out much needed machinery at their Nissen hut opposite Norwood Park on Lower Kirklington Rd. **John Watts**

Life was even harder for my father when the government set up Local Agricultural Committees. The War Ag's role was to make sure more food was grown in their local area. I remember one of the members, Mr Reynolds from Farnsfield, coming up to our farm and telling my father what crops had to be grown. He would turn up later and check my father had carried this out. They had a depot in one of the fields next to the Army Camp off the road to Kirklington. There certainly was an International tractor there and three sets of threshing equipment. **David Hutchinson**[8]

Often pasture which had remained inviolate since medieval times was ordered by the local War Ag to be ploughed.

Ploughing up Norwood Park

The plough has claimed the picturesque acres of Norwood Park. This was formerly one of the four parks owned by the archbishops of York and is notable for its fine old timber. Here, of course, stood Cludd's Oak under which Edward Cludd performed the marriage ceremony for local couples during the Commonwealth and many oaks still flourish there which must pre-date that by many a year.[9]

Much of the meadow land used for grazing had been ploughed up at the start of the war. There was no farming by the family during the war. The farming was undertaken either by existing tenants or the War Agricultural Executive. **Sir John Starkey**

461/NK/204		SCHEDULE.	
DISTRICT	NEWARK.		
Parish, O.S. Map No. and Edition	Area	Description	Required Cultivation
	Acres		
Rolleston			
	15.021	Grassland	To be ploughed by 31st December, 1940, cultivated in an approved manner and sown with an approved arable crop for the harvest of 1941.
			These directions are in substitution for and in cancellation of directions 461/NK/204 dated 14th October, 1940.

Schedule for ploughing land in Rolleston.

(Frank Mitchell)

---

[8] Stevenson.
[9] *N/Adv*, 29th October 1941.

Another well-known piece of land that came under the plough, under somewhat controversial circumstances, was Southwell Golf Club. Play at the Golf Club was restricted in the early war years, because many of the members who travelled from the Nottingham area no longer had petrol. However, not all the land was lost as the following article, a week later, showed.

Southwell Golf Links - some land saved for Minster School

Further to last week's remarks about the ploughing of Southwell Golf Links, it is pleasing to hear that a small portion of the links at the bottom of the hills - that which used to comprise the 9th fairway - has been saved and is to be used by the Minster Grammar School as a sports field.

This will maintain the old sporting association of this field for, prior to the time when it was taken over by the Golf Club, the old Southwell City Football Club - and I believe a second team, too - had their pitch there.[10]

Nevertheless, the ploughing campaign nationally was a success. By 1944 the country had increased its area of arable land by 50%, its pasture land by 66%, had nearly doubled its output of wheat and barley and more than doubled its output of potatoes.[11] It was such achievements that ensured the country never starved, and by the end of the war was importing only one third of its food, rather than two thirds.

HARVESTING ROOT CROPS and POTATOES

For harvesting potatoes, beet and all root crops the Fordson Tractor is the farmer's biggest aid. Hundreds of growers have demonstrated that it shows valuable savings in *time* and *cost* over other methods.
Remember, too, the immense value of the Fordson for haulage at this season, when every hour counts.

In the fields or on the road there is no greater asset.

Look ahead and ORDER YOUR

Fordson TRACTOR-*NOW!*
BROOKS' MOTOR CO.
23/5, Castlegate and Farndon Road
Tel. 179   **Newark**   Tel. 179

(Newark Advertiser)

---

[10] *N/Adv,* 2nd December 1942.
[11] *N/Adv*, 11th July 1945.

Nottinghamshire had already been largely an arable county before the war, so could not be expected to show a spectacular reduction in the area of permanent grass, as occurred in many of the grassland counties. However, as Alderman G E Walker pointed out, much was achieved by the Nottinghamshire farmers by the end of the war.

A very substantial area of permanent grassland has been ploughed up - 77,743 acres to be exact. This had decreased the pre-war grass area from 224,281 acres to 146,538 acres, a decrease of 34% as compared with a national decrease of 38%. In 1939 44% of Nottinghamshire was arable land and 56% grass. In 1944 the arable area had increased to 63% and the permanent grass had decreased to 37% of the total agricultural area.

Turning to the main food crops - wheat, potatoes and sugar beet - we can show some remarkable figures. Wheat in the county has increased between 1939 and 1944 from 45,522 acres to 69,069 acres, a gain of almost 30%. ... Potatoes show a truly remarkable increase in the county. In 1939 7,576 acres were grown as compared with 24,022, an increase of 217%. Sugar Beet, of which this county is one of the principal producers, shows an increase from 7,882 acres in 1939 to 11,564 acres in 1944, an increase of 47%. It will be noticed that the main increase in food crops have been in those crops - potatoes and sugar beet - which have the heaviest labour requirement.[12]

Partly as a result of this ploughing success, there was a dramatic rise in agricultural investment funded by the government, which helped bring about an increase in mechanisation. Domestic production of tractors doubled in 1941 alone, whilst imports of tractors trebled. In 1939 56,000 tractors could be found on British farms; by 1942 the number was 111,000. Gradually more farm machinery was introduced, especially under the control of the local War Ag.[13]

Later in the war, both at Brockilow Farm, Laxton and at Breck's Farm, Maplebeck, there were tractors to pull the machinery where previously there had been horses.   **Bob Reeves**[14]

Solving the Labour shortage - Land Army girls, POWs, 'Displaced Persons' and Lowdham Borstal boys

The labour shortage was a major problem for local farmers in 1939. Agriculture was a reserved occupation, but many male farm workers were nevertheless joining the armed forces. The labour shortfall was partly made up by the young women of the Land Army. Recruitment began in January 1939 and women were already helping with the harvest in August 1939. By the time war broke out in September 1939, 17,000 volunteers had registered.

Land Army girls

Many local women joined the WLA after the National Service Act of December 1941; training the girls before placing them on farms was obviously important, and four- to six-week training programmes were established on 'model' farms and at agricultural colleges. To avoid the problem of homesickness, LA hostels were set up, usually housing around 20-40 girls, located in requisitioned buildings as diverse as manor houses, converted stables and Nissen huts. In the

---

[12] *N/Adv*, 25th July 1945.
[13] Longmate, p. 236.
[14] Stevenson.

nearby district there were WLA hostels set up at Hockerton, Hoveringham, Farndon, Brackenhurst and Collingham, as well as other hostels further afield. Many girls had never been away from home before and were not local. Each hostel had its own warden, cook, daily cleaner and handyman to maintain the building.

Nationally, the Land Army was run by its director, Lady Trudie Denman, who generously handed over her family's country home, Balcombe House in Sussex, as its headquarters. Locally, Lady Sibell Argles was appointed Chairman of Nottinghamshire Women's Land Army and the county office was established at The Kennels, Thoresby Park, Ollerton. To promote the work of the Land Army in the county, Lady Sibell invited Lady Denman to a meeting at Newark in December 1940.[15]

"WRONG AGAIN!"

(Bombers and Mash)

Lady Denman meets Land Army girls at Newark

Tributes to the efficiency of girl land workers were paid at a rally of the Notts. section of the Women's Land Army, held at the Technical College, Newark on Saturday. 'They cannot take the places of key men, but they do fill in the gaps when the boys have gone', said one speaker. The rally was organised under the auspices of the Notts. County Committee, and on arrival at the Midland Station the girls marched to the College via Stodman Street and the Market Place. ... During the proceedings Lady Denman presented good service badges to 56 girls who had earned the distinction by six months, and in some cases a year's good work on the land.

Lady Sibell Impressed

Lady Sibell said she thought it was a great occasion because it was the first large gathering for the Land Army in the county. ... 'The life of a land girl during the dark winter months was not exactly attractive, but she was sure the girls who passed through the awful weather of last winter would encourage those who had joined up since, by telling what a tremendous lot of good it did them.'

British Women's Grit

'You may not be as hefty as men', said Lady Sibell, 'but remember British women have always been foremost in pluck, grit, determination and staying power. England today is in the hottest corner she has ever been in her history. ... Let her grit her teeth, put her back into her work and do her duty just as the soldiers, sailors and airmen are doing. Then will the cruel Nazi regime be overthrown and peace be restored to the world.' (Applause)

---

[15] Longmate, p. 239.

Variety of Jobs

Lady Denman ... said she did not believe there was a job on the farm that some member of the Land Army had not undertaken.

'There is no doubt that the members of the Land Army are doing magnificent work in helping to grow the nation's food. Volunteers are driving tractors, milking cows, tending sheep, hedging and ditching: in fact, I know of no job which has not been carried out satisfactorily by a member of the Land Army.' (Applause)[16]

There are many positive memories of Land Army girls working on nearby farms.

Jesse Featherstone Women's Land Army
(Peter Marrison)

Margaret Peet was one of the Land Army girls who came to Norwood. She was selected by my mother as she would present no temptation to my father. He was not like that anyway, so she need not have worried. **Sir John Starkey**

I can remember the Land Army girls who came to the Rolleston farms came mainly from the Hockerton hostel by cycle but were sometimes brought by a Hillman truck with a canopy on the back. WLA hostels were established at many locations in the district, forming pools of labour available to the local farmers.

However, some girls lived on the farms, in fact we had some at our farm. Some Land Girls married local men. This changed their way of life, opening up new horizons for some of the Land Army girls. But inevitably, for those who were not used to it, some found the work too hard. It certainly was very hard. Perhaps also the farmers who worked very hard themselves expected too much from the girls. I remember Mary Voce telling me that she had done every kind of job and had enjoyed the companionship of her contemporaries at the camps and the outdoor life. **Frank Mitchell**

We had Land Army girls at Lodge Farm, Upton, too. I have a vivid memory of being invited, as a young boy, back to their hostel at Hockerton for a film show. **Geoff Riley**

Our best remembered Land Army girl at Springs Farm, Edingley was Kathleen 'Paddy' Storer, who, though a town dweller, picked up the management of a herd of cows quickly and efficiently. After the war she married a Canadian soldier. **John Watts**

---

[16] *N/Adv*, 18th December 1940.

Joyce Trueman was a Land Army girl based at the WLA hostel on Lodgefield Lane, Hoveringham. ... She had been born in London and five members of her immediate family were killed in the Blitz. ... The hostel housed twelve girls, who were under the care of a female warden. The girls slept on straw mattresses in three bedrooms and there was always a hot meal at the hostel in the evening. When Joyce was stationed there in 1943, a rota ensured two girls did the washing up each evening. This was a particularly unpopular chore as it meant missing a dance at the Old Elm Tree 300 yards away and packed with personnel from RAF Syerston.[17]

They used to come to the local farms and help with threshing and milking. I especially remember a very attractive Land Army girl from Sheffield called Ellen. I met her on the Thoresby Estate picking potatoes. A group of Land Army girls had come there from Hockerton.   **Bill Kemp**

"*Now, Miss Fforbes-Wattson, have you had any experience of agricultural work?*"

(Home Front)

We had two Land Army girls at Westwood Farm, Normanton; one of them was a Lincolnshire farmer's daughter. She knew exactly what to do. The other was a machinist out of Jessops and she had stickability. The girls came from very different backgrounds.

David Hutchinson[18]

My mother had an aunt called Helen Pease who was housekeeper for the Land Army at the Hockerton hostel. We walked to see her quite often and she brought several Land Army girls for tea. I remember they were all beefy girls and I loved their baggy trousers and thick brown knee high socks.   **Barbara Page**

I remember Jean Arnold from Halloughton joining the Land Army and she worked at Stubbins Farm. I can remember seeing her in uniform. She married one of the Voce family.

Elizabeth Riley

---

[17] Helen Nall, *The Courage of the Small Hours* (Mansfield: Linney Group, 2010), p. 37.
[18] Stevenson.

Inevitably, close relationships were formed between WLA girls and the local men, sometimes in unusual surroundings.

> It is said that one of the Land Army girls fell in love with a member of the 'Society of the Sacred Mission' at Kelham Hall. The monk was expelled from the Order and promptly joined the Armed Forces.[19]

For further information and memories of Land Army girls in the Southwell district, see *Southwell and District at War 1939-45, Volume 1, Keep Smiling Through*, Chapter 6 pp. 167-171.

Prisoners of War (POWs) and 'Displaced Persons'

Apart from the WLA, what really came to the rescue of the area's farmers was the use of prisoners of war and 'displaced' Eastern Europeans on the land. As with the WLA hostels, a number of POW camps were set up in the Southwell area, notably at Caunton, Carburton, Little Carlton and Walesby. The first POWs were Italian, captured in the North African campaign, coming in the summer of 1941 in time for helping with the harvest. More Italian POWs came in greater numbers once the Allies had broken out of Tobruk.

The normal procedure was that the Italians were taken out to the farms, at first by armed soldiers in lorries, each morning and returned to the camp each evening. Each POW received 6 shillings for eight hours a day, six days a week. However, after its surrender in September 1943, Italy became an ally and the men no longer needed to be imprisoned, so arrangements were soon made to have them billeted on the farms where they worked, or close by.

Once the Italians had left the Nottinghamshire camps, German POWs moved in, and they too were taken out of the camps by lorry to the local farms. After the war had ended, some of the German POWs began to live at their place of work, because it wasn't until 1947 that most German POWs were repatriated. It was highly unusual for both Italian and German POWs to be at the same camp together because of potential conflicts between them; German soldiers were angry that Italy had surrendered in 1943.

Bob Reeves clearly remembered the POWs at Breck's Farm.

> Towards the end of the war we had POWs to help on the farm. They came from a camp in Caunton, just off the Norwell road, in a lorry at first, but then they were allowed to cycle. The first POWs were Italian; one, Cesare Camione, was a really nice man. Then we had a German called Venzel. Both were great workers. We were not supposed to feed them but my aunt always took them what we had for lunch. They were not allowed inside the house. I remember hearing that Venzel had decided to stay permanently in this country after the war. He once said to me that he had nothing to go back to in Germany. Later we had more POWs and I remember that one POW cut his foot, so we had to go into the village to phone the Caunton camp and they came and collected him. There were occasions when I went to the Caunton POW camp and I remember seeing some lovely paintings that the POWs produced hanging on the walls of their huts.
>
> **Bob Reeves[20]**

Amazingly, Caunton POW camp is still clearly visible beside the Norwell Road. The concrete bases and frames of the dormitory huts, with some of the asbestos wall panels, are still standing.

---

[19] Brian Robinson, *Averham, Staythorpe and Kelham* (Newark: Partners Press, 1997), p. 133.
[20] Stevenson.

Caunton POW Camp - water tower with one of the sleeping blocks at the back (Su Dobson)

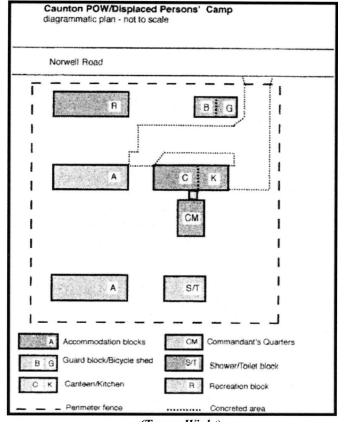

(Trevor Wight)

The brick huts - shower block, cookhouse and latrines - are mostly intact, as is the water tower. It is strange that POW camp buildings that were put up so quickly and never intended to last long are still with us after 70 years. At Caunton this was largely because the village took over at least one of the huts for dances and social events, and later owners of the site used other huts for storage and keeping poultry. The plan of the POW Camp, opposite, shows that there were three main sleeping huts, all of which had concrete uprights and asphalt/asbestos panels on the exterior and interior, with an asphalt roof. Near the Caunton-Norwell road was a recreation hut, a wooden structure which had plasterboard on the inside. Here, the Italian and German POWs had done paintings on the interior walls, usually of local landscapes, parish churches or scenes back home; sadly, these were later destroyed. In the middle of the camp was a catering hut with an adjoining kitchen, whilst at the back were a shower block and latrines. The small building close to the road was likely to have been the Guard's hut, whilst the one in the centre was possibly the caretaker's quarters. If you walk to the west of the POW site, the original concrete posts can still be seen, marking the camp boundary.

> We bought the old Caunton camp in 1961. I think it might have been owned by Major Hole before it was probably requisitioned by the Army. The Recreation Hut had been used by the village for many years after the last Displaced Persons had left. In fact, the title of the property for sale was 'The Village Hall, Caunton'.
>
> We found that the huts had been well built with metal posts, concrete bases, asbestos roofing and hardboard lining round the walls. This made the huts reasonably warm. I remember the wonderful paintings that were still on the walls of the Recreational Hut. One really good painting was of a quayside, probably from somewhere back home in Europe. It was a great shame that the paintings were never kept.
> **Bill Cranidge**

As well as Bill Cranidge, Bob Reeves and Pauline Branston have vivid memories of the images on the walls at the Caunton camp. At other Nottinghamshire POW camps, a number of Italian and German POWs spent much of their spare time sketching local scenes or scenes from their continental background. Whilst these paintings have sadly disappeared, one sketchbook remains, which belonged to Wolfgang Scheffler.

Sketch of Caunton by German POW Wolfgang Scheffler (Ruth Robinson)

Wolfgang Scheffler from eastern Germany had been admitted to the Little Carlton POW camp in the latter stages of the war. Until the war ended he probably worked on farms and was not granted the freedom in his spare time to sketch scenes in the local area. However, after the war ended, POWs were allowed to visit the immediate district in their spare time. Wolfgang used this opportunity to sketch some of his favourite local scenes and later in his life, after he had returned to Germany, he created a series of sketchbooks.

I have chosen 36 sketches which should characterise the richness and individuality of this lovely Midlands cultural landscape. We see monasteries, churches, vicarages, cemeteries, manor houses, hotels, windmills, forges, farms, dovecotes, barns as well as poor-houses.

Christmas 1946 was when we German Prisoners of War were allowed to fraternise. We were allowed to go twelve kilometres from the camp by ourselves. From Little Carlton onwards, where I was from the 21st April 1947, I was able to go and see systematically the surrounding area, making an inventory as it were, a bike being available to me, and in many places I was received with hospitality. The localities further north I got to know by being driven there by English civilians, so that I had a chance to draw.

To all who helped me, I am heartily grateful - for me Summer 1947 in England is unforgettable.
Wolfgang Scheffler, Berlin 1st October 1987[21]

There are several vivid memories of POWs from other camps in the area.

Both Italian and German POWs worked on our farm and at other Rolleston farms. The Italian POWs were very cheery and friendly, but generally they didn't seem too keen on hard work, whereas the German POWs, Marcus and Carl, were real hard workers. They used to cycle to the farm from their camp in Little Carlton.
Frank Mitchell

The Mitchell family and workers at Rolleston in WW2

Back Row: Gilbert Mitchell, Karl Klohr (German POW), Geoffrey Mitchell. Front Row: Edna Mitchell, Guy Mitchell, Arthur Proctor, Margaret Dowse, Marcus (German POW).

(Frank Mitchell)

[21] Wolfgang Scheffler, *Sketches of Villages in the Southwell District,* Berlin 1987.

I came across two POWs at Smith's Farm at Normanton. There was one Italian and one German and they worked pretty hard. They were based at a camp at Carburton because I remember once taking them back with Mr Smith. Many of them were very skilled at creating things, like making slippers out of string.

Quite a number of POWs settled here after the war. One, an Italian, Mr Tome, set up his own agricultural contractor's business based north of Hockerton. He had a store of tractors and would take on ploughing jobs on various farms.

Roy Scoffield

The POWs we had at Lodge Farm, Upton were mainly Italian with some German, too. They were usually brought by lorry but sometimes we needed to fetch them from their camp. I remember they only brought with them a chunk of bread with a little butter. To keep them happy, we used to give them some meat to supplement this meagre ration.

Geoff Riley

Our second billet was at Coulthard Farm, Kirklington. The farmer had German and Italian POW workers and they were very kind to me. They used to drive me round the farm on a tractor, and some of them used to tell me that when the war was over they were going to move back to Italy and open ice cream shops.

Harry Brown[22]

According to a number of Southwell residents, both Italian and German POWs worked in the fields around Southwell, and also on road and drainage work in the town itself.

I used to see Italian POWs working in the fields near Norwood Park. I remember watching them cook hedgehogs by covering them in mud and then putting them over a fire.   **Tony Hayward**

I met some Italian and German POWs when they were digging ditches and working in the fields. They taught us how to make whistles out of willow sticks, by cutting the bark and slicing the bark off. They seemed to be well versed in craft and were permitted to sell what they made and could keep the money.

John Postle[23]

Italian POWs were often seen in the countryside around Southwell. They were identified by the diamond shape patches on their shirts - yellow on brown - on the back, so they were clearly visible if they ran away.

Ray Bush

A lot of POWs, mainly Italian, worked on the farms around Westhorpe. Latterly my father worked for Judge Capthorne at The Elms. He came across POWs and I remember him saying he felt sorry for them because they weren't treated very well, so mother would occasionally give them food parcels. To thank her, the POWs would make objects for the family out of wood.   **Rosa Cooling**

I can remember seeing POWs working on the local farms. They would come on very ropy bikes from Little Carlton; they would walk down the street in their khaki dungarees. We were told not to talk to them as they wouldn't understand us.

Mary Hall

Once the German POWs returned to Germany, their places at the Nottinghamshire camps were taken by 'displaced' Ukranians or other nationalities from Eastern Europe, who had managed to escape from the chaotic situation resulting from many countries being taken over by either the

---

[22] *N/Adv*, 10th May 2002.
[23] Birks.

Nazis or the Russians. Local farmers were happy to employ these displaced persons as there was still a labour shortage, since many British servicemen hadn't yet been demobilised. A number of these displaced men stayed on after the war and settled permanently in the area, including Ukranian John Peglis, and from Eastern Europe Albert Bergmanis. (See Vol. 1, Chapter 4, p. 125).

There were also displaced persons who worked on the farms. I especially recall that the sister of Jack Starbrook, the Norwood Farm manager, married a man who had fled to England from Eastern Europe.
Sir John Starkey

We had a number of displaced persons working at our farm at Halam. I remember two men from Eastern Europe working for us. One of them was heavily tattooed and I remember hearing he had witnessed his parents being shot, presumably by the Germans.
Olive Kitts

Apart from the POWs there were also Ukranians and Rumanians, displaced people, working locally. We had a Ukranian, Jonny Duda, who I remember having a bike crash one day as he left the farm. One local girl, Margery Wesson, married a displaced person, Adam Sottenberg.
Frank Mitchell

It appears that the POWs and Displaced Persons were good workers, and in many cases close friendships were established with the farmers' families. There were several examples of marriages to local girls.

The other source of labour for the farmers came from Lowdham Borstal.

Borstal boys came to Lodge Farm, Upton from Lowdham Grange. They always had a supervisor with them to check they didn't 'scarper'. He was a big, thickset man, 'Punch' Greenwood, so called because he had been a professional boxer. There was never any trouble when he was about.
Geoff Riley

Due to the labour shortage we had help on Westwood Farm from Borstal boys at Lowdham Grange. I remember one of the boys listening to the 1 p.m. news with me while we were having our dinner in the kitchen.
David Hutchinson[24]

Helping the war effort

For the local farmers life in wartime wasn't always all work and no play. There were lighter moments and, as with other groups, farmers recognised the need to support worthy causes.

Local Farmers raise £262

Congratulations to the Southwell local farmers who recently organised a mammoth whist drive and sale at the Ideal Cinema which yielded the astonishing total of over £262. The affair which was unanimously acclaimed as the most successful ever held in Southwell was in aid of the Red Cross Agriculture Sale Fund. Forty-three tables were in play and the number present was considerably increased for the sale which followed. The expenses of the whist drive were defrayed by the organisers. Mr T Gledhill proved himself to be an extremely capable MC.

Winners were: Ladies - 1. Mrs Storer (Halam) 2. Mrs Thatcher (Winkburn)
3. Mrs T Smith
Gents - 1. Mr G Tipple 2. Mr Underwood 3.Mrs McGowan [*sic*]

---

[24] Stevenson.

Consolation - Miss Edith Field and Mr George Harvey

A lucrative sale of gifts took place. Mr H Selby was unable to be present owing to illness, but fortunately a most able deputy was found whose capabilities resulted in the total of over £120. Two competitions were arranged during the evening.

Winners: Pig - Mr J Hewson, Whiskey - Mr G Mosedale.

In the second competition a large toy engine was won by Miss Molly Butler, who subsequently gave it to the children at Winkburn School. Mrs Chilton of Normanton organised a separate competition for a tablecloth and presented substantial proceeds to the local farmers to incorporate in their effort.

Thanks are due to the organisers and to their helpers, too numerous to mention in this column, whose unstinting efforts achieved such gratifying results. The organisers wish to thank the Southwell public for their most generous support.[25]

Looking Back

When the war broke out in 1939, local farmers had two big problems facing them, the urgent need for a dramatic increase in food production and a shortage of labour. Further difficulties arose when War Ags were introduced to give 'direction and advice'. Many farmers didn't take kindly to either direction or advice.

Nevertheless, by their wholehearted commitment to the war effort, they did assist by doubling investment in mechanisation, and increasing the percentage of land under the plough in Nottinghamshire from 44% to 63%. Despite initial strains, a substantial degree of cooperation grew between local farmers and the 'War Ag'.

The employment of Land Army girls, POWs and Displaced Persons also contributed to this success by supplementing the labour shortfall, despite the strong reservations some farmers had when the WLA first arrived on the scene. The fact that so many of the WLA and POWs settled in Nottinghamshire after the war is an indicator of how well the majority integrated into the local community.

Despite the pressures on them, most farmers found the war profitable; they got guaranteed prices for as much produce as they could grow or rear. They also gained, as did businessmen, from the full employment that war brought, after the economic depression of the pre-war years.

---

[25] *N/Adv*, 19th May 1943.

CHAPTER 8

'A Long Face Never Won A War'

'A long face never won a war. ... This is the year when we should think ... that in being cheerful and gay we are paying tribute to life itself, which must go on, and after all is what man is fighting for.'[1]

Being 'cheerful and gay' had to be worked at in those first few weeks of the war. With theatres and cinemas shut and almost all venues for sport and entertainment closed down as an immediate response to the declaration of war, there wasn't much on offer to help. The wireless was the main source of entertainment in the autumn of 1939.

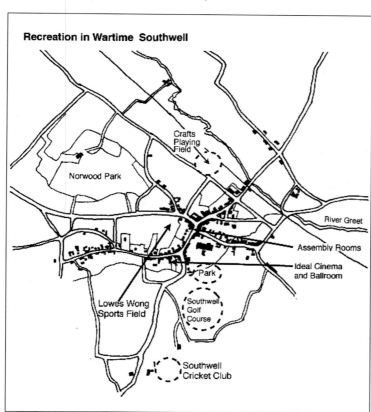

(Map by Trevor Wight)

The wireless

The government and the BBC realised that wireless programmes could play an important role in keeping up spirits. When at six and nine o'clock every evening throughout the war, the chimes of Big Ben introduced the news, they commanded instant silence - 'This is Alvar Lidell.' A ritual surrounded news programmes and many wartime children were puzzled because their normally indulgent parents insisted on absolute quiet at these times. However, operating a radio could be a bit of a performance in itself.

As long as we could get the accumulator charged, usually every Friday, we would listen to the radio. **Bill Kemp**

We had a Cossar radio; you had to warm up the filaments with a lead acid battery before it worked.
Bob Hardstaff[2]

---

[1] *Picture Post,* 10th December 1939.
[2] Stevenson.

We had to get the battery for the accumulator from Mr Barlow down Kent Row. I think it cost 2d to get the battery charged. **Billy Mitchell and Cynthia Patterson née Mitchell**

Most people made sure they were gathered round their wireless set when Winston Churchill was due to make an evening broadcast. No matter how grave the news, many families were inspired, and the great man made them believe that come what may, Britain would eventually prevail. However, some also listened to the Nazi propaganda broadcasts by William Joyce, 'Lord Haw Haw'.

Mother and I listened to radio programmes and I well remember Churchill's broadcasts. He was a strong leader; I think he was the right man for the job at that moment in time. After the war when we were in Switzerland, a Dutch lady came to us, 'I really did admire your Winston Churchill', she said. **Joan Hallam[3]**

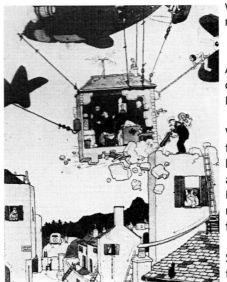

Kidnapping Lord Haw Haw (Home Front)

At home, we listened a lot to the radio. There were ... of course, Churchill's broadcasts. We all thought a lot of him. He kept our spirits up. **Jean Hallam[4]**

We first heard of my father's capture from a friend of the family who came to our house and said that he had just been listening to Lord Haw Haw on the radio and he had read out a long list of names of captured British servicemen in Norway. My dad had been mentioned. A week later my mother received the official letter notifying her of my father's capture. **John Stephenson**

Some nights we would tune into Lord Haw Haw, broadcasting from Germany, with all his propaganda news; not because we were interested in fascism, but because we might get news not provided by the BBC. Lord Haw Haw was eventually hanged as a traitor. **Jim Bentley[5]**

Comedy is a powerful weapon in fighting despair, and the BBC created a number of radio shows designed to poke fun at Hitler, the Nazis, authority and austerity. By common consent *ITMA*, with its star Tommy Handley, was the one everyone listened to. *It's That Man Again* actually referred to Hitler, but the butt of the sketches was the Ministry of Aggravation and Mysteries (Agriculture and Fisheries), where Handley worked in the office of Twerps, coping with the persistent disapproval of the hidebound civil servant Fusspot, and his constant lament of 'It's most irregular'. The German, Funf, played by Jack Train, would announce himself on the 'phone as 'Funf, your favourite spy', to which Handley retorted, 'It may be funf for you but it's not much funf for me!' This kind of word play, along with catch phrases such as Mrs Mopp's immortalised 'Can I do you now, Sir?', soon became absorbed into everyday speech.[6]

---

[3] Stevenson.
[4] Stevenson.
[5] Thurgarton History Archive.
[6] Gardiner, p. 135.

We enjoyed listening to the radio, especially *ITMA* with Tommy Handley and characters such as Colonel Chinstrap and Mrs Mopp. I think 90% of the population must have tuned in on a Thursday night. **David Hutchinson**[7]

(Wartime Britain 1939 - 45)

My father thought having the wireless on was good for business. He used to have the radio on all the time in his barber's shop and many customers would come in regularly just to listen to radio programmes like *ITMA*. I remember always switching on to *Just William*. **Malcolm Gough**[8]

One of the most successful innovations on the radio was the five minutes of *The Kitchen Front*, broadcast at 8.15 every morning from June 1940. The programme made the name of the Radio Doctor, Dr Charles Hill, famous. With his rich, reassuring, fruity tones exuding good humour and common sense, he was a British Medical Association official who soon became the GP everyone would have liked to have had. One of his favourite themes was the need for regularity in bodily habits, and imitations of him talking about the bowels were a frequent turn at wartime concerts. His favourite expression was in praise of 'that humble, black-coated worker, the prune'.[9]

The Ideal Cinema, Southwell

(Peter Cant)

The Ideal Cinema on Westgate was the hub of entertainment in wartime Southwell, with something to attract all ages and interests. In autumn 1939 all cinemas were closed by government order, mainly because there was concern that many lives would be lost if a bomb hit a building where a large number of people were gathered. The future of the Ideal was far from certain.

However, it was soon realised that as well as keeping spirits up by allowing cinema-goers to escape the drab reality of wartime Britain, there was a perfect opportunity to disperse

---

[7] Stevenson.
[8] Stevenson.
[9] Gardiner, p. 187.

information and propaganda. The Ministry of Information produced weekly short films on subjects such as *Salvage, Careless Talk and Food Flashes*. Newsreels were heavily slanted reports on the progress of the war, but were hugely popular, raising cheers for the heroic efforts of 'our boys', and jeers at the Italian and German troops surrendering and being taken prisoner.

Both Hollywood and the British Film Studios recognised that box office success during wartime was guaranteed by films which raised morale, particularly by appealing to patriotic feelings, or were pure glamour and escapism to a fantasy world where everything came out right in the end. Films such as *Lady Hamilton*, with Vivien Leigh and Laurence Olivier, reduced members of the audience - including Churchill - to tears, as they watched Nelson die saving his country from invasion at Trafalgar. The idealised Hollywood view of upper middle-class family life in wartime Britain, *Mrs Miniver*, was an enormous success, as were American musicals starring Judy Garland, Fred Astaire and Ginger Rogers, and the visual extravaganzas of Busby Berkley. The biggest blockbuster on both sides of the Atlantic was *Gone With the Wind*, with its spectacular battle scenes and tempestuous love story.[10]

By December 1939 cinemas were open almost as normal, although all screenings finished by 11 p.m. However, it was not until 1942 that the pattern of twice-weekly programmes was restored with a newsreel and supporting 'B' film, as well as the main feature.

In early 1940 more people than ever before packed into the cinema, to enjoy three hours or so of blissful escapism. It was not unusual to see long queues, with the local cinema manager chatting with wartime friendliness to those waiting. Indeed, it was common for local residents to visit the cinema more than once a week, to see films, dance in the upstairs ballroom, and attend special talks and lectures on topics intended to raise people's awareness of the war effort.

1939 Film Poster (Home Front)

---

[10] Longmate, p. 406.

Gaiety! Glory! Glamour!

THE WIZARD OF OZ

JUDY GARLAND
FRANK MORGAN
RAY BOLGER
BERT LAHR
JACK HALEY

BILLIE BURKE
MARGARET HAMILTON
CHARLEY GRAPEWIN
THE MUNCHKINS

A VICTOR FLEMING Production

VICTOR FLEMING   MERVYN LEROY

It's
METRO-GOLDWYN-MAYER'S
TECHNICOLOR TRIUMPH!

(Home Front)

The Ideal Cinema was very popular during the war, and there was often a queue waiting outside. I really enjoyed going there, though I do remember the films sometimes breaking down, because the young men operating the equipment didn't seem very experienced. But when Mr or Mrs Tuck were in charge the equipment never broke down. They had a good grip.   **Freda Kirby**

There were usually two different programmes - Monday to Wednesday and Thursday to Saturday. To enter the Ideal, you went through the two pillars into the foyer. On the left was the ticket office and straight ahead the entrance into the cinema. There was a wide staircase to the seated area below. To go to the Ballroom upstairs, you could only get access from the outside - to the left of the building and up some concrete steps. You can still see the IDEAL CINEMA sign to this day.   **Robert Beckett**

The only leisure time my parents had was spent going to the cinema. There were two 'houses' on every Monday and Thursday; I went to the first one with my mother and father passed us the door key going to the second.
Malcolm Gough[11]

Local builder Jack Tuck had built the cinema back in the 1930s, on the footprint of the Old Brewery. Jack's parents managed the cinema and they clearly had a reputation for demanding high standards of behaviour.

My husband Jack Tuck built the Ideal Cinema. I can remember that putting blackouts up in all the windows was a huge job. The blackouts had to be all put on frames, you know. My husband's mother, Mrs Tuck, would be in the pay box and my father-in-law, as the proprietor, would walk round and see everything was working well. They wouldn't put up with any nonsense.
Addalane Tuck

Our family would spend a fair amount of time at the Ideal, as Louisa Tuck was my mother's godmother. Mother would take me down to see Mrs Tuck, and I can remember seeing her at the Ticket Office on the left. If mother lifted me up I could see what film was on, because there was a square clear pane of glass, which I suppose allowed the staff to see if the film was finished.
Keith Lee

Early in the war going to the Ideal was a real thrill. I used to go there with my sweetheart from the Essex Yeomanry. We would try and get the double seats at the back of the cinema, but the Tuck family, who ran the Ideal, would allow no 'hanky-panky'.   **Nancy Harrison**

For many Southwell youngsters, the Saturday matinee at the Ideal was their event of the week. These film clubs were very popular. Children flocked to see 'westerns' with the likes of

---

[11] Stevenson.

Roy Rogers, Gene Autrey and Hopalong Cassidy. A number of local residents have fond memories of their Saturday afternoon treat.

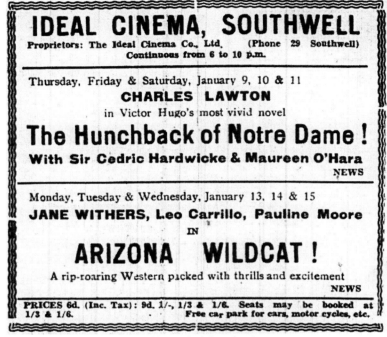

IDEAL CINEMA, SOUTHWELL

Proprietors: The Ideal Cinema Co., Ltd.   (Phone 29 Southwell)

Continuous from 6 to 10 p.m.

Thursday, Friday & Saturday, January 9, 10 & 11

CHARLES LAWTON

in Victor Hugo's most vivid novel

The Hunchback of Notre Dame!

With Sir Cedric Hardwicke & Maureen O'Hara

NEWS

Monday, Tuesday & Wednesday, January 13, 14 & 15

JANE WITHERS, Leo Carrillo, Pauline Moore

IN

ARIZONA WILDCAT!

A rip-roaring Western packed with thrills and excitement

NEWS

PRICES 6d. (Inc. Tax): 9d. 1/-, 1/3 & 1/6. Seats may be booked at 1/3 & 1/6.   Free car park for cars, motor cycles, etc.

(Newark Advertiser)

It was quite usual for young children to go to the Ideal Cinema two or three times a week, as it was only 5d. I normally went on Monday and Wednesday nights and then for the Saturday matinee. Apart from the films you could see, it was a good place to congregate as there was a fish and chip shop at one side and a sweet shop on the other.

Tony Hayward

It was always fun going to the Ideal Cinema in the 2d seats. I used to go often to the Saturday matinee and as well as the main film there was always the Pathé News.

Douglas Gascoine

Edith Plummer and I used to look forward to going to the cinema on a Saturday afternoon when there would be films for children shown. I can remember enjoying the early Disney films and also 'westerns'. We couldn't afford to go any other times.

Rosa Cooling

I especially remember going to the Ideal for the Saturday matinee. The programme always seemed to be either Laurel and Hardy or Buster Keaton followed by a cowboy and Indian film. I loved 'westerns'.

John Lukehurst

I loved to go to the Saturday 'rush' which cost 2d. But sometimes I didn't have any money so I would sit outside and listen by the emergency exit.

Harry Cooling

I remember going to the Ideal on a Saturday afternoon to see *The Last of the Mohicans* serialised.

John Stephenson

The Saturday matinee was very popular. I always remember that the better seats above the gangway were 3d and the seats below were 2d, but they were still good. They also used to have a lucky draw and the winner got a bag of sweets.

Betty Millard

I used to go with friends to the Ideal on Saturday afternoons and sit in the front seats, costing 2d, I think. I remember seeing a lot of propaganda films showing how well we were doing in the war.

Keith Marshall

During the week, the Ideal only allowed entrance to children if they were accompanied by an adult. This could be a problem if no adult was available, but Southwell children were not easily put off.

We occasionally went to the cinema but, other than on the Saturday matinee, unless you had an adult with you, you wouldn't be admitted. I used to say to people as they came into the cinema, 'Take us in, Mister, please.'
Billy Mitchell

Cinema foyers became popular places for displays in aid of 'Wings for Victory', 'Save for a Spitfire' or a war workers' recruitment drive. The Ideal Cinema was happy to support these community war efforts.

I remember seeing a dud bomb in the Ideal foyer, about 4 feet long, complete with fins and with stamps stuck on it. There was an appeal laid across the bomb, 'Pay for a Spitfire'. **Brian Pacey**

Mrs W H Hardy organised a series of special film shows and illustrated talks on topics relating to the war, and these were well attended.

Ideal Cinema Talk - Fifty Days On A Raft

Kenneth Cooke, who is to speak under the auspices of the Ministry of Information at the Ideal Cinema, Southwell on Sunday April 9th, went to sea more than eight years ago as a ship's carpenter. He was at Gibraltar when the war broke out and has been in many convoys to all parts of the world during the whole of the war years.

He was in Montevideo when the Graf Spee limped in after her encounter with the British fleet and he saw the German crew finally destroy their ship.

In September 1942 he sailed from England on a voyage which was to bring him new and testing experiences of the war. The vessel was attacked and sunk by an enemy submarine in the South Atlantic and for fifty days Kenneth Cooke lived on an open raft. Of the thirteen other men who were his companions on this incredible voyage only one besides himself survived. The programme will include a film show. The Chairman will be Admiral of the Fleet Sir Osmond de Beauvoir Brock, GCB, KCMG.[12]

My father took me once to a talk at the cinema, given by a man who had been cast adrift from a boat in the Atlantic Ocean.
Keith Marshall

On 5th January 1944 a Chinese visitor, Miss Lai Po Kan, gave a talk about the terrible conditions in China following the Japanese invasion in 1937. Two months later a French woman, Madame Jeanne Biddulph, related to a large audience 'the grim experiences of life under the Nazi regime'. Following the illustrated talk, a collection realised £10-3s-6d, which was forwarded to the 'Fighting French Fund'.[13]

---

[12] *N/Adv*, 5th April 1944. Note: Admiral Brock (1869-1947) retired from the Royal Navy in 1934. He stayed with the Starkey family at Norwood Park during 1944-45.
[13] *N/Adv*, 1st March 1944.

Wartime Dances and Concerts

There was a real hunger for social life and entertainment, be it whist drives, beetle drives, local concerts or dances. The day-to-day conditions of life were hard and anything that provided relaxation was very welcome. Dances and dance halls cheered up the population. Holding a dance was an immediate response as a fund raiser for all the special 'weeks', such as 'Save for a Spitfire'. There was one almost every week wherever there was a village hall or assembly rooms. Dance halls were a favourite meeting place and, as well as attending dances at the Assembly Rooms and the Ideal Cinema, local girls were prepared to travel some distance to meet the young RAF servicemen stationed at the nearby Bomber Command airfields at Syerston and Ossington. The arrival of the 'boys in blue' brought excitement to the female population of the area. After all, many of the local young men had been called up.

IDEAL BALL ROOM

Dancing Twice Weekly. **Tuesdays & Saturdays,**
7.30 to 11 p m.
Admission—CIVILIANS 1/6, FORCES 1/-.

WHITEHEAD'S DANCE BAND

CAR PARK   BUFFET

(Newark Advertiser)

Songs Won Great Reception

SUPERB ARTISTRY

'DONT CLAP, IT'S TOO HOT"

WITH that superb artistry which has gained for her an international fame, Miss Gracie Fields gave two entertainments in Newark on Sunday. At mid-day her audience consisted of workpeople, and during the afternoon, under the sponsorship of the Northgate House Social Committee, she gave further items from her extensive repertoire to another enthusiastic assembly.

On both occasions she had a magnificent reception, fully merited by the quality of her performance, and, as is customary with her, she pleased all tastes.

The afternoon programme began with the works band's rendering of a medley march, "Sousa on Parade," and then the well-known baritone, Mr. Charles True, sang "Lonely Road" and "I'll Walk Beside You." Both these items were beautifully rendered and at their coynclusion Mr. True introduced the famous star with a wealth of laudatory adjectives.

(Newark Advertiser)

Our favourite dancing places were the Corn Exchange in Newark and at Hazleford Ferry. I would go on the train to Newark with my bike, leave it at a shop in Kirkgate, and cycle back home after the dance. If the sirens started up, I would have to put the bike light out. When I cycled to Hazleford my two friends and myself hoped to meet up with some of the airmen from across the river at Syerston airfield. I got to know a Canadian airman who was based at Ossington airfield in north Nottinghamshire. He would travel to Syerston Airfield, opposite the Hazleford Ferry dance hall, for pilot training. I was invited by the Canadian airman to go down to London on the train for the day. When I asked permission from my father, he immediately said, 'You should go, he's fighting for us'.

Later it was at Syerston that I met Colin Leisk who I eventually became engaged to.   **Nancy Harrison**

TUNES OF TO-DAY

The White Cliffs of Dover
By Candlelight ★ Rose O'Day
Elmer's Tune ★ Green Eyes
Apple Blossom Time ★ Yours
Ma, I Miss Your Apple Pie

RECORDS OF THESE AND HUNDREDS MORE NOW
IN STOCK

There's nothing like Recorded Music

From SWING to CLASSICS

You can Please Yourself !

TRY **COYNE'S** FIRST

LARGEST STOCKS — QUICKEST SERVICE

(Newark Advertiser)

The arrival of the troops brought new interest in Lowdham, especially among the girls. Regular dances were held at the Old Elm Tree, Hoveringham and Burton Joyce, to which they would cycle on a Saturday night. These dances were so popular that the RAF personnel at Syerston crossed the river in a boat to attend. The dances are remembered as bringing a great deal of enjoyment to the village at a difficult time and when so many of the local men were away in the forces.[14]

However, there were occasions when the presence of American servicemen at local dances led to disputes.

There was a regular Sunday night dance in Bilsthorpe Village Hall when busloads of young people would pour in from Farnsfield, Ollerton and even Mansfield. The dance also attracted American servicemen stationed in the area. The American forces operated a policy of segregation at that time, which was a potential source of conflict since the white soldiers made it clear that they were not prepared to remain at the dance if the black servicemen were allowed entry. Mr Wardle, who organised the dances as well as working at Bilsthorpe Colliery, would have nothing to do with such attitudes, letting the black Americans know that they were very welcome, and even introducing them to local girls, as they were rather shy. **Pam Field**

For Southwell girls there were plenty of opportunities to meet eligible young servicemen within the town.

I used to go dancing in the early days of the war. We went to either Trebeck Hall or the Assembly Rooms. I can remember once a busload of airmen came all the way from Cranwell and then a return bus trip was arranged.
I first met my future husband at a dance at Old Trebeck Hall. He was doing an apprenticeship at Ringer's chemist's shop. We got married in September 1943 at Southwell Minster. The Rev. Conybeare married us and we had the reception at the Saracen's Head. **Margaret Harrison**

We used to dance all evening at the Assembly Rooms, next to the Saracen's Head, and then congregate round the huge chimney designed to provide central heating for Southwell Minster. The Essex Yeomanry were such nice young men. Then we'd have a quick kiss and cuddle before going home. My father always seemed to be walking the dog at this time. **Nancy Harrison**

The top floor of the Ideal Cinema was a Dance Hall on Saturdays, but mother wouldn't let me go there. I had to be home by 8.30 p.m. each evening. On a few occasions, I went with friends to dances in the Assembly Rooms and there was live music by a trio of musicians. If I had a boyfriend I knew I could take him home. **Jean Hallam**[15]

[14] Lowdham, p.41.
[15] Stevenson.

There was so much community spirit during the war. I enjoyed dancing the Gay Gordons at The Assembly Rooms and I also belonged to the Old Time Dancing Club. **Margaret Ringrose**[16]

For the young girls in the town a big attraction was Miss Joan Thomas' Dancing School at the Admiral Rodney. The school became noted for its successful pupils, including Cynthia Parker of Burgage Lane.

SOUTHWELL GIRL'S ACADEMY SUCCESS

CYNTHIA PARKER — AGE 9

The above photograph is of Cynthia Parker of Southwell who at the age of only nine years has passed the Intermediate examination of the Royal Academy of Dancing which is the second of the three major examinations of the Academy. Cynthia passed all five grades before she was eight and was accepted as a member of the Royal Academy just over a year ago. She is one of the youngest children in England to have reached this advanced standard. She is a pupil of Miss Joan G. Thomas of Southwell.

(Tim Warner)

My friends and I liked to go and watch the girls dance at Miss Thomas' Dance School at the Admiral Rodney. I remember one evening we sat on the wall beside the dance room looking in at the girls when a policeman came by. We jumped off the wall and ran away. He chased us all to the park, caught us and gave us all a clip. Some of the girls at Miss Thomas' Dance School became quite famous. There was Cynthia Parker and Joan Bradley, who eventually married a well-known night club owner from London. Miss Thomas herself was a tall dark-haired lady, very attractive. **Bernard Driscoll**

Occasionally we would be taken to the Assembly Rooms to watch a show put on by the Joan Thomas' Dancing School. My sister, Ruth, was and remained a close friend of one of the local stars, Cynthia Parker. **Rosa Cooling**

A number of wartime concerts were also held in the town, usually with the purpose of raising funds for one of the many local organisations engaged in supporting the war effort. Details of two of these concerts were covered by the *Newark Advertiser.*

'Happy Days' a comedy

Large audiences attended the presentation of a comedy at the Assembly Rooms last week, one of the best shows seen in Southwell for a long time. It was performed by Farnsfield Players and was produced by Mr J Bullock.

The cast was: Reginald Bledisloe Blougham - Claude Sledger, Leslie Royston - Freda Shipgood, Ruth Elthingham - Jesse Kennedy, Mrs Lash - Elsie M Webster, Jimmy Harbottle - Bert Parrish, 'Bagshot' Pilkington - Jack Bullock, 'Twinky' Farrell (artist's model) - Marjorie Carding, Miss Twinge - Molly Gillsespie, Miss Cattermole - Dorothy Hill, Cordelia B Parkenstacker - Nancy Nairn, Ramshaw Skentlebury - John B Robinson (of the *Daily Comet*), Stage Manager - J Cliffe, prompter - M Shew; Lighting Effects - R Stephenson, J Cooper.

The performances were in aid of the NSPCC and the Southwell Ambulance Fund. The mileage of the latter during

---

[16] Stevenson, p. 32.

1942 amounted to 11,488 miles and 373 cases were moved. All the drivers are local volunteers. The proceeds of the entertainment totalled between £30 and £40. On Monday Mrs P H Warwick expressed thanks to the promoters and audience on behalf of the NSPCC and on Tuesday Mr N A Metcalfe returned thanks on behalf of the Southwell Ambulance Fund.[17]

'A Play for Ronnie', Trebeck Hall

(Newark Advertiser)

Youth Discussion Group

A programme of comedy music and drama was presented in the Grammar School on Saturday evening by Southwell Youth Discussion Group. Those who took part were:

Jean Bowes, Mary Cooper, Pat Osborne, Mary Woodward, impersonation by Patrick Atkins, Raymond Long (at the piano), John Kirk (impersonations), Mary Woodward and Neville Peacock (songs), Jean Bowes and Neville Peacock (duet).

Scene 111 of 'Abraham Lincoln' by John Drinkwater was produced by Mrs Dowling.

The cast was: The President - Peter Wendels, Mrs Lincoln - Margaret Berg, Mrs Goliath Blow - Mary Cooper, Mrs Otherly - Mary Woodward, Mr Frederick Douglas - Ian Shepperson, Susan - Judy Shepperson. The proceeds in aid of the Red Cross amounted to over £15.[18]

---

[17] *N/Adv*, 17th March 1943.
[18] *N/Adv*, 2nd May 1945.

Some of the stars who visited the area

Ethel and Doris Waters were regular visitors to The Saracen's Head when on tour
(Home Front)

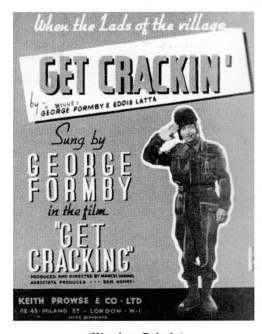

(Wartime Britain)

Vera Lynn (Home Front)

Playtime outdoors

Whilst wartime brought many problems for adults, for children it was a time when they could roam over the fields and in the streets without anyone minding or the children feeling unsafe. Many of the pastimes were seasonal. Marbles, whip and top and hoops were usually brought out in spring when the weather warmed up. Skipping was popular with girls; a piece of old clothes line made an excellent skipping rope. Southwell then had only half the population it has today, there was hardly any traffic, and the town was surrounded by open countryside. Popular playground games were hopscotch and flicking cigarette cards.

The streets were our playground then. There was so little transport on the roads because, unless you had an essential vehicle, you could get very little petrol. We used to get very annoyed when about every hour and a half we had to get off the street and let a car go by.

Anything we could get our hands on we'd use, like car tyres, which we'd roll down the street. Making smokescreens was great fun. During winter we'd gather 'touchy wood' from the inside of dead trees and then fill treacle tins with it. When you lit it up it wouldn't burn but it would smoulder. When you ran along the road you held the tins up in the air and there'd be a glow and smoke used to come out the back. So if you added grass to the tin then you'd made a great smokescreen - lovely for the environment. Basically, as there was nothing for you to buy, you had to make things up for yourself.

Nowadays children expect to go to faraway places on school trips. Then you could only go to places by walking to them. Going to Norwood Park or the eight miles to Newark would be a great adventure. You could always cycle, but you had to be a 'rich' family to own a bike.

Most weekends we'd roam in the fields and eat sugar beet and turnips. We'd go into the barns and find oats which were for the horses. Farmers didn't mind. We'd build dens in the hedgerows, but always made sure we did no damage. We were brought up to remember that if you were in the countryside you never left gates open in case livestock got out onto the roads. In those days I might be out from 8.30 a.m. to 9 p.m., and my parents would never have worried about me being molested or anything. We used to go out to Westhorpe and Easthorpe, which were quite separate in those days from the town. We'd play games of 'Hide and Seek' with the children there. It was a very free existence. **John Postle[19]**

Living close to Westhorpe it was so easy to access the open countryside. We would play in the fields around Westhorpe and often go as far as Norwood Park, mischievously attracted by fruit in the orchards and the presence of soldiers in or around the hall.

Tony Hayward, Brian Pacey, David Hall

Our main enjoyment out of school-time was playing out in the fields of Westhorpe. Mother would pack us a little picnic and at the weekend we'd go out all day picking primroses, bird watching and blackberrying. Occasionally, the Westhorpe estate gamekeeper would chase us if he thought we were up to no good. **Rosa Cooling**

You had to make your own provision in those days. Living at the north end of the town we used to play by the River Greet, in the open fields next to Dornoch Avenue, or by Potwell Dyke at the bottom of Burgage Lane. **Margaret Pulford**

---

[19] Birks.

There were few kids around where I lived on the Burgage and so I would go across to Cecil Hall's farm after school and help out. I would feed and milk the cows, wash their udders, generally muck out the cowsheds. I would then turn out the cows on the Burgage and take them down Newark Road to certain fields. In winter I would take out the horse and dray and go to the fields where Leeway Road is today; I'd then cut cabbage, load it on the dray and return to Cecil Hall's farm. I'd give the cows the cabbage. Tommy Fairholme and I would also use the dray for delivering milk.
Roy Scoffield

It was the same in the villages of Thurgarton, Bilsthorpe and Upton. It was a great time to be a child, because there was so much to get up to throughout the year.

The games seemed to go in seasons. In spring it was skipping for the girls, marbles and whip and top for the boys. In winter there was sliding on frozen ponds, sledging on Booker's field, roller skating and tracking. In summer it was cricket, rounders and cycling and in autumn, of course, it was conkers and fox hounds - a great time was had by all.
Jim Bentley

In Bilsthorpe the favourite street or playground game for young girls was 'Kerb or Wall'; it was a running race game intended for two children. My friend and I would toss to choose whether to make the first run either to the 'wall' or 'kerb'. If I won I always chose to run from the starting line to the 'kerb', then I ran back to the line, then to the 'wall' and finally back to the starting line again. My friend would start at the same time but do the run to the 'wall' first and then to the 'kerb' afterwards. The winner was the first back to the starting line, having visited both 'kerb' and 'wall'. It was great fun.
Pam Field

A group of about a dozen of us would play for hours on the main road with whip and top or we'd play marbles.
Mary Hall

One outdoor activity that was particularly enjoyed by both children and adults was skating. Norwood Park had been a favourite location for local children for many years. However, this article in the *Newark Advertiser* in January 1945, suggested that the war had possibly reduced its popularity.

Outdoor Skating at Norwood Park

In spite of the fact that the recent cold snap lasted several days, only a few local people availed themselves of the opportunity of outdoor skating under very good conditions. There were few boys and girls equipped with skates on the ice. There were one or two good stretches of frozen water and conditions were unusually good on the large ponds in the district.

Norwood Park has for generations been the most popular resort of local skaters. Time was when such a week would have found the ice thronged with skaters of all ages. Where are today's enthusiasts? Many of course are in the Forces. But what of the teenage boys and girls? Lack of skates may be partly responsible. Winters are not what they used to be, they say. Skating spells are of short duration and young folk who have no access to an indoor rink have not had sufficient opportunity to indulge in this exhilarating pastime.[20]

---

[20] *N/Adv*, 3rd January 1945.

Ball games and bird's-nesting

Even though new balls were hard to come by, boys were always inventive in finding alternatives so they could still enjoy their games of football and cricket. An inflated pig's bladder could be used as a football and the players were not put off by the irregularity of bounce and flight. Both cricket and football were played in the road, one of the few places where vegetables were not grown, and there was no danger to life and limb as traffic was virtually non-existent.

> We used to play a lot of football and cricket with our friends in the fields around the town. A favourite field was at Lowes Wong, where the school is now, though my brother Keith remembers that after the army camp had been there, it was a nuisance having to constantly retrieve the football from the trenches which had been dug round the camp. We also played on the Burgage and on Craft's field, off Lower Kirklington Road. **Eric and Keith Marshall**

> I used to like to kick a football around with some of the evacuees from the Brighton School for the Blind at Upton Hall. We used to play in a field at the back of the Hall. Not all the children were blind; some were partially sighted and were quite able to kick a ball around. **John Stephenson**

> In my leisure time I played sport, especially tennis and rugby. When young, we all gathered on the Burgage to play games. I played rugby for the Minster School and we played up on the top ground. **Malcolm Gough**[21]

Although frowned upon today, bird's-nesting was a very popular pastime in wartime.

> I went 'bird's-nesting' around the Dumble at the back of Holy Trinity Church. We would also try and catch little fish there by creating a dam in the stream. **Keith Lee**

> I would go looking for owls' eggs up Micklebarrow Hill, near Upton. We'd put holes in the eggs and blow the yoke out. It was a popular activity to collect birds' eggs. **John Stephenson**

> Most people in the countryside would make up their own entertainment. I loved to kick a ball round with my Rolleston friends and then we'd go bird's-nesting. **Frank Mitchell**

SANTA CLAUS DEPARTMENT

NO TOYS

'The usual guff about Sub-Section 253, Allocation of Raw Materials Order, Board of Trade ...'

(Home Front)

---

21 Stevenson.

Toys, games, books and comics

December, 1944 THE AERO-MODELLER

"TRUSCALE"
1/72 Solid Model Kits
ROYAL AIR FORCE
AMERICAN AIR FORCE
and GERMAN WARPLANES

Wellington Price 3/4

Boulton Paul Defiant
Price 1/10

Airacobra
Price 1/10

Spitfire Price 1/10

All KITS contain fuselage cut to outline shape, wings cut to shape, tail-plane, rudder, and where necessary nacelles printed on balsa, hardwood cowls and wheels, metal propellers, transfer insignia, cement. Also full-size detailed plan.

Hawker Hurricane
Price 1/10

Messerschmitt 110 Price 2/5

Westland Lysander
Price 2/5

Whirlwind   Price 2/5

Blenheim Price 2/5

SUNDRIES :
Hardwood cowls, 5/8 in., 3/4 in. diameter ... 1d. each.
Plated metal propellers, 2-blade, 2 in. diameter, 1½d. „
Plated metal propellers, 3-blade, 2 in. diameter, 2½d. „
Plated metal propellers, 3-blade, 1½ in. diameter, 2d. „
Targets and swastikas, tail markings, complete
set of transfers 3d. „
Wheels 1/2 in. and 7/16 in. diameter ...   ½d. „

Avro Anson   Price 2/5

Heinkel H.E. III K
Price 3/1

Handley Page Hampden
Price 3/1

ADD ½d. Postage on all
Kit Prices.

Tomahawk .. ce 1/10

Buffalo   Price 1/10

Messerschmitt 109
Price 1/10

ADD 2½d. Postage on all
Sundry Prices.

MODEL AIRCRAFT STORES (Bournemouth) LTD.
27b HANKINSON ROAD, BOURNEMOUTH   Phone : 1922 WINTON

Kindly mention THE AERO-MODELLER when replying to advertisers.

(Wartime Britain)

Toys and games were considered non-essential in wartime, and the factories that manufactured them were more likely to be making parts for real aircraft and fighting vehicles than toy ones. New toys virtually disappeared from shops, and before long even the toy-shops themselves disappeared.

Despite the shortage of new toys, there were many ways of acquiring second-hand ones. Relatives and neighbours were always willing to pass on any that their own children had grown out of, and in those days children didn't care if they were brand new or not. Second-hand Hornby trains were sought after, as were second-hand dolls' houses.

Some new toys could be found, but with difficulty. Lead models of farm animals and toy soldiers were popular with boys, and most had one or two 'Dinky' toys, usually military vehicles, which they would tow along the pavement with a piece of string.

Often fathers, relatives and friends with practical skills made toys for their children from any odd bits of material they could find, forts or castles for boys and rag dolls for girls. A favourite toy for both boys and girls was a kaleidoscope, made from pieces of mirror and scraps of coloured glass or coloured foil taken from sweet wrappers.

Generally, home entertainment was simple - regular sessions of playing cards, board games and doing jigsaw puzzles. Reading was always a great standby.

I remember my father making lots of jigsaw puzzles for me from wood. He would stick a picture on some 3-ply wood and then he created lots of different pieces.   **Ruth Robinson**

Peter Wendels, my friend and desk-mate for three years, and I were keen aero-modellers; he was inducted into basic gliding in the ATC, and between us we seriously started, at our farm, to build our own full-sized glider. I had calculated that it could be towed into the air by our tractor, which had a high top gear. By a merciful providence this project was never completed, for in the first place we ran out of old tea chests, and in the second my father put his foot down. **John Watts**

As a substitute for toys, many boys collected anything to do with the military. Fathers and uncles might bring them army helmets, regimental badges or captured German caps, belts or badges from the battlefront or from training camp, and they would scrounge other memorabilia from troops stationed near their homes. These were treasured possessions. Opportunities opened up whenever there was an aircraft crash. As soon as news got round, boys would rush to the scene of the accident in the hope of finding a collection of shrapnel and twisted pieces of aluminium. When a Lancaster crashed on School Lane, Halam in 1943, it was astonishing how rapidly boys in the district were on the scene. Fragments of parachutes occasionally surfaced in the classroom.

The collection of shrapnel became almost the holy grail for children. Whether it was parts of shell cases, ammunition cases, lumps of wrecked aircraft, bits of bombs, indeed anything connected with battle that was lying around was picked up and treasured. The larger and more varied the collection, the higher the status of its owner became.

The war also encouraged an interest in games with a military theme. Air-raid shelters were used as bases for 'attacks' on the 'big house at the end of the road'. Boys imagined they were soldiers, dressed up in makeshift 'uniforms' and enjoyed 'let's pretend'.

A regular activity for our Westhorpe gang was looking for war memorabilia like shrapnel and bullets and then 'swapping' them for badges and servicemen's hats, brought home by family members. I remember getting an SS helmet and, keen to test its strength, I shouted to my friends, 'Hit it harder, harder, harder.'
David Hall

Like most boys I often pretended I was a soldier. I used to go and talk to them at their camp down Mill Lane. One day I got hold of a bullet from a soldier and took it up to Burrows Farm, put the bullet in a vice, struck a nail in it and hit it with a hammer. It exploded - not surprisingly. Fortunately, I wasn't hurt. I was lucky.
John Stephenson

There was a plane crash near Halloughton. I'm not sure whether the plane was ours or German. The crash attracted a lot of attention and several of the family went up to see it. At the time one of the most sought after pieces of booty was a piece of Perspex from a plane's windscreen.
Barrie Doar

For Doug Rose and Brian Johnson at Maplebeck the wartime years seem to have been an idyllic 'Boys Own' adventure. In between helping on the farm, they skipped off school to cycle to Ossington airfield and, best of all, to visit the site of plane crashes (looking for memorabilia). Doug recalls how one afternoon at school word went round that a plane had crashed near the road between Hockerton and Kirklington. Three boys piled onto one bike and Doug described how, 'I'd got one on the handlebars and one on the crossbar and I couldn't turn and went straight into the dyke. I smashed me bike up and I couldn't move.' Doug broke his leg.[22]

---

[22] Gardner, Rachel, p. 46.

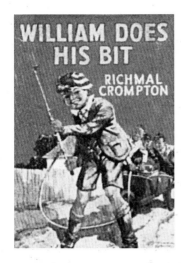  

A popular book and wartime comics   (Home Front)

Reading books and comics was another popular activity for children, though it would be rare to expect a book other than as a birthday or Christmas present. Amongst boys, *Biggles* and *William* books were great favourites, and comics both boys and girls enjoyed were *Dandy* and *Beano*. Two other well liked comics for boys were *Wizard* and *Hotspur*. As family income was limited, it was usual for children to pass the comics around, so they were well thumbed before they were put in the bin.

Collecting cigarette cards, train numbers, stamps and coins

30. Joe Hardstaff jnr, a more complete player than his father, scored 83 centuries and over 31,000 runs for Notts between 1930 and 1955. Card no. 13 in Player's *Cricketers* 1938 set.

(Roger Dobson)

Making a collection of a particular interest was another popular and relatively inexpensive hobby. As it was common for people to smoke at that time, there was a plentiful supply of cigarette cards. There were sets of cards for virtually every subject you could think of, and on the back were colourful snippets of general knowledge on all subjects.

I had sets of flowers, trains, footballers, cricketers, animals, film stars, ships and aeroplanes, to name but a few. We used to go to a building site in Thurgarton on Sundays when the workmen were off and collect almost a full set of cards from all the empty cigarette packets - a few 'swaps' completed the set.   **Jim Bentley**[23]

We would play a game with cigarette cards by flicking the card against a wall and if you landed your card on top of all the others you would win all the cards.   **Frank Mitchell**

[23] Thurgarton.

(Roger Dobson)

The rules were simple, each player had to stand to flick; a card had to cover more than half the one on which it landed, and it had to be picture side up to win. Once the game had concluded, the winner would eagerly scoop up the pile of cards by the wall.

Like other boys, Jim Bentley was a great collector of train numbers, and being so close to the LNER station at Newark was a huge advantage.

Trainspotting, taking steam locomotives' names and numbers, was another popular pastime. Newark was the place to go to see such famous engines as *The Flying Scotsman, Mallard, Silver Fox, Sir Nigel Gresley* and *Silver Jubilee*. Not many 'names' passed through Thurgarton on the Derby to Lincoln line but quite a few could be seen at Nottingham's Midland Station, especially the 'City Class' locomotives. Some Sundays 'Uncle' Harry, a train driver on the LNER, would take us to Colwick marshalling yards and give us rides round on the steam loco around the yards. The engines were always coaled up and serviced on Sundays with grease gun, oil can and oily rag. **Jim Bentley**[24]

Wartime journeys to visit family and friends were difficult to organise because of petrol rationing and limited public transport, so people kept in touch through letter writing. The arrival of letters from those in the services, who saw their loved ones only rarely, was eagerly awaited, as was news from home sent through the post. Not surprisingly many children and adults became keen collectors of stamps. Ruth Robinson, Frank Mitchell and Mary Hall all recall their collections with some pride. Foreign coins brought back from postings abroad were also a novelty and avidly collected.

Occasions and Celebrations

Local parents made great efforts to keep Christmas a very special occasion for children, with presents, decorations and a celebratory meal that meant planning and scrimping on the rations for months. Christmas presents were most likely toys passed down by older children, which could be cleaned, mended or repainted. Alternatively, family members made presents from any odds and ends they could find.

My grandma made me Christmas presents from scrap materials she had, once I got a lovely needle case. **Cynthia Woolley**

Decorations for the big occasion had to be home-made. Paste made from flour was the general choice as glue or gum was rarely obtainable. Lengths of colourful chains in primary colours were quickly made and adorned many houses.

The Christmas meal called for the greatest reserves of ingenuity on the part of housewives. As Southwell district was mainly rural, poultry of some sort was available, and maybe a piece of pork. The actual creature chosen could produce trauma in the children as they were encouraged to keep poultry or rabbits as pets. The pudding was another headache. As little dried fruit was available a 'one fruit' pudding - namely prunes - was often the answer. As for Christmas cake - occasionally there might be a real one if it had been possible to save some fruit over the year;

---

[24] Thurgarton.

sometimes there was a sponge cake substitute, with icing if there had been a delivery to the shops. Marzipan was simply a memory. Birthday teas again proved a tough challenge. Many mothers hoarded tins of peaches and jellies to make a lovely birthday tea.

Southwell Golf Club

Most local sports clubs were adversely affected by the war, mainly as a result of members being called up to join the armed services, which in turn led to difficulty arranging fixtures with other clubs. Petrol rationing was also a factor, indeed Southwell Rugby Club had no fixtures during the conflict. No club was more affected than Southwell Golf Club, based at their nine-hole course at the bottom of Park Lane. Local butcher George Harvey was a member there and played off a handicap of nine when the war broke out.

Southwell Golf Club, before closure (Southwell Civic Society)

Mr Partington, the Manager of Carey's Lace Factory, was the President. Nottingham players came out on Sundays as the Southwell club had Sunday golf. Membership was three guineas. Clubs were made of hickory, had leather grips and cost about one guinea each. All players wore plus fours. After some time artisans from Carey's Factory were allowed to join the club.

George Harvey

At the start of the war there was as yet no hint of the threat to the golf club that lay ahead. In fact, the ruling body of the game indicated that, in its view, golf clubs should carry on as best as they could since people needed the opportunity for leisure and social activities. Hence, Southwell Golf Club continued as usual. The *Newark Advertiser* gave two reports of the trophy winners in late 1939.

Golf Competitions

Three finals of golf competitions have been played during the last few days. The winner of the 'Meaby Bowl' was Mr F P Gosling, who beat Mr H Kirkby by one hole. Mr R Walker and Mrs Turner beat Dr Wallace and Mrs T Bond by a similar amount in the 'Titchfield Cup', and Mrs Kirkby won the 'Hicking Cup' by beating Miss Adamson.[25]

Family Golfers

Brother and sister carried off the honours on Southwell golf course on Saturday when two cups were competed for. Mr Reg Walker won the Kirkby Cup, this being his second such success this season, as he had previously won the Titchfield Cup in partnership with Mrs Turner; and his sister Mrs H Kirkby added to her long list of triumphs in the Ladies' Club by winning the cup given by Mrs Turner, which was competed for the first time. These successes are part of a notable series of family golfing feats this season as Mr Hugh Walker and his brother-in-law have been cup winners.[26]

By March 1940 it was obvious that Southwell Golf Club was in difficulties. At the Annual General Meeting, held at the Saracen's Head, Alderman Charles Caudwell was elected President, Dr Wallace, Captain and Mr K G Blair, Vice-captain. An appeal was made to members for donations to enable the club to carry on during the war. However, this clearly wasn't enough to save the club, as the following year the sad decision was taken to wind it up. The *Newark Advertiser* carried the story.

Southwell Golf Club Closes

Owing to the difficulties which have arisen since the outbreak of the war it has recently been decided to wind up Southwell Golf Club. This will be regretted by many people as the club has weathered many periods of depression to come through with flying colours.

After being founded in 1911 by a very small band of enthusiasts - golf was then a game for a very few - the club was carried on in a restricted form during the 1914-18 war years. Although it has never laid claims to being a good course, since then it has always provided excellent fun for about 150 and the club had had an annual fixture list with most of the other clubs in the county.

Its nine holes have as pleasant a view as one could desire, overlooking as they do the Minster and the town. Petrol rationing dealt the club a hard blow early in the war and since then those who were carrying on have found it increasingly hard to devote time to its affairs. That so small a town as Southwell should have been able to run a golf club at all, was often a source of wonderment to visitors and it is hoped that in the not too distant future the old club will come to life again.[27]

---

[25] *N/Adv*, 11th October 1939.
[26] *N/Adv*, 1st November 1939.
[27] *N/Adv*, 29th November 1941.

This was not to be. Probably influenced by the national 'Dig for Victory' campaign, which stressed the need to use any available land, it was decided to plough up Southwell Golf Club the following year. The *Newark Advertiser* reported:

Ploughing Southwell Golf Club Links

With the ploughing of Southwell Golf Club Links last week, the Constitutional Hills take on an appearance they have not had within the living memory of the oldest inhabitants and the prospects of the Golf Club's being revived on the same scene fade almost completely away. The present position of the Club seems rather vague but most people had hoped that the suspension of activities was only for the duration.

However, the ploughing that has taken place is not the more usual fifty-fifty business that has taken place on so many links, for rough, fairway and greens have all gone under the plough. The whole length of the Constitutional Hills has been permanent grassland since the golden age of corn-growing, perhaps, it is 'sheer luck' that the 'links' are the only fields to revert in these days of need.[28]

A section of the lower part of the course, known as Pentelows, was saved, so that it could become an additional sports field for the Minster Grammar School, needed because of the sudden expansion of the school in wartime. This maintained the old sporting association of the field as it had earlier been part of Southwell City Football Club.

Southwell Cricket Club

Southwell Cricket Club, before the War   (Southwell Civic Society)

---

[28] *N/Adv*, 2nd December 1942.

Like most cricket clubs, Southwell Cricket Club, based at the top ground at South Hill, Brackenhurst, was greatly affected by the coming of war. Many of its members were called up and a limited fixture list was inevitable. Nevertheless, the club continued to play games in the early years of the war as the scorecards from the *Newark Advertiser* and Southwell CC show. Though several key members of the team were absent, the batting line-up featured German Whysall, brother of W W Whysall, who played for Nottinghamshire. German kept the Plough Inn at Halam and was grounds man at the Brackenhurst ground until he retired. Missing were two stalwarts, John Merryweather and William Leek.

Cricket - Southwell v Players Athletic
Players Athletic 180 for 6 dec.

Southwell 97 for 6

G Whysall	c Hurst b Christie	11
G A Sheppard	c Wood b Hurst	12
A E Lukehurst	c Call b Hurst	22
G E Foster	b Bradford	17
C Holden	lbw Christie	24
H Middleton	no	3
R D N Clarke	c Gosling b Bradford	3
M Waddington	no	0
W Smith, D H Doy, R Singleton did not bat		
Extras 5	**Total 97 for 8**[29]	

The following year, the issue of whether to continue playing competitive games came up at the Southwell Cricket Club Annual General Meeting. It was decided to keep the flag flying. Although so many members of the old team were serving in the armed forces, the nucleus of a good side remained, and it was hoped that the team would be made up with men on leave, or stationed within reach, and possibly with schoolboys. Major J K Lane was elected president, Mr Bill Freeman, Hon. Secretary and Treasurer and Messrs D H Doy and C Holden, Captain and Vice-captain respectively.[30] Seven fixtures had already been arranged for the next year. Two of those fixtures were with Newark Cricket Club, the local 'derby' always taken most seriously by both sides. The *Newark Advertiser* covered both matches. The first 'derby' match ended easily in Newark's favour.

Cricket - Newark beat Southwell
At Southwell on Saturday, Newark 153 for 6 declared.
Southwell

G Whysall	c Johnson	b Bourne	0
H J Schumach	c Beckett	b Bourne	1
A E Lukehurst	c Johnson	b Richards	1
W Taylor	c Maule	b Bourne	27
H Singleton	b Bourne		12
J Dimock	c Trowsdale b Johnson		6

---

29 *N/Adv*, 28th August 1940.
30 *N/Adv,* 9th April 1941.

E Bancroft	b Johnson	2
J K Lane	b Johnson	0
C Holden	c Richards b Wood	25
T Templeman	b Bourne	1
D M Clarke	not out	0
Extras		1
	Total	**75**[31]

In the rematch at Newark a month later, the result was in doubt until the last few minutes. 'Southwell opened shakily and lost seven wickets for 55. The Rev Turner and Tom Templeman, however, changed the situation with innings of 62 not out and 26 respectively. Eventually Southwell reached 140 for 9 wickets. The homesters were left with one and a quarter hours, and by excellent batting they passed the visitors' total, scoring 156 for the loss of three wickets. ... It was a brilliant win, just beating the clock by 2 ½ minutes.'[32]

Southwell St Mary's Football Team, late 1935/6 (Peter Cant and Pat Johnson))

Back row standing: 'Ginger' Brailsford, Joe Gibson, Walter Smith, 'Buller' Foster, Arthur Crouch, George Foster, Bill Leek, Bob Ward.
Front row sitting: Neville Ross, Harry Bradbury, Bert Paling, The Very Revd W J Conybeare, Unknown, Tom Foster.

---

[31] *N/Adv,* 15th July 1942.
[32] *N/Adv,* 19th August 1942.

Southwell St Mary's Football Club

In 1939 the town had only one main football club, Southwell St Mary's, which played in the Nottingham Spartan League. Southwell City, the oldest club in the town, had temporarily closed down between the wars and re-emerged in the 1950s.

The football season in late August 1939 commenced as usual with no suggestion of the problems that lay ahead.

Football Commenced

The first match of the football season produced a very even game when the Colwick Sugar Factory FC and St Mary's made a draw on the new ground. The visitors started well and had most of the play, taking the lead from a rebound. The Saints improved after 30 minutes and M Smith equalised just before the interval after a good solo effort. The defences on both sides were seen to advantage in the early part of the second half, A Handley, the Southwell right-back and the Colwick keeper doing particularly well. D A Keetley eventually got away on the right wing, and placed a lovely shot in the corner of the Colwick goal.

Southwell held this lead until a few minutes from the end, when the visiting forwards combined nicely to get a clever goal, misjudged by the Saints' keeper. The last part of the game was keenly contested and the result, a draw, was satisfactory.[33]

However, once war had been declared and the young men in the district had begun to be called up, it was inevitable that most sports clubs suffered. Whilst many football clubs in the area ceased to have regular fixture lists, friendly matches were played when the opportunity arose. One obvious source of opposition was a team got together from the servicemen camped around the town. The *Newark Advertiser* reported one such 'friendly' match.

Football Report - Win for Southwell St Mary's

On Saturday, Southwell St Mary's played a Royal Army Medical Corps side. Southwell started off well by keeping the play in their opponents' half. After about ten minutes hard play the first goal for Southwell St Mary's was scored by H Bradley. This was followed very shortly afterwards by Philip Fox, the Southwell outside right, scoring the second goal.

Half time: Southwell St Mary's 2 R.A.M.C. 0

At the beginning of the second half play became more even, and it was not until 20 minutes from the finish that Southwell scored their third goal through L Fry, the outside left. The Army were now counter-attacking with more vigour; however, Southwell managed to break through their opponents' defence to score yet another fine goal, the scorer again being P Fox. A word of praise must be added to the Army goalkeeper who made many fine saves during the match.
Result: Southwell St. Mary's 4 The Army 0[34]

Clearly, Southwell St Mary's possessed some potential stars as this article in the Rural Deanery Magazine suggested.

The many friends of Dennis Davidson and supporters of St Mary's Football team have been delighted to hear that following his trial match last week with the 'Colts' he has been signed up by Derby County. He is very fast, a good shot, and has played some very fine games for St Mary's,

---

[33] *N/Adv*, 30th August 1939.
[34] *N/Adv*, 27th March 1940.

and in League matches. Among the good wishes received by the Chairman was a message from Mr Sam Radford, late of St Mary's, Bulwell, who prior to entering Kelham to be trained for the priesthood, was selected for Aston Villa. The St Mary's Committee and supporters will watch his future with interest. Good wishes, Dennis.[35]

Tennis Party at The Chestnuts, Fiskerton, early 1930s. (Peter Pickup)

Looking Back

It is clear that children in and around Southwell were able to keep themselves entertained throughout the war. The freedom they enjoyed in the surrounding countryside more than made up for the lack of manufactured toys, which many families could not have afforded anyway, and they were happy using their ingenuity and imagination to devise games for themselves. Both adults and children listened to the radio and were transported to a world of adventure and escapism by the films screened at the Ideal Cinema. The wireless played a extremely important role for children and adults alike, helping people forget the problems that the war had created for them. Compared with their great-grandchildren today, many of those who grew up in the war were able to enjoy a freedom without constant adult supervision.

Organised sport in Southwell and district was inevitably very much affected by the war, as a result of the petrol shortage and the absence of so many team members who had joined the armed forces. The local golf club had to close because of the 'Dig For Victory' campaign and was never re-opened. The football and cricket clubs were forced to have a severely restricted fixture list, though this returned to normality after the war with the gradual return of many of the servicemen.

Nevertheless, the lack of organised sport didn't stop younger residents enjoying kicking a ball around in the town park or on Burgage Green. Football and cricket could still be played - there were, after all, plenty of open spaces. It was an age when people of all ages made their own entertainment, whether it was collecting stamps, cigarette cards, birds' eggs or war souvenirs, gathering round the piano for a sing-song or the radio to listen to a favourite show, going out for a walk as a family, or playing in the street or in the fields.

[35] *Southwell Rural Deanery Magazine*, April 1944.

CHAPTER 9

Business as Usual

'Bramley's Seedling, the finest Apple on Earth and now well-known as certainly the best cooking variety grown.'[1]

The Nottinghamshire coalfield and Newark munitions factories

Apart from people employed in agriculture and the associated trades, many men and women from Southwell and district in 1939 worked in some form of industry, whether in the Nottinghamshire coalfield or the Newark factories.

There was a substantial number of men from the Southwell area working as miners in the Nottinghamshire coalfield, at pits as close as Bilsthorpe and Ollerton. When the war broke out the government, underestimating the value of experienced coalminers, conscripted them into the armed forces. By mid-1943 the coalmines had lost 36,000 workers, and it became obvious that these miners needed to be replaced as a considerable supply of coal was required both for the war effort and for the 1943-44 winter at home. Hence the Minister of Labour and National Service, Ernest Bevin, devised a scheme whereby a proportion of conscripted men (roughly one in ten) were directed to work in the mines, rather than serve in the armed forces. These conscripts were given the nickname 'Bevin Boys'.

Bevin Boys
(Private Collection)

It was not easy for these young conscripts as many had set their sights on a career in the armed forces, and some were horrified at being sent to the collieries instead. They frequently suffered taunts as they wore no uniform and were wrongly assumed to be avoiding conscription, which was mandatory for young men in the UK. There was also sometimes an assumption that all 'Bevin Boys' were 'Conchies', as a number of conscientious objectors were sent to work in the mines as an alternative to military service. In addition, 'Bevin Boys' suffered resentment from local mining families, who had seen their own sons drafted into the armed services only to be replaced by 'outsiders'. Not surprisingly, therefore, some 'Bevin Boys' didn't take kindly to being conscripted as coalminers and made their resentment very clear.

Three Bevin Boys before Bench at Southwell
Three Bevin Boys were summoned at Southwell Magistrates Court on Friday for 'absenteeism'. John Robert Fox, working at Bilsthorpe Colliery, was fined £2 for absenteeism on 7th November. Two other summonses were adjourned for six weeks.

---
[1] Henry Merryweather and Son Catalogue 1942-3.

Major Kirkland, who prosecuted for the Ministry of Labour and National Service, said the defendant when first interviewed said he could not say what the reason was. On another occasion he gave the excuse that he went home to a birthday party. The Chairman, Ald. J H Freckingham, pointed out the defendant could be fined £100 or be sent to prison for 3 months. 'You are directed to this work, which I hope and trust won't be long, and you must really make an effort. I don't think I should like to work there, but then that is not the question.'[2]

Pam Field's father was Underground Manager at Bilsthorpe Pit, so it was inevitable that he had dealings with Bevin Boys.

Father had a number of 'Bevin Boys' working at Bilsthorpe Pit. They used to drive him mad. They hadn't wanted to work down the mine in the first place and often used to arrive late, wearing necklaces and bracelets. They hadn't a clue what they were supposed to do as they showed no interest. Many of the local miners got very annoyed at the Bevin Boys' casual attitude, and the foreman once told my father, 'If I were you I'd give them a good clout.'   **Pam Field**

The finished product from Worthington Simpson (Private Collection)

Many people from the area travelled to Newark finding employment in the numerous munitions factories. 'Mechanised warfare means machines, and machines need bearings, so there is little wonder that the products of Ransome and Marles Ltd found a vital place in almost every instrument of war.'[3] Locals also worked at Worthington-Simpson, who supplied thousands of pumps to the Navy, Farrar Boilers manufactured heavy turrets for tanks, and Blagg and Johnson produced 'pressings' for pontoon bridges and amphibious vehicles. Much of the work had to be kept secret, but when the war came to an end the valuable contribution made by the workers was fully recognised.

Newark's Worthy Industrial Contribution to the War

An illuminating record of Newark's worthy record in producing goods needed for the prosecution of the war was given at Saturday's opening ceremony in connection with Thanksgiving Savings Week.

... Mr Bruce Thompson said: 'For the past six years every worker in industry has been exhorted to "go for it", ask no questions and keep his lips sealed. Apart from a few "Very Important Persons" nobody has known exactly what part his job has played in the whole war effort, and practically nothing about the other fellow's job.'

'Gradually the veil of secrecy is being lifted and we are learning of the mighty achievements of British industry, of British brains, hands and machines. In this as in other tasks, Newark has played a part, which for its size, is second to none.'[4]

It is interesting to note the use of 'his' - at least as many women worked in munitions as men.

---

[2] *N/Adv*, 31st January 1945.
[3] *N/Adv*, 3rd October 1945.
[4] *N/Adv*, 3rd October 1945.

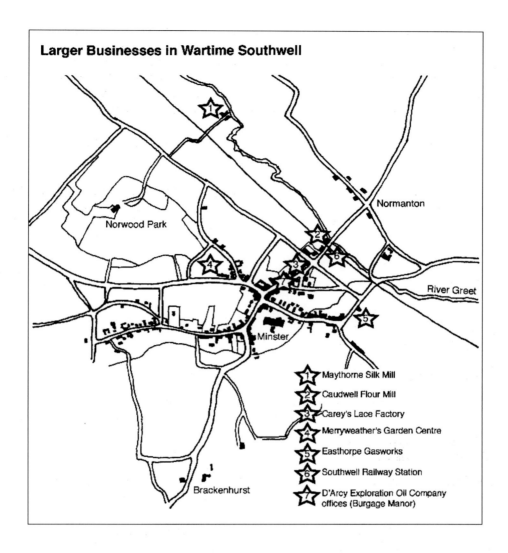

(Map by Trevor Wight)

The Eakring Oilfield and the D'Arcy Exploration Oil Company

The war had a positive impact on the Nottinghamshire oil industry based round Eakring. Much greater yields were needed from British oilfields in wartime as German U-boats were sinking merchant ships carrying imported oil. Consequently, there was a search for potentially productive British deposits, resulting in the selection of Eakring oilfield as a major area to be developed. This took place in the utmost secrecy, so as not to attract enemy bombers to the site. The D'Arcy Exploration Oil Company's office was a few hundred yards up from the Lace Factory, at Burgage Manor. The company was an offshoot of the Anglo-Iranian International Oil Company.

In 1942 the Noble Drilling Corporation from Tulsa, Oklahoma was brought in as a partner so that their experience, equipment and money could be used to advantage. Managers of both the Anglo-Iranian Oil Company and the Noble Drilling Corporation were based at Burgage Manor; the forty or so Oklahoman drillers, fondly known as 'Roughnecks', were billeted at Kelham Hall, then a monastery.

However, this 'secret' presence of the American and Anglo-Iranian Oil Companies was hard to keep from curious youngsters who were either working or living nearby.

Eugene Rosser and Brother Edgar at Kelham Hall
(Secret of Sherwood Forest - both images)

My job at Burgage Manor was to carry out various secretarial tasks. ... Working with the Americans was a lot of fun. The two bosses I got to know were Mr Eugene Rosser and Mr Donald Walker. Donald Walker was in the office more as he was responsible for the administration of the American Company. Mr Walker used to say, 'I have 40 big babies (the 'Roughnecks') to look after.' The Roughnecks were all based at Kelham Hall and they travelled each day to Eakring to the Duke's Wood oilfields. But after their work shift they often called in at the company headquarters at Burgage House.

Freda Kirby

Americans Drilling for Oil at Eakring

I used to see the American drillers when they brought their two big vehicles to the garages near our house at the back of the Police Station. They had a big, grey lorry with a grill on the back and the second vehicle was a grey seismic Box Wagon; its purpose was to find oil. Late in the afternoon I would see the Americans bring the vehicles back from the oilfield. They were quite young, wore tin hats and grey boiler suits and they were always very welcoming; they let me get in the cab with them as they washed the two vehicles down.

The local drillers, like my later father-in-law Samuel Vast, worked very hard for many years at Eakring, but never got proper recognition for their drilling like the Americans did in their one year there. The American and the British drillers were in separate teams; the Americans always joked at how long the local drillers took to sink wells. But it was much easier for them as they had the better equipment. **Roy Scoffield**

It was supposed to be dead secret that there were American oil drillers working at Eakring, but I used to see them going into the D'Arcy Oil Company Office at Burgage Manor. I also used to go regularly into Mr Keetley's saddler's workshop and I remember several times seeing distinctively 'American' boots being lined up for repair. **Tom Fairholme**

We lived at Blair's Newsagents in the Old Market Place in the war. I remember one day looking out the bedroom window and seeing a load of Americans in a derrick lorry pull up outside. They used to come into the shop to buy cigarettes on their way to the oilfield at Eakring. **Barrie Doar**

The Anglo-Iranian Oil Company made a positive contribution to the war effort in Southwell by holding a number of well attended fund-raising events in the town.

D'Arcy Exploration Oil Company Garden Fete
The D'Arcy Exploration Oil Company raised the large sum of over £310 in their effort of supporting the Red Cross Sale, when they held a Garden Fete at Burgage Manor. ... Over 800 people were present. Lady Starkey, wearing the uniform of Commandant, Red Cross, opened the proceedings.
... Many attractions were offered. In spite of wartime difficulties, wonders were achieved by the Catering Committee and between 300 and 400 teas were served. During tea an American visitor entertained the guests by playing a guitar and a mouth-harp. An outstanding attraction was children's sports. Mrs Lefroy presented the prizes. ... Gifts which had been contributed by the Southwell public for the Red Cross Sale and which were exhibited in the windows of Messrs Dowse, King Street, were included in the sale.[5]

Because of the need for the utmost secrecy, no reports were made of this Anglo-American initiative until post D-Day, in September 1944, when the story was broken. Even then no mention was made as to the exact whereabouts of the Nottinghamshire oilfields.

'Roughnecks' 1943
(Secret of Sherwood Forest)

---
[5] *N/Adv*, 9th June 1943.

OIL FROM BRITISH FIELDS
Millions of Gallons

A British oilfield is now yielding oil at the rate of 100,000 tons or 26,000,000 gallons per year. This news has only just been released to the public.

An 'Advertiser' reporter was allowed to visit one of these oilfields in a part of the country which cannot be named, and found scores of pumps working at intervals of every few hundred yards over a stretch of farmland two miles long by half a mile broad.

Mr Geoffrey Lloyd, Secretary of Petroleum, said, 'This secret oilfield came into operation just when we needed every ton of oil to carry this country through the crisis of war. These were supplies which the U-boats could never sink.'

Statue of the Oil Patch Warrior
(Eakring Oil Museum and Kevin Topham)

A Dozen Tankers

This particular field is now yielding very high-grade oil which would require a fleet of about a dozen tankers to bring across the Atlantic. When war broke out the output of this particular field was 238 tons a month: today more than 200 wells are in production and so far 300,000 tons of oil have been obtained.

The crude oil is described as of excellent quality, providing raw material for the manufacture of high quality petrol and lubricants, including aviation grades. On the completed fields the pumps are only seven feet high and they are worked by silent electric motors.

Main Oilfield

At the main oilfield, offices, stores, workshop and geological and engineering laboratories have been erected at the headquarters of these operations on the oilfield, and road construction totalling 25 miles has been necessary. Pipelines have been laid to a nearby railway siding, from which the oil goes by rail tank cars to the refinery. A considerable number of British workmen have been trained in oilfield work by skilled British technicians from foreign oilfields. There are about 1,000 men employed at one field.[6]

In March 1945 there was at last public recognition from Philip Southwell, Manager of the Anglo-Iranian Oil Company, that the 'mystery oilfield' was indeed the Duke's Wood area of Eakring.

---

[6] *N/Adv,* 27th September 1944.

Large local employers

In 1939 many Southwell people were employed in industries in the immediate locality, at Caudwell's Mill, Maythorne Silk Mill or Carey's Lace Factory. However, only one of these three employers was economically vibrant by 1945.

Caudwell's Mill

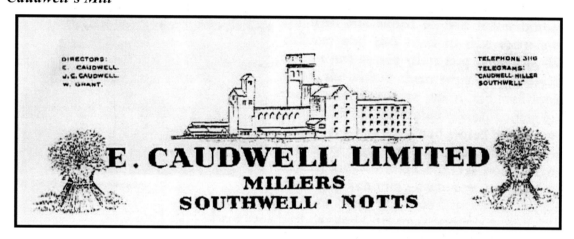

Letter Heading, Caudwell's Mill
(Ruth Robinson)

The flour mill on Station Road had been in the Caudwell family for a number of generations.

Father was a flour miller, which was a reserved occupation. He ran the flour mill during the war whilst his brother, Uncle Edward, was in the services. Local farmers would bring the wheat to the mill and then flour was distributed to many areas of Nottinghamshire as well as places in Lincolnshire, including Cranwell RAF station. Locally, flour was distributed to various bakeries, including Mosedale's. The mill ran 24 hours a day, operating an eight-hour shift system.

With the war the workforce had changed somewhat, with more women at work, replacing male workers who had joined the services. My father cycled to work and back and he would usually come back for lunch. **Ruth Robinson**

I remember spending many hours sitting on the bridge by Caudwell's mill and watching fish swim underneath. There seemed to be a lot more water depth then. It has silted up a lot since then. The mill seemed to be fully working throughout the war. **Keith Marshall**

Jimmy Gemmel had been a sales representative for Caudwell's, a job which required him to visit his customers, usually bakers, on a regular basis. He was also a close friend of John Caudwell. Despite being away in the services, his letters to John show his thoughts were never far away from the milling business.

Capt. J.A.B.Gemmel

> *No. 1 Ordnance Workshop Company, RAOC*
> *Middle East Forces, March 10th 1941.*

Dear Mr Caudwell,
Many thanks for your letter of Dec. 6th, which I got two days ago. I was glad to learn that the mill is full-time and especially that we are doing so well ... I expect that in time of war the local mills will come into their own a bit. I also heard some time ago that Rusks and Spillers' mills in London had been knocked for six.

... Nottingham seems to have been pretty lucky up to date regarding air raids, though I heard that Judge's at Mapperley had had an incendiary bomb on them. Are we doing much now with Mason's of Russell Street?

Please give my kindest regards to Oscar and Robert Longmore, Mr Jones and Mr Harwood. ... Please remember me very kindly to your father and to your mother, when you write, and all good wishes to yourself.
> *Yours sincerely,*
> *J.A.B. Gemmel*[7]

Edward Caudwell, who before the war ran the business along with his brother John, also showed a keen interest in how the mill was operating whilst he was away in the armed services in North Africa.

Dear John,
I am afraid I have not written much to you of late, but what with work and the hot sun, one only feels like sitting after the day is over. I paid a very interesting visit to a Tunisian grain silo the other day. It is a very large concern and deals with all the wheat grown in the country. Apparently, all wheat goes through the silo direct from farmers and not to the millers and the reason being that the country is trying to improve its quality and so obtain a better international price. A lot of the wheat now being grown is from Manitoba ...
> *Kind wishes to Joan,*
> *Edward*[8]

---

[7] Jimmy Gemmel to John Caudwell, 10th March 1941. (Ruth Robinson).
[8] Edward Caudwell to John Caudwell, 6th June 1943. (Ruth Robinson).

Maythorne Silk Mill

Unlike Caudwell's Mill, which seemed to be thriving, by the beginning of the war Maythorne Silk Mill was facing closure. In April 1940 the *Newark Advertiser* reported on difficulties facing the mill owners.

Maythorne Silk Mill

At 7.30 a.m. each morning, a covered lorry draws up in the Market Place and is quickly filled with girls whose destination is Nottingham. They are the last remnant of a large number of workpeople, who, up to a short time ago, were employed at Maythorne Silk Mill, where silk throwsting had been carried on for more than a century. The future of the mill seems uncertain, for we understand that the best of its machinery has been transferred elsewhere.

Thus the silk industry in Southwell is likely to sink into the oblivion, which has overtaken the stockingers of Westhorpe, the Tanyard near Holy Trinity Church and the various brickyards in the district. The history of the Maythorne Mill takes us back to the days before steam power was known, when the River Greet, on which it is situated, had the reputation of being seven miles in length and of supplying water power for seven mills on its course.[9]

This sad report is supported by the memories of London evacuees Bernard and Dennis Driscoll, whose family had settled in Maythorne around 1942.

The Silk Mill had not been closed long before we arrived, and there were still plenty of bobbins to see in the mill, though most of the building was now occupied by army personnel. Some rooms were used for storage of army equipment and tools. I remember on the left-hand side of the buildings there were two cottages rented by local people, Gertie Smith and the Caladine family. The former mill owner's house, where the Butler family live today, was occupied by George Cross who worked on nearby farms.

Bernard Driscoll

I just remember wherever you looked around Maythorne there were troops. The whole line of mill buildings opposite us had been requisitioned by the army for accommodation. Funny thing was that some of the mill machinery had been left although the mill was never used again.

Dennis Driscoll

Maythorne Mill never re-opened after the war.

Carey's Lace Factory

Lace making was established in Southwell in 1885, on the former House of Correction site at the bottom of the Burgage, by W G Gregory. By 1895 the factory was bought by E Carey & Sons Limited of Nottingham who moved their manufacturing unit into the premises.[10] At its peak it was the largest employer in the town with a workforce of between 150-200, many of them highly skilled.[11] The men at Careys were very patriotic and at least 80 served in the First World War, 16 lost their lives.[12] There are, unfortunately, no details of the number who served in the Second World War.

---

[9] *N/Adv,* 17th April, 1940.

[10] Sheila A Mason, *Nottingham Lace* 1760s-1950s (Stroud: Alan Sutton, 1994), p. 266.

[11] Hutchinson, *Southwell, The Town and Its People, Vol.1* (Southwell: Southwell LHS, 1992) pp. 54-6.

[12] Michael Austin, Michael J Kirton, Lance Wright, eds., *Southwell at War, 1914-1919* (Southwell and District Local History Society, 2014), pp. 83-201.

Before the start of the war the lace factory was also facing hard times. Demand for traditional lace products fell and factories concentrated on what was needed for the war effort. As early as December 1939, it was reported that the 'lace trade has had an unusually bad time for the early winter and the factory workers have had quite a series of weeks with three days off work. This had led a number of them to find other employment and the boom in engineering works at Newark has been fortunate for them.[13] However, it did manage to limp on until 1942, when it closed temporarily.

Carey's Lace Factory workshop at Southwell

(Rob Smith)

Christine Raithby has in recent years researched the history of Carey's lace. She became aware that a decline in the lace manufacturing trade took place after WW1, especially during the Great Depression of the late 1920s and early 1930s. At the start of WW2 the economic outlook was no better.

In WW2 only 50% of curtain machines were allowed to be in production. In 1941 Carey's were part of British Lace Furnishings Ltd with their warehouse base on Broad St in Nottingham. Carey's had 2.79% of the curtain making business during the war.

The Board of Trade's wartime action was to concentrate and organise industries that might be needed in the war effort. Southwell needed to support the war effort by turning over production to sand-fly and mosquito net and camouflage face veils. The machines needed care and attention so that they could be put back into production after the war for commercial purposes.

At the start of the war women worked in the industry mainly in an auxiliary capacity in mending the lace and finishing it in the upper rooms on Carey's site. Could women take over the running of the machines as they did in other war industries? I do not have an answer to this. But the twist hands who manned the machines were skilled at setting the thread and working the machines, which were of industrial capacity, sometimes 10 yards wide and heavy duty. That is not to say that women could not do it but, from what I have read, it takes quite an apprenticeship to work at lace manufacture. The manpower would not have been available during the war even if the supply of yarn was.[14]

Christine Raithby

---

[13] *N/Adv,* 20th December 1939.
[14] Mason, p. 109.

Carey's in Southwell played an important role in the war as the conglomeration of companies forming British Lace Furnishings Ltd were based at the factory, and controlled the industry making mosquito, sand-fly and camouflage netting. This allowed some of the machinery to be kept running and maintenance of the rest.[15] However, in July 1942 it was reported that the lace factory had temporarily closed down. It is unclear as to how long the factory was closed for, but the evidence above suggests that the production of military netting was carried out for the duration.

Carey's Lace Factory has shut down

After many years of active and useful work Southwell's Carey's Lace Factory has closed down. The Southwell Rural Deanery Magazine comments: 'The closing down of our lace factory is a serious matter for the economic welfare of the town and we are particularly sorry for those who have worked there all their lives.'

It is fortunate that under wartime conditions workers can be absorbed in other trades but we hope the factory will re-open before long. The machinery is intricate and heavy and is only good for making lace. We shall await anxiously any future development. The factory will recall to most of us the name of Mr Partington who did much for the welfare of our town. Many of us connect him with our golf course which he did so much for. Those were happy days when the artisans under his inspiration were the backbone of the Club. Now, alas, the course, like the factory is closed down.[16]

(Rob Smith)

The lace factory building was a landmark in the town.

I used to pass the lace factory on the way to and from school. My grandfather was a foreman there. We used to stand by the entrance and look at the workers lift materials off the lorries and haul them up to the various floors of the factory - it was five storeys high. I can remember there were a lot of women who worked there and some older men who were not called up for national service. **Keith Marshall**

Many local women and men worked at Carey's Lace Factory on the Burgage where they made very fine lace, on a par with what was produced at Nottingham. A large number of the employees lived in cottages where King's Court is today and also on Spring Terrace, off Fiskerton Road. **Steve Pulford**[17]

Unfortunately, labour was very short during the war. Carey's Lace Factory didn't have a permanent blacksmith on the staff, so my grandfather was called for most days and did all the repairs needed on the machinery. I remember it was more or less on the same footprint as Rainbows today, but the Lace factory was much taller - up to four or five storeys. **Robert Beckett**

[15] Mason, p. 109.
[16] *N/Adv,* 15th July 1942.
[17] Stevenson.

There were mostly women working there in the war although some men worked the big machines. These were in the old prison wing in the middle of the site. The modern building at the front on the right was used for the making of curtains and for mending lace. **Roy Scoffield**

Cyril Flowers had worked at the Lace Factory for many years before 1939; he then joined the army, returning to his job there after being 'demobbed'.

Before WW2 Cyril started work at Carey's on the Burgage as a threading boy. There were 46 machines; some capable of producing lace 360 inches wide with 54 threads to the inch, so some machines had 3,000 bobbins or shuttles that needed threading.

To start with Cyril earned 7s 6d a week, working 7.30 a.m. to 5.30 p.m. Three hours' extra work on a Saturday morning earned an additional 6d, but there were no paid holidays nor paid Bank Holidays. The factory could produce any order in lace and, each day except Sunday, lorries fetched large sacks of tablecloths and bedspreads for finishing in Nottingham.

When the war came Cyril Flowers joined the army and wasn't 'demobbed' until 1946. However, Carey's had kept his job for him, but after the war the demand for lace fell drastically. Cyril had to work any machine that was suitable for the order and it was rare, Cyril Flowers said, that 46 machines were in production prior to WW2. He said 20 women were employed as menders.

He did return to the factory in 1946 as Carey's had kept his job open for him.

Cyril Flowers to Doreen Stevenson[18]

The Southwell factory finally closed in 1956, due to a lack of demand for curtain lace, and because of cheap imports from Scotland and abroad. Cyril Flowers was the last man to be paid off.[19] The company, which had facilities in Nottingham, finally ceased business in the 1970s.[20]

Market gardening, agriculture and associated trades

H Merryweather and Sons Ltd

Before the war, H Merryweather and Sons Ltd employed around 90 staff and enjoyed a wide international market for its products. The business owned about 130 acres of nursery land in several parts of the town and district, including Halam Road, Halloughton Road, Micklebarrow and Brinkley.

However, whilst the business continued throughout the war, the war did cause problems for the well-known local business. Firstly, the 'Dig For Victory' national campaign led to nearly two thirds of Merryweather's land having to be ploughed up, so that food production could be increased in the district. For most of the war, therefore, the cultivation of flowers and fruit made up less than half of their annual crop. Secondly, Merryweather's lost many of its permanent staff to the war effort.

---

[18] Stevenson, pp. 64-6.
[19] Stevenson, p. 66.
[20] Mason, p. 267.

A group of Merryweather employees in 1946
(Roger Merryweather)

We are working under great difficulties with a much reduced staff; a number of our best men are serving with HM Forces, and of those that remain some still have to go, others are engaged in food production, to which we have devoted many acres of our Nurseries, and all have part-time duties with the local Home Guard platoons and Civil Defence organisations.[21]

Staffing had to be reduced from around 90 to 45 due to the loss of men to the Armed Forces and to the conversion of nursery land to food production. More women were employed, especially doing office work, such as despatching all the orders and checking labels for flowers and fruit trees; women also worked in the potting sheds organising beds for the small alpine plants.

Roger Merryweather

The war impacted on the Merryweather business in two other ways. Enjoying such a world-wide market, the business relied on being able to send out regularly to its customers general catalogues of roses, fruit trees and shrubs. However, the economy drive in the use of paper prevented the inclusion of many illustrations, much descriptive matter and the hints on their plants which were to be found in their peace-time editions. In 1943-44 Merryweather's were obliged to make a charge of 2d for the catalogue, as a wartime measure only.

The other difficulty facing Merryweather's concerned transport. Most of their deliveries were by rail, but wartime priorities often caused delays in the arrival of products. The shortage of petrol also meant that they could no longer guarantee to visit customers to give advice.

There is sometimes delay in transit due to the Railways giving priority, as they quite rightly should, to traffic of national importance (troops and equipment) but you can rest assured of all goods arriving in good condition.

(Roger Merryweather)

---

[21] Merryweather and Sons.

... Owing to shortage of staff and transport difficulties (petrol rationing) we are unable to make personal calls on our customers or undertake planting and pruning as we do in normal times. **Catalogue of Roses, Fruit Trees 1943-44, H Merryweather and Son**

In the early years of the war Merryweather's would have horse-drawn transport to carry the deliveries of roses from our nurseries to Southwell Railway Station. The roses would be in bundles, all packed in straw. You didn't see many tractors around at that time. **Roger Merryweather**

I used to visit Southwell Station each day in term time and I can remember seeing masses of flowers and plants from Merryweather's Nurseries being sent off by rail to various places.

Jack Inger

Saddler - Harold Keetley

Keetley's business ran for four generations. In wartime Harold Keetley's shop was at 54 King Street (now a carpet shop). 'Harold Keetley produced a great variety of leather goods and every item of tack for horses, all made to the horse's individual measurements. Repairs were a major part of the business and they also stocked some sports accessories.'[22]

Harold Keetley, Saddler in King Street (Elizabeth Riley)

---

[22] *Southwell, The Town and Its People*, p. 70.

My father was the local saddler and had two German POWs working for him. Max wasn't a Nazi and he was a lovely man who worked well. Father corresponded with Max for several years after he was repatriated. The other POW was called Hans and definitely had been a Nazi, but I believe he returned home to Germany with very different views. **Elizabeth Riley**

Harold Keetley repaired shoes and sold saddles, harnesses, binders and other farming equipment. The word 'Saddlery' was over the windows. **Malcolm Gough[23]**

I used to go into Keetley's saddler's shop to get my football blown up. **Eric Marshall**

Harold Keetley got plenty of business repairing servicemen's boots, as did Arthur Musson's uncle in Farnsfield.

When I left school I went to work for my uncle in Farnsfield and trained to be a shoe repairer. As the war was on we had a lot of Army and RAF contracts, repairing the boots and shoes. We repaired hundreds a week. … The army boots were all nailed on and they had heel plates on, which was like a horseshoe. They had studs in the sole and a toe plate on the toe. You could hear them coming.

Of course, we had to be quick because there was a time limit on the contracts. You never knew how many they were going to bring; they could bring fifty pairs one week; the same unit might bring a hundred pairs the next week … You'd got to keep the army on its feet.

Arthur Musson[24]

Wheelwright – Gerald Marrison

Gerald Marrison and daughter Maureen at his depot, off Bishop's Drive (Peter Marrison)

Wheelwright Gerald Marrison, his wife Margaret and children Maureen and Peter, lived at 60 Westgate. Margaret's sister, Jesse Featherstone, also lived with them; she worked around the town as a Land Army girl, mainly driving tractors and reporting to the Hockerton LA hostel.

My father was a wheelwright, a 'reserved occupation' then. He had his workshop in the Memorial Park where the children's play area and Squire's Pond is today. He rented the land from the church at £3 a year. There were about four acres, including a number of outhouses which he used for his business. His main job was to make wheels, often for vehicles needed for war use, and he worked closely with local blacksmiths Arthur Beckett of Westgate and Edwin Cottam. **Peter Marrison**

---

23 Stevenson.
24 *Memories of Farnsfield*, pp. 15-16.

Blacksmiths – George and Arthur Beckett

George Beckett's family had been blacksmiths on Westgate since the late nineteenth century. By WW2 George was still involved in the trade, but increasingly his son, Arthur, was taking more responsibility. The war brought extra work to the business as land locally had to be ploughed. Most of the farming equipment was horse-drawn, so George and Arthur Beckett had regular visits from local farmers such as J Kirkham, W Hare of Church Farm Upton, Jo Arnold, Harry Butler of Maythorne, Mr Fox of Halloughton, and Osmanthorpe Manor Farm, Kirklington.

Usually George concentrated on repairs to the agricultural equipment, whilst Arthur did a lot of 'shoeing'; he was also good at repairing binders. Arthur was often called to a local farm to mend some machinery or other, and travelled there on his motorbike and sidecar.

A J Beckett (2nd right) and young Robert Beckett with employees at smithy. (Robert Beckett)

The blacksmith's day was usually a long one. Farmers wanted pretty quick service when machinery broke down and when their horses needed shoeing. Mind you, they weren't always so prompt themselves when the blacksmith's bill arrived on their doorstep.

To complete the required tasks, it needed a team of people on the job. My father A J Beckett usually forged the metal, whilst Jack Ware, standing on the opposite side of the anvil, struck the metal. Also giving assistance was George Beckett, Frank Plummer and 'Frenchie', a young lad, who had come to the town as an evacuee and decided to stay on after the war, working at the blacksmith's.

Apart from the local farmers, other tradesmen such as Gerald Marrison, the wheelwright, were regular customers. Gerald brought broken wheels to the workshop and usually asked A J, 'Could you work on the rim, Arthur, I've just finished mending the wheel?' Other local tradesmen the blacksmith worked closely with in the war years were Bob Lee, builder, whose workshop was at the bottom of the yard, Tom Buckels, decorator, George Mosedale, butcher, and L Steel, butcher.

Robert Beckett

A year before the war ended George Beckett died and the coverage in the *Advertiser* reflected his personal service to the town and the importance to the community of the blacksmith at that time.

Old Tradesman's Death

Southwell has lost one of its oldest tradesmen by the death of Mr George Beckett, farrier and agricultural smith, of 45 Westgate, which occurred on Wednesday after an illness of some months, at 74 years of age. Mr Beckett went to Southwell as an apprentice to his grandfather in the present premises 60 years ago and ultimately took over the business. In his younger days he was an enthusiastic cricketer and one of his favourite pastimes was the art of bell-ringing, and for many years he was a ringer at the Minster and travelled to various parts of the country with a team of ringers. Mr Beckett was secretary of the Newark and District branch of the National

Master Farriers and Blacksmiths' Association up to the time of his death. He was also secretary of the Southwell Sick and Annual Society. He is survived by a widow and three sons, the youngest of which is serving in the Royal Navy.

The funeral took place at Holy Trinity Church on Saturday. The service was conducted by the Vicar of the Holy Trinity, the Revd A R Grant. Flowers were received from the following: Wife and family - 'At Rest': from Arthur, Sadie and Robert; Cynthia and John; Auntie Nellie; Mrs T Buckels: Southwell Sick and Annual Society; J Stevenson; Edwin and Ronald; Mr and Mrs Ware; Frank and Nancy Plummer; Mr and Mrs Hayes and family; Mr and Mrs Belfield; Mr and Mrs Pickard and family; Mrs Steel, Hector and Annie; Mr and Mrs W Burroughs and family, Normanton; G and R Mosedale; Mr and Mrs Hare and Michael; Annie and family; Harry, Fred, Jim and Bert; Newark and Southwell Farriers' Association; E and K Woodruff. [25]

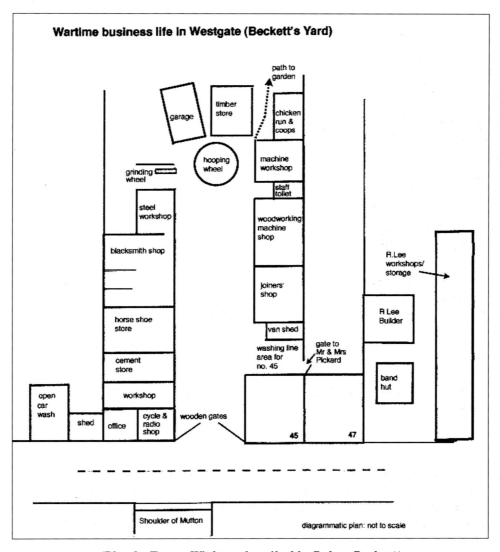

(Plan by Trevor Wight as described by Robert Beckett))

[25] *N/Adv*, 9th August 1944.

Bishop's Gardener and Goatherd - Cecil Marrison

Cecil Marrison and his wife Gladys lived at the top of Church Walk.

My Uncle Cecil was too old for the services, but he did volunteer in his spare time to join the local Home Guard battalion. His main job though, was gardener for the Bishop of Southwell and he served a number of them. If the bishop had difficulty finding transport, given that it was wartime and petrol was in short supply, Uncle Cecil would take him around his diocese in his horse and trap; he also helped out when Dr Warner needed urgently to visit one of his patients out in the villages.

Uncle Cecil's other job was tending his goats on the land he owned off Halloughton Road, close to Holy Trinity Church. He would call in to the nearby Shoulder of Mutton at lunchtime and the locals always knew Cecil was in because his clothes had a 'goaty' sniff about them.

Peter Marrison

Smaller industries, public amenities and trades

Southwell Railway Station

Doreen England's [née Barwise] father worked as a fireman on the Southwell 'Paddy' and Mr Burns was the engine driver. Alice Gascoine worked in the ticket office.

The Paddy's last run (Peter Cant)

Southwell railway station was very busy during the war; early in the war evacuees were coming into town on the railway and later there was a lot of army activity. I can remember seeing all the platforms being filled with field guns, probably just before D-Day. Local people had to use the train more often as petrol was rationed.

Keith Marshall

Southwell Gasworks

In 1852 the Southwell Gas Company had been established in Easthorpe next to the former Easthorpe School.

> There was little electricity in Southwell. Most people used gas. We used to have to go to Newark on the 'Paddy' to get gas mantles. I can remember collecting fuel (coke) from the gasworks.
> **Keith Marshall**

Southwell Gasworks

(Peter Cant)

Motor Garages - Moore's Garage, Parker's Garage

There had been two garages in King Street for many years; Moore's Garage was were Southwell Library is now and Parker's Garage was where the Minster Garage is.

Builders/ Engineers - W D Tuck, G C Nevitt, B Lee,

During the war, what is now the Church Street car park was a commercial space used as a builder's yard by W D Tuck, who had previously built the Ideal Cinema in Westgate.   Addalane Tuck recalls her father-in-law building an air-raid shelter for his workers at the depot.   There was also a builder's yard on Westgate, behind George Beckett's smithy.

> Close by The Ideal there were a number of businesses. The Beckett family had the blacksmithy and also a cycle/electrical shop opposite. Behind the cinema Mr Nevitt had a business, later taken over by Bunce's, which made prop shafts for mines. Further down the lane was Bob Lee's builder's yard.
> **Douglas Gascoine**

Hotels - The Saracen's Head, The Admiral Rodney, The Crown, The Newcastle Arms

Southwell shops and businesses

The Saracen's Head Hotel

SOUTHWELL

FIRST CLASS CATERING

LUNCHES . TEAS . DINNERS
PROVIDED

FULLY LICENSED

RESIDENTIAL

All enquiries to the Manager

Telephone: Southwell 3143

(Peter Cant)

Local businesses faced mixed blessings at the outbreak of war. Many men left the town to join HM Forces, followed by the exodus of the young women, who were conscripted. This clearly depleted the staff of many of the town's shops and businesses, but was partly offset by more married women taking jobs. However, there was still a healthy demand for goods from the local shops as a result of the town's temporarily inflated population with the arrival in the autumn of 1939 of evacuees and helpers, and servicemen.

Unlike today, most residents shopped exclusively in Southwell for food, clothing and most general needs. At that time, most people possessed far fewer clothes than we do now. What clothing they had was often passed down through the family, or altered by home dressmakers. Many women knitted jumpers, scarves, hats, gloves and socks for themselves and their family, and made their own clothes. The same applied to food, most housewives cooked from fresh ingredients and did their own baking. Throughout the war, people were able to find ideas for making clothes as well as ingenious recipes from magazines and from advertising campaigns, to get round rationing and shortages.

There was no real urgency to go outside the town for food or clothing as shops here provided the essential needs. With the introduction of rationing there was even less reason to shop elsewhere. People needed to be registered with local traders. This meant residents had a very close relationship with their local grocer, butcher, greengrocer and other traders. It also meant that the town had a wide variety of independent shops, for a relatively modest population.

There was a wide range of local shops working for the local community. In King Street alone were grocers, butchers (one also selling cream cheeses), sweet shops, fishmongers, a shoe shop (owned by a German family who changed the pronunciation of their name), leather goods, fish and chips, a Gas showroom, a ladies' and a men's hairdresser, a gents' outfitters, a radio shop, which also charged accumulators for people not connected to electricity, a plumber, a watchmaker, Dowse's department store, and three tobacconists and stationers. **Malcolm Gough**[26]

As far as the shopkeepers were concerned, whilst they could count on many regular local customers, the war brought some frustrations. Rationing brought with it countless hours of counting coupons and checking ration books. There was also the problem of food and clothing shortages. The shopkeeper would constantly be looking to persuade customers to consider alternative choices. Despite these frustrations, shopkeepers had a profitable first winter. 'Christmas trade in the town had been well up to business and was developing beyond normal proportions in some lines of business.'[27]

---

[26] Stevenson.
[27] *N/Adv*, Jan 1940.

Department Store/Men's and Ladies' Outfitters/Drapers - W Dowse, C Bond, W Loughton, 'Jeannette', A Francis, G W Edwards

Dowse's in King St (now Lloyd's Chemist) was Southwell's nearest thing to a department store and occupied two floors. It not only served the town, but customers came from the surrounding area. It is fondly remembered by many residents for the quality of the goods and service, and for its fine staircase. The Dowse sisters were strong Methodists and were hugely influential in setting up the recreational facilities at the Methodist Church for army servicemen billeted locally.

I remember Dowse's department store. They had a cylinder on wires. You put your money in the cylinder and the change came back to you! **Mary Hall**

I worked at Dowse's, the draper's. Marjorie Dowse was the fairest trading woman in the county. 'If the rich can have credit then so can the poor', she said to me once. **Chris Rippin**[28]

I used to enjoy going to Dowse's department shop. The products always seemed classy and I would often go and buy stockings for my mother. I remember there were separate Men's and Women's departments. I was always curious about the piped system for delivering change. **Jean Hallam**[29]

I just remember the fine staircase they had. It gave it a 'classy' feel.

Margaret Harrison

Dowse's Draper's shop

(Both images Peter Cant)

---

[28] Stevenson, p. 5.
[29] Stevenson.

Frederick Bond had a draper's shop at 21 Easthorpe.

Beyond the Hearty Goodfellow was Bond's draper's shop, where Easthorpe News is today. We used to love to look in the window of Bonds. Around Christmas time it would be full of small gifts which you could buy for your family for under 6d. Our mum would regularly send us to Bonds to buy wool because we did so much knitting then. I remember the bell would ring when you opened the door and you usually had to wait quite a while before old Mr Bond would appear.

Bridget Clarke and Janette Barrett

Also on King Street were Alice Francis's Ladies' Outfitters, at No. 43, and G W Edwards Men's Outfitters, at No. 16.

Grocers - J H Kirkby and Sons, Star Supply Stores, S Key, M Patterson, Johnson and Peace, Co-operative Stores, M E Dodsworth

There was no lack of food shops in wartime Southwell. The largest business was J H Kirkby's, on the corner of Church Street (now Catherine's), which prospered in wartime. Kirkby's also had a transport depot and warehouse on the Ropewalk. They had a large enough staff to be able to provide a Fire Service for the business and also to hold annual dinners at The Saracen's Head for nearly 100 people.

J H Kirkby's Annual Dance 1944 (Southwell Civic Society)
Front Row: Fred Mosedale, Freda Mosedale, Reg Marshall, Beattie McAllister, Percy Davis, Sydney Kirkby, Mr Johnson, Nora McGowan, Ian Thompson, Nev Rose. **Second Row:** George Brown, May Grant, Mr Allan, Mary Marriott, Bob Walker, Margaret Bell, Arthur Crouch, Iris Cooling, Mr Ware, Joyce Lloyd, Chris Rippen. **Third Row:** Harold Wynne, Hilda Starbrook, Albert Postle, Audrey Lister, Ainsley Postle, Louie Brown, Eric Walker, Win Pitchford, Chippy Flowers, Alwen Lister, Ernest Ware. **Back Row:** Irene Randall, Molly Postle, Nellie Butcher, Reg Wright, Lily Brown, Dot Reville, Connie Bateman.

I regularly visited J H Kirkby's. I remember that George Brown, the manager, sometimes gave me special treatment - 'Jellies' were kept under the counter for the family. **Nancy Harrison**

My father, Reg Marshall, drove lorries and cars for Sid Kirkby. The transport depots were on the Ropewalk. Opposite where the 'Coop' is today was Kirkby's Garage and Stables where they kept a number of lorries, and further down the Ropewalk, on the other side of the road, was Kirkby's Loading and Maintenance depot where they stored their foodstuffs. There was also a grain store.

With working for Kirkby's, father had several farmer contacts and so got some extras on the side. At Christmas we always had a big pork pie and chicken. I remember often going to Sid Kirkby's house on Halam Road after school to pick up milk, because Sid kept a cow.

Keith Marshall

Our family regularly went to Kirkby's grocer's. When you went in there was a big counter facing Church Street. The cheese counter was on the left, general groceries were in the centre of the shop and there was a cooked meat counter on the right. An office was on the right with a small glass window where you went to pay your weekly account. **Keith Lee**

Chris Rippin worked at J H Kirkby's for 25 years, six loads of bread were delivered to Newark each day. Chris Rippin operated the machine for repairing wheat bags, and later worked in the shop, finally becoming one of the 4 travellers in a 50-mile radius. Chris admired J H Kirkby. 'He bought in bulk in Hull; he bought 1,000 bags of wheat and never saw it. Got 6d a bag out of it. He was quite happy.' **Chris Rippin speaking to Doreen Stevenson**[30]

J H Kirkby and Sons Ltd 4th Annual Staff Social and Dance
This was held at the Saracen's Head. 88 staff and friends were present. It was good to see the Armed Forces were represented too. It was hoped Mr H Grafton, another member of staff, would be home soon after recovering from his wounds. Dancing was to Willis Wells and his Band and Jimmy Newton entertained. The evening ended with the Last Waltz - the prize was won by Mrs E Walker and Mr A Postle. The MCs were Mr R Marshall and Mr J Twells.[31]

At 4-6 Queen Street was Patterson's grocer's shop. On Westgate there were many more shops and businesses than there are today, especially in the area around the Ideal Cinema. There were two grocers, Sarah Key's and the Cooperative Stores.

We used to get our rations at the 'Coop' on Westgate. I can still remember our 'divi' number, 282090. **Harry Cooling**

My family registered at Key's grocer's shop on Westgate. The shop was close to where Hillside Drive is now. It was owned by Mrs Smith, who was about 80, so her daughter tended to run the shop. I can remember taking my sweet coupons there, and I also remember the gas light just inside the shop. **Douglas Gascoine**

Jackson's was on Queen Street and at 67 Church Street there was Johnson and Peace's grocers. Further down, at 47 Easthorpe was Dodsworth's grocery and sweet shop.

---

[30] Stevenson, p. 4.
[31] *N/Adv,* 14th February 1945.

There were a lot more shops and businesses on Church Street and Easthorpe compared with today. Beyond C Bond's draper's shop was my grandparents', the Dodsworths, general shop, at 47 Easthorpe, where we lived. The shop sold groceries and sweets. The bread would be delivered by Mosedales.   **Jean Hallam**[32]

Mr Jackson on Queen Street was a lovely chap. On cold days he'd hand you a free cup of soup.
Billy Mitchell

Butchers - S Reeves, G Cumberland, G Harvey, L Steel, G Burrows, M Steel

In 1939 there were many more butchers than there are today - Reeves (now One Stop), Cumberland's (Pitchford's) on King Street, Harvey's (private residence) on Church Street, Steel's (kitchen shop) and Burrows', both on Westgate. There was also a pork butcher - Madeleine Steel at 28 King Street.

Butchers in wartime always had a substantial clientele, but because of meat shortages and few deliveries they could only open on certain days. They were often allocated poor quality meat, which wasn't always appreciated by their customers.

S. REEVES & SON

FAMILY BUTCHER

AND POULTERER

Registrations Welcomed   Personal Service

55. KING STREET . SOUTHWELL

(Southwell Minster Library)

There were many occasions when a delivery of meat would come early in the week on a Monday or Tuesday and the next delivery wouldn't arrive until the weekend. I remember the meat delivery for all the butchers would always go to Cumberland butcher's shop because they had a slaughter house behind the shop. The rest of the butchers would go there and agree on the allocation and then make arrangements to get their meat transported to their shop.   **Bob Reeves**[33]

People living in the centre of Southwell were more likely to be regular customers at Sid and Sophie Reeves' or Graham Cumberland's shops.

I can remember old man Reeves, a big man, standing behind the counter with his hands inside his 'bloodied' apron. As kids we were a little in awe of him.   **Mary Hall**

There were so many butchers in the town. I would usually go to Steel's, but sometimes I would buy our meat at Cumberland's because Mrs Cumberland and I were members of the WI.
Margaret Ringrose[34]

Harry Harvey ran the family butcher's shop on Church Street during the war, whilst George Harvey worked at Ransome and Marles' ball bearing factory in Newark, though he would help out in the shop in the daytime if he was on nights.

---

[32] Stevenson.
[33] Stevenson.
[34] Stevenson.

H Harvey, Butcher of Church Street Southwell
(Southwell Civic Society)

For their meat rations my parents went to Harry and George Harvey's shop on Church Street. I would help the Harveys clean up after the slaughtering in the yard at the back of the shop. In return they would give us lads a pig's bladder to kick about in the nearby fields. Dad did joinery for them so we never went without. **John Lukehurst**

Family butchers were affected by the changes in legislation regarding meat. Independent slaughtering was stopped and much of the allocated meat was of poor quality. Some of it came in solid lumps from the Argentine. I didn't know what some of the meat was. It must have been reindeer because it had long tails [*sic*].

In 1941 Mr Tweedale Meaby, Clerk to Notts County Council, who lived at Burgage Court, formulated an Emergency Feeding Plan. Derelict buildings used previously for storing wheat at Fiskerton were renovated by Notts CC. George and Harry Harvey were requested to supply 250 lbs each of sausages, stewing steak and mince every week. The food was cooked in Fiskerton and used to feed Nottingham if and when the city was bombed. Meanwhile the food (including rice pudding that was produced in three large coppers) was sent to schools in Nottingham for children needing dinners when their mothers were working as part of the war effort.

For 3 months, no bills were paid. Eventually a cheque for £1,500 arrived and a letter signed by Mr Whipple, Director of Education, apologising for the delay. After a time, the contract went to Beeston along with the cooking. George Harvey closed the butcher's shop in 1953.
George Harvey to Doreen Stevenson[35]

People living in the Westgate and Westhorpe area of town were more likely to take their custom to Steel's at 22 Westgate, or to George Burrows' at 67 Westgate.

We would go to Steel's on Westgate for our meat and I remember that if my mother wasn't satisfied with the joints she was given, she would take them back. I can remember that lard was so hard that my mother set me on grating it for pastry. **Jean Quickenden**

We shopped at Steel's, butchers. I can remember queuing up for a sheep's head. Mum would boil it and we used the tongue in a sandwich. The sheep's brains would be fried and put on toast - quite a delicacy! Soup would be made from the rest. **Harry Cooling**

Burrows' butcher's shop was opposite Holy Trinity Church. The butcher was sweet on my mum and we knew this, so when we went in we used to say to Mr Burrows, 'Me mam says have you got any treats?' Mr Burrows would usually pack some meat together under the counter and pass it quietly to us. **Billy Mitchell**

35 Stevenson, pp. 12-13.

Steel's Butchers, Westgate, Southwell

(Southwell Civic Society)

Bakers - G F Mosedale, J Jones, H Foster (Upton)

George Mosedale's bakery was on the north side of Bull Yard in King St; in recent years a baker's business has opened on the same site, using the original name for their business. George Mosedale bought Greet Lily flour from Caudwell's Mill and delivered to town shops and the outlying villages by horse and van. Jones's baker's shop was at 8 Queen Street (Birds). In Upton, the bakery was run by the Foster family who lived in the thatched cottage at the front.

'Phone 3176.

G. F. MOSEDALE & SONS

Bakers and Confectioners

: Reynold's Wheatmeal, Cremalt Sultana :
Hovis Bread, Farmhouse Bread, Madeira Cakes

First Prize Newark Agricultural Show, 1908 and 1914 – Open to all England. Winner of the Nottinghamshire Bakers' Cup (value 40 Guineas), 1914. First Prize for Cremalt at Birmingham and Aylesbury, 1937.

"Crown Bakery," King Street
SOUTHWELL

(Jenny Clay)

One Minster GS memory which sticks out was the 'bun rush'. At breaks we would all rush out the school door and race across the road to Mosedale's bakery to buy a 1d bun. Local residents would sometimes get knocked over in the rush! When Mr Rushby-Smith took over from Mr Matthews he put a stop to the 'bun rush' and organised for four prefects to collect the buns.
John Clarke, evacuee

On Fridays, as a treat, we went to Jones the baker on King Street for a cream bun. One day I was walking back to school with a cream bun in hand behind my back when a dog pinched it out of my hand.
Jim Bentley[36]

---

[36] Thurgarton.

Father, Harry Foster, being a baker had plenty of contacts especially with farmers and millers. I remember he worked very long hours. Once I remember him being prosecuted for baking bread outside the permitted hours. It all came about when a man came in the shop and asked him for a loaf and spun him such a yarn about his family being in difficulties. Father thought he would do a good deal and ended up being taken to court.

Father had a lucrative contract for bread sales with the Workhouse. I can remember loaves, fitting into long tins, being loaded into one of our vans by Mr Lowe on their way to the Workhouse. 'Skip' Brailsford drove our other van.

Mary Hall

I had a job with Foster's bakery in Upton village on Saturdays. I would assist Alf Lowe in the baker's van. We first loaded the van with the freshly baked loaves; after that we would visit all the villages and farms delivering it. Often we would bring back pork pies from some of the farms for baking. This delivery took all day.

John Stephenson

Greengrocers/fruiterers - J Leek, H Ellis, H Roberts

There were a number of greengrocers in town. Jack Leek's shop was on Queen Street (now the Pet shop) and Ellis the greengrocer was on King Street (the Hen House). Jack Leek came from a well-known Southwell family, who owned land and orchards in the Private Road/Leeks Close area. Jack's brother, William, was Rating Officer at Southwell RDC. The Leek and Merryweather families were very close, in particular John Merryweather and William Leek junior were good friends, regularly playing for Southwell cricket team before the war at the top ground at Brackenhurst. In the event of a daytime siren alert, Jack Leek opened his shop up to children from the Methodist School. The greengrocer on King Street, next to Bullyard, Herbert Ellis, offered his spare rooms during the war to local organisations, especially youth groups. Hubert Roberts had a fruiterer's business on the corner of Nottingham Road and Westgate.

Jack Leek used to put his money in a basin because he never had a proper till. I was very fond of him. He was kind to everybody, didn't overcharge you and sorted out the potatoes for you.

Margaret Ringrose[37]

Cafés - A Ridgeway, F M Punchard, Pallishall House

There were at least three cafés in the town during the war. Ridgeways 'Central' café (now an Italian restaurant) was next to where Robert Beckett's electrical shop is today. Frances Punchard ran The Tuck Shop at 15 King Street; at the end of the war it had become Gooch and Hill's electrical shop. Doreen England remembers a tea room at Pallishall House on the corner of Church Street and the road leading to what is now the Church Street Car Park.

The Tuck Shop
SOUTHWELL
FRANCES M. PUNCHARD

LIGHT
LUNCHEONS

TEAS and HOME-MADE CAKES & SWEETS
HAND-MADE POTTERY

(Southwell Minster Library)

37 Stevenson.

Confectioners - E Greatorex, K Lee, E Lichfield, E Jackson, G Baxter

Greatorex's and Baxter's sweet shops were at 52 and 44 King St respectively. Jackson's sweet shop, opposite what is now Bramley Close, is especially well remembered.

> There were a lot of shops in Easthorpe. We often visited the shop opposite Bramley Close; the shopkeeper used to be known as 'Paraffin' Jackson because his ice cream always smelt of paraffin. 'Paraffin' sold a bit of everything. **Bridget Clarke and Janette Barrett**

Fish and Chip shop - Mary Baker

On VE Day 1945, Mary Baker entered into the spirit of the celebrations by bringing out her piano on to King Street from her Fish and Chip café. Very soon the street was full of people drinking and dancing.

Fishmonger - W E Bush, 32 King Street

Gents' and Ladies' Hairdressers - J Gough, F Robinson, Miss Harrison, L C Roe

Jonny Gough, Barber, King Street, Southwell
(Malcolm Gough)

'Jonny' Gough at 48 King Street and Frederick Robinson at 12 Queen Street were the two gentlemen's hairdressers in town. Their different clientele reflected the strong social divisions of the time. There were also two salons for ladies.

My father 'Jonny' Gough managed to make a lot of money as a hairdresser. Southwell was very much a strata society. The gentry and higher clergy, including the bishop, went to the other barber, Robinson's, on Queen St (gift shop today). Sometimes Mr Robinson saw them in their houses, at other times they visited the shop. All the other men in town went to my father. When the soldiers were camped on Lowes Wong field, if they had no barber there, then they lined up on Sundays at my father's.

He also sold cigarettes and tobacco, hair stuff and contraceptives. If men glanced in a particular direction, my Mother left the counter and my Father served the contraceptives. Mother wouldn't serve them! Sometimes my father would work until 10 p.m., carrying on until all had been served. The radio was always on and many customers came in regularly to listen, especially when something serious was going on, like the Battle of Britain. They all smoked; the place absolutely stank of cigarettes and smoke, that wasn't unusual. The carpets and curtains were full of hair. The fact that things were discoloured didn't cross your mind as secondary inhalation wasn't known. I fortunately haven't suffered. **Malcolm Gough**[38]

An old man, Charlie, who lived at the Workhouse, would be seen in King Street with his cabinet barrow. I remember sitting in Jonny Gough's waiting for a haircut when Charlie came in and asked for packets of Craven A and Woodbine cigarettes. He took them back to the Workhouse for some of his fellow inmates. **Ray Bush**

Haircuts cost 2d, 3d if you opted for Brylcreem! **Harold Goodwin, evacuee**

Opposite, on the north side of Church Street/Easthorpe, was a hairdresser's shop, Miss Harrison's, next door to the George and Dragon; she used to sell nail varnish for 1s 6d. Miss Lottie Roe's salon was at 27 King Street. **Bridget Clarke and Janette Barrett**

F Robinson, Barber, Queen Street, Southwell

(Southwell Civic Society)

---

[38] Stevenson.

Chemist - A A Ringer

YOU'LL BE PROUD

of your prints if you send your Films to us. We make our prints on "VELOX" the "KODAK" quality paper. Look for the name "VELOX" on the back of every print . . . . . .

A. A. RINGER

PHARMACEUTICAL CHEMIST

MARKET PLACE, SOUTHWELL.

Telephone 2241.

(Southwell Minster Library)

In 1939 the chemist's shop was at the corner of King and Queen Streets. The chemist was Mr Alec Archdale Ringer, a huge man of 6' 7'', who also sold wine and spirits.

After school on weekdays and on Saturday mornings, I worked for Mr Alec Archdale Ringer. As an errand boy, I would go and collect the items, often wine and spirits, from the warehouse across the road where the Handicentre is now, and put them in a carrier bicycle. Then I would take them to shops and houses all over the town. As well as giving me a wage, Mr Ringer would regularly barter with me - ¼ lb of tea for half a dozen eggs. Being a large family, our ration of tea was more than we needed and anyway I preferred lemonade to tea so it was a good deal for me. I would ride up to Mr Ringer's house on Westgate with the tea ration and collect the eggs from his wife, who kept chickens in the garden at the back of Beckett's shop. **Bernard Driscoll**

Stationer - K G Blair

George Blair's stationer's shop was in the Old Market Place where Violet Rose is today. George was the uncle of evacuee Barrie Doare and was very prominent in town affairs.

(Southwell Minster Library)

Telephone : 3148.

K. G. BLAIR

MARKET PLACE
SOUTHWELL

NEWSAGENT and STATIONER
: LOCAL MAPS and VIEWS :

Branch of the **"Leisure Hour"** Library

Shoes/Bootmaker - A Bramwell, A Atkins, F Elliott, T Revill

Bramwell's shoe shop (now a home decor shop) was at 30 King Street and was noted for its high quality shoes.

Watch and Clockmaker - H Clulow

Clulow's Clock Repairs shop always felt very spooky. Mrs Clulow was quite frightening to look at and Mr Clulow would be sat at a table, wearing rimless glasses, mending clocks. I could never understand how he could see in there as it was so dark. **Mary Hall**

Cycle Agent - A J Beckett

(Robert Beckett)

During the war years Arthur Beckett's cycle and radio shop at 43 Westgate was next to his father's blacksmith's business. After the war he moved his shop across the road and took the premises at 34 Westgate.

In wartime most people with bikes used them to get to work rather than for recreational purposes. Few people possessed cars and anyway petrol rationing made transport difficult, so a lot of people regularly cycled from Southwell to the Newark munition factories, to Bilsthorpe pit, to local farms and to factories in Mansfield and Nottingham. Most days my father worked next door at his father's blacksmith's until around 5pm when he moved to his cycle shop to be there when cyclists returned from work bringing him punctures to repair. He might have as many as twenty repairs to do before he went home for his tea.

Not surprisingly, being so close to the Raleigh Cycle factory in Nottingham, father stocked plenty of Raleigh and Rudge bicycles but he also sold Humber, Robin Hood, Hercules, Triumph and BSA cycles.

He also did a good trade in radios, especially by charging batteries. At that time most radios had both a wet and a dry battery. The 'wet' battery lasted about a week whilst the 'dry' battery would operate for about six weeks. People brought in their flat battery, which father put on a slow charge on his accumulator; often at the same time the customer took back the battery he had brought in earlier. **Robert Beckett**

Electrical Appliances - Wm Carey, 13 Queen Street.

Music - Thomas Brookfield, 14 Queen Street.

Hardware Store - R C Roe

Roe's Hardware store was at the corner of Burgage Lane and King Street, where the Riverside Church is today.

(Southwell Civic Society)

Then and Now - Changes since 1939-45 of retail premises.

During World War II Southwell had a busy business community catering for the needs of its inhabitants and visiting troops. The previous pages have provided a summary of the main business and shops in the town. All these years later it is difficult to be absolutely accurate about the situation of all of the businesses, as some premises have been physically re-structured and others have been demolished. In addition some of the street numbering has changed. However, unlike many towns the character of the town centre has changed very little.

However, with the help of a small group of residents, in particular Janette Barrett, Bridget Clarke, Robert Beckett, David Hutchinson and Trevor Wight, it has been possible to identify most of the business premises. In an effort to demonstrate the evolution of the commercial businesses since the war, the following lists attempt to show the 'Then and Now' situation.

KING STREET (West)		
Number	**1939-45**	**2016**
1	A A Ringer - *Chemist*	Hyde Barker Travel
3 & 5	H Ellis/Pearsons - *Greengrocer*	Mix Mix - *Clothing* The Hen House - *Interiors*
7	G F Mosedales - *Bakers*	Mosedales - *Bakers*
9 & 11	Admiral Rodney - *P/House*	Admiral Rodney - *P/House*
13	Gooch & Hill - *Electrical*	Wardrobe - *Ladies' Wear*
15	F Punchard, The Tuck Shop - *Café*	Mughal Rasoi/Shashi Kebabs - *Restaurant & Takeaway*
	(Waterloo Yard)	Epona Art & Tattoo Ultimate Nails & Beauty
17 & 19	Baker's - *Fish Café* Food Office	Boots - *Chemist & Beauty*
19 & 21	Moore's - *Garage*	Southwell Library
21 & 23	Portland Arms - *P/House*	Turnaround Charity The Chocolate Shop
	(Portland Arcade)	Divine Body - *Hair & Beauty* Osteopathy Southwell Building Cosmetic Services
25	A Wood - *Grocer*	Healthwell Beauty Salon
27	Mrs L C Roe - *Ladies' Hairdresser*	Aspire - *Hairdressers*
29 & 31	W Cook - *Chemist* Cottage Sweet Shop Cottage	Southwell Dry Cleaners Country Home Interiors Market Place Market Place Market Place
43	Cottage Alice Francis - *Ladies' and Children's Wear* Health Clinic	Market Place
	Wheatsheaf - *P/House*	Wheatsheaf - *P/House*
49	F Tinley - *Plumber*	Ross Elliott - *Hairdresser*
55	S Reeves - *Butcher*	One Stop - *Supermarket*
		Jillings Estates - *Property* White Room - *Bridal Wear*
	Parker's Garage	Minster Garage (M Ward)

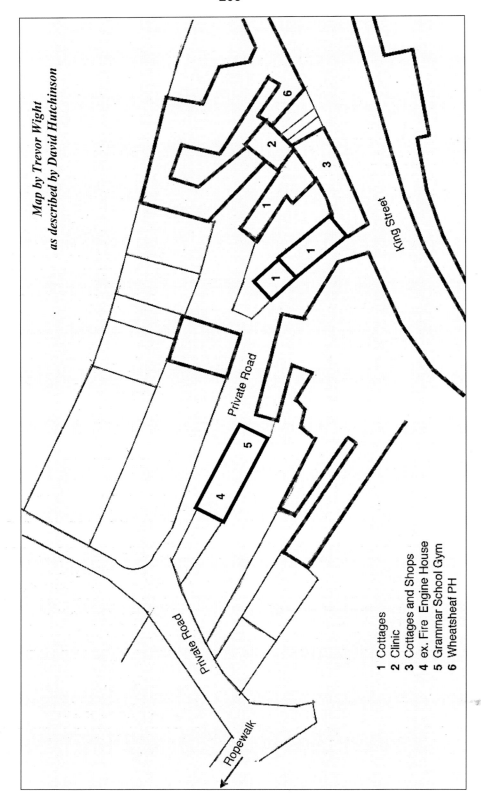

Southwell Market Square 1945

*Map by Trevor Wight
as described by David Hutchinson*

Private Road

King Street

Private Road

Ropewalk

1 Cottages
2 Clinic
3 Cottages and Shops
4 ex. Fire Engine House
5 Grammar School Gym
6 Wheatsheaf PH

KING STREET (East)		
Number	**1939-45**	**2016**
2,4, & 6	W Dowse - *Draper's and Department Store*	Lloyds - *Chemists* Paper Kisses - *Cards*
8A	H Clulow - *Clock Mender*	King Street Interiors
10	F Stout - *Harness Maker*	En Vogue - *Ladies' Wear*
12	Robert Ellis - *Plumber*	The Barber's Chair
14		La Parissiene - *Café and Restaurant*
16	G W Edwards - *Clothing Outfitters*	Woodlanders - *Gifts and Furniture*
18 & 20	Star Tea Co - *Grocers*	Labels - *Ladies' Wear*
22	L C Roe - Ladies Hairdresser	Real Clothing - *Ladies' Wear* Move Pilates
24	Gas Showrooms	A Morrison - *Estate Agent*
26		Gossips Coffee House
28	M A Steel - *Pork Butcher*	Flowers by Susan
30	A Bramwell/W Wyer - *Shoes*	Country Home Interiors
32	W E Bush - *Fish merchant*	
34	The Tuck Shop, F Punchard (1941 at 15 King Street)	Old Sweet Shop
36-42	Residences	Residences
44	Baxter/Litchfield - *Sweets*	Residence
46	Howells - *Electrical*	Kyhber Pass - *Restaurant and Takeaway*
48	J Gough - *Hairdresser*	Cantonese & Chinese - *Takeaway*
50	O Wendells - *Radio/Electrical*	Home Bake - *Baking Supplies*
52	Emma Greatorex - *Sweets*	Southwell Fish and Chips
54	J Keetley - *Saddler*	Carpet Connection
60		T G's - *Hair Salon*
62		D J Hall - *Funeral Director*
	R C Roe - *Hardware*	The Riverside Church Centre

QUEEN STREET (North)		
Number	**1939-45**	**2016**
2		Bookwise/Beaumont House - *Charity Shops*
4 & 6	Jackson/Patterson - *Grocer*	Sue Ryder - *Charity Shop* Birds - *Bakers*
		(Harman's Walk)
8	J Jones - *Baker*	Last Night I Dreamt - *Jewellery*
10	Penny Bank/Free Library	Alfresco Caffé
12	F Robinson - *Hairdresser*	A Fly Went By - *Gifts*
14	T Brookfield - *Sheet Music*	Memory Lane - *Antiques*
16 & 18	J Leek - *Greengrocer*	The Pet Shop
20		Little Herbert - *Children's Shoes* Blades - *Hairdresser* Pinders - *Opticians*
QUEEN STREET (South)		
5	Loughton - *Haberdasher*	Theatre Deli Minster Flowers
7	Suter - *Newsagent*	Handicentre
9	Sandaver - *Junk Shop*	Residence/Office
11	Post Office	Post Office - *P. O. & Store*
13 & 15	Carey's - *Electrical*	Goff's - *Butchers*
17		Fletchers - *Surveyors* C & C - *Interiors* Mr & Mrs Fine Wine
CHURCH STREET (North)		
1		Gascoines - *Estate Agents*
3 to 7	J H Kirkby's - *Grocers*	Catherine's - *Ladies' Wear*
9	Westminster Bank	NatWest Bank
	Palishall House - *Tea Rooms*	Residence (Next to Car Park)
	W D Tuck - *Builders*	Church Street Car Park
	Residence	A Spybey - *Optometrists*

Number	1939-45	2016
CHURCH STREET CONTINUED		
17	Kirkland & Lane - *Solicitors*	Kirkland & Lane - *Solicitors*
43	E F Scales - *Sweet Shop*	Residence, Bridge House
49	Harrison & Lee - *Dressmakers*	Residence
	The George & Dragon - *P/House*	Bramley Apple - *P/House*
65	Peace & Johnson - *Food Shop*	Residence
	Harry May - *Coal Merchant*	Inn Yard
	Hearty Goodfellow - *P/House*	Hearty Goodfellow - *P/House*
CHURCH STREET (South)		
54	R Harvey - *Butcher*	Residence
64	Schumach House - *Labour Exchange*	Residence
	J Avery/Linney's Farm	Farthingate - *Housing*
EASTHORPE		
21	Abdo Bond - *Draper and Gen. Clothier*	The Old Shop - *Newsagents and Food*
31	H Roberts - *Greengrocer*	Residence
39	H E Cottam - *Milk and Haulage*	Residence
43	Hursts - *Market Gardeners*	Residence
47	Mary Dodsworth - *Grocer*	Residence
69	The White Lion - *P/House*	The Coach House - *Public House*
103	'Paraffin' Jackson - *Sweet Shop*	Residence
	Foster's - *Market Gardeners*	Residence
	Taylor's - *Market Gardeners* (Corner of Newark Road)	Residence

WESTGATE (North/West)		
Number	**1939-45**	**2016**
2	Stenton & Metcalfe - Solicitors	Tallents - *Solicitors*
	Dunham House - *RDC & Fire Stn*	Diocesan H Q
	Booth - *Coal Merchant*	Residence
22	L H Steel - *Butchers*	Minster Interiors - *Fitted Kitchens*
24	Reindeer - *P/House*	Reindeer - *P/House*
34	Beckett's Cycles	Residence
40	Shoulder of Mutton - *P/House*	Residence
44	A Ryalls - *Greengrocer*	Residence
46	Residence	Portofino - *Ladies' Wear*
48	T Buckle - *Decorator*	MJN - *Hairdresser*
52	W Butler - *Plumber*	Residence
58		Beeley & Hawley - *Business Services*
72	Cooperative Stores	Apartments
92	Plasterer	Residence
96	Mrs S E Keys - *Sweets*	Residence
114	T Peacock - *Basketmaker*	Residence
	The Vicarage	The Old Vicarage - *Hotel*
	The Grapes - *P/House*	Antique Shop/Residence
WESTGATE (South/East)		
17	Kelham House - *Food Office*	Residence
31	C Warner, Norwell House - *Surgery*	Residence
	Monumental Mason	Demolished
	Roberts - *Greengrocer*	Residence
	J Beckett - *Builder*	Demolished
43	A Beckett - *Cycles*	Demolished
49	R Lee - *Builder's Workshops* Nevitt - *Metal Worker*	Demolished
Ideal Cinema	Ice Cream/Fish & Chips Bond - *Radio*	Apartments
67	G Burrows - *Butcher*	Residence
	E Taylor - *Garage*	Housing
	Whitton's Fish and Chips	Residence

THE OLD MARKET PLACE (East)		
Number	**1939-45**	**2016**
	Cumberlands - *Butchers*	Pitchford's - *Butchers*
	Residence	Birleys - *Gifts*
	Maltby's - *Toys*	Real Clothing - *Menswear*
	National Provincial Bank	Gascoine's - *Estate Agents*
	Crown Inn	Crown Hotel
13	G Wilson - *Decorator*	Becketts - *Electrical*
15	A Ridgeway - *Central Café*	Scoozi - *Pizzeria*
17	F Elliott - *Boot Maker*	R Watkinson - *Estate Agents*
THE OLD MARKET PLACE (West)		
2	A Loughton - *Draper*	Demolished Theatre Deli, front - *Café*
4	A Loughton - *Whitesmith*	Demolished
6 & 8	K G Blair - *Stationer*	Violet Rose - *Ladies' Wear*
	Saracen's Head Hotel	Saracen's Head Hotel
	Assembly Rooms	Saracen's Head Hotel
16	A Atkins - *Boot Maker*	Smiths - *Estate Agents*
18	Jackson - *Cakes/Café*	Bamboo Garden - *Restaurant*

Recent Changes

In recent years the retail provision in the town has expanded with a large Cooperative Supermarket built on the Ropewalk and additional shopping in Bull Yard/Harman's Walk, together with Leeway Stores to the west of the town. Most recently, a Marks and Spencer's Food store has been established at the petrol station on Upton Road.

Looking Back

War inevitably produces casualties in all aspects of life, including the commercial world. Two major industries in the town which were adversely affected were Carey's Lace Factory and Maythorne Mill. In both cases, however, especially in the case of the latter, the writing was on the wall well before the war started; the Lace Factory did re-open, but only for a brief period. The urgent need for oil resulted in a boost in employment for people in the district in the 'secret' Nottinghamshire oilfield.

For smaller businesses and shops, it appears that generally trade was particularly buoyant in the war. Why was this? The war effort certainly created new jobs, especially for women, many of whom had not worked before. This meant that some families had a higher income than they had been used to, which could be spent on local goods and services. In addition, there was an influx of servicemen in and around the town throughout the war, who spent money in local shops. Finally, due to petrol rationing and limited public transport, most people shopped exclusively in Southwell for food, clothing and most general needs. This is clearly a very different picture from the difficulties experienced by businesses today in many town centres, though Southwell currently appears to be thriving.

CHAPTER 10

When the Lights Go On Again

'Until the end of May you may buy cotton bunting without coupons, as long as it is red, white or blue and does not cost more than one and three a square yard'.[1]

If the war had been slow in starting, it seemed even slower in finishing. After the advance from Normandy in July 1944, there had been high hopes that it would all be over before the end of the year, but the Germans' breakthrough in the Ardennes in December put paid to that.

However, by late March 1945 General Montgomery's forces had crossed the Rhine and on 25th April the Americans, advancing from the west, and the Russians, from the east, joined forces and cut Germany in two. Then, on 1st May, the news broke that Hitler had killed himself. For years the public had sung of that joyous day

> When that man is dead and gone
> Some fine day the news will flash,
> Satan with a small moustache
> Is asleep beneath the tomb.[2]

WHEN THE LIGHTS
GO ON AGAIN
ALL OVER THE WORLD

Written by Eddie Seller,
Sol Marcus
and Bennie Benjamin

When the lights go on again all over the world,
And the boys are home again all over the world,
And rain or snow is all that may fall from the skies above,
A kiss won't mean "goodbye" but "hello to love".

When the lights go on again all over the world,
And the ships will sail again all over the world,
Then we'll have time for things like wedding rings
and free hearts will sing,
When the lights go on again all over the world.

(Home Front)

---

[1] Board of Trade, 7th May 1945.
[2] Longmate, p. 497. (Words adapted from *When That Man Is Dead and Gone,* Irving Berlin), (Al Bowlly, 1941.)

It was still not the end. Though Berlin had fallen on the 2nd May, there was no official announcement that Germany had signed the surrender terms. Later it was discovered that the British government had, somewhat surprisingly, promised to keep the news of victory quiet until a time that suited the Russians and the Americans. Finally, at 7.40 p.m. on 7th May, it was announced on the BBC that the following day, 8th May, would be celebrated as Victory in Europe Day and the next day, 'VE plus 1', would also be a national holiday.

On VE Day the BBC put out a special victory radio programme, with a cinema organ playing tunes such as *Keep Your Sunny Side Up* and *Victory Parade*. The climax of the day was Churchill's broadcast at 3.00 p. m. from the same room at 10 Downing Street where Chamberlain had announced the declaration of war in 1939.

> Yesterday at 2.41 a.m. … the representative of the German High Command … signed the unconditional surrender of all German land, sea and air forces in Europe. Hostilities will end officially at one minute past midnight tonight. … The German war is therefore at an end. … Long live the cause of freedom! God save the King![3]

(Daily Mail)

With so little notice given for the two-day national holiday, there was hardly any time to organise official celebrations for VE Day; nevertheless, street parties were hastily set up all over the country, with everyone contributing drinks and food. People sang and danced, they climbed lamp posts, lit bonfires, burnt Hitler's effigy, let off fireworks, and drank whatever was available. They certainly enjoyed themselves.

---

[3] Prime Minister, Winston Churchill's broadcast to the nation, 8th May.

VE Day Celebrations, May 1945

Left 4th April 1945

THIS HOUR OF VICTORY

LET the BELLS RING

but . . .

Let the bells ring for the half is done!
But after the bells a task remains.
The roof is safe, the fireside smiles,
but sons are away from their homes,
away ten thousand miles;
Burma, Borneo, Hong Kong, Singapore
Though half is done still half remains.
While they still fight shall we forget—
with a world to mend and wounds to heal?
The bells that ring to bid us rejoice
they also ring with a graver voice:
a sterner summons no man may shirk
to new beginnings and nobler work.

(Newark Advertiser)

Naturally, there were celebrations in Southwell and the surrounding villages, though there were many absent faces as most servicemen hadn't been 'demobbed' and weren't likely to be home for some time. The parties in the town centre were especially memorable.

What parties there were on VE Day! I saw people drunk that night who I'd never seen drinking before. We must have burned two inches of tarmac off Private Road after the bonfire we had there. There didn't seem to be a street which wasn't closed off for a party. Everyone turned out, in those days you didn't send invites, there was a real closeness.
John Postle[4]

On VE Day I remember staying around Maythorne, but my father, sister's husband and brother went into the town centre and wined and dined at the Crown Hotel. They celebrated so well that my sister's husband got lost on the way home. The family went to look for him and some of the local troops helped, too. Eventually we found him in a field, fast asleep!
Bernard Driscoll

There was a big bonfire on Burgage Green and then in the evening dancing all night long. On the morning of 13th May a huge parade to the Minster had taken place from Burgage Green that went the long way round the town to allow time to get all those parading to get into the Minster. The parade went down Newark Road, Easthorpe and Church Street.
Keith Marshall

I remember people in Palace View and Church Street organising a big party in Harvey's Field, opposite our house. There was a long table with all the children sitting round it and the mothers brought out cakes and jellies and all sorts of treats we had not had for a long time. There was a really festive mood and everyone was in great spirits.
John Lukehurst

We lived on Newark Road when VE Day was celebrated. I remember going with my mother and sister to a party at the Drill Hall, up the road. Unfortunately, we had to leave the party early as my sister and I were crying too much!
Barbara Page

I can remember going to a victory party for children at the Portland Arms.
Peter Cant

People living on the edge of the town and in the nearby villages have similar strong memories of their VE Day celebrations.

---

[4] Birks.

THIS HOUR OF VICTORY
BELLS RANG OUT IN BEFLAGGED NEWARK

(Newark Advertiser)

We had a big bonfire in front of the church at Edingley. I remember them sawing some big yew trees and a telegraph pole down for the bonfire. It led to some arguments. After the bonfire we had food provided in the school.
Bill Kemp

VE Day was celebrated in Edingley with a party at the school for everyone. It overflowed into the street. Many people became 'somewhat lit-up'. Some of these took it into their heads to light a bonfire on the pavement and a good bonfire it was, too. It melted the telephone wires! That was the last bit of war damage to be sustained in Edingley.
John Watts

On VE Day I was present at the celebrations on the Racecourse, organised, I believe, by the villagers of Rolleston, Fiskerton and Morton. I can also remember the celebration at my Uncle Fred's farm at Maplebeck sometime later. There, a local farmer, Tommy Duffin, gave a sheep to be slaughtered. The villagers duly prepared it and it was followed by a 'big knees-up' in the village hall.
Bob Reeves[5]

There was a big celebration at Bilsthorpe School. A village queen was chosen and quite a few girls dressed up as 'Maids of Honour'. This festive scene was mounted on a float and horse-drawn transport took it round the village many times. I can still see the scene now.
Pam Field

I recall VE Day, particularly, because it happened to be my 7th birthday. I can remember decorating my bedroom at Norwood with flags and things.
Sir John Starkey

The end of the war was celebrated in Maplebeck with a party in the Henfrey's field where the cricket matches were held. Dorothy Cupitt, then 7 yrs old, recalls that her mother made her a dress out of a Union Jack flag. A cricket match was held and the village brass band played for the last time.[6]

I was still working in the Land Army, living in a hostel near Retford. I remember when the news came through, most of the Land Army girls went into Retford and headed to the Market Place to a big party. Everyone was so happy.
Rosemary Lockley

Victory was announced at 3 p.m. on May 8th and at 7 p.m. there was a service at St Mary's Church, Lowdham, followed by fireworks. Dancing in the streets followed this. All week, there were bonfires, fancy dress parties, parades, sports events, donkey rides and a 'devastating TEA'. The following poem appeared in the parish magazine:

---

[5] Stevenson.
[6] Maplebeck, p. 46.

Five long years in enemy hands
Long, weary years away from heart and home
What thoughts were yours in Norway and the Eastern Reich?
May we too, when wandering in lands of bondage
Learn patience such as yours,
And so deserve a homecoming as glorious,
When we arrive in our Land of Promise.[7]

FOOD SUPPLIES FOR VE-DAYS

The Ministry of Food is confident that food traders, having served the public well throughout the war years, will provide a service during the V Holiday that will enable the public to obtain their essential minimum food supplies. The Ministry makes the following suggestions to food traders and housewives:—

GROCERS should remain open on VE Day for at least one hour after the Victory announcement has been made and, if possible, two hours. If VE Day is a Friday grocers should open on Saturday and close on Monday, but grocers selling bread and milk should act also in accordance with the following paragraphs.

DAIRYMEN are expected to deliver *milk* on both VE Days just as they normally do on Good Friday or a Bank Holiday.

BAKERS should make arrangements in advance to ensure that after the announcement *bread* will be made and delivered to private houses and retail shops in sufficient quantities to provide at least for normal requirements. Wherever possible bakers should in addition make bread as usual for sale on VE+1 Day and on this day open their shops for one hour or possibly two hours for the sale of bread only.

Although it is expected that the public will be able to obtain bread supplies during the V Holiday housewives are advised to carry in their homes slightly more bread than usual.

SHOPS DEALING IN PERISHABLE FOODS should remain open on VE Day long enough after the official announcement to ensure that perishable goods are not wasted.

RESTAURANTS AND CAFÉS are expected to be open on both VE Days.

Every food trader is asked to display in his shop a notice telling his customers at what hours his shop will be open during the V Holiday, together with any further details useful to his customers. Retailers expecting deliveries from wholesalers on VE Day should arrange for the reception of these goods.

(Newark Advertiser)

Mr Hughes, Headmaster of Brighton School for the Blind evacuated to Upton Hall, said that his boys would be having sports in the afternoon of VE Day followed by a really good feast, and he very kindly offered Upton Hall Ball Room for that evening and the grounds on the day following for the use of Upton villagers. Arrangements were concluded for the sports followed by tea in the Parish Room at 5 p.m. and the gift of a Savings Stamp to each child.[8]

In June a dance was held at Upton Hall in aid of the Welcome Home Fund for members of HM forces. £42 was raised and the Ladies' Committee ran a buffet which 'did a roaring trade'. Girls from the village married their sweethearts as they were demobbed home. Jose Suter married Charles Aslin RAF, Margaret Keyworth married Bernard Clarke.[9]

One nearby community that had every reason to celebrate VE Day was Syerston Bomber Command Airfield. Plenty of steam was let off and who can blame them?

[On VE Day, May 8th], there was a parade at the big hangar after lunch with an address by the 'Groupie', followed by a service and then Churchill's speech -

'In war, resolution, in defeat magnanimity'.

The sports started and a wagon load of ATS came into the camp. Tea followed the sports and then a station dance in the hangar with cheap beer, but curiously no glasses ... More and more barrels of

---

[7] Lowdham, p. 113.
[8] *Upton Notes, Rural Deanery Magazine*, June 1945.
[9] Upton, p. 52-3.

beer were rolled out from the Sergeants' Mess. Things apparently got quite rowdy and the erks got tight (who can blame them?). At the end of the dance, the aircrew turned up the heat and began to drive cars right through the hangar. They also fetched the Very Pistols from every aircraft and let them off ... The aircrew proceeded to start a big fire in the middle of the parade ground, the flag pole being one of the items burnt with great ceremony, whilst everyone stood around and sang to the music of two accordions.[10]

Arrangements for a service in the Minster at 11.00 a.m. had been made beforehand, on whatever day was ultimately fixed for VE Day. So on Tuesday May 8th, the service took place.

Led by the Parish Council, the people of our town filled the Nave for a service conducted by the Bishop. Again in the evening the bells rang merrily and the Nave was well filled. The rejoicing was naturally subdued because the war continues in the Far East.[11]

The following Sunday, 13th May, a special Thanksgiving Service took place in the Minster. The Provost preached the sermon, which was most appropriate as he had preached at the Victory Service in 1918. There was a large representation of the Armed Forces and local organisations, parading from the Burgage, and returning there after the service, where a military band played. Mr Matthews thanked the Armed Forces on behalf of the town. Local people commented that it was good to hear the Minster 'chimes' again, as well as the bells, not heard since Dunkirk days. After a long absence, once again there was floodlighting of the Minster. This reminded people of Vera Lynn's well-known song, '*When the Lights Go On Again All Over The World*'.

On the Sunday morning, 13th May, our great Parade Service was held, with the High Sheriff, J Holland Walker, Esq., present. The bells rang again, those bells which for so long a time were subdued, only to be used in case of invasion.

The outstanding and unique feature of our service was that Private John Stephenson, who had sounded the Last Post and Reveille year by year at our Armistice Services, arrived back after five years as a POW the evening before, and so was able to sound his bugle in the Minster just as well as ever he did. We were truly thankful to see him back and many others, too.[12]

Shortly after VE Day the local Women's Institute held a celebratory meeting:

Women's Institute

The 28th birthday party of the Southwell Women's Institute was held at the Institute, Mrs Davies, president, being in the chair. The president welcomed visitors from Collingham, Fiskerton, Farnsfield and Caunton. The Institute was decorated and the tables arranged to form the letter 'V'. The president wished the members many happy returns and referred to the coincidence of celebrating the Victory in Europe.

The Government have warmly praised the work of the National Federation of Women's Institute during the war. The wish was expressed that all would work in the same way for the reconstruction of the country. It was gratifying that after six years of war the members could provide such a splendid tea and a two-tier cake to celebrate the event. Lady Sibell Argles was the guest of honour and as Chairman of the County Federation of Institutes, Lady Sibell thanked

[10] Syerston Airfield Command Station website.
[11] *Rural Deanery Notes*, June 1945.
[12] *Southwell Deanery Notes*, June 1945.

the members for the part they had taken in winning the peace and referred to the difficulties ahead and wished the Institute a prosperous new year.

Mrs Alvey and Miss Elston, two of the oldest members, lighted the 28 candles on the cake. The evening was spent in games and Mr Percy Holland's Concert Party gave a programme which was much appreciated.[13]

In all the villages church bells rang out joyfully, and services attracted large congregations.

At 10 a.m. on VE Day the Flag of St Andrew was hoisted and broken on the Upton Church staff, by a colour party comprising Cub Barry Pailing, Scouts Harold and Richard Stevens with Guides Barbara Stevens and Jane Pritchett. The church bells were rung immediately after, and again at 2.45 p.m.

At the special Service of Thanksgiving for Victory, Miss Grace Trueman was at the organ, Professor Chesters read the Lessons, the Rev Eric Wheeler led the Thanksgiving.[14]

The VE celebrations began with a Service of Thanksgiving in Bleasby-with-Halloughton Parish Church on Tuesday, May 8th at 11 a.m. after the bells had been rung an hour before. A splendid congregation assembled and the offertory, which was given to the bombed churches of Nottingham, amounted to £3-8s-6d. ... We were all the more so grateful because of the safe arrival of John Woodsend of Goverton House, who was captured at Tobruk and endured a long captivity.[15]

It was an inspiration to see our Eakring Church full to overflowing on VE Day and as the news leaks through, many are beginning to realize for the first time how great has been our deliverance and how mightily the hand of God has sustained us.[16]

This was not the end of the rejoicing. It was, to quote Winston Churchill, merely the end of the beginning. On 5th June a Victory Dance was held at the Assembly Rooms, attended by the Mayor and Mayoress of Newark. This was in aid of the Sherwood Foresters Benevolent Fund; music was provided by Percy Staveley's band. It was followed a few days later by the first of a number of parties for local children. Southwell RDC had planned a party for each area of the town. The first was for the children from the town centre; the second for the Westgate community, and the third for children from Westhorpe.

Victory Party!

A successful party was held at the Assembly Rooms on Wednesday when nearly 100 children were entertained. The area they came from comprised Burgage Lane, King and Queen Streets and Kirklington Road. The party was held to celebrate the victory over Germany in which many young people from Southwell had served.

Guests of honour were Pte Ernest Bell, Corp. A Smith and Pte Lowe who have returned from German POW camps.[17]

---

[13] *N/Adv*, 23rd May 1945.
[14] *Upton Parish Rural Deanery Notes*, June 1945.
[15] *Bleasby Parish Rural Deanery Notes*, June 1945.
[16] *Eakring Parish Rural Deanery Notes*, June 1945.
[17] *N/Adv*, 13th June 1945.

Another Victory Party!

A second Victory Party was held last Saturday for those children residing in the area of Westgate, Nottingham Road to Brackenhurst and Halloughton Road. Initiators were Mr Stephenson and Mrs Best. Numbers assembled were well over 100.

Meeting at the Cathedral gates they proceeded to the Orchard Field, Tanyard Farm, then this was followed by a lavish tea at Holy Trinity School.[18]

Third Victory Party at Westhorpe Hall

Most children in the town have now been entertained to a Victory Party. Those children resident in Westhorpe were guests recently at a party in the grounds of Westhorpe Hall, lent by Group Captain Hanmer and Mrs Hanmer. The children assembled in the gardens at 2.30 p.m. when Mrs Hanmer opened the party. After a programme of sports and games the children were provided with a lavish tea. More games followed and an entertainment by a conjuror. At the close each child was presented with a bun and a half crown. Beryl Firth gave thanks to Group Captain and Mrs Hanmer for the use of the grounds. She also thanked all who, by their generosity and support, had made such an enjoyable party possible.

Winners of Competitions were;

Bowling for the Pig - Mr H Underwood; Darts - Mr H Underwood and Mr Wilson. The committee responsible for the party were Messrs Lynds, S and W Scraton, G Kirk, S Mitchell, J Smalley; Mesdames W Scraton, T Todd, J Smalley, G Kirk and A Merrin. The secretary was Mr A Rushby and Treasurer Mr T Todd. The committee thank all those who gave food, cash or help to make such an enjoyable occasion.[19]

A number of the children who attended these parties have clear memories of what went on, especially the children at the Westhorpe VE Party.

I have a vivid memory of a big party given by the Hanmers on the front lawn at Westhorpe Hall. I especially remember the lemonade and assume that the Westhorpe people clubbed together to bring baking for the party.

Brian Pacey

Group Captain Hanmer and his wife invited all the Westhorpe children to a Victory Party at Westhorpe Hall. A photograph of the children was taken but I didn't get on it. Mrs Hanmer was on the photograph, but sadly she died soon after.

Jean Quickenden

I remember going to the Victory Party at Westhorpe Hall. I had earlier crossed swords with Group Captain Hanmer when he caught me collecting wood from the Westhorpe estate.

When he physically threatened me I turned to him and said, cheekily, 'Well, alright, but you realise your shirts won't be washed and you'll have to do the coal fires yourself 'cos my mother won't be coming to help!'

Harry Cooling

All the children were invited to the VE Day party at Westhorpe Hall. There were some good games and races. I remember Alec in one race; he got to the line first, then stopped and John Rushby broke the tape.

Billy, Ted and Cynthia Mitchell

---

[18] *N/Adv,* 27th June 1945.
[19] *N/Adv,* 25th June 1945.

V E Party at Westhorpe Hall, July 1945 (Jean Quickenden)

Back Row: Megan Merrin, Ruth Cooling, ? Stacy, Dot Stacy, Billy Mitchell, Evelyn Postle, Beryl Firth, Edith Plummer, Rosa Cooling, Ray Plummer, Derek Sanderver, Ken Radford, Mosie Halifax, Tony Walker, Harold Pacey, Eric Loughton (?), Peter Wilson.

Middle Row: Harold Cooling, ?, Tony Todd, Malcolm Todd, Pat Nettleship, Janet Wilson, Cynthia Mitchell, Nora Barlow, Janet Rushby, Chris Postle, Mary Cooling, Alec Mitchell, John Hanmer, Billy Hanmer (?), Beryl Rushby.

Front Row: (Those identified) Yvonne Hewitt, Olive Pacey, Elizabeth Hanmer, Eileen Barlow, Donald Seven, Sean Cooling, Frank Cooling, Jean Barlow, John Radford.

However, it has to be remembered that many Southwell men and women in the services at home and abroad hadn't yet been demobilised. Some fathers, sons and boyfriends were never to return. It was inevitable that in many households' celebrations were somewhat muted.

I just remember everyone was so pleased the war was over, though it was hard to celebrate too much when members of your family were still away from home. We were all happy when Hilda came back to Southwell from her important job in the ATS. **Freda Kirby**

Not surprisingly, for me there were mixed emotions at the Victory Celebrations in May and August 1945. My fiancée, Colin Leisk, never came back - the last I saw of him was saying goodbye on Peterborough Station. **Nancy Harrison**

VJ Day Celebrations, August 1945

Merely a few weeks after these prolonged victory celebrations for the end of the war in Europe, there began another period of jubilation. On 14th August Japan surrendered, following the dropping of atomic bombs on Hiroshima (6th August) and Nagasaki (9th August). Just as for the VE celebrations Victory in Japan, VJ Day, was proclaimed a two-day national holiday. Once again, the government gave people very little notice and this news took many people by surprise.

However, as with the VE Day celebrations, there were impromptu street parties, a Thanksgiving Service was speedily arranged at Southwell Minster and bonfires were lit on the Burgage, on Landseer Rd and on the fairground at Palace View. However, the event which was remembered most was the music and dancing on King Street in the evening.

(Daily Mirror)

Victory against Japan Revels!

Some young revellers roused people early in the morning, reminding them it was VJ Day, this resulted in getting them out of bed.

At Southwell Minster there was a big attendance for the Thanksgiving Service and it was attended by Southwell Parish Council and various local youth organisations. The service was conducted by the Rev. Heywood.

In the evening there was much merriment. Revellers were in the streets which were bedecked with singing and dancing. A piano was taken into King

Street to accompany the dancing with a crowd of about 200 present.

Thursday was the main day for revellers. There were bonfires on the Burgage and on waste ground in Landseer Road and on the fairground in Easthorpe. Fireworks followed - the whole place seethed with jubilated spirit!

In the evening there was '*Din and Clamour*'. The whole thing climaxed at 11 p.m. There should be an award for the soldier violinist - he gets the 'pat on the back'. Thanks are extended to Mrs Baker of King Street for the loan of the piano on VJ 1 and VJ 2 nights. Mrs Baker is well known for her never failing hospitality to men and women of his Majesty's forces.[20]

I do remember the announcement at the end of the Japanese war. There was a party in King Street. I can see the tables now all down the street and also down Army Yard opposite my father's barber's shop.   **Malcolm Gough**[21]

Our family started celebrating at the George and Dragon because my parents knew the publican, Mrs Johnson-Cooper. We then moved up to King Street where there were celebrations in the road outside the Fish and Chip shop. Mrs Baker brought out a piano from the shop and soon the street was full of people drinking and dancing.   **Margaret Pulford**

In many corners of England, VE Day was really the end of the story because far more families had members serving in the forces in Europe than in the Far East. However, there was certainly no lack of celebration on the VJ Days. In the middle of September there was a special VJ Day party for the children and adults of Church Street and Easthorpe. It is possible that this had been delayed until some of the local servicemen and prisoners of war returned. Not surprisingly, a number of residents have not forgotten where they were on VJ Day.

Fourth Victory Party!

A fourth Victory Party was held in the town, this time at the George and Dragon. Tea was given to 140 children living in Easthorpe and Church Street. There was a Punch and Judy Show and races in Harvey's Field.[22]

At Halam on VJ Day we had a bonfire. It was near the Plough and I remember the fire got so hot that it caused some bike tyres to burst and make a big bang!   **Olive Kitts**

I was called up in March 1945 when I was 18 yrs old and chose to join the Royal Navy. I did my training in Malvern in May at the time of VE Day so I missed the celebrations back home. I was then posted to Malta, and in August picked up my ship and was told that the intention was to sail to do service in the Far East in the war against Japan. Virtually the next day the announcement came that Japan had surrendered.   **Douglas Gascoine**

I was called up for National Service at the end of the war. Together with Geoff Marshall from Westgate I was sent to Ireland and think I might have been there when the celebrations on VE and VJ Days took place.   **Ray Bush**

On VJ Day we were with the Southwell Boys' Brigade on camp near the Yorkshire coast. I can remember Eric Marshall was also with us. The reserve fleet came off Bridlington and was

[20] *N/Adv*, 22nd August 1945.
[21] Stevenson.
[22] *N/Adv*, 26th August 1945.

welcomed home. The ships fired their guns to celebrate the end of the war in the Far East. The Boys' Brigade group was taken out to board a minesweeper.   **Bernard and Dennis Driscoll**

VJ parties were enjoyed in the local villages, too.

The Morton and Fiskerton village VJ Day party was held at the big barn at Morton Manor Farm, the property of Mr Wright. I became Housekeeper to Mr Wright at the farm, staying for 24 years so I have good memories of the event.
  There was such a large crowd of people there - many adults, even though the party was meant to be mainly for the local children. There were tables with cakes and sandwiches and I remember a lot of games being played on the cricket field. There was even a parents' race.

Marjorie Parker

VJ Day Party, Morton and Fiskerton - See opposite for names of the group.
(Jo Blaney)

The Return of servicemen and women

In many cases, servicemen and women didn't return until 1946, or even 1947. Sometimes the homecoming was fine - on the surface - but at other times there were dramatic physical changes, and mental ones too. Fathers arrived home with all their possessions packed in kitbags and wearing their brown 'demobbed' suit, but for many children these men were 'strangers'. What a shock it must have been for the returning servicemen - meeting a 17-year-old teenage daughter was vastly different from the little 11-year-old girl to whom they had said goodbye in 1939. It often took a long time for father and child to get to know each other.

List of names - Morton and Fiskerton VJ Party

1. Marjorie Longden	16. Mrs Astley	32. Alwyn Goy
2. Barbara Stevens	17. Edward Astley	33. Janet Martin
3. Marjorie Parker	18. David Taylor	34. Ruth Ratcliffe
4. Barry Beardsley	19. Philip Taylor	35. Mary Joad
5. Pearl Michael	20. Peter Voce	36. Brian Johnson
6. Pat Beard	21. Eric Howard	37. Robin Beard
7. Joan Parker	22. Doug Parker	38. Pauline Jennings
8. Geraldine Beardsley	23. John Starr	39. Peter Pickup
9. Barbara Brothwell	24. Ena Brothwell	40. Jean Thurlby
10. Judy Snushall	25. Doreen Brown	41. Violet Gilliatt
11. Rita Elliott holding Neville Chapman	26. Eileen Andrews	42. Ann Woodward
12. Sonia Houghton	27. Murray Taylor	43. June Voce
13. Sally Beard	28. Brian Williams	44. Sylvia Gilliatt
14. Betty Pead	29. John Walton	45. Celia Thurlby
15. Eddy Staunton	30. Brian Walton	46. Penny Beardsley
	31. George Starr	47. Jackie Beardsley

NOTTS. F.A. Minor Competition
CHALLENGE MATCH
Newark Minor League XI
VERSUS
Mapperley VILLA
(Champions Nottm. Section, 1943-44, 1944-45)
On CRAFT'S FIELD, SOUTHWELL,
SATURDAY, MAY 12th, 1945
Kick Off 3-0 p.m.   Admission 3d.

(John Stephenson)

After the war is over,
When all our boys come home,
Travelling will be so easy
No need to groan or moan.
Punctual will be the driver,
Unharassed will be his mate,
For we'll have enough staff to serve you,
After the "Berlin" date.

(Newark Advertiser)

I didn't see my father for four years as he was in the services, so when he did finally come home, I couldn't really take to him and it took me a long time to come to terms with the fact that he was the 'Boss' and not my mother.[23]

Dad returned on the train from London one Saturday morning. We went to meet him at Northgate Station, Newark. I still have a ticket for a football match at Southwell, which I had bought for 3d, for that very day. Because we went to meet Dad I never used it.   **John Stephenson**

I vividly remember 'Giddy' Smith, a local farm worker, who had been a POW in the Far East, appearing at the Maplebeck celebration, looking very ill. He'd suffered badly at the hands of the Japanese.   **Bob Reeves**[24]

The great excitement of Cyril Flowers' arrival was marred by his appearance; he was now 9st 6lb, having lost 2 stone. He had brought home a spare kitbag full of tinned fruit and sugar that he had been able to buy on the boat. Doll had also kept tinned food for the welcome-home party.   **Cyril Flowers**[25]

When I came back home from Italy I was demobbed in Lincolnshire and given a 50s suit. Back at our cottage I couldn't believe it. I was half mad. I couldn't believe there were flowers in the garden; couldn't believe there was paper on the walls and carpets on the floor. I walked about our fields for hours. I couldn't believe I had survived.   **Bert Ulyatt**[26]

I remember vividly when my father first came home. He carried a pack in which he had soap flakes, which presumably were scarce, and the bag had broken and all the flakes spilt out over the carpet. Father had never met his second daughter, Janet, my younger sister. Mother had invented little tricks to show her girls that Father was always expected. After boiled eggs we always turned them upside-down and said, 'An egg for Father when he comes

---

[23] *Nottinghamshire Federation of the WI, p. 206.*
[24] Stevenson.
[25] Stevenson, p. 66.
[26] Stevenson, p. 35.

home.' I remember so well that evening he finally arrived. When it was bedtime he lifted me up and pretended not to know where I slept. He opened every drawer and cupboard in the house and asked, 'Barbara, do you sleep here?' I was alarmed and found him the craziest man I had ever known but eventually we found my bed.   **Barbara Page**

After the war Ernest and John Bentley returned to work on the farm with Phil. Hilda married and moved to Burton Joyce and Mary moved to Daventry after marrying Philip Benton. At least everyone came through the war safely but life was never the same again.   **Jim Bentley[27]**

However, the end of the war resulted in one local resident moving back to Europe rather than returning.

Back in Southwell in the autumn of 1945 there was a letter from Save the Children Fund asking me to go out to Germany and run a Children's home for displaced persons. It was for Latvians, Lithuanians and Estonians near Hamburg. They had been in UNRRA camps so had been well fed but they were terrified of Russia. Some children had lost their families. One Polish girl I kept in contact with had been caught in Germany, potato picking. In the end they went to Australia. When I came home I thought that no-one has any true idea of what it's like to be displaced. Your imagination doesn't really cover it, does it?   **Mary Beaumont[28]**

Returning from the War (Home Front)

27 Thurgarton.
28 Stevenson, p. 58.

Those evacuated families who had been uprooted from their homes in the South East and moved to Southwell for the duration had to decide whether to return or stay here.

We never seriously considered returning to Bermondsey, because everything we had owned had been destroyed in the war damage to our apartment. Most of us stayed in Nottinghamshire. Ron went to Arnold, Irene to Collingham, Dolly to Balderton, Pat to Suffolk and Bernard and I stayed in Southwell. A lot had happened to us. Apart from having to be evacuated, we had lost Jean in the Blitz and then Bob, too. He had been in the TA before the war, joined the Royal Artillery and was then involved in the retreat from Dunkirk, escaping in a fishing boat. After getting re-kitted, he went to fight in Italy and got as far as crossing the Rhine before he was killed. In these circumstances we felt it was best to stay on here.
Dennis Driscoll

Post-war situation – Rationing, Holidays, NHS

Gradually normality returned. There were still food shortages, rationing, coupons and a black market. Whilst it was true that bananas re-appeared, they were generally strictly rationed, and there was still a shortage of meat. Hence, many of the food economy practices encouraged during the war continued afterwards. The pig swill bins were a feature of most streets, which continued until the early 1950s, the contents being religiously collected daily and passed to local farmers.

Many car owners looked forward to being able to replace their vehicles once the war had ended. However, it wasn't as simple as they thought. Although production of civilian cars resumed quickly, the nation had to start repaying the American lend-lease aid, so a huge proportion of national production went for export, to raise the necessary cash flow.

It was possible to go to the seaside for holidays again, but mines remained a potential hazard. Although the seas had been 'swept', many mines had been missed and for many years were brought in on the incoming tides.

In 1947 one postwar change, which was a huge improvement for the vast majority of the population, was the introduction by the Labour Government of the National Health Service. People no longer had to pay to see a doctor, and medical prescriptions were free; this was a big step forward.

Roll of Honour

List of men who died on active service in the 1939-45 War

Southwell Parishes

Becher, John Henry. Squadron Leader, RAF; killed at Aden, 10th August 1940; buried in Maala Cemetery, Aden

Beckett, Alan. Private, King's Own Yorkshire Light Infantry; killed by enemy action, 29th November 1943; buried in Sangro River War Cemetery, Italy

Brailsford, Harold. Leading Cook, RN; lost at sea presumed drowned, December 1942; remembered on Lowestoft Naval Memorial

Browne, J M Godfree. Flying Officer, RAF; killed in a flying accident, 9th September 1939; buried in Southwell Minster churchyard

Doubleday, Charles. Private, Welsh Regiment; killed in action in France, 15th August 1944; buried in Ranville War Cemetery, France

Drury, Herbert. Sergeant, Royal Artillery; killed in action Hong Kong, 24th December 1941; remembered on Saiwan Memorial, Hong Kong

Fox, James Crosby. Corporal, RAF; killed in plane crash March, Cambridgeshire, 24th November 1941; buried in Southwell Minster churchyard

Haywood, Albert. Sapper, Royal Engineers; Prisoner of War of Japan; died 2nd October 1943; buried in Chungkai War Cemetery, Thailand

Hemstock, Harold. Guardsman, Grenadiers; killed in action Anzio, 9th February 1944; buried in Anzio War Cemetery, Italy

Hopewell, Herbert. Able Seaman, RN; missing presumed drowned Atlantic convoy, 25th December 1943

Inglis, Robert. Sergeant, RAF; Air Gunner; shot down over Berlin, 23rd November 1943; remembered on Runnymede Memorial

Keetley, Arthur. Sergeant, RAF; killed in action over Dutch coast, 18th July 1940; remembered on Runnymede Memorial

Matthews, Robert Henry. Pilot Officer, RAF; killed in action, 22nd December 1941; buried in Malta Naval Cemetery

Mosley, Michael Henry. MC Captain, Rifle Brigade; killed at El Alamein, 2nd November 1942; buried in El Alamein War Cemetery, Egypt

Picker, George William. Sergeant, RAF; killed in action Coignieres, Rambouillet, France, 26th July 1944; buried in Coignieres churchyard, France

Scraton, Ernest Harry. Sergeant Air Gunner, RAF; shot down over Hanover, Germany, 18th October 1943; buried in Becklingen War Cemetery, Soltau, Germany

Sheppard, George. Able Seaman, RN; missing presumed drowned, 1942; remembered on Chatham Naval Memorial

Smith, George. Lance Bombardier; killed in action, 15th December 1941; buried in Knightsbridge Cemetery, Tobruk, Libya

Spencer, Howard. Flying Officer, RAF; shot down over Germany, 22nd June 1944; buried in Rheinberg War Cemetery, Germany

Suckling, Michael. Pilot Officer, RAF; missing on flight from St Eval, 21st July 1941; remembered on Runnymede Memorial

Thorne, Robert. Sub-Lieutenant, RNVR; missing presumed drowned North Atlantic, 11th March 1943; remembered on Chatham Naval Memorial

Ulyatt, Benjamin. Private, Highland Light Infantry; killed in action, 7th April 1945; buried in Reichswald Forest War Cemetery, Germany

Voce, Dennis. Private, Sherwood Foresters; killed at Dunkirk, 1940; remembered on the Memorial Column, Dunkirk

Whyatt, Ben. Private, 2nd Glasgow Highlanders; killed by enemy action in Germany, 7th April 1945

Ex-Minster Grammar School students/staff resident outside the district

Eccles, Gordon Scott. Pilot Officer, RAF; killed in action, 1st September 1941; buried in Waterbeach Cemetery

Harrison, Carlton. Fl Lt, RAF; died in a flying accident 19th October 1945; buried in Dely Ibrahim War Cemetery, Algeria

Hayward, Robert Norman. L. Cpl, Lincolnshire Regiment; killed in action, 19th August 1944; buried in St Desir War Cemetery, France

Morris, Philip Edwin. Fl. Lt, RAF; died 14th November 1945; buried in Caserta War Cemetery, Italy

Tansley, William Middleton. Fl. Lt, RAF; killed in action, 7th November 1942; buried in Abson churchyard, USA

Walkden, James Patrick. Lt, Northamptonshire Regiment; killed in action, 15th February 1945; buried in Taukkyan War Cemetery, Burma

The Villages

Averham, Kelham and Staythorpe

Cherrington, Peter Ralph. Captain, Northamptonshire Reg.; killed in action, 20th January 1945, buried in Taukkyan War Cemetery, Burma

Esam, John Arnott. Lt, Sherwood Foresters; killed in action, 28th April 1940; buried in Lillehammer Northern Civil Cemetery, Norway

Hatton, John. Sgt, RAF; killed in action, 3rd April 1943; buried in Averham churchyard

Tandy, Kenneth Edward; Mechanic, RN; died 16th March 1944; buried in Bergen-Op-Zoom War Cemetery, Netherlands

Bilsthorpe

Capewell, Samuel. Sgt, RAF; killed in action, 13th April 1942; buried in Bilsthorpe churchyard

Hallam, George Victor. Seaman, RNPS; killed in action, 19th November 1942; remembered on Lowestoft Naval Memorial

Hatton, George. Pte, Oxford and Bucks Light Infantry; killed in action, 11th November 1943; buried in Cassino War Cemetery, Italy

Mellors, Stanley. Fl. Sgt, RAF; killed in action, 25th June 1944; buried in Fruges Communal Cemetery, France

Mendham C. No details known

Oliver, Lionel. Pte, Pioneer Corps; died 25th August 1945; buried in Bilsthorpe churchyard

Richards, John Osborne. Pte, Royal Army Medical Corps; died, 19th January 1940; buried in Sutton-in-Ashfield Cemetery

Spencer, Roy. Cpl, East Lancs. Regiment; killed in action, 1st August 1944; buried in Ryes Cemetery, Bazenville, France

Steele, Harry Ernest. Sgt, RAF; killed in action, 2nd December 1943; buried in Esbjerg Cemetery, Denmark

Storer, N. No details known

Thorpe, George. L-Sgt, Gloucestershire Reg; killed in action, 13th February 1945; buried in Taukkyan War Cemetery, Burma

Todhunter, E. No details known

Bleasby

Graham, William Monteith. Wg Cdr, RAF; killed in action, 9th May 1941; buried in Reichswald Forest War Cemetery, Germany

Hall, Roy. Sgt, Royal Artillery; no details known

Morris, Robert Varley. Captain, Sherwood Foresters; died 13th November 1945; buried in Bari War Cemetery, Italy

Eakring (No entries)

Epperstone

Allen, Gerrard Griffin. Sgt, Royal Artillery; killed in action, 30th December 1942; buried in Imtarfa Military Cemetery, Malta

Brindle, Arthur. Pte, Essex Regiment; killed in action, 25th December 1940; buried in Leeds (Armley) Cemetery

Seely, William Evelyn. Lt Col, South Notts Hussars; killed in action, 6th June 1942; remembered on El Alamein Memorial, Egypt

Farnsfield

Davis, Cyril. Pte, Hampshire Regiment; killed in action in North Africa, 15th March 1943; buried in Oued Zarga War Cemetery, Tunisia

Dexter, Charles William. Cpl, Sherwood Foresters; killed in action, 28th May 1940; buried in Oostaverne Wood Military Cemetery, Belgium

Hucknall, Horatio. Pte, Leicestershire Reg.; died as a POW, 18th August 1943; buried in Kanchanaburi War Cemetery, Thailand

MacAskill, Angus. L-Sgt, Sherwood Foresters; died 12th September 1944; remembered on Kranji War Memorial, Singapore

Fiskerton/Morton

Dudley, Thomas Kem. Fl. Sgt, RAF; killed in action, 29th January 1944; buried in Aabenraa Cemetery, Denmark

Fox, Cedric Charles. Fl. Lt, RAF; killed in action, 25th May 1944; buried in Rheinberg Cemetery, Germany

Garland, John William. Sgt, RAF; killed in action, 2nd December 1943; buried in Berlin War Cemetery, Germany

Hibbard, John Vessey. Pte, Home Guard; died 28th December 1941; buried in Morton churchyard

Raisin, William Arthur. Pte, Sherwood Foresters; died 24th November 1939; buried in Morton churchyard

Gunthorpe (No entries)

Hoveringham/Caythorpe

Allwood C S. Pte, Northamptonshire Regiment; no further details known

Summers Albert, Creighton. Leading Airman, Fleet Air Arm; died 13th January 1944; buried in Flatrock Oak Ridge Cemetery, USA

Kirklington

Burton, R C. RASC. No details known

Lowdham, and Gonalston

Allwood, George Samuel. Pte, Northants; killed in action, 4th May 1944; buried in Imphal War Cemetery, India

Greaves, James Samuel. Pte, Worcesters; killed in action, 6th July 1941; buried in Khartoum War Cemetery, Sudan

Reeve Arthur. Sgt, Sherwood Foresters; killed in action, 20th June 1942; remembered on El Alamein Memorial, Egypt

Watts, Stanley. Cpl, Household Cavalry; killed in action, 27th August 1940; buried in North Sheen Cemetery, Sudan

Wright, John. 2nd Lt, Sherwood Foresters; killed in action in Norway, 24th April 1940; buried in Lillehammer Civil Cemetery, Norway

Maplebeck (No entries)

Norwell

Adamson, James. Gunner, Royal Horse Artillery; killed in action, 3rd July 1942; buried in El Alamein War Cemetery, Egypt

Cary, Wilfred Alan. Cpl, Royal Armoured Corps; died 23rd October 1944; buried in Cesena Cemetery, Italy

Greasley, Frank Frecknall. Pte, Sherwood Foresters; killed in action, 12th February 1942; remembered on Singapore Memorial

Rolleston (No entries)

Thurgarton

Allwood, John Edward George. Sgt, RAF; killed in action, 26th September 1942; buried in Ramleh War Cemetery, Israel

Fletcher, Geoffrey. Pte, South Staffordshire; killed in action in Italy, 9th July 1943; remembered on Cassino Memorial, Italy

Upton (No entries)

BIBLIOGRAPHY

Primary Sources:

Catalogue 1942-3, Henry Merryweather and Son

Daily Sketch, 17th November 1941

Daily Telegraph, Obituary of Patrick McCraith June 1998

Diary of John Merryweather 1942

Interviews with Paul Birks - Janette and Stella Barrett, Dallas Doy, Julia Paling, John Postle, Steve Pulford,

Interviews with Roger Dobson - local residents (c. 120)

Interviews with Doreen Stevenson – Malcolm Gough, Jean Hallam, Joan Hallam, Bob Hardstaff, David Hutchinson and Bob Reeves

Letters between the Air Ministry and Mrs Suckling

Letters from servicemen home: Edward Caudwell, Ted Kendall, John Kirkland, John Merryweather,

Logbook of Ian Linney

Memoirs and logbook of Frank Barrett (Unpublished)

Memoirs of Harry Taylor (Unpublished)

Memoirs of Alan Yates, *Find Station X* (Unpublished)

National Archive Records for Battle of Britain Pilots, Norman Norfolk

Newark Advertiser 1939-46

Operations Records Book, 608 Squadron

Southwell Civic Society: photographic archive

Southwell Cricket Club Scorebooks 1939-45

Southwell Rural Deanery Magazines 1939-45

Secondary Sources

Austin, Kirton and Wright, *Southwell at War 1914-19* (Southwell: Southwell/District LHS, 2014)

Bartley, Olivia, *Wartime Songs and Music* (London: Caxton Publishing, 2002)

Beevor, Antony, *D-Day, The Battle for Normandy* (London: Penguin, 2009)

Bentinck, Michael, *Forgotten Heroes* (Cambridge: M Bentinck, 1995)

Bowman, Martin, *Mosquito Bomber/Fighter-Bomber Units 1942-45* (Oxford: Osprey, 2010)

Briggs, Susan, *Keep Smiling Through - The Home Front 1939-45* (London: Fontana, 1975)

Brown, Michael, *Wartime Britain* (Oxford: Shire Living Histories, 2011)

Bryant, Mark, *Original Posters from the Home Front* (London: Thames and Hudson, 2012)

Church, Judith, *Beating the Invader – Beeston and Chilwell in WW2* (Nottingham: Chilwell Publishers, 2006)

Dimbleby, Jonathan, *Destiny in the Desert* (London: Profile Books, 2013)

Downing Taylor, *Spies in the Sky* (London: Little Brown, 2011)

Epperstone Local History Society, *Epperstone in the 20th C* (Nottingham: Minta's Print, 1992)

Farnsfield Local History Society, *Memories of Farnsfield* (Nottingham: Farnsfield LHS, 2000)

Gardiner, Juliet, *Wartime Britain* (London: Headline Book Publishing, 2004)

Gardiner, Rachel, Maplebeck, *Continuity and Change* (Mansfield: Nottinghamshire Living History Archive, 2002)

Ginn P, Goodman R, Langlands A, *The Wartime Farm* (London: Mitchell Beazley, 2012)

Hardstaff, R E, *Reminiscences of Southwell in the Early 20th C* (Southwell: Southwell & District LHS, 2007)

Hickman, Tom, *The Bevin Boys* (Stroud: History Press, 2010)

His Majesty's Minesweepers (HMSO: 1943)

Housley, Cliff, *First Contact: History of the 8th Battalion, Sherwood Foresters, 1939-45* (London: Miliquest, 1997)

Hustwayte Marjorie, Young, Penny, *Holy Trinity Church 1846-1996* (Southwell: Self published)

Hutchison, David, *The History of the Minster School* (Southwell: Southwell Minster School, 2009)

Jackson, John, *A Living History - Halam 1900-2000* (Farnsfield: Unwin Print, 2001)

Longmate, Norman, *How We Lived Then* (London: Arrow Books, 1973)

Lowdham History Society, *The 20th C in Lowdham* (Nottingham: Adlard Print, 1999)

Mallory, Robert, *Newark in the WW2* (Nottingham: NCC/N SH, 1995)

Mason, Sheila A, *Nottingham Lace 1760s- 1950s* (Stroud: Alan Sutton, 1994)

Minns, Raynes, *Bombers and Mash* (London: Virago Press, 2012)

Mitchell, Frank, *A Window on Rolleston in the 20th Century* (Local)

Nall, Helen, *The Courage of the Small Hours* (Mansfield: Linney Group, 2010)

Nicholson, Virginia, *Women's Lives in War and Peace 1939-49* (London: Penguin Group, 2011)

Northway, BS, *A History of 107 Squadron* (107 Squadron: unpublished, c 1963)

Nottinghamshire Federation of the WIs, *Within Living Memory* (Newbury: Linney group, 1995)

Old Mansfield Society, *Mansfield in WW2* (Nottingham: Old Mansfield Society, 2003)

Otter, Patrick, *Lincolnshire Airfields in the Second World War* (Newbury: Countryside Books, 1996)

Payne, Richard, *Frank North of the 8th Sherwood Foresters* (Nottingham: Milford Printers, 1994)

Robinson, Brian, *History of Averham, Staythorpe and Kelham* (Newark: Partners Press, 1997)

Smith, Brian and Warner, Tim, *Home Front Newark* (Nottingham: NCC, 1995)

Southwell, The Town and Its People, Volume 1 (Southwell: Southwell and District Local History Society, 1992)

Stevenson, Doreen, *Twentieth Century Lives of Southwell* (Southwell: Stevenson, 2001)

Storey, N and Housego, M, *Women's Land Army* (Oxford: Shire Library, 2012)

Taylor Downing, *Spies In The Sky* (London: Little Brown, 2011)

Thorburn, Gordon, *Luck of a Lancaster* (Barnsley: Pen and Sword Aviation, 2013)

Upton Local History Society, *Upton in the 20th Century, A Lingering Look Behind* (Nottingham: Upton LHS, 1999)
Watts, John, Edingley, *A Description of a Nottinghamshire Village* (Farnsfield: John Watts, 2000)
Webb, Kay, *Lilliput Goes To War* (London: Hutchinson, 1985)
West, Mary, *In the Sound of Southwell Bells* (Southwell: Mary West, 1990)
Wilds, Trevor, *Warriors of Farnsfield* (Mansfield: Linneys, 2015)
Woodward, GH and GS, *The Secret of Sherwood Forest Oil Production in WW2* (Oklahoma: Red River Books, 1973)
Wright, Beatrice, Mary, *Bleasby in Wartime* (Bleasby: Beatrice Mary Wright, 1994)

Internet Sources

Reginald Cook: www.thisdayinaviation.com/2-august-1947
National Archives Records for Battle of Britain: AIR-50-30-19_1Norfolkcombatlog.vol1.pdf
Robert Sherbrooke: wikipedia.org/wiki/Robert_Sherbrooke
Sherwood Foresters: wikipedia.org/wike/Sherwood_Foresters
608 Squadron RAF: Wikipedia.org/wiki/No._608_squadron_RAF
Special Wartime Dishes: www.cookit.e2bn.org/historycookbook

INDEX - PEOPLE

INDEX - GENERAL